Jewish Writing and
the Deep Places of the Imagination

This book was published with the support of
THE UNIVERSITY OF CHICAGO

Jewish Writing and the Deep Places of the Imagination

Mark Krupnick

Edited by
Jean K. Carney
and
Mark Shechner

THE UNIVERSITY OF WISCONSIN PRESS

The University of Wisconsin Press
1930 Monroe Street
Madison, Wisconsin 53711

www.wisc.edu/wisconsinpress/

3 Henrietta Street
London WC2E 8LU, England

1   3   5   4   2

Printed in the United States of America

Library of Congress Cataloging-in-Publication Data
Krupnick, Mark, 1939–
Jewish writing and the deep places of the imagination /
Mark Krupnick ; edited by Jean K. Carney and Mark Shechner.
          p.   cm.
Includes bibliographical references and index.
ISBN 0-299-21440-0 (hardcover: alk. paper)
1. American literature—Jewish authors—History and criticism.
2. Jews—United States—Intellectual life.
3. Judaism and literature—United States.
4. Judaism in literature.   5. Jews in literature.   6. Imagination.
I. Carney, Jean K.   II. Shechner, Mark.   III. Title.
            PS153.J4K78   2005
        810.9´8924—dc22   2005008262

To

JEAN,

who kept me alive

and to

JOSEPH,

who made me rethink my writing

Contents

V. LAST WORDS

Acknowledgments

Shortly before his death on March 29, 2003, Mark Krupnick asked his wife, Jean Carney, to take care of his acknowledgments. He left a working note on the computer, but, since there was not time to discuss details, there are, no doubt, friends and colleagues whom Mark would want to thank but whom we do not mention.

Mark wishes to thank Jean, who kept him alive, and Joseph, whose suggestions caused him to rethink his writing; Mark Shechner, who at key moments encouraged him to plumb his own "deep places," and Eric Homberger, who so vigorously lent mind and heart in continuing conversation about this and so many other works in progress.

For help on particular essays Mark thanks: Richard Stern (Roth), Daniel Aaron (Kazin and Howe), Allen Grossman (Hartman), Anne Fadiman (obituaries), Daniel Asa Rose (Morrie Schwartz); for comments and reactions: Elaine Safer, Richard Rosengarten, and Peter O'Leary; for extra hand- and legwork essential to his writing: Jeremy Biles, Sandra Peppers, Sandra Crane, and the reference librarians at the University of Chicago Regenstein Library; for heartening during the difficult days: David Terman, Bruce and Louise Lincoln, Scott Heller, Raymond Roos, and Ben Carandang.

The book would not have been possible without the correspondence and help of many people. The editors would like to thank in particular Eric Homberger, Mark's dear friend who was generous with his time as a reader and advisor from the beginning of the project right through until the end. Among the many others who generously shared their reflections on Mark and saved us from many errors are Gerald Graff, Norman Finkelstein, Allen Grossman, Geoffrey Hartman, Michael Lieb, Richard Rosengarten, Bruce Lincoln, Elaine Safer, Herman Rapaport, Elyse Krupnick, Gene Goodheart, Joel Porte, Patrick Parrinder, and Cynthia Ozick.

The editors are especially grateful to Dean Richard Rosengarten and the Divinity School of the University of Chicago for timely and generous assistance when it was most needed to bring out Mark's last book.

Jean Carney wishes to thank Joseph Carney Krupnick, who upon learning of his father's diagnosis set about developing the muscular strength that carried his parents through, Lucy Carney, Nina Bernstein, and Sanford Weisblatt, for their steadfast hopefulness throughout, and Constantin Fasolt for invaluable help in the end.

Foreword

JEAN K. CARNEY

After he was diagnosed, the first thing my husband, Mark, did was to clear out the shelf at the University of Chicago library devoted to amyotrophic lateral sclerosis (ALS). The next thing Mark did was to start this book. The working title, "How to Die," reflected his intention to produce a how-to manual that would draw on his experience of living with the certainty that he was going to die—not just in the abstract—but in a year or two and in a way that seemed, well, unseemly.

There is not much on the "How to Die" disk, so quickly did Mark turn to the New York intellectuals, mostly Jewish, whom he had discovered in the Harvard library at seventeen. Away from family for the first time, he literally had picked through shelves looking for writers whose language and manner of expression made him feel at home.

His conversation with these writers had sustained him well enough into his fifties, over the years as a literary critic and professor of English literature. Then, about ten years ago, after several frustrating efforts to pull together a book on the group, he announced, once and for all, that they had nothing more to say to him. He was through with them. Never again. He had been calling his attempt to write, finally, what the group had meant to him "Whatever Happened to the Jews?" So recently when I found a disk so named I had to laugh. It was blank.

This book, *Jewish Writing and the Deep Places of the Imagination,* is how-to-die meets whatever-happened-to-the-Jews. What is so moving to me is how, as Mark would say, under "a death sentence," he returned to this community of writers who had brought him so much stimulation and energy at earlier periods of his life and wrestled with the particular kind of death he knew was coming by wrestling once more with them.

With ALS there was plenty to dread. It is a disease of progressive neurological degeneration that leaves muscles useless. Over two and a half years ALS chipped away at Mark's physical capacities, leaving him, in this order, unable to speak, swallow, walk, lift, and breathe.

The first symptom, slurred speech, sent us to the emergency room and a workup for stroke, which proved to be negative. It took nearly six months to get a diagnosis. By then the volume of his voice was failing. It was a day of intense grief when he had to ask a student to read the poem for a class in the last course he taught. I had to read his "retirement" party farewell to colleagues and students. He used a voice amplifier for a short while, then written notes, then a voice synthesizer on a laptop computer.

Mark loved the physical slip and slide of language on the tongue, the shape of words in the mouth. He got a kick out of reading poetry to me and our son, Joseph, but he especially delighted in reading long passages to us of Roth, Nabokov, Dickens, and Bellow. In this volume, the chapter on Bellow, "Listmania in *Humboldt's Gift*," celebrates the "operatic . . . verbal performances," the "spiels."

The problem with computer-generated speech was that everything sounded the same. "Humboldt could really talk," wrote Mark at a time when he soon would not. With no variation in volume, rhythm, and tone, how could Mark suggest nuance, emphasis, irony, wit? He had wild animal calls on the computer that he used to herald the desired emotional effects. He tried the machine at different speeds (as fast as Humboldt?), pitches, volumes, even sexes, anything to create drama. But the most effective to me was the exaggerated use of his eyes, as in the silent films, to express wonderment, skepticism, disapproval, and the like.

Small talk and pleasantries disappeared from Mark's speech early on. They did not feel cost-effective. Yet using his eyes gave him so much pleasure that he exerted himself almost to the end, when he was so worn out one day from the effort that he slept the rest of the day. A poem Mark wrote the month before he died celebrates the pleasure of flirting with an ER nurse using only his eyes.

He had always worked at the epigram. Now in conversation he tended to the single highly distilled word. And, from outward appearances, he lived to an astonishing degree in the present. He took in and seemed to enjoy Joseph and my reminiscences about our shared past, but he rarely added anything. Nor was he interested in looking at pictures of our past life or his life before us. When I asked him about it he said that it just didn't occur to him to look backward or forward. On those occasions when he did speak about the life he would miss with me and Joseph — especially the prospect of missing out on any future grandchildren — the grief was truly overwhelming. Likewise, when his mother and sisters visited before he died there were similar staggering moments. Day to day, though, he seemed sunny, remarkably without complaint, and simply in the present.

In this book, however, he was nimbly moving back and forth between past, present, and future: remembering, anticipating, tying up loose ends, weaving it all into meaningful and heartfelt experience. He could have said of himself, as he says of Alfred Kazin, that it is difficult "being in religion without being religious," and "that spiritual longing plainly had its source in his traumatic experience of silence as a young boy: 'Speak, Father, speak!'"

As his speech faded, so did his swallowing. He was on a feeding tube for the last year. Yet he also was melting up to a pound of thin chocolate on his tongue over the course of a day, using a suction machine to mop up most of it — until I couldn't tolerate the choking episodes and the sweaty and blue close calls. He used a noninvasive ventilator to rest his weakening lungs.

One of the few things that didn't change was the work on this book. He worked every day, reading and thinking in the afternoon, writing in the morning. He kept the texts nearby for reference but used no notes. Compared to his earlier work, there were few revisions. I think he knew that the power of his experience was such that highly glossed language, which he treasured and used to effect on other occasions, was not the point. Nor were indirection or understatement. Bold, even blunt, he was sure-footed in his writing (though certainly not on his feet). The physical act of typing was labored, but the writing flowed more easily than at any time of his life. He wrote un-self-consciously and matter-of-factly, and was surprised that visitors were surprised at the number of hours he worked. E-mail correspondence was a lifeline, particularly the back-and-forth with fellow scholars exchanging ideas and manuscripts in progress.

Some of the book I did not read as it was being written. Mark said he wanted me to have it for later. I did know which texts he was using, because part of tucking him in for the night was my setting out books for the next day. He woke between three and five and used a flashlight so that he could type without waking me. In the last several months, he was typing with the single finger that was strong enough to depress the keys.

Joseph read some chapters while Mark was writing. It was immensely gratifying to me that Mark found Joseph's reactions helpful in a particular way: Joseph encouraged him not to be hard on his fathers, the New York intellectuals, but to understand that they did the best they could with what they had been given and not to fear his tender love for them.

Early on, Mark seized on a televised comment by fellow-ALS-patient Morrie Schwartz, the subject of Mitch Albom's best-selling *Tuesdays with Morrie,* that needing help "wiping one's ass" might be the ultimate humiliation of the disease. Mark read and reread Philip Roth's *Patrimony,* including the "shit-filled scene" where Roth scrubs the bathroom, cleaning up after his father. By the time Mark needed help himself, it was anticlimactic. He had worked and reworked the dread through writing about Roth's preoccupation with "shit-filled life." It felt less toxic.

Roth's *Sabbath's Theater* guided Mark through the humiliation intrinsic to human physicality, especially the bodily degeneration of ALS and increasing physical dependency on me, Joseph, and his caregiver. In the final month, before what turned out to be the last visit from friends, Mark asked me to read aloud from Morris ("Mickey") Sabbath's self-written obituary. Such tearful, wordless laughter, the articulation of which I find in Mark's chapters on Roth and his iconoclastic review of *Tuesdays with Morrie,* the lessons of Morrie Schwartz. When looking for guidance on living and dying with ALS, Mark preferred Morris Sabbath to Morris Schwartz.

Mark quotes Roth's Sabbath, "For a pure sense of being tumultuously alive, you can't beat the nasty side of existence." And Sabbath's outrage: "Why does life refuse me even the *grave* I want!" The day I took Mark to the cemetery to review four potential family plots I'd selected mostly on the basis of aesthetics, it could have been a scene out of Roth. Mark barely looked at the trees, monuments, or pathways, so busy was he taking down and pondering names and dates of prospective graveside companions. "I don't have any choice where I'm headed," he grumped, "but at least I want to know in whose company." He finally settled on a spot near a Filipino congregation, in honor of a cherished caregiver.

Mark looked also to Geoffrey Hartman, the writer and the man. His first symptom, though he had no way of knowing what it foretold, actually occurred on a trip to Hartman's beloved Wordsworth country. A deepening friendship with Hartman the man, as the two of them talked of Hartman's personal and literary life, had brought Mark back to reading Wordsworth closely and sparked a trip to the Lake District. Like Hartman, Mark was to become "a stranger in a strange land": Hartman in his childhood new land of the English countryside, Mark in his new land of ALS.

When Mark describes Hartman's fortuitous use of literature as "a means of emotional survival," Mark knows this territory from daily experience. When he admires Hartman's "strong, even survivalist attachment to English poetry," it resonates with Mark's own stay-alive attachment to the New York intellectuals. Writing about the way Hartman "transformed his personal trauma," Mark works toward transforming his own.

Perhaps most significantly, Mark appreciates that Hartman struggled for years to find a way to deal with the Holocaust "that did not cast the Jews in the role of passive victims." Passivity was much on Mark's mind.

A good seven months before Mark died I returned home one afternoon to find him face down in a plush carpet unable to move his head to draw breath. A substitute caretaker had left a few minutes early, and Mark had tried to reach across to the controls of his hospital bed and had kept on rolling, out of bed and onto the floor. Glasses broken, blood pooling in his face, he could move neither head, nor neck, nor shoulders, nor arms, nor legs, nor anything else to shift his body enough to get some air. He told me later that in those terrifying minutes he had conceded to himself that he would die—right there in utter ignominy—if I did not return on time. And he showed me a poem by George MacBeth that cited the long list of indignities of ALS, ending "worst of all, my wife's become my nurse."

No wonder Mark found kinship with Cynthia Ozick, the essayist, in her nobody's-fool depiction of vulnerability and awkwardness, embarrassment and shame. Mark writes, "The figure of the humiliated woman sometimes appears frankly in Ozick's essays as a figure for herself." He knew the unspeakable humiliation of involuntary passivity. He drew on the human strength in this personal—he calls it womanly—side of Ozick, embarrassed, but capable of withstanding embarrassment well enough to expose herself unvarnished as a specimen of human nature, subject at every turn not only to vulnerability but, more woundingly, to the humiliation of being vulnerable and knowing it.

Mark painted a portrait of Ozick, the portraitist, who—just when he needed it—highlights vulnerability in any number of men and women dear to both Mark and Ozick, including Henry James, Lionel Trilling, Virginia Woolf, Edith Wharton, and T. S. Eliot. Through Ozick's essays, Mark meditates on James's life-changing public humiliation, Woolf's shamefully queasy physicality and her loss of autonomy to her caretaker husband. On Alfred Chester's humiliating physical defect and on Ozick's embarrassment at her attraction to him notwithstanding. Through it all, Mark allies himself with Ozick's Edith Wharton and with Ozick herself, writing their way out of humiliation.

An image remains with me: Mark on flamingo legs, in the old house sorting and packing his own books. Leaning on his cane, he would bend the opposite knee, lift and plant the leg precisely, toes, then heel on the floor, while snagging a book. He teetered and tottered and refused all help, except to be picked up and put back on his feet in front of the bookshelves. Four months later he would be in home hospice care. I think it was the last thing he insisted on doing by himself.

There was a sensuous elegance to his system, characteristic but for its astonishing slowness. He put aside the cane and took each book in his hands, feeling his way into its upholstery by pressing his fingertips into the cover, the binding, the paper. I have seen him make those moves thousands of times. It's the way that his father taught him to feel his way into fabric when he took him to New York's "rag district" on buying trips for the family textile business. Mark always said that he "felt his way into a text," and the process with every new book began with gently creasing the front and back covers, going through the book page by page, folding pages back and forth, getting the book ready to rest in his hands.

We were selling the house, so Mark knew that he would never again touch most of these books, which were headed for storage. But he wanted to decide their allotment. He set aside hundreds of Jewish books—apart from the writers who are the subject of this book—to be kept for Joseph, for whom he became more consciously Jewish as Joseph grew. He saved dozens of Henry James and Nabokov volumes for me.

Most of the Roth, Bellow, Ozick, Trilling, Howe, Kazin, Hartman, Harold Bloom, and Joseph Brodsky were already at the new place, but any stragglers he packed for the trip. It took him weeks to sort and pack his books, not long given that he said directly that he was deciding which ones he needed to have at hand as he got ready to die.

The day after Mark died I found a note on his computer written the previous week to Joseph and me. The file was called "bookjoejean." Of these writers he wrote:

> They are important to me not for their ideas but for their presence; their humanity. I am critical; how they created themselves; self-definition; separate self-studies . . .
>
> They came from similar roots; provided me with a community; so why am I critical? They provided me with help on the journey. But I became like them: critical . . .
>
> They were like friends. Conversation. A continuing conversation in my head.

Jewish Writing and
the Deep Places of the Imagination

Introduction

A reader's relation to the body of work to which he has devoted the greater part of his career is likely to be complex. It is certainly so in my own case. I first began reading Jewish writers and critics as an undergraduate in the late 1950s. Never fully engaged by my college courses, I used to slink away from my solitary carrel in the library in favor of the Reading Room at Harvard, where I would pick out a few magazines from the current periodicals shelves and settle in for an hour of relaxation. The magazines I favored—among them *Partisan Review, Commentary,* and the British periodical *Encounter*—all featured argument, although they published short stories and poetry, too. I was looking for explanations in those days.

A scholar's attitude to his lifetime subject is usually multidimensional. If that subject is mostly composed of intellectual father-surrogates, those attitudes are likely to be ambivalent as well. The authors I read most were figures who, in the wake of Irving Howe's well-known essay of 1968, are known as the New York intellectuals. Although most were Jewish, I did not always understand them as much as I wished. That was because their writing always seemed to rely on masked assumptions and hint at shared experiences about which they were not explicit. And there was a political component to their discourse, even when they were discussing literature that was coded and hard to penetrate.

I had grown up in a family that was indifferent to politics, communist or anticommunist, Democrat or Republican, Zionist or anti-Zionist. My mother used to vote for the person running in municipal elections who she thought would receive the least votes. She wanted to protect that person's feelings when, as was inevitable, he came in last. My father had emigrated from the Ukraine around 1920. The formative events of his early life had been traumatic: pogroms, the Bolshevik Revolution, and the civil war that followed. The traumas included witnessing the rape of his older sister by Cossacks in the course of a pogrom. He never recovered from this rocky start. Although he was to live six decades in his adopted land, he never learned to speak the language well, and his relation to American culture was tenuous at best. Life had been too hard to allow him much space for worrying about politics.

So I grew up in the 1950s, a postradical decade, in a family that was basically apolitical. I had difficulty with the articles that attracted me because the Jewish intellectuals I was reading had been radicals in the 1930s and later avoided being explicit in the postwar period about their former party and institutional commitments. Their cautiousness made for a style that held younger readers like me at a distance.

I did not, in any case, read these writers to learn what to think about the contemporary political scene. I read the literary critics among them to learn how to read and think about literature and thereby how to think about life. I should add that the persons I read in those magazines were almost all men. There were simply not many women writers admitted to their pages. The early careers of Mary McCarthy and Elizabeth Hardwick at *Partisan Review* were typical in that they were consigned to reviews in the "back of the book." In the late 1930s, McCarthy covered the theater scene, about which the editors could not have cared less. What they cared about was McCarthy, keeping her around for her beauty and slashing intelligence.

As my desire grew to become a critic myself, I increasingly studied my models to learn how to write about literature. But there was always something else. I read them and recognized myself in them in a way that was both comforting and liberating. They were like me in some ways I found difficult to specify, but they were also ahead of me, and inevitably I read them as a person searching for a path. The way I needed to take was obvious in certain respects. I needed to get beyond the vacuum of my beginnings. I had been raised in a household without religion, politics, worldly sophistication, or learning. Neither did we have more than a few phonograph records or more than a dozen books. One kind of book I remember is the *Reader's Digest* volumes in which four or so contemporary books were condensed.

Neither did I have the support of an extended family that might have made up for the vacuum at home. Nor did I have to liberate myself from a ghetto; indeed, I grew up envying those who had experienced the sustaining nourishment of a community in which nearly everyone was Jewish, like the nearby Jewish section of Newark that Philip Roth has made known in his fiction. At the same time, I lacked the self-confidence of assimilated upper-middle-class kids my age who had grown up among like-minded friends in the suburbs.

Geographically, I lived in a town that was alternately boring and scary, especially because my very first years of life corresponded to the years of World War II. Irvington, New Jersey, was populated mainly by working-class and lower-middle-class people with Polish and German roots. Even at the edge of my own, mostly Jewish street, I encountered anti-Semitism in the grandfather of my friend Stevie. Irvington was a town of about a hundred thousand on the road that led from Philip Roth's Jewish Newark to suburban South Orange, with its beautiful houses and lush lawns.

I recall a story of Roth's in which he refers to "semi-industrial" Irvington. I had never thought of it this way, but if, like Roth, you knew my town only as the railroad tracks and Dairy Queen you encountered in crossing the boundary out of Newark, that description was accurate. My own street was wholly residential, but only a few blocks away was Coit Street, with its strip of small tool-and-dye factories. And at the end of Webster Street, where we lived, was a waste area where kids rode their bikes and there was the plant where Lionel miniature electronic trains were manufactured.

Because of where we lived, I could not attend Weequahic High School, where Roth matriculated six years before my time; nor could I go to Columbia High School, where teenagers from South Orange and Maplewood were educated. All that remained for me was Irvington High School, with its sorry record of failure in helping its graduates gain admission to good colleges. My mother might have to reconcile herself to living in Irvington, but she would not suffer her son's going to the local high school. She removed me from the public-school system and enrolled me in Newark Academy, a small private day school with a history of getting its better graduates into Princeton. The school had been founded in 1774, but things had changed since the glory days. Now it was in the same industrial neighborhood as Newark Vocational-Technical High School; I can still remember how students from Vo-Tech glared at me as I stood on the corner after school waiting for the public bus that would take me back to Irvington. No wonder. During those four years, but never after, I often wore a tweed sport jacket from Brooks Brothers and white-buck shoes.

My parents did not have much formal education—my mother had a high school degree—or religious orientation. Their strongest sense was of being Jewish. The first thing my father did after coming home from work was to read the Yiddish paper, the *Forward.* When he immigrated to America, he eventually learned a trade and spent the Depression years as an upholsterer. By the 1940s he had become a boss in his own right. He ran a wholesale textile firm. He had few employees, four or five, of whom two were women who handled the bookkeeping and bills. But he ran the business well; it supported my family for almost thirty years until Newark as a whole went up in flames after the assassination of Martin Luther King.

He was at least ten years older and earned more money than the fathers of other kids my age on Webster Street. We could have afforded a larger life, including a modest house in Maplewood or the Oranges, but my mother could not get my father to budge. History's terrors had glued him to the spot where we lived—which as social terrain and as the ground of my being was effectively nowhere.

My mother had grown up on the Lower East Side, the daughter of immigrants from Galicia in the former Austro-Hungarian Empire; her father had worked in sweatshops and had died of tuberculosis at fifty. My mother had powerful ambitions for me, although she was hardly original among Jewish mothers in hoping that I would become a medical doctor. However, her aspirations were so woolly that the idea of becoming a physician never imprinted itself on me as an assignment or distinct wish of my own. I always interpreted her wishes as having more to do with my doing well in school than with anything else.

At the start I regarded with simple admiration the Jewish writers and intellectuals I had first become acquainted with in the Lamont Library Reading Room. But that phase ended in the later 1960s. Then, like others of my generation, I became disillusioned with the Jewish intellectuals for having nothing to say about the war in Vietnam, or saying the wrong things.

My feelings about that war have not greatly changed, but my feelings about my intellectual father figures have modulated. During my twenties and thirties, my resentments were those of my generation. Things have changed for me, and I am not likely to have time to modulate further. My feelings at present are more personal than they were thirty years ago.

On the day after Thanksgiving in 2000, I was rushed to the emergency room of the University of Chicago Hospital. I had symptoms that the neurologists there thought to be signs that I had suffered a stroke. Four months later my illness was authoritatively diagnosed as amyotrophic lateral sclerosis (ALS, more familiarly known as Lou Gehrig's disease). ALS is a fatal neurodegenerative disease for which there is no known cure. It affects all the voluntary muscles and some that feel involuntary. Death looms when the muscles that regulate breathing become too weak. I am currently in the hospice care phase of the illness, which means that my days are numbered.

One effect of ALS has been to intensify my interest in the most elemental ideas, fantasies, and feelings of the persons I discuss in these essays. I had always been something of a moralist who sought to arrive at bedrock by an untheorized approach that combined close reading, a study of social-cultural contexts, attention to individual temperament, and other factors. Some of the essays in this collection were originally published when I was healthy; indeed, one of them, on Philip Rahv, goes back to 1976. However, half of these essays, including all of the longer ones, belong to the last few years. That accounts for the more intense focus in those essays—on Trilling, Saul Bellow, Cynthia Ozick, Geoffrey Hartman, and Philip Roth—on the most elemental issues: life and death, love and hate, sex, gender, and the like.

I have found that the imminence of death has concentrated my mind; it has also speeded up the flow of my thinking and writing. Fortunately, ALS usually does not affect cognitive functioning although it does attack the brain stem. In the latter stage of ALS I have not been able to speak, ingest food by mouth, hold my head up without the mechanical support of a neck brace, dress myself, walk about, or do much else. I am mostly stuck in bed, apart from some time in my wheelchair. I can still read, but mostly I use my time to write.

When I read Lionel Trilling as a young man, I was struck by his style and tone. His essays were convertible, for someone with social aspirations, into a Miss Manners guide for the purposes of upward cultural mobility. I do not think I was particularly conscious in those years of the practical social implications of Trilling's work, but I think now that was part of its unconscious appeal. My mother had social aspirations on which she never had a chance to act—she dreamed, for example, of changing the family name to Palmer—and I wanted to learn the moves that would gain me favor in the upscale educational institutions to which I had been lucky enough to be admitted.

However, I had a prior and more elemental wish. I read the Jewish writers—my memory is of reading the critics before I read the novelists—to learn how they thought and felt about things. That is vague because as a young person I was vague. In my early life there had been no intimate community, charismatic persons, or watershed events that had decisively shaped me. Mostly I read literature not to get ahead but to learn about the world—I felt as if I knew so little. I read my Jewish elders in search of an identity and a way to do things.

They formed my intellectual community, and each of them functioned for me as a surrogate father. But it was not only their ideas that mattered. They saved my life by providing me with a world, and their writing gave me access to their presence as persons. Over the years I came to take them for granted as if they were like other literary critics, persons to learn from or agree or disagree with. But, even when I did not adequately appreciate their actual importance in my life, they were always more to me than persons with whom to argue. I sensed that they were like me in that they had put themselves together somewhat in the way I had. They had their books, their cultural context—which in my own case, as I have said, was desperately thin; they had their personalities, traumas, needs; and they had the ongoing theoretical-intellectual debate into which to insert themselves. It was hardly the ideal way to cobble together a moral self or literary-critical identity in that we all had to rely on ourselves more than individuals ideally should.

From the foregoing a reader might surmise that the essays to follow will all be acts of homage. After all, these writers offered me models of how to conduct myself in a world where I had no mentors at closer hand. But one of the things I learned from them is to call things as I see them. There is the further matter of the ambivalence one feels toward persons who have influenced one as they influenced me. They were fiercely competitive and judgmental, in part because they had no pre-existing role in society or in the literary community. Lacking a defined place, they had to carve one out. People who belong to a club have a stake in good manners; they are likely to be generous toward fellow members. The Jewish writers and critics who came of age in the 1930s belonged to no club except in one or two instances the Communist Party, and that was not a club much concerned with refined manners.

I have judged my various persons by the standards I would expect to be judged by myself. Reconsidering the essays in this selection, I see that my emphasis in every case has been on individuals, either a single literary performance or their careers in general. I have not taken up individual persons as occasions to consider questions in theory or large cultural issues. It has been common in the past four decades in academic literary studies for a professor to wheel out a complicated theory to show how it can illuminate one or another poet or literary situation. On the contrary, I have not sought to foreground any theory. My focus has been on how writers and critics have constructed themselves out of their reading and discourse. I regard what I have done in most of these essays as literary criticism, but my sense of the writer has always remained central.

What I have found myself coming back to are issues of the self: its wounds, its commitments, and its way of negotiating the complicated relationships that exist among its needs, the texts one studies, the social-cultural context, and the complex of dominant fantasies, drives, and emotions that underlie more accessible matters. Such an undertaking involves guesswork and intuition as well as learning and close analysis of style.

The New York intellectuals represented a sharp alternative to my college professors. I did not aspire to be a university teacher through the greater part of my doctoral training. I was in graduate school because I did not know what else to do; also, during the 1960s I was subject to being drafted and sent to Vietnam, and that was a fate I sought to avoid. But staying in graduate school was an uncertain affair. I knew the New York intellectuals did not hold professors of literature in high esteem. Philip Rahv happened to be on my MA oral examination committee at Brandeis. A young professor friend who was also on the examining committee told me that when I completed the exam and had left the room, Rahv had commented: "There goes a professor." My medievalist professor friend thought that would please me. In fact, I did not take it as a compliment. No doubt I had taken too literally Rahv's generally dismissive remarks about professors, but at the time, given what I knew of his prejudices, I experienced his comment as a put-down rather than as praise.

I thought that most of the professors I had been exposed to were unsituated in relation to the world; nothing they ever said in their lectures appeared to draw on daily life outside the academy. No doubt what I really felt at the time was that they were not situated in relation to me. That is, their lectures did not confirm me in my sense of personal reality. But the personal and emotional nature of my alienation can be measured from the fact that at Harvard I had been exposed to several figures who were as situated as academics could have been at the time. My time was not the worst of academic times. I was in college at the end of the 1950s, as the fresh tide began that mounted higher with the election of John Kennedy. My teachers included the cognitive psychologist Jerome Bruner and the historian of American politics Arthur M. Schlesinger Jr. There were few professors more plugged into extra-academic actuality than these.

Later, when I myself began to write about Jewish writing, I often placed it in a political-cultural context. That seemed justified because my authors seemed, even the most literary of them, to think of themselves as political persons. A legend of the old-left intellectuals already existed. That legend had to do with their courage in breaking with Stalinism and setting up as independent radicals in the waning years of the 1930s. In fact, their break with the official Communist line did not entail great risk. Nobody then anticipated the rise of McCarthyism and the fervent anticommunism of the postwar years, but, in any case, breaking with the Communist Party, which had sponsored the old *Partisan Review,* turned out to be prudent in light of the subsequent Red Scare.

It is true that the independent Marxists of the reorganized *Partisan Review* paid a price for breaking with their old associates. They became objects of contempt and exclusion by the much more numerous readers of the Stalinist *New Masses* and the officials of the Communist Party. But there were no gulags to which any of the *Partisan Review* rebels could be sent. At worst, they might find their book manuscripts rejected out of hand by the several big publishing houses then dominated by fellow travelers.

The legend grew and turned into a great cultural myth when the younger generation made the old left the objects of scholarly research in the 1970s and '80s. Before then, in the years of the anti-Vietnam protest, the old left had been roundly denounced by Tom Hayden and other leaders of the radical Students for a Democratic Society. But after the end of the Vietnam War the mood changed. The 1970s brought with them the defeat of radicalism and the beginning of the eclipse of the liberalism that had dominated intellectual life in the first half of the twentieth century. With the accession to power in the 1980s of Ronald Reagan and the Jewish neoconservatives who provided a rationale for his administration, the 1930s radicals, even the old liberals, were looking better than they had in the 1960s. My own book on the 1930s generation, *Lionel Trilling and the Fate of Cultural Criticism* (1986), proceeded on the assumption that Trilling and his contemporaries were, above all, political intellectuals.

Nowadays I value the political side of their work much less than I once did. In fact, Trilling had wound up writing much more about ideas of culture and politics than he had himself advised in his polemical essays of the 1940s on the liberal (lack of) imagination. So my interests have changed since the 1980s, and with them my appreciation of the cohorts of Jewish American novelists and critics before my own. In the essays that follow I touch on politics here and there, but my main interest in the people I write about lies elsewhere.

I have studied their imaginative lives, "the deep places of the imagination," a phrase I have taken from Trilling. In my initial essay, on Trilling, I gloss that phrase and attempt to clarify the framework I have devised for the essays that follow. By "imagination" I do not refer to a faculty all to itself that appears only in "creative" writing. Although many of the following pages are given over to the novels of Saul Bellow and especially Philip Roth, I regard the critical writing I discuss as also the products of their authors' imaginations.

By "imagination" I have in mind a fusion of ideas with fantasy and emotion. I have written mainly about the inner lives of my subjects as that inwardness shows up in their writing. I have not sacrificed literary criticism to amateur psychologizing, but I have not hesitated to draw on what I know of my subjects' lives and personalities to understand and evaluate their writing. I have wanted to understand them in a way different from how they have been understood before, which has been in terms of their politically oriented ideas and opinions. Ultimately, I am interested in the ways in which they have integrated their intellectually elaborated ideas and moral sentiments with their deepest personal experiences and needs. That personal emphasis has meant privileging literary persons over those who devoted themselves mostly to politics, and in the case of those who attempted to bridge the two worlds giving my attention more to the literary imagination.

I have mostly referred to the New York intellectuals here. But a substantial portion of this book is given over to three literary figures who to a greater or lesser degree are heirs of the New York school. Geoffrey Hartman, Cynthia Ozick, and Philip Roth could not be more different, but they were all born around 1930 and represent some of the best of Jewish writing of their cohort.

I hope that the essays that follow are persuasive and shed new light on fairly familiar figures. In the end, what I seem to myself to have done is to follow up on my boyhood aim, which was to discover how persons like myself—Jewish, of immigrant origins, living chiefly in their heads—contrived to form a self-identity through their reading and in their writing. To be sure, that literary self-identity has often not been perfectly congruent with their quotidian selves, but it is the identity that has concerned me.

I

JEWISH WRITERS

"A Shit-Filled Life"
Philip Roth's *Sabbath's Theater*

I.

What do we find in the deepest places of imagination? Obviously different people find different things, and some are too occupied with the worldly world to search for or find anything at all. Western philosophers have mostly found spirit, or the ideal, at the foundation of things. Others who also find ultimate reality there find forms of matter, and not necessarily economic modes of production. Some find love, others hatred.

In his writing during the past fifteen years or so, Philip Roth has continued to be a writer with little interest in dreams or traditional ideas of beauty, except if represented in the shape of the female breast. He has increasingly found loss, humiliation, and death at the heart of things. And increasingly reductive in his sense of reality, he has found the most basic, most elemental principle of things in excrement. The protagonists of his most recent books have been in the end overcome by storms of shit. It might seem excessive to say that Roth was invoking shit as more than a metaphor, but it is an important literal fact in the doomed careers in some of his main characters.

Mickey Sabbath, the satyr-victim of *Sabbath's Theater*, refers to his "shit-filled life" and thinks to himself at one point: "You besmirch yourself in increments of excrement." It is not the case that actual excrement plays an important role in this novel, although Sabbath, the irrepressible fornicator, does have a taste for anal intercourse. The chief pleasures of his final affair with his Croatian mistress, Drenka Balich, are not excremental in the narrow sense of referring to feces. But they are undinist: Sabbath and Drenka piss on each other and drink each other's urine. Well, this *is* a novel intended to combine farce and outrageousness.

It is also a novel about humiliation and defeat. At the height of their joy in each other, Drenka, in her early fifties, dies from cancer. Her death is the latest devastating loss in Sabbath's life of disappointment and deprivation. Roth's critics have justifiably emphasized the saturnalian element in this novel of sexual transgression and Rabelaisian comedy, but they have not done enough by way of acknowledging Sabbath's grief, rage, and madness. Indeed, it has been a "shit-filled life."

Sabbath's career enacts on a huge scale the "increments of excrement" that figure so importantly in Roth's writing, beginning in 1991 with *Patrimony,* his memoir of his father's struggle with a brain tumor that eventually killed him. In the most remarkable scene of that book, Roth describes a visit by his father to the son's rural Connecticut home. There Philip conducts himself with a filial devotion and love that are a rebuke to readers who have regarded the father-son relation in *Portnoy's Complaint* as a direct imitation of Roth's actual relations with his father. With Claire Bloom to help him, Philip does all that a son can do to make his father as comfortable as possible despite his terminal condition.

But at one point Herman Roth slips away from the company to go upstairs. When he does not reappear, Philip mounts the stairs himself and discovers his father in a state of shock. Repeatedly moaning "I beshat myself," the old man stands in his son's bathroom surrounded by the effects of the volcanic eruption of his bowels: "The shit was everywhere." Philip ends his inventory of stain with striking detail: "It was even on the tips of the bristles of my toothbrush hanging in the holder over the sink."

His father is consumed by shame: "Don't tell the children. . . . Don't tell Claire." To honor his father's wish, the son seeks no help in cleaning up the mess. He even gets down on his hands and knees, and with a bucket of hot water and Spic and Span goes to work with that toothbrush trying to clean flecks of shit from where they have lodged in the crevices between the planks of the old farmhouse floor.

A scene like this one has to have a point, even if Roth as a writer is nominally as disdainful of symbols as the Mark Twain of *Huckleberry Finn.* Watching his father sleep, the son contrives a life-affirming meaning for this horrendous occurrence: "I couldn't have asked any-thing more for myself before he died—this, too, was right and as it should be." And he goes on: "Once you sidestep disgust and ignore nau-sea and plunge past those phobias that are fortified like taboos, there's an awful lot of life to cherish." Nothing could sound more unlike Roth's unillusioned remarks on the shit-filled lives of Mickey Sabbath and the victims of his other subsequent, fictional narratives.

"So *that* was the patrimony. And not because cleaning it up was sym-bolic of something else but because it wasn't, because it was nothing less or more than the lived reality that it was." So shit, Philip's patrimony, is a positive. The conviction that life will finally leave us stripped of any-thing that might protect our dignity—somehow that belief appears to the son as liberating in the present context. And that is partly because he looks upon his father from the point of view not only of a son but also of a writer. Remarking on his father's lack of refinement, his bluntness and stubbornness, which now seem graces to the son, the novelist in him sums up the lesson of the messy scene he has led us through: "[My father] taught me the vernacular. He *was* the vernacular, unpoetic and expressive and point-blank, with all the vernacular's glaring limitations and all its durable force." Ask where Roth learned the punchy vernacu-lar style that is so great a part of his success as a novelist, and you get the answer in the shit-filled scene of *Patrimony* I have described.

Ten years later, in *The Human Stain*, we have another shit-filled novel, but the connotations of human waste are very different. Perhaps the most curious character in that novel is Faunia Farley, who becomes the mistress of Coleman Silk after he has lost his wife, his teaching po-sition, and his respectable standing in the academic community where he had been for many years a leader. Coleman's politically correct ene-mies have, figuratively, shit all over their innocent victim. But in the case of Faunia the shit is not merely figurative: she is intimately associated with excrement as the janitor at the college and the local post office. Not only does she clean the school toilets; to supplement her meager in-come, Faunia also milks the cows at a local dairy and mucks their stalls.

Faunia herself is a living expression of the later Roth's will to reality. She has been stripped by life: as a small child, she has been sexually abused by her stepfather; as a wife, she has been battered and hounded by her husband, Les, who returned from combat in Vietnam rabidly insane;

as a mother, she has suffered the loss and shame of having lived through the death of her own small children caused by a fire in their house that occurred while Faunia was blowing a relative stranger in the front seat of his truck. But Faunia has been degraded not destroyed. She has learned to take things as they are.

In *The Human Stain* that means being reduced to one's unbuffered physical condition. Faunia pretends to be illiterate to escape from human things, but she actively identifies with animal life. She is given a long—four-page—stream-of-consciousness reflection on crows, the scavengers that somehow never miss a meal, although that means they often are seen eating the dead in the middle of the highway: "The thing about them is that they're all practicality. In their flight. In their talk. Even in their color. All that blackness. Nothing but blackness." That blackness associates the crow not with practicality alone but with death and excrement.

If Faunia is identified with the outcast crows, so is she associated with the muck of cows. After her regular workday of cleaning up the human shit at the college and post office, she goes to a nearby organic dairy farm to milk the cows and clean up their waste. In turn she gets to live at the farm rent-free. Faunia is skillful and matter-of-fact in managing the cows—she is hardly a figure out of Greco-Roman pastoral or love poetry. But Coleman, the ex-professor of classics, is transfixed as he watches her at work. She is his "Voluptas." Nathan Zuckerman, the observer of their affair, offers a glimpse of the seventy-one-year-old Coleman visually ravishing his thirty-four-year-old lover as she goes about her mundane chores. Whatever may be Coleman's fantasies, Zuckerman, who is telling Coleman's story, limits his own lyricism. He describes the cows eating and at the same time being milked by "four pulsating, untiring mechanical mouths. . . . Each of [the cows] deep into a bestial existence blissfully lacking in spiritual depth: to squirt and to chew, to crap and to piss, to graze and to sleep—that was their whole raison d'être."

This passage appears near the beginning of *The Human Stain* and prepares the reader for the intimate Faunia-Coleman scene in which Roth most dramatically defies the "coercions of propriety." The novel's events occur in the year of the House Republicans' attempt to impeach Bill Clinton for what Zuckerman and Coleman feel to be the minor impropriety of his secret affair with Monica Lewinsky. How better for Roth to outrage such sanctimonious hypocrites than to portray a scene of transgression that deliberately subverts the values of "love" and "spirit." This scene is the set piece in which Roth tries hardest to dramatize the countervalues of a novel that exists to affirm "the contaminant of sex, the redeeming corruption that de-idealizes the species and keeps us everlastingly mindful of the matter we are." Or, how to be a cow.

This time Faunia does not excite Coleman's lust in the course of milking cows. Rather, she has just milked him, and her face and body are smeared with his semen. This old ex-dean, shunned and discredited by his former colleagues, feels alive again, and he says, "Come on, dance for me." And, without experiencing anything degrading about his request, Faunia proceeds to dance before Coleman for the next nine pages.

This scene ought to be erotically exciting, but it turns out to be about as stimulating as an earlier image of the cows "reposefully sprawled in a mix of hay and shit." That is only partly because of Roth's reductive emphasis on the vegetal and fleshy at the expense of fantasy. It is also because what here takes the place of fantasy is even more inert than excrement. I refer to this novelist's irrepressible zest for sermons. While dancing, Faunia is thinking the whole time about what her lover may be thinking and what he should be thinking about the relation of sex-unredeemed-by-meaning to an illusion called love.

Faunia's thoughts to herself and her words spoken to Coleman while he gazes at her alternate with description of her naked gyrations. The ideas appear to emerge spontaneously, but they have their effect as argument; Faunia moves from fairly concrete reflections to large generalizations about sex, society, suffering, life, and death:

> Faunia thinking: [Coleman's] going to pretend that the world is ours . . . but he has to remember. This is only what it is, even if I'm wearing nothing but the opal ring, nothing on me but the ring he gave me. . . . That's a lot. But that's all it is. . . . Don't fuck it up by thinking it's more than this. . . . It doesn't *have* to be more than this.
>
> "A man and woman in a room. Naked. We've got all we need. We don't need love. Don't diminish yourself—don't reveal yourself as a sentimental sap. You're dying to do it, but don't. Let's not lose this. Imagine, Coleman, imagine sustaining this."

And what is it that sustains Faunia, that energizes her message and her dancing? It is the "irreversible futility" that has been her life, "the chaos and callousness." By comparison Coleman's fall has been the fall of the privileged. But he too has been plunged into hatred and rage. Their shared hatred for the respectable world sustains their animal passion. Faunia, who affects ignorance, is actually quite adept at reading Coleman. She knows that "you're with *me*. Why else would you be with me, if you weren't so fucking enraged? And why would I be with you, if *I* wasn't so fucking enraged? That's what makes for the great fucking, Coleman. The rage that levels everything. So don't lose it." Faunia has a wisdom lacking to Coleman. She has lived with degradation and bitterness for so long that she recognizes evil and perversity not only in the world and her oppressors, but also in herself.

After leaving Coleman's place, she visits the local Audubon Society to commune with Prince, the crow. At the society she runs into a little girl feeding the snake. She offers the child bits of her wisdom and reflects to herself: "We leave a stain, we leave a trail, we leave our imprint. Impurity, cruelty, abuse, error, excrement, semen—there's no other way to be here." She is not lamenting Original Sin; on the contrary, she means, as does Roth, to recommend the dissoluteness, the depravity, the perversity—the sensual adventurousness—that are part of her redemptive nihilism.

The transvaluation of values can make for great literature. In accord with Coleman Silk's academic specialty, Roth offers a jazzed-up understanding of Greek tragedy. He might also have mentioned Blake's *Marriage of Heaven and Hell*. But it does not work well in *The Human Stain*, where the message remains inert on the page. Faunia remains an idea, just as the characterization of Coleman does not progress much beyond the original conceit of having a black man pass as a Jew, with the bitter ironies that follow. He says "spooks" in class and is hounded out of the Athena College community as white racist; and the death of his reputation is followed by his physical death, when Faunia's ex-husband sets him up for killing.

Roth has always had a flair for classroom teaching, and in her dance scene Faunia appears as a professor of desire. Repeating her lesson while she performs naked in front of her seventy-one-year-old student, Faunia at one point exclaims, "That's my boy. . . . Now you're learning." To which Coleman replies, "Is that what this is — you teaching me?" Faunia answers: "It's about time somebody did. Yes, I'm teaching you." At this point she controls Coleman's thoughts in much the same way that Mickey Sabbath, the puppeteer, seeks to control everyone in his life as he had his actors as a theatrical director.

2.

I have written about *The Human Stain* because of its intrinsic interest, but also because I have wished to prepare the ground for a discussion of *Sabbath's Theater*. The latter seems to me much the best novel Philip Roth has written and one of the best American novels altogether. Morris Dickstein has written about *Sabbath's Theater* as a later version of *Portnoy's Complaint,* *the* rollicking novel of sexual transgression that emerged from the cultural revolution of the sixties.[1] Certainly there is continuity, but it is possible to overemphasize it. Sexual transgression is Roth's great subject as the "transatlantic theme" is Henry James's, but *Portnoy,* finally, has about the relation to *Sabbath* that James's *The American* has to *The Golden Bowl.*

Roth's personal crisis during the early 1990s, which bears comparison to James's a century earlier, encouraged an extremism of subject matter and style that goes far beyond the artistic self-liberation he achieved in *Portnoy's Complaint.* I have preferred writing about *The Human Stain* to discussing *Portnoy's Complaint,* because the later novel is much more like the story of Mickey Sabbath than anything he wrote during the early phase of his career. It seems to me relevant even though it appeared six years and two novels after *Sabbath's Theater.* But if Sabbath's story resembles Coleman Silk's in having to do with disappointment and humiliation, it differs in that Sabbath is not a classicist in any sense, particularly not in the way he regulates his emotions and conduct. Even when he sinks into despair and weighs whether "to be or not to be," he is still the manic, reckless, self-subversive satyr. Superabundance, extremism, excess, these are Sabbath's defining features as

1. Dickstein's discussion of Roth is part of his excellent recent book, *Leopards in the Temple: The Transformation of American Fiction, 1945–1970* (Cambridge, MA: Harvard University Press, 2002).

he confronts the imminent end to his ability to fornicate, which is his reason for being. As far as Sabbath is concerned, death itself will be an anticlimax once he is no longer able to have erections and climaxes.

Two of the finest appreciations of *Sabbath's Theater* are by British critics Frank Kermode and James Wood.[2] Understandably, both put Sabbath's sex life at the center of their considerations of his story, and they both quote from this passage: "You must devote yourself to fucking the way a monk devotes himself to God. Most men have to fit fucking in around the edges of what they define as more pressing concerns: the pursuit of money, power, politics, fashion, Christ knows what it might be. . . . But Sabbath had simplified his life and fit the other concerns in around fucking. . . . The Monk of Fucking. The Evangelist of Fornication."

But if Sabbath is the "monk of fornication," that hardly makes him a paragon of piety. Rather, as Wood argues, Sabbath's irrepressible lust is allied to his defiance and nihilism; it is his way of inverting the values of respectable society. Sex for Sabbath is inseparable from his impulse to affront and antagonize; it is inseparable from the hatred that fuels his will to live. Sabbath's primary motive is to "fuck the world."

An essay on this novel would be incomplete that leaves out this fucking and Sabbath's misery in facing the end of his career as a dedicated fornicator. But his manic sexual energy plays itself out in the context of his massive losses and defeats, and his overwhelming grief, hatred, and madness are as central to this novel as sex. Indeed *Sabbath's Theater* is an uneven novel, and some of its weakest parts, coming at the beginning, involve Sabbath's perverse pleasures with Drenka Balich. On the other hand, it is hard to think of many American novels that convey with such intensity Sabbath's despair and disgust and offensiveness. During the last, better half of the novel, Roth draws on *King Lear* and *Hamlet*. The denouement of Sabbath's story obviously relies more on sex than do those of Shakespeare's heroes. However, where sexual transgression pops up in this phase of Sabbath's "shit-filled life," it is only in memory.

2. Frank Kermode, "Philip Roth," in *Pleasing Myself: From "Beowulf" to Philip Roth* (London: Allen Lane, 2001); James Wood, "The Monk of Fornication: Philip Roth's Nihilism," in *The Broken Estate: Essays on Literature and Belief* (London: Jonathan Cape, 1999).

The second half of this novel, titled "To Be or Not to Be," starts with a hilarious obituary Sabbath has written for himself. This death notice helps us get a handle on the trajectory of this life, which is presented in the novel as a series of flashbacks on the screen of Sabbath's memory, interrupted by scenes in the present. A review is helpful because the narrative is anything but chronological.

Sabbath has been a reckless, self-subversive character from the start. But for a decade, from the mid-fifties until the mid-sixties, he had been a promising figure on New York's avant-garde theater scene. He attracted attention as a puppeteer, using his fingers rather than marionettes as characters; and he had founded the Indecent Theater, in which he directed his talented wife, Nikki, who had once played Cordelia to Sabbath's Lear. But in 1964 Nikki disappeared, at a time when her director-husband had been seducing Roseanna, who had just graduated from Bennington. Despite Sabbath's infidelities, his great love, and his tie to the stage, has been Nikki.

Her loss proves devastating. So, after a long period of searching everywhere for her, he takes the radical step of forsaking New York altogether and following his new lover to Madamaska Falls, where she had lined up a job at an obscure New England college. Sabbath becomes an adjunct instructor in puppet-work, making a few thousand dollars a year. Otherwise, he lives off the Bennington lady. Sabbath's real activity at that college is seducing undergraduates, while an embittered Roseanna, who has become his second wife, adapts to Sabbath's derelictions by becoming an alcoholic. They have dwelled together for decades in mutual enmity, without the pleasure and consolation of sex.

In the meantime Sabbath has suffered other disappointments. Osteoarthritis in his hands has forced him to give up puppeteering. However, that loss is compensated by Sabbath's discovery of Drenka Balich, a married woman with her own flair for sexual excess. Other than the family in which he grew up as a boy, Drenka is the greatest love of Sabbath's life. She dies of cancer at the age of fifty-two, when their relationship has reached a perverse perfection. Memories of Drenka are among the few things that sustain Sabbath in his latter-day despair. Other memories that keep him going are of his early teen-age years in a close-knit Jewish family living in a small town on the New Jersey shore. When Sabbath is fifteen, during World War II, his older brother

Morty, who had been his guide to the great world, is killed on a flying mission over the Pacific. That death, the originating loss in Sabbath's personal history of losses, is followed by another tragedy, the irreversible breakdown of Sabbath's mother, who never emerges from mourning.

Following Drenka's unexpected death from cancer, Sabbath ravished a girl from the college in a running phone-sex relationship. The girl unintentionally left a tape of their conversation—the novel provides a long transcript—in the women's restroom of the college library; the administration confiscated it; and the Japanese-born woman dean led the successful charge for Sabbath's ouster from the faculty. Roseanna hears of the scandal and has a psychotic breakdown requiring that she be institutionalized. We have learned previously about her obsessive interest in a newspaper story about an unhappy wife who had cut off her abusive husband's penis while he slept. When Roseanna re-emerges, she kicks Sabbath out of their home. Since her job had been the main source of his money, he is now practically broke as well as well as lacking all the other things that more conventional human beings rely on to shore up their dignity. In addition to these setbacks, there is the impotence that Sabbath experiences as life's final insult.

With so little to keep him in Madamaska Falls, he heads to New York to attend the funeral of an old friend who has committed suicide. He stays at the apartment of Norman Cowan—both Norm and the dead man had backed Sabbath when the young puppeteer set out on his once-promising career. Sabbath flees Cowan's place after rifling through the underclothes of his friend's college-age daughter, Michelle, in whose room he has been sleeping. He has also acted outrageously in trying to seduce the wife of his well-meaning old friend. A scene that combines pathos and grotesque comedy occurs when Sabbath makes another sexual bid, but again fails. This time he chases the Cowans' terrified Hispanic maid around the apartment in an attempt to bugger her.

When Sabbath leaves the Cowan place, he heads for the Bowery to observe the ways of the bereft; it is not out of the question that he may become one of them. He thinks of himself as "wifeless, mistressless, penniless, vocationless, homeless." Roth has a flair for portraying his main characters as the quintessence of "-lessness." In *The Counterlife* (1986), Nathan Zuckerman is explaining to his English wife, Maria, why he is leaving her. It has to do with his discovery of the importance to him of his Jewish identity. Maria is skeptical about what appears to her as his belated conversion to Jew-craziness. Refuting her challenge that he is a "human being" not fundamentally different from herself, Zuckerman defines his sense of himself in terms of antagonism. England, with its upper-class anti-Semitism, has "made a Jew of me." But what kind of Jew? At the end of *The Counterlife,* Zuckerman sums up his essence as he now understands it: "A Jew without Jews, without Judaism, without Zionism, without Jewishness . . . a Jew clearly without a home, just the object itself, like a glass or an apple." Lists like Zuckerman's inevitably imply abundance by virtue of their additiveness, but Roth likes to use them to evoke a condition of nakedness, a life or an identity stripped of qualifiers. In *The Counterlife,* that stripped-down, "without" condition suggests a kind of purity about Zuckerman's way of being a Jew. In *Sabbath's Theater,* the protagonist's "-lessness" is intended to convey his self-image as the most of the least. In one of his conversations with his dead mother, who is more present to him than most of the living, he tells her, "I am a failure. . . . I am at the very pinnacle of failure." At another time, Sabbath thinks to himself that he has been such a failure that he has even failed at failure. His litanies of loss are a unifying element in his anarchical internal monologue: "He was drained of skepticism, cynicism, sarcasm, bitterness, mockery, self-mockery, and such lucidity, coherence, and objectivity as he possessed — had run out of everything that marked him as Sabbath except desperation; of that he had a superabundance."

Sabbath's emphasis on his desperation bears on the question of whether Roth is laying out a message in this novel. James Wood argues that *Sabbath's Theater* is a metaphysical novel, an exposition of European-style nihilism. Indeed, in his view Mickey Sabbath is so consistently subversive that he is a quasi-religious figure in his performance of the "sacrament of infidelity" and his attack on everything that is decent, normal, and ordinary. Wood's citations all come from Christianity, but Sabbath's name need not be associated with his inversion of all that is represented by the sabbath or the Roman Catholic Mass. Roth's "monk of fornication" could be associated with the Jewish false messiah, Sabbatai Sevi, who transformed Jewish history in the seventeenth century. Gershom Scholem has written an authoritative study of Sabbatai, who was quite convinced that he was the messiah for whose arrival

Europe's Jews had grown increasingly impatient. And Scholem has written an essay on a movement inspired by Sabbatai. The chief goal of that movement was the same as Sabbath's reason for being: as Scholem's title has it, "Redemption by Sin."

The problem with Wood's interpretation and my hypothetical Jewish variant is that Sabbath lacks the self-certainty of a messianic figure. He is not in a position to offer an antitheological theology such as Wood attributes to this novel for the simple reason that he is so little sure about what matters most. He is a suffering skeptic whose only conviction concerns the incoherence of things. He is even unsteady in the hatred that fuels his will to live. Philip Roth does not seem to me to be any more concerned than Mickey Sabbath to present a consistent philosophy.

At bottom, Sabbath's sense of the incoherence of existence is a matter of his incoherent sense of himself. That disoriented state gives rise to an endless internal monologue in which he tries out various self-descriptions. It is remarkable how much of this novel is given over to *naming* Sabbath. He silently describes himself as he sees himself in the distorting mirrors of self-reflection, and he plays various roles (Lear, the beggar, the hapless victim when it is convenient, and so on). Roth, with his habit of supplying reviewers with useful tags for his characters, also has others describe Sabbath to himself. One of the most illuminating of these descriptions from outside, because it is both a challenge and a critique, is uttered by Norm in the process of expelling Sabbath from his home. He is "the walking panegyric for obscenity . . . the inverted saint whose message is desecration." Norm's point is that Sabbath's stance, his "pitch," is out of date. Norm's own pitch is, in effect, "Come off it. Come in out of the cold; be more like me and find some middle-class comfort."

Sabbath's reply is a refutation of his friend's labels: "You're going to feel dashed by this, Norman, but on top of everything else I don't have, I don't have a pitch. . . . I am flowing swiftly along the curbs of life, I am merely debris, in possession of nothing to interfere with an objective reading of the shit."

3.

The second part of the novel gropes to define the impulses and ideas that are at war within Sabbath. There is little space here between some putative external author and an "implied narrator." The reader has access only to Sabbath's consciousness, what he calls "the turbulent inner talkathon." That metaphor calls to mind the annual TV talkathons of the film comedian Jerry Lewis on behalf of victims of muscular dystrophy. Lewis grew up a few years earlier in the same Jewish neighborhood as Roth, and Roth, the younger comedian, knew Lewis's work in the movies, where he became famous as the partner of Dean Martin. The point about Lewis is that his comedy, mindless as it is, relied on a turbulence and excess that are the leading qualities of Sabbath's performance art and his inner world. Sabbath's earthy style goes along with comfortable recourse to a broad range of art and entertainment: he much prefers Ava Gardner to Virginia Woolf.

After imagining a Mount Rushmore adorned by huge rock carvings of Gardner, Sonja Henie, Yvonne de Carlo, and Grace Kelly, Sabbath shifts to another mode of consciousness: "So Sabbath passeth the time . . . seeing all the antipathies in collision, the villainous and the innocent, the genuine and the fraudulent, the loathsome and the laughable, a caricature of himself and entirely himself, embracing the truth and blind to the truth." Sabbath's self-conscious self-division is not the state of mind of a man in much of a position to be advancing metaphysical arguments.

Ultimately, for Sabbath the question of "to be or not to be" is inseparable from his doubt as to who he is: "a caricature of himself and entirely himself, . . . self-haunted while barely what you would call a self, ex-son, ex-brother, ex-husband, ex-puppet artist without any idea of what he now was or what he was seeking." Whenever in doubt, Sabbath sums up his totally stripped condition in terms of "-less" or "without" or "ex-." Well, that is certitude of a sort. The question, however, stands, "about what he was seeking, whether it was to slide headlong into the stairwells with the substrata of bums"—Sabbath has been walking lower Manhattan's mean streets after his getaway from the Cowans—"or to succumb like a man to the-desire-not-to-be-alive-any-longer or to affront and affront and affront till there was no one on earth unaffronted." So Sabbath's choices boil down to whether to slide passively into a condition of homelessness or to commit suicide or to take up arms against his sea of troubles, his chief weapons being hatred and insult.

An exclusive concentration on Sabbath the satyr and affronter must have the effect, however, of missing out on the pathos that is engendered by Sabbath's memories as he haunts the New York scenes where he had once flourished. Some of his most tearful memories have to do with his younger self and the security he once knew. Now he cannot even hold himself upright: "He clutched the edge of a street vendor's stand, waiting for the coffee to save him. Thought went on independently of him, scenes summoning themselves up while he seemed to wobble perilously on a slight rise between where he was and where he wasn't. He was trapped in a process of self-division. . . . A pale, pale analog to what must have happened to Morty when his plane was torn apart by flak: living your life backward while spinning out of control." Roth's narrative method in this half of the novel is an attempt to conjure up such a perilous condition, rather like that of Lear, of a mind assaulted by delirium and situated at the edge of a cliff. Rarely have writers succeeded as well in conveying emotions like Sabbath's grief and despair with the threat of outright madness hanging over everything.

James Wood mentions Celine; Frank Kermode likens Sabbath the con man to Thomas Mann's Felix Krull; and Sabbath himself remembers reading Dostoevsky, who may well have helped Roth in creating a consciousness for his own Underground Man. In addition, Roth edited for many years a series of translations of books by modern Central and East European writers. Still, apart from formal influences, *Sabbath's Theater* seems to me a very American book and Mickey Sabbath a very American type. The reader is given a man with an extreme talent for messing up his life, at the very end of his tether. But what was Sabbath at the beginning? He was yet another much-loved Jewish child of the (lower) middle class. Nothing in his youth had prepared him for the losses that are inherent in existence; his rage and outrageousness are partly reactions that such things should have happened to him. His is an extreme instance of a familiar American fate, of innocence violated. Drenka was certain of Sabbath's Americanness. In a deathbed scene, which Mickey remembers near the end of the novel, Drenka tries in her broken English to sum up what he meant to her: "To have the lover, Mickey, to be very close that way, to be accepted by you, the American boyfriend. . . . You *are* America. Yes, you are, my wicked boy."

Another American feature that is especially marked in view of the politically oriented novels that Roth composed right after this one is the lack of social context for Sabbath's crisis. He himself is indifferent to the news—hooked on fucking, he has not even cared who is the president. His ordeal, the end to his career of fornication, this is a private matter. Neither is the novel remarkable for its sense of place. Rather, to use a familiar American expression, Sabbath is simply "up shit's creek," which can be anywhere, depending upon one's personal history. Who is he? That is the question Sabbath puts to himself. What has it meant to have a self? How did his life turn out this way? Is there any reason to continue? No doubt characters in the novels of other nations ask such questions, but the emphasis on personal identity, with so few strings attached, is an American specialty.

So is the "road novel," the rollicking ride away from the normal and commonplace, the ride always being what counts rather than the destination. Sabbath's ride is infused by hate and hopelessness, so he comes across as belonging to a different species than the road-loving Beats of the fifties. But he shares with them an enthusiasm for "wow!" experiences. His consistent ability to create huge hilarity out of grotesque and heart-breaking situations gives this novel a strangeness that puts it in an entirely different league from anything by Jack Kerouac.

Sabbath's Theater is very American, also, in being a "redskin" rather than a "paleface" novel. It emerges from the cult of experience, not the Great Books program associated with Robert Hutchins's University of Chicago. Unlike Saul Bellow's Moses Herzog, Mickey Sabbath is not an intellectual; he lives much closer to the bone. Bellow's contemporaries fell over themselves in praising *Herzog* when it appeared in 1964. The response was so keen that Irving Howe was able to find ten excellent essays to include with Bellow's text in the Viking Critical Edition. Commentators especially recognized the title character as representative of his generation of ex-radicals in that, deprived of a politics of ideas to engage him during the Eisenhower years, he had filled the void with "private relations." Specifically, Herzog had become a womanizer and then received his comeuppance when his wife cuckolded him with his best friend.

Sabbath, on the other hand, could not care less about Herzog's ideal of "a politics in the Aristotelian sense." He belongs to a generation that is post-political. Whereas Herzog chastises himself for investing in his girlfriends the attention he should have given to the public sphere, Sabbath regards obsession with the private and personal as inevitable. Talking to himself in his own version of Lear-speak, he says: "The personal's an immensity, nuncle, a constellation of detritus that doth dwarf the Milky Way; it pilots thee as do the stars."

The story of Herzog and his women is punctuated by a steady stream of unsent letters, many of which read like brief sermons or newspaper op-ed pieces. These letters are not uniformly serious in tone, but Herzog's sometime absurdity only made it easier for intellectuals to exult in the novel's intellectualism. At the same time, the general reader was able to identify with his predicament. *Herzog* became a best seller, was translated into many languages, and its self-consciously humanistic affirmations contributed to Bellow's winning the Nobel Prize in Literature in 1976. For its part, *Sabbath's Theater* did not go unrecognized: it won the National Book Award for Fiction in 1995. But its reception was otherwise muted compared with that of Bellow's novel. In the universities, it was met largely with indifference. Cultural studies specialists were writing about *The Sopranos,* and academic theorists had their own problems, like that of "the subject"; feminists detested the book as they have most of Roth's work; and, finally, middlebrow readers, who have made up the larger part of his audience, seem to have been either at the movies or watching DVDs at home.

Sabbath's Theater will someday receive the honor it deserves. It is not didactic fiction propelled by argument like *Herzog* and is free of Roth's own tendency in recent novels to preach cultural jeremiads. Also, its nihilism is not doctrinal. Rather, it is a triumph of fantasy, emotion, and instinct. Roth was able to reach down far into the deep places of imagination. In this unique novel, Roth reached down within himself to the deepest springs of his being, which freed his imagination as never before or since. The result, as with Mickey Sabbath himself, was a giant surge of energy, but, unlike in the case of Sabbath, energy not so anarchical that it ran away with itself and turned the book into a mess.

4.

Sabbath is still in New York, on the IRT subway that will carry him uptown from the Bowery to Grand Central Station. Dressed like a homeless person, he lumbers from car to car with a beggar's cup in his hand. Now, as he plays Lear to onlookers, he recalls his immense satisfaction at having Roseanna out of the way. In reaction to the phone-sex scandal at the college, she had gone on a terrible drinking binge and had to be confined to the detox unit of a fancy local hospital. Sabbath remembers driving and playing on his radio an old recording of "The Sheik of Araby." What makes Sabbath distinctive is his paradoxical ability at times to feel exultant in the midst of defeat: "Maybe it was knowing that he'd never had to please and wasn't starting now. Yes, yes, yes, he felt uncontrollable tenderness for his own shit-filled life. And a laughable hunger for more. More defeat! More disappointment! More deceit! More loneliness! More arthritis! . . . God willing, more cunt! More disastrous entanglement in everything. For a pure sense of being tumultuously alive, you can't beat the nasty side of existence."

Apart from the prayer for more sex, Sabbath is eager for more negativity: more loss, more emptiness, more loneliness, more arthritis-caused incapacity to practice his art. The lust in this remembered scene belongs to a time before his present impotence, which has spread from his sex life to affect everything. Still, he remains irrepressible. He equals Lear in his self-will, but his kind of defiance marks him as an original. Now he is playing Lear in the subway while enduring something like Lear's own degradation, which goes beyond anything he has known before. As always, Sabbath has the illusion that he retains some control, that he is only *acting* the part, as he is only pretending to be a beggar.

On the subway to his friend's funeral, Sabbath is nearly overcome by memory. When Lear's lines come back to him from his stage performance with Nikki thirty years before, he thinks on the "huge mnemonic surprise." He can leave nothing behind: "The mind is the perpetual motion machine." What it now brings back are the sorest griefs and the rawest emotions. Sabbath alternates between memories of his family in the period right after learning of Morty's death and thoughts of Nikki as his Cordelia. He recalls the last scene of act four, when a broken Lear is reunited with the daughter who has remained true to him despite his cruelty to her at the start of the play. Sabbath plays his part to a college-age girl dressed all in black. She surprises him by feeding him lines when he gets stuck.

He says, "I think this lady / To be my child Cordelia," and the girl replies, "And so I am, I am." Sabbath is nearly as overawed by the experience as Lear himself. He identifies the girl with Nikki and whispers to her, "Who is your mother?" Convinced in his Lear-like madness that the girl is Nikki's daughter, he turns her face with his gnarled hand. The girl, suddenly horrified, screams as she flees from Sabbath, and a male passenger grabs him and throws him off the train. We see him at the end of this scene alone and lost, abandoned by the girl as he had been by Nikki. He has been thoroughly disabused of his fantasy that by play-acting he can bring back his dead.

Where Sabbath comes closest to Lear is in his dramatization of humanity radically stripped of all those things that separate us from bestiality. He differs from Lear, however, insofar as he combines in himself the pathos of the wretched king *and* the hilarious detachment of the king's Fool. Still, allowing for the comedy, to which I will return, the passages from *Lear* that seem to me to have inspired Roth most, although he does not quote them, have to do with human life stripped of dignity and honor. When Lear visits the daughters on whom he has conferred his entire kingdom, they shock him by insisting that he divest himself of his entourage of knights. At first Goneril and Regan demand he cut back from one hundred to fifty. Then, after he curses Goneril for her filial disobedience, the sisters reduce that number to twenty-five and finally to none. The king must rid himself of all the appurtenances of kingliness. In act two, scene four, Goneril puts to him this rhetorical question: why does he need his own retainers when she has plenty of her own to care for him?

Grief-stricken and enraged, Lear launches forth on one of his many great speeches: "O, reason not the need! Our basest beggars / Are in the poorest thing superfluous. / Allow not nature more than nature needs, / Man's life is cheap as beast's." In the next act, Lear is led out of the storm into the hovel of another figure driven to madness by adversity. This is Gloucester's natural son, Edgar, unclothed in raiment and name, pretending to be Tom o' Bedlam. The king reflects on this mirror of himself as a person deprived of all appurtenances: "Is man no more than this? Consider him well. Thou ow'st the worm no silk, the beast no hide, the sheep no wool, the cat no perfume. . . . Thou art the thing itself; unaccommodated man is no more but such a poor, bare, forked animal as thou art."

Sabbath's rhetoric of negative qualifiers—he has been rendered wife*less* and mistress*less* after having been an *ex*-son and *ex*-brother—makes for the same effect as the plot in which Lear is deprived of his entourage by Goneril and Regan, is then betrayed by Edmund in collaboration with those evil daughters, and finally is reduced to madness by the storm on the heath, or perhaps, as Gloucester says, by "th' gods, / [Who] kill us for their sport." Roth enters into the spirit of the Lear-Cordelia reunion in his subway scene. His fiction has seldom communicated tenderness, but in this instance Sabbath's situation evokes pathos more than outrage. At the same time, I would admit that the tenderness does not extend much beyond Sabbath himself; the compassion he feels for his Cordelia, the drama-student girl in black, is limited. Sabbath never overcomes his absorption in himself. Even in his worst moments, Lear is never without company.

King Lear is the play of Shakespeare's that most resonates with the twentieth-century experience of genocide, "ethnic cleansing," and mass death caused by starvation and pestilence. Roth, in his individualistic American way, depicts "unaccommodated man" stripped of his dignity, and *Lear* was clearly an influence. But in Shakespeare there is a countervailing vision. In the case of humanity, not allowing nature more than nature needs is unnatural. Humankind has a natural right to silk and leather and woolens and perfumes. He speaks on behalf of a Renaissance-humanist conception of what is appropriate to the human condition. And the Christian influence is evident in Lear's discovery of love and sympathy as a consequence of his purgatorial suffering.

Roth is not without his own ideal of honor and dignity. But he is relentless in depicting the process of stripping, to which his victims respond with bitter rage and more and more sex, the more perverse the better, so long as they remain capable of it.

The dominant spirit, then, is of defiance. At the end, Mickey Sabbath is changed also: he has decided not to commit suicide. Love—remembered love for Morty and his parents—is part of it, but Roth seems embarrassed by that four-letter word. What ultimately keeps him going is his dark laughter and hatred of the world.

It would be an exaggeration to characterize Roth's view of human nature as totally bestial: his characters are always thinking overtime, and shame and humiliation are psychological not physical wounds. But neither is he a humanist. His emphasis in *Sabbath's Theater* and since has been on rawness and nakedness, on that "poor, bare, forked animal" to which his leading characters are reduced. That is the truth and reality of things, and society will make sure that we all get to know it first-hand.

Sabbath sums up the idea as part of his speech of defiance after Norm Cowan orders him out of the apartment after learning that his guest has been going about, including to their friend's funeral, with Cowan's daughter's underpants stuffed in his pocket. Norm still cannot grasp what appears to him as simply his guest's self-destructiveness. Sabbath counters: "It's always been hard for you, Norman, hasn't it, to imagine me? How he does it without protection? How do any of them do it without protection? Baby, there *is* no protection. It's all wallpaper. . . . What we are in the hands of *is not protection*." He describes, when he was a sailor coming into Latin American ports, visiting Catholic churches and being erotically stimulated by the sight of kneeling maidens at prayer: "Watching them seeking protection. . . . Seeking protection against the other. Seeking protection against themselves. Seeking protection against everything. *But there isn't any*." As Lear had affirmed a Renaissance-humanist conception of man clothed in appurtenances that distinguish him from the beasts, so Sabbath repudiates a certain well-meaning modern liberal humanism summed up in Norm. There will be no protection for him, despite his having money in the bank, the respect of the business community, and a lovely family. Sabbath is about to outrage Norm by revealing how close he came to seducing his wife: "Even you are exposed— what do you make of that? Exposed! Fucking naked, even in that suit! The suit is futile, the monogram is futile—nothing will do it. *We have no idea how it's going to turn out*." The truth is that unaccommodated man is the reality of things behind the wallpaper that is the veil of Maya. Briefly put, life is shit or will turn out to be shit if we live long enough.

5.

Now, that experience and conviction may, I suppose, constitute the basis for a religion of sorts. James Wood certainly discerns a religious meaning in *Sabbath's Theater*. But if such an intention informed this novel, it might be expected to disclose itself in the scene in which Sabbath visits the Jersey cemetery in which his parents and Morty lie buried. I have looked for a positive countervailing force to oppose the anarchy and incoherence that Sabbath discerns as the only meaning of things. But if the countervailing force is here in the cemetery scene, it is not supernatural. It is comedy, dark comedy to be sure, but not less hilarious for that. Laughter is both an expression of Sabbath's despair and his means for overcoming it. There is much to overcome, at the funeral in New York and now, at the cemetery near the Jersey shore: the fact that the dead cannot be brought back.

"Alas, Poor Yorick!" Hamlet did not get to Yorick's burial site by driving "an ancient Chevy with a broken-down tailpipe" south on the Garden State Parkway, but it was conceivably *Hamlet* that led to Roth's writing his cemetery scene, one of the funniest in this novel. He sets the dominant tone of Schadenfreude from the start. The cemetery is not where it is supposed to be. The dead have been relocated so that the ground in which they have been buried could be asphalted over to serve as a parking lot; a supermarket has been built where Sabbath's parents had been previously laid to rest. He assails the store manager: "Where the hell did you put them?" Asked whom he is talking about, Sabbath exclaims, "The dead. I am a mourner! Which aisle?"

When he gets to the cemetery, he locates the Sabbaths' new four-grave plot. His mother, father, and Morty have been laid to rest, and Sabbath plans to commit suicide and join them. But he finds that two years ago his place in the plot had been filled by the coffin of his mother's maiden sister from the Bronx: "Had everybody forgotten the second son?" Being exiled from his final resting place with the family comes as a stunning blow to Sabbath. He again envisions himself as the most of the least: "King of the kingdom of the disillusioned, emperor of no expectations, crestfallen man-god of the double cross, Sabbath had *still* to learn that nothing but *nothing* will ever turn out—and this obtuseness was, in itself, a deep, deep shock. Why does life refuse me even the *grave* I want!"

The cemetery manager shows him what is available and offers a variety of advice. The cemetery has a special section reserved for single plots, and Crawford the manager recommends one plot there because, although Sabbath would be at some distance from his own kin, "you're across from a very fine family." But the manager also pushes two-grave sites: "I would rather see you up with the two. You won't be crammed in up there." Sabbath agrees: "There's definitely more legroom." But he is not enthusiastic about any two-grave plot. Crawford is agreeable: "Okay. You just look around and see where you'll be comfortable."

Frustrated by the distance he will have to lie from his family, Sabbath thinks about being buried back in New England "as close to Drenka as he could get." That has its down side, too: "But whom would he talk to up there?" Sabbath has been communing with his mother's spirit, and he expects his conversations with his significant dead will increase once he is dead. If he returns to be buried in Madamaska Falls, he will lose the company of his family and tens of other members of the extended family also buried in this Jewish cemetery. It would be fine to converse with Drenka, but who is buried near her? "He had never found a goy yet who would talk fast enough for him. And there they'd be slower than usual."

One of the jokes of this scene is how Sabbath pays in advance the charges for his plot, monument, the inscription, funeral arrangements, and the rabbi. He had stolen from Michelle Cowan's chest of drawers a packet of hundred-dollar bills along with another envelope containing Polaroid shots of Michelle in the nude. Both envelopes lay concealed and pointed to the possibility that she thought she might one day run off with one or another of her lovers.

So Sabbath's family reunion is of a piece with the rest of his life in being bitterly disillusioning. But emotions come intermingled, and memories of his great happiness from eight to thirteen rejuvenate him. He reflects that he should have reached out to Morty in the grave and shared a joke with him: "Rapture itself, to reach out my hand and give him a laugh, a body, a voice, a life with some of the fun in it of being alive, the fun of existing that even a flea must feel, the pleasure of existence, pure and simple, that practically anyone this side of the cancer ward gets a glimmer of occasionally, uninspiring as his fortunes overall may be."

That rapture and other such moments do not cause Sabbath to change his mind: he remains determined to take his own life. He cruises in his Chevy for one last time past remembered places from his childhood. He comes upon the house of Cousin Fish, who had been close to his family when he was a boy. Amazingly, his ancient cousin is still alive at one hundred, and Fish still feels that mysterious resistance to death that Sabbath had noted among all the Jewish men of that generation in the family. Cousin Fish remembers how things had been a half-century before, and he stirs up in Sabbath a renewed desire to live.

However, the cousin also has in his house a carton of Morty's things, and going through those memorabilia—from Morty's childhood and his time in the air force—affects Sabbath with grief that even he has never known. Cartons, packets of cash and Polaroids, conversations on tape, concealed letters and diaries; such items are as necessary to Roth's plot as the narrative conventions Dickens made famous. They provide the structure for Mickey Sabbath's intense feelings, generated in this instance by the reminders of Morty: "The pure, monstrous purity of the suffering was new to him, made any and all suffering he'd known previously seem like an imitation of suffering. This was the passionate, the violent stuff, the worst, invented to torment one species alone, the re-membering animal, the animal with the long memory."

There follows a description of Sabbath's frenzy of grief on the beach. He is crying, ranting, chanting aloud sentences that even he does not understand: "He figured the only thing that could ever swallow him up like that again would have to be the ocean. And all from only a single carton. Imagine, then, the history of the world. We are immoderate because grief is immoderate, all the hundreds and thousands of kinds of grief." Surely some have experienced a fate even more horrendous than Sabbath's. Perhaps he is immoderate because he is immoderate; he is intense and superabundant in everything, especially where feelings of every kind are concerned.

In these pages about Morty, Roth wants to emphasize the theme of "unaccommodated man" from *Lear*. He is driving back to Madamaska Falls with the American flag draped about him that he had found in Morty's carton. He wears on his head another item from the box: "the red, white, and blue V for Victory, God Bless America yarmulke." How better to affirm the identification of America's Jews with their adopted homeland. But Sabbath draws no such moral from his costume. Rather, he thinks the outfit appropriate in his present role as a tragicomic version of *Lear*'s Fool and Yorick the court jester: "A man of mirth must always dress in the priestly garb of his sect."

Sabbath affirms the lesson Huck Finn learns going down the river with Nigger Jim: "Clothes are a masquerade anyway. When you go outside and see everyone in clothes, then you know for sure that nobody has a clue as to why he was born and that, aware of it or not, people are perpetually performing in a dream. It's putting corpses into clothes that really betrays what great thinkers we are." The conviction that man is most himself as the "naked, poor, forked animal" intensifies Sabbath's sense of futility. But as regards committing suicide, he is not so resolute; he is constantly leaning one way and then the other. His latest thought on the matter is this: "How could he kill himself now that he had Morty's things?"

He cannot kill himself simply because he has such intensity about him. It is possible to feel that Sabbath has not committed suicide at the Jersey shore because of the solidarity he experiences with his family at the cemetery, in particular his memory of love for Morty that is evoked by the relics he discovers at the home of Cousin Fish. There is also the inspiration he derives from that good cousin.

I am myself disposed to think that Sabbath has to keep going not because he discovers love that had long been buried inside but because he has too much energy to stop. His adventures might end at any point, but Roth is not ready to wind things down until Sabbath makes his return to Madamaska Falls, where this peculiar variant of a road novel began. Still given to illusion despite his image of himself as the "King of the kingdom of disillusionment," Sabbath imagines moving back in with Roseanna. To stimulate himself he creates a detailed fantasy of her masturbating; but then, approaching the house, he finds his place has been usurped by Roseanna's lover, who turns out to be a woman. Then, still unsubdued, Sabbath hauls himself up to Drenka's grave in the woods for one final act of homage. It is dark out, but, having found the spot, Sabbath is performing his version of honoring his lost lover when he is interrupted by a tap from behind and the glare of a powerful flashlight in his eyes: "Stop what you are doing, sir! *Stop now!* . . . You are pissing on my mother's grave!" It is Drenka's policeman son, Matthew.

It appears that Matthew and the trainee in his patrol car will take Sabbath off to jail. Then Matthew changes his mind, takes off his prisoner's handcuffs, and orders him out of the patrol car. Sabbath is sure Matthew or his partner will now kill him, and he longs for such an ending. But, no, it will not be so easy for him to exit this world. The language of the ending does not point to Sabbath's conversion to love, but it does affirm energy and the life force in things.

Matthew has left his mother's lover "ankle-deep in the pudding of the springtime mud, blindly engulfed by the alien, inland woods, by the rainmaking trees and the rainwashed boulders—and with no one to kill him except himself." That "pudding" evokes the security of Sabbath's early life about which he was reminded when he visited his family's graves; and "springtime mud" suggests birth and the inevitable cycles of life. The passage in general conveys a sense of life pushing itself through whatever obstacles winter may put up. The "alien, inland woods" that engulf Sabbath are not like the ocean of suffering he had imagined earlier; they refer, rather, to the mystery of things that we cannot know: life goes on despite our blindness. And the "rainmaking trees and rainwashed boulders" are beautiful images that again contribute to a sense of life being fed and watered so that it may push through that pudding of mud into visibility. The rain may also refer to the undinist pagan tribute Sabbath was paying to Drenka when he was interrupted by the law in the person of her son.

If this sounds too positive and sentimental, there are the final words of the book to keep us on course. Energy is not a sentimental concept. Sabbath has been left by Matthew "with no one to kill him except himself." But as on all previous occasions, he wriggles out of the fate he thinks he craves: "He couldn't do it. He could not fucking die. How could he leave? How could he go? Everything he hated was here."

"We Are Here to Be Humiliated"

Philip Roth's Recent Fiction

Philip Roth's most recent novels have created a problem for his critics. Earlier in his controversial career, during the phase of *Portnoy's Complaint* and the following decade, readers worried whether Roth was the Real Thing or only a popular entertainer determined to repeat over and over an updated Borscht Belt comedy routine. I think it is evident by now that Roth always wished to be considered a serious artist, even, perhaps especially, when his fiction was most outrageous. In recent years he has developed into a kind of novelist of ideas, but it has remained unclear what his commitments are and what, finally, his novels are about.

Opposing evaluations of *I Married a Communist* help to pinpoint the problem. John Leonard, writing in the *Nation,* judged that novel to be a failure. Taking for granted that Roth's subject is politics, which seems reasonable enough, Leonard attacked the novel for being a "soap opera" and for being insufficiently sympathetic to the Left. Norman Podhoretz, ever attentive to ideology, also interpreted Roth's novel politically, but as having the opposite intention, as an expression of the anti-anticommunism of the 1950s.[1]

---

1. John Leonard, "Bedtime for Bolsheviks," review of *I Married a Communist* in *Nation,* December 28, 1998. Norman Podhoretz, "The Adventures of Philip Roth," *Commentary* 106 (October 1998).

The article by Podhoretz, "The Adventures of Philip Roth," appeared in the October 1998 issue of *Commentary*, the monthly of which he was editor for three decades. According to Podhoretz, in the first phase of Roth's career there was "an extraliterary and even a narrowly political dimension to [his] work and to his popularity as well," and in his new novel Roth was returning after twenty-five years to the political stance that had made him the "laureate of the New Class." Anti-anti-communist, fellow traveler of the counterculture, laureate of the New Class . . . in the eyes of Podhoretz, with his zest for simplistic political categories, Philip Roth is a type. Which is to say that he is just like Podhoretz himself, but on the opposite side.

But Roth is not like Podhoretz. His novels are literary performances, not statements of a "position." He is consistent in railing against the fanaticism of communal virtue, but the tribal pieties he attacks change from one novel to another such that, if one looks for their political implications, it turns out that Roth is totally undependable, not at all a solid party man. That makes it frustrating if you are a partisan like Podhoretz, who is above all determined to know which side you are on.

The assumption that in *I Married a Communist* Roth was trying to write a political novel might seem to be self-evident. Why else write a novel about the activities of communists and anti-communists during the early cold war? But there are other possible motives, and Roth suggests one answer in Murray Ringold's account of the betrayal that destroyed his brother Ira, the novel's central figure and the "Communist" in its title. Murray declares that "more acts of personal betrayal were tellingly perpetrated in America in the decade after the war—say, between '46 and '56—than in any other period of our history." Betrayal happens to be a great theme of Roth; it plays a large role in his imaginative life quite independent of national politics. An artist starts with his obsessions and searches for contexts that allow him to objectify them. That is what T. S. Eliot had in mind by the term "objective correlative."

The theme of betrayal bubbles away in the deep places of Roth's imagination; presumably it exists there both as a traumatic experience and as an obsessive fantasy. Formalists argue that meaning follows form. On this view, Hemingway's clipped style, an amalgam of his early journalism and literary models, produced the attitudes that inform his fiction: the code of the stiff upper lip, the allergy to emotional expressiveness, the high valuation placed on technical expertise, and so on. Similarly, writers search for situations to write about that allow them to inject their ruling passions and fantasies. Ideological anti-communism in the post–World War II period was to Roth's purpose for the reason Murray Ringold mentions, the flood of betrayals it encouraged. Roth, having found his theme, has run with it, especially in his fiction since *Sabbath's Theater.*

Murray brings Ira's story into association with sexual transgression, another favorite Roth subject, by urging the analogy between the pleasures of sex and the gratification of destroying an enemy by exposing him. Ira was betrayed by his embittered wife, who conspired with fanatical anti-communist friends of hers to expose him. That exposure involved a memoir, *I Married a Communist,* supposedly written by Ira's wife, Eve, but actually concocted by his wife's friends with the specific purpose of destroying him. Contrary to Eve's supposed "confession," Ira had never been a Communist spy.

Eve Frame's fabricated exposé of Ira inevitably calls to mind *Leaving a Doll's House* (1996), which might be regarded as Claire Bloom's exposé of Roth. Bloom had lived with him for two decades and had persuaded him to marry her toward the end of their relationship. These last years obviously were ghastly, and Roth's conduct was hardly admirable. Bloom was clearly aiming to get her version of events on the record; Roth had revealed his version of their story in fictional terms that in the case of one novel, *Deception,* barely bothered to draw a curtain over their actual lives. In general, Bloom exceeded the bounds of taste in her memoir but managed to keep her anger in check. In *I Married a Communist,* on the other hand, vengeance is a great simplifier: Roth renders Eve Frame as a version of the Great American Bitch.

The battle over communism and anti-communism, then, is only the *occasion* for this novel, not its deeper subject. Roth's historical trilogy— *American Pastoral, I Married a Communist,* and *The Human Stain,* published in a fury of creativity between 1997 and 2000—is about great social-political turning points in American life since World War II. But even though Roth was writing here on a much broader canvas than in the earlier part of his career, I do not regard him as either a political novelist or a novelist with large general ideas about society or history. If Roth has any philosophy of history to propose in this novel, it is that betrayal—of father by son, husband by wife, mentor by protégé, friend by friend, and so on—is what life is about and has always been about.

Critics lacking in literary sensibility try to compensate for a tin ear by finding portentous political implications in novels that may have been written with very different intentions, for example, as formal experiments in narrative. Norman Podhoretz announces in "The Adventures of Philip Roth" that he had read Roth's previous novel, *American Pastoral,* as evidence of the novelist-prodigal's coming home to right-thinking Jewish middle-class values. That novel showed Swede Levov's adolescent daughter as an evil monster, blowing up innocent people in the name of opposition to the Vietnam War. In contrast to the radical daughter, Roth limned a sympathetic portrait of Swede's old-fashioned Jewish parents, especially emphasizing the work ethic, patriotism, and devotion of Swede's father. According to Podhoretz, *American Pastoral* marked the second birth of Roth the writer, this time as a *Commentary*-type neoconservative. It had taken a long time, but Roth had finally seen the wisdom of Podhoretz's way.

Given such a reading, it is not surprising that *I Married a Communist* should have seemed to Podhoretz a lamentable case of backsliding. But the fact is that *American Pastoral,* which appeared only a year earlier, is not that much different in its true subject. In the earlier novel, Swede is betrayed by his daughter and then by his Catholic beauty-queen wife, who allows herself to be seduced by a loathsome neighbor. The difference perhaps is that although both Swede and Ira are the victims of specific individuals, Swede is made to appear more as the victim of life itself.

American Pastoral is on its face a story of violence and terrorism occurring against the background of the antiwar movement of the late 1960s. But if Roth's central concern was political, it might have involved itself far more with the actual radical movement. Instead, that movement appears here as a Gothic nightmare, akin to Hollywood horror movies about serial killers. What Roth actually offers the reader is grotesquerie in the person of Swede's mad daughter, Merry, and the adolescent witch, one Rita Cohen, under whose spell she has fallen. Roth depicts Swede's one-on-one confrontation with Rita, who shows off her private parts and mockingly suggests he have sex with her if he would like ever to see his daughter again. Later in the novel Swede catches up with Merry. Still in her teens, she has now participated in the killing of several innocent people. When her father discovers her living in primitive conditions in the heart of devastated Newark, she has long been a fugitive from justice and has degenerated into an image of horror as far beyond the reach of sanity as she is beyond any kind of rational politics. She has become a Jain and lives in elective squalor. What Roth wants to show is not social conflict but metaphysical evil, cosmic disorder on a grand scale, his purpose being to reveal the impact of that disorder on an innocent man, Swede Levov, little prepared for it.

But, then, Roth asks, who *is* prepared for it? In short, this is another novel, like *I Married a Communist* and all of Roth's novels, about someone's "life as a man." A man grows older and expects the shocks of life to decrease, but in Roth's recent novels they occur more frequently. In the novels of the historical trilogy, these shocks end only with the man's destruction.

Ira's story, however, does not have the feel of tragedy. Rather, it is a very American story about the rise from violence and obscurity of a Jewish tough guy from Newark's Italian First Ward. Ira is a resourceful street fighter, but socially he is an ignorant drifter. He enlists in the army, and there he meets a fiercely disciplined communist, Johnny O'Day, from whom he absorbs a ready-made system for thinking about the world. Put into practice, that system gives Ira's life a structure, but it also discourages the independent thinking that might have saved him from the worst effects of his illusions.

After the war Ira, at six-foot-six, becomes famous for his imitations of Abe Lincoln at trade union events. From there he moves up to become the star of a radio serial, *The Brave and the Free*, in which he impersonates a host of legendary American heroes, Abraham Lincoln in particular. This is the period of the Popular Front, when it was possible to be a communist like Ira and simultaneously think of oneself as 100 percent American. After this point in Ira's career, however, it is mainly downhill. He is not blessed with good sense about many matters. Above all, he is helpless when it comes to women.

He marries Eve Frame, a silent-film star several years older than himself. Eve has been married several times before, and she brings to her union with Ira a daughter in her twenties to whom she proves more devoted than to her new husband. The marriage falls apart, as it is clear it must, because Eve's hysteria as a mother is matched by Ira's implacable rages and small-time philandering. Eve runs for sympathy to her op-portunistic anti-communist friends, the Grants, who persuade her to lend her name to the exposé I have mentioned, which effectively de-stroys Ira's life. This memoir, devised by the Grants, falsely portrays Ira as the "mastermind" of a "ring" of Communists who have infiltrated the media to disseminate their subversive message. The consequence of Eve's "revelations" is Ira's utter ruin. By the end his only motive for keeping alive is to exact revenge against Eve.

I have said that Roth shows his hand early as far as his intentions are concerned. On page three, Murray Ringold describes his brother's story as "a grave misfortune replete with farce." Ira's rise and fall dramatize the idea that we are alive to be shamed, stripped of our dignity and every comfort that might assuage the loss. Life as betrayal, humiliation, and internal exile have been the central themes of Roth's most recent phase.

That theme surfaced early in his career, in his agonized response to a powerful attack on his work by Irving Howe that appeared in *Commentary* in 1972. Howe had praised *Goodbye, Columbus* when it came out in 1959, but after *Portnoy's Complaint* Howe decided that Roth was a rootless Jew with no ties to the tradition and a nastiness the critic attrib-uted to the novelist's "thin personal culture" and underlying depression. Howe's "reconsideration" was right in picking up a note of bitterness that would be sounded more fully in Roth's later writing, but the cri-tique was wrongheaded in denying Roth's positive identification with his Jewishness.

However, Roth's fiction in the seventies shows how little he was able to shake off the hurt. He kept nursing the wound until *The Anatomy Lesson,* which appeared eleven years after Howe's article. Howe, in *The Anatomy Lesson,* is given the name of Milton Appel, a character who is subjected to the furies of Nathan Zuckerman's rage, in person and by proxy. On a plane flight to Chicago, Zuckerman, liberally dosed on al-cohol, Percodan, and marijuana, introduces himself to his seatmate as Milton Appel, professional pornographer, and assails the man with the most outrageous sleaze imaginable. However, despite what should be a final exorcism of the Appel-wound, Nathan continues to worry whether the actual Appel may have been correct in what he wrote: "What if my writing's as bad as he says? I hate his guts, and obviously the sixties have driven him batty, but that doesn't make him a fool, you know. He's one of the few of them around who make any sense at all. Let's face it, even the worst criticism contains some truth. They always see something you're trying to hide."

The Anatomy Lesson is important in showing how demoralized Roth could be by negative criticism. Howe's attack had left him paralyzed as a writer. He understood that his only subject was himself and that he lacked the capacity to enter into the consciousness of others. That incapacity would in fact weaken all three novels in the historical trilogy of 1997–2000. Not one of his central characters—Swede Levov, Ira Ringold, or Coleman Silk—comes across vividly. In *The Anatomy Lesson,* Zuckerman seems to accept that he has only himself to write about, and he wonders whether, as some critics have complained, he has exhausted that subject. Zuckerman's self-doubt causes him to entertain the idea of quitting writing altogether and going to medical school.

That self-doubt issues in a reflection that makes explicit the problem of imagination that will be central to Roth's fiction in the wake of *The Anatomy Lesson.* In that book Zuckerman ponders the secret of self-understanding, sounding for all the world like Roth himself: "If he wasn't cultivating hypothetical Zuckermans he really had no more means than a fire hydrant to decipher his existence. But either there was no existence left to decipher or he was without sufficient imaginative power to convert into his fiction of seeming self-exposure what existence had now become. There was no rhetorical overlay left: he was bound and gagged by the real raw thing, ground down to his own unhypothetical nub. He could no longer pretend to be anyone else, and as a medium for his books he had ceased to be."

What is wondrous is that by 1995 Roth would seem in his personal life to have been truly "ground down to his own unhypothetical nub," yet prove able imaginatively to convert "what his existence had now become" into a marvelous picaresque comedy about an aging artist-buffoon like and unlike himself. Reflecting on his brother's ravaged life in *I Married a Communist,* Murray Ringold says to Zuckerman: "Maybe, despite ideology, politics, and history, a genuine catastrophe is always personal bathos at the core. Life can't be impugned for any failure to trivialize people. You have to take your hat off to life for the techniques at its disposal to strip a man of his significance and empty him totally of his pride."

Roth's own career has been marked from the start by attempts to mortify him. *Goodbye, Columbus* (1959) stirred up the indignation of rabbis and other spokespersons of the organized Jewish community. The familiar cry of anti-Semitism went up, and it has been heard since then at various times. *Commentary* magazine in particular has found it hard to forgive Roth for not celebrating Jewish "family values," as if he ought to be a Jewish Dan Quayle.[2] But there was another, more positive side to the reception of Roth's first book. The young author was welcomed into the fold by the most respected figures of the New York literary community. Among those who wrote glowingly of the stories in that collection were Howe, Alfred Kazin, and Saul Bellow, and when the *New York Review of Books* got underway a few years later, Roth was its favorite younger novelist. Since then he has remained the fiction writer most consistently celebrated in its pages. In the year after its publication, *Goodbye, Columbus* won the National Book Award. Roth was all of twenty-seven. Since then he has probably received more honors than any living American novelist except for Toni Morrison and Saul Bellow, whose Nobel prizes have set them apart.

But Roth has seemed to hang on to his humiliations in order to exploit them in his writing. As an instructor at the University of Chicago in the fifties, he got involved with a highly neurotic divorced woman with children who was a few years older than he. The affair turned into a marriage when the woman deceived him about being pregnant. Roth lived with her only a few years and fitfully thereafter but was not able to shed her completely until she was killed in a car accident roughly a decade after they had met. Plainly, this hysterical and unscrupulous woman caused him great anguish. Also plainly, only a highly unusual writer would have rehashed their story in one version or another in novels of the sixties (*Letting Go* [1962] and *When She Was Good* [1967]); in endless detail in *My Life as a Man* (1974); and yet again in *The Facts* (1988), Roth's "true" account of his early life. At the end of the mad wife section of that memoir, Roth owns up to her usefulness as a prod to his imagination: "Without doubt she was the worst enemy ever, but, alas,

2. Dan Quayle was the forty-fourth vice president of the United States from January 20, 1989, to January 20, 1993, under the presidency of George Bush Sr. Famous for his malapropisms, he was a figure of fun among political liberals.

she was also nothing less than the greatest creative-writing teacher of them all, specialist par excellence in the aesthetics of extremist fiction."

It may happen, however, that less-than-earthshaking wounds that have been nurtured for their literary uses come to be taken uncritically by a writer as tragedies on a vast human scale. Understandably, readers become impatient waiting for that writer to take on new subject matter. But in the late eighties, reality itself upped the ante for Roth. Those years witnessed the start of a series of personal disasters that he has been drawing on ever since for his fiction. As *The Anatomy Lesson* shows, Roth has known physical pain for a long time. He had chronic back pain from an injury suffered in basic training at Fort Dix in the fifties, but that pain was only a mild prelude to the disasters that began thirty-five years later.

In 1988 his father died, after considerable suffering, of a brain tumor—the son tells the story in a very affecting memoir, *Patrimony* (1991). Roth himself had to undergo quintuple by-pass surgery during the period of his father's decline. More devastasting was a nervous breakdown he suffered as a consequence of taking the drug Halcyon for pain after failed knee surgery. According to Claire Bloom, Roth suffered another breakdown, this time as a result of John Updike's highly critical review of *Operation Shylock* (1993) in the *New Yorker*. Around the same time, Bloom, feeling her grip on her lover to be slipping, put pressure on him to formalize their relationship, which had gone on for twenty years without their marrying. But marriage had the effect of throwing Roth into a panic, and the relationship suffered a quick meltdown. Roth's abusive treatment of Bloom, his psychotic episodes, and other intimate details were exposed in her memoir. These were the disasters, Bloom's revelations being not the least of them, that Roth converted into art in *Sabbath's Theater*.

One way in which that novel differs from the historical trilogy is that Roth does not treat Mickey Sabbath with the sentimentality in which the protagonists of the trilogy are draped. Roth, never shy about loading the narrative deck to win sympathy for his suffering heroes, went farther than usual in rendering the big, unskeptical Swede Levov and the physically even larger Ira Ringold as grown-ups with the moral simplicity of children. Roth does not deal well with the innocence that was J. D. Salinger's forte; as a result the reader finds it hard to believe in Swede and Ira or to care much about them.

I have been discussing the first two novels of the trilogy that follows *Sabbath's Theater*. The weaknesses of that trilogy are illuminated by comparison with *Zuckerman Bound,* the individual novels of which appeared between 1979 and 1983. Those novels are vivid and spirited, and nothing in Roth's body of work is as formally perfect as *The Ghost Writer* (1979), which brings together the influences of James and Chekhov. The novels of that trilogy, which includes *The Anatomy Lesson,* are entertaining, but may be judged as limited by their focus on the hijinks and vicissitudes of Zuckerman, their artist-hero.

However, in my own view Roth is almost always better at imagining the hijinks of persons like himself than in imagining characters who stand out for their otherness. The later trilogy was a brave narrative experiment after the more autobiographical *Operation Shylock* and *Sabbath's Theater.* But however ambitious they may appear in widening the scope of his fiction, they are far less successfully realized than the more narrowly focused novels of the earlier Zuckerman trilogy.

The new trilogy is an attempt at a higher degree of objectivity and broader social reach, and in his rhetoric of ranting and raving Roth seems to want to appear as original in his views. But what is new about the bias of these novels? The anti-anti-communism of the fifties that informs *I Married a Communist,* the detestation of the Weathermen that fuels *American Pastoral,* and the skepticism about French feminism in *The Human Stain* were and are conventional opinions among the ever-so-slightly-left-of-center liberals who came of age in the late forties and early fifties. In that respect, Roth, if not the laureate of the "new class," whatever that is, has been the laureate of the *New York Review of Books.*

The refinements of cultural politics in New York during the past several decades are largely irrelevant to Roth's unique abilities as a novelist. For the fact is simple: no, he is not a political novelist and is least interesting in his rants and homilies about the state of American culture. On the contrary, he appears at the top of his form when he writes tragical-farcical saturnalias about individuals who are at least a little like himself. It seems to me clear that the best of these carnivals of outrageousness, like *Portnoy's Complaint, The Anatomy Lesson,* and *Sabbath's Theater,* do not illuminate politics or history. They reflect, rather, a typically American anxious uncertainty over who one really is. They are not informed by original social thought but by Roth's manic defense against being dragged down by the wounds suffered by his fragile narcissism. Of course, narcissistic vulnerability has become as commonplace as apple pie. What, at his best, makes Roth special is what in his fiction he does with his wounds.

Roth's obsessive sense of always being humiliated led after his break with Claire Bloom to his exit from the world of daily personal relationships into Flaubert-like solitude. Alone, at least most of the time, he has been able to write new novels at a prodigious rate and protect himself from most externally generated traumas. Keeping to himself and not facing the frustrations a recalcitrant world offers to our imaginative designs, Roth invents fictions of betrayal and revenge, currently his richest vein of material. These stories are given a realistic literary format, but they appear to well up from deep sources of personal fantasy, which plainly occupy more of Roth's mind than the cycles of history.

Sometimes Roth has escaped from obsession by way of ironic detachment. Harold Bloom tells this story: "It was 1990 at Symphony Space in New York City. Claire Bloom, then married to Roth, was giving a reading from my *Book of J*. I went on after her, to make some remarks . . . on the work's reception. Some *Orthodoxen Ochsen* in the audience called out insulting remarks—I would not respond. Afterwards, in the Green Room, Roth came over to me and said: 'Harold, my motto is: We are here to be humiliated.'"[3]

---

3. Personal communication to the author, July 3, 2002.

Geoffrey Hartman,
Wordsworth, and
Holocaust Testimonies

Up to the 1950s, it was no easy thing for a Jewish scholar to find a place in university departments of English. There had previously been Jewish professors of mathematics and chemistry. That was because professors of math and science were not as concerned about "culture" and "refinement" as were their colleagues in English. "Refinement" was one of those code words to justify excluding the unwashed, above all Jews who had the right intellectual gifts but often lacked what were felt to be the appropriate manners. After World War II, however, that genteel anti-Semitism was no longer socially acceptable, and it became harder to keep out the Jews.

Then another trend began. The first Jews to gain acceptance in the best university departments of literature had been persons wholly assimilated in their taste and style. Indeed, pioneers like Harry Levin at Harvard and Lionel Trilling at Columbia had quite complicated feelings about being Jewish. With the rapid expansion of the universities in the sixties, many more Jewish literary scholars found places available, and they did not have to overcome the prejudices that had often made things bitter for earlier cohorts. The attitudes of many Jewish literary academics who arrived on the scene in the sixties and after were quite different as well. Often the newcomers, having been raised in securely assimilated circumstances, recovered the positive Jewish self-identification from which their parents had fled in the thirties and forties. Some were even dedicated to the Judaic learning that had been a matter of indifference to secular-minded and politically leftist intellectuals of the preceding generation.

In most cases those Jewish interests did not emerge full blown. The younger cohorts started, as had the pioneering generation, with doctoral dissertations on Milton and Wordsworth and Matthew Arnold and other established figures in the Anglo-American canon. Only gradually did their interests become sufficiently consolidated and their confidence sufficient that they offered courses specifically on Jewish themes and writers. Those interests ultimately evolved into a new area of concentration: Jewish studies. Except at a few places, like Brandeis, Jewish studies was not a self-standing academic department but a committee composed of scholars from a variety of traditional departments. The courses taught by these scholars—perhaps a course in the literature of the Holocaust, but also a required course on Milton's poetry—reflected their dual interests and commitments.

One can study the transition to Jewish studies in a compilation of personal essays, mainly by baby-boomer academics: *People of the Book: Thirty Scholars Reflect on Their Jewish Identity* (1996).[1] It is notable that hardly any of the contributors write of suffering in their careers on account of their Jewish identity and overt Jewish interests. In fact, many of them gained far more visibility as Jewish-oriented scholars than they had before.

There is the occasional scholar, not represented in that collection, who had achieved preeminence in his or her traditional literary field and risked the skepticism of friends and colleagues by a major shift in direction. Many writers and painters have reinvented themselves in their work, but radical changes are less common in the careers of literary scholars and critics. And academics, far more conservative as a group than the writers they study, tend to stick to their areas of expertise.

---

1. Jeffrey Rubin-Dorsky and Shelley Fisher Fishkin, eds. *People of the Book: Thirty Scholars Reflect on their Jewish Identity* (Madison: University of Wisconsin Press, 1996).

Indeed, some rarely venture beyond a thirty-year period of literary history that is their specialty. Trilling certainly worked in a broader range. Still, as I wrote earlier, he felt he could not violate the boundaries he had set for himself, as a cultural critic, to take a chance again at writing fiction. I have discussed in another essay in this book the habitual cautiousness that trapped him in the public role at which he excelled but which did not allow him to express his unique individuality.

There is a case of another Jewish critic who has been more bold. During the first quarter-century of his career, Geoffrey Hartman was one of a handful of leading reinterpreters of Romantic poetry in the academy. It is a peculiar fact that it was mainly Jews, like Hartman and his Yale colleague Harold Bloom and Meyer Abrams at Cornell, who led the way in bringing the Romantics back into scholarly prominence after the mainly Episcopal and Catholic New Critics, influenced by T. S. Eliot, had edited them out. Hartman's work as an interpreter of poetry and critic-historian of trends in literary theory accounted for eight books from 1954 to 1985, not including the many volumes he edited. Three or four of these books alone would have been sufficient to establish a place for him among the leading literary academics of his generation. And that does not include his contribution to the prestige of comparative literature as a new framework for literary studies with departmental legitimation.

But then, when other critics were consolidating and extending their achievements, Hartman seemed to take a new direction altogether. Starting in the 1980s, Hartman created a new, less narrowly academic identity for himself. He became a founder of the Fortunoff Video Archive for Holocaust Testimonies at Yale and has remained its faculty advisor and project director. As of the year 2000, well over four thousand Holocaust survivors had granted video interviews; the archive includes more than ten thousand hours of testimony. Hartman has contributed to the success of the project by his academic prestige, but also by his energy. He has traveled all over America, Europe, and Israel to present lectures bearing on the testimonies and related issues; he has organized major conferences on the Holocaust that turned into edited books; and he has written a series of influential essays that inquire into the testimonies as a new genre that has importance not only for Holocaust historians but also in the general culture.

Hartman's work on the testimonies does represent a fresh start, but it did not require his becoming an entirely different person. My focus here, drawing on heretofore-unknown details of Hartman's life, is on the continuities that link his early literary studies, especially on Wordsworth, with his Holocaust studies. What I offer is necessarily speculative: Hartman is an elusive writer. Logic has never been his strong suit, and in his essays on Holocaust testimonies he especially depreciates what he calls the "positivities" of verifiable fact.

2.

In May 2000, Hartman visited the Divinity School of the University of Chicago, where I was myself a professor, to offer a short course on some Romantic poems. I conducted three interviews with him in which I asked mainly about his Jewish background and current interests.

One question that always arises in my mind about older Jewish intellectuals concerns timing: why did their Jewish concerns intensify at the time that they did? Hartman pointed out that he had long been concerned with the Holocaust but had not until the eighties found a way to engage it as a scholarly subject. That was because he had not found a way of dealing with the subject that did not cast the Jews in the role of passive victims. After all, the photographs of concentration camp life were taken by Nazis, who intended to represent the Jews as defeated and degraded. The survivor testimonies at Yale have a very different aim. As Hartman said, "They restore the sympathy and humanity systematically denied by the Nazi footage." People who view the videos "see the testimony of a thinking and feeling person, rather than of a victim."

Hartman can hardly be said to be disinterested in relation to the question of how these survivors are seen. He came close as a child to being a concentration-camp internee himself. He was living in Frankfurt, Germany, his birthplace, as late as 1939. After the pogrom of Kristallnacht, in December 1938, his mother secured a visa to America for herself but was not able to obtain one for her nine-year-old son. He was rescued in March 1939 by a Children's Transport *(Kindertransport)* financed by British Jews, and he wound up spending the years 1939–45 in the countryside of Buckinghamshire.[2] That may seem an idyll compared with the fate other Jewish children suffered in the concentration camps. But being separated from one's mother for so long in a situation of great uncertainty can hardly not have been traumatic. Moreover, Hartman lacked other nourishing human ties in England. None of the other Jewish German boys at his English foster home shared his intellectual interests or spiritual sympathies. Neither was he open to the kindness of strangers. In *The Longest Shadow*, he describes how little he felt for James and Dorothy de Rothschild, major financiers of the *Kindertransport* and patrons of the group home in Waddesdon where he spent the war years. He writes: "Brought up without father and mother, I would let no one else fill the vacuum."

Young people, awed by the glamor of success, are apt to believe that their heroes are persons who have, from their beginnings, enjoyed blessed lives very different from their own. In fact, America has increasingly become a nation of family dynasties, in which it sometimes appears that most of the people at the top have started out with a leg up. But the older we get, the more we see things differently. Not all the great ones, not even the suavely sophisticated members of the Republic of Letters like Hartman, have had flowers strewn on their paths. In his case adversity had been the main theme long before 1939.

Geoffrey Hartman started out life as Gert Heumann. He acquired his present surname when, in his second year of life, his father and mother divorced and she reverted to her own family name. After her husband left her, Hartman's mother had great difficulty supporting herself, so that when Gert was seven she placed him in an orphanage, although she continued to see him on weekends. So the young Hartman had experienced the loss of his father at the age of one and the loss on a

2. These details are not as clear as they might be, and so we requested clarification from Hartman, who wrote the following: "Mark did not mention that my mother had made sure that I would be taken to England with the orphanage; she also had my name put on a list for being provisionally adopted by, or rather placed in, an English family. This actually came about, a month or so after arriving in England; but because that family lived close to Coventry, the authorities decided, after war broke out, that I would be safer in the countryside of Waddesdon, so I was returned there in September of 1939." Eds.

domestic basis of his mother at seven before his most profound loss: being shipped out of the country of his *Muttersprache* to a strange land in which he lived out six crucial years of the transition from boyhood to adolescence. This traumatizing childhood sounds more like something out of Dickens than any story we conventionally think of as "romantic."

As a new arrival in New York, Hartman discovered that in America people named Gert are usually women. So he renamed himself Geoffrey. Why did he did not call himself Jeffrey, the more familiar variant of that name in America? It probably had to do with his identification with British literature. He never published on Chaucer, as far as I know, but he had by age sixteen formed a strong, even survivalist, attachment to English poetry.

In *The Longest Shadow* Hartman confesses to the effect on him of having been torn up by the roots, dispatched without parents at such a young age to be a stranger in a strange land: "An organic relation to place is what I lacked and would never recover. I rarely experience strong feelings of attachment, whether to people or to soil." Hartman is brief and matter-of-fact in confessing this sense of unreality in *The Longest Shadow*—it comes up also in the more impersonal context of his later studies of contemporary media culture in *Scars of the Spirit*. But I have no doubt of the grief that informs such an admission.

3.

So where does literature enter this story? It enters first as a means of emotional survival. Hartman is the author of two books on Wordsworth. The first, published in his midthirties, is a big, very original study that drew on Continental phenomenology and thereby marked a milestone as one of the first books to introduce "theory" into American literary studies. He had already published a long essay on "Tintern Abbey" that had appeared a decade earlier, in 1954, in his first book, *The Unmediated Vision*. He wrote his book and independent essays on Wordsworth in the sixties, then more in the seventies, and in every subsequent decade. A former student put together a collection of some of the best of these essays in 1987. Hartman has hugged Wordsworth's poetry to himself as children sometimes hold their dolls or pets or fantasy-friends to themselves. Literary critics and scholars typically have a favorite author with whom they have a close relationship, but Hartman's tie to Wordsworth is remarkable for its intimacy. The poet of the Lake District propped him up when he was a child and his supports were few, and it is as if he has continued to be part of Hartman's being.

Hartman followed Wordsworth in celebrating the trust in nature that protected him from trauma. In *The Prelude* Wordsworth sounds a similarly wishful note, as when he writes of witnessing the dragging from a Cumbrian lake of a decomposed corpse. On that occasion, Wordsworth says, his youthful self was able to avoid trauma by casting a glow of make-believe, "Of faery land, the forest of romance," over the scene. Fairy tale, and psychological denial, defuse a threat to the boy's imagination. What we nowadays are disposed to think of in terms of repression and the unconscious, Wordsworth thinks of in terms of the imagination threatened and restored.

As a boy, Hartman recalls, he felt no debt to the patrons of the foster home, because he was "always aware of a greater debt: to creation itself." People were unreliable—they might come and go—but his loneliness did not matter because it was "as if God had wrapped me about and kept me immune from the worst." He was "at home in the gentle countryside of Buckinghamshire, my life somehow part of its life, and sheltered by an active sense of belonging."

The feelings toward nature here are very similar to the feelings Wordsworth describes in his greatest poem, *The Prelude,* which in its 1850 edition was subtitled *Growth of a Poet's Mind: An Autobiographical Poem.* Hartman writes of his youthful experience of nature as preceding his actual reading of the poet in school. He writes about his solitary joy in "berrying or hunting or on long, aimless walks, leaping over hedge and stile." He says that his experience of happiness in the English countryside so protected him that when he began studying the British Romantics as a schoolboy, "Wordsworth opened himself to my understanding as soon as I read him."

Hartman does not mention in *The Longest Shadow* the resemblance between his early years and that of the poet with whom he felt such an affinity. Hartman was left by his father at age one and lost his mother at nine. Wordsworth's mother died when he was eight, and the death of his father, one of the losses recorded in *The Prelude,* occurred when he was thirteen. Altogether, I do not doubt that Hartman's experience preceded his reading, but it is self-evident to me that he drew on Wordsworth for his personal myth of loss and restitution as Wordsworth had drawn on memory and nature in elaborating his own paradigm.

I hope that goes some way toward explaining the way in which literature contributed to Hartman's emotional survival during his English years and has contributed to his spiritual nourishment ever since. Of course, the Wordsworthian paradigm I have described is altogether too positive to describe how Holocaust survivors deal with their traumas in the video testimonies. There is nothing in these testimonies like the "spots of time" in *The Prelude*. One would nowadays think of the latter as traumatic experiences that Wordsworth was able, almost magically, to convert to positive account. No such imaginative transformation occurs in the testimonies. Yet there does occur a reexperiencing in some of these interviews that leaves the survivor, and the viewer, transformed. It is like a process of writing in which the poet, remembering what is past, emotionally responds to his or her subject and discovers something new in the midst of composing. Hartman is not interested in the Holocaust testimonies as straightforward historical narratives. Rather, he watches for the surfacing of a long-forgotten trauma, and the subject's self-reflective imaginative response in the present. Here, too, Wordsworth's poems provide some clues and constitute the link between the earlier and the later Hartman.

4.

Before going on to Hartman's account of Holocaust testimonies, I want to interpolate a few thoughts about his "answerable style," the way he has lately transformed his personal trauma into a discourse that is at once philosophical, eschatological, and literary-linguistic, and also enables a critique of nonliterary media culture. Much of his recent book, *Scars of the Spirit*, is taken up with critique of our contemporary culture of exposure and disclosure. In Hartman's heartsore sense of the present, people go about haunted by an inner sense of unreality due in part to the proliferation of "simulacra" generated by electronic media. What he has in mind is phenomena like "reality TV," which has the perverse effect of putting our experience of actual reality in question. We inhabit a world of ghosts, in which the hunger for immediacy of experience is increasingly frustrated.

The question, then, becomes one of authenticity. Ultimately, the question is fundamental: can one be real to oneself? In his essay "The Virtue of Attentiveness," Hartman presents no simple solution. Instead, he describes a posture to experience, an attitude. It inevitably involves suffering but is normative all the same. That posture is not one of "looking for" but one of "waiting for."

Hartman quotes Simone Weil: "Absolute, unadulterated attention is prayer." This mode of attention stands in contrast to our Internet-driven lust for information and rejects Hegel's suggestion that consciousness can achieve completeness. Here he cites Maurice Blanchot on "the imposture of finalized meaning." In general, Hartman's language is eschatological, the idiom of the religious watcher and waiter. He writes of "hopeless, helpless waiting." Our fate is "to lie in wait in an anguished temporality . . . on the *qui vive* as to exactly when revelation will occur."

Curiously this language presumes a latency that is as relevant to trauma, even the trauma of the Holocaust, as to an inward conviction of an imminent divine revelation. Gerard de Nerval, whom Hartman takes up in his essay on attentiveness, writes of his intimations of the return of the pagan gods, but Hartman's language defines the possible mind-cast of a survivor who has chosen to be part of the Yale video testimony project: "From a phenomenological point of view . . . there is a feeling that a lost chance, a lost world, remains present, although hidden and waiting to emerge." What he says in relation to Baudelaire's theory of "correspondences" might also be said of these testimonies: "As a heightened form of attention, vigilance is spurred by the absence of a presence whose numinous imprints (traces, vestiges, footsteps) remain. Thus the possibility of communication is never completely cut off."

The resonance of the language of attention is great. On this topic Blanchot, the author of récits as well as theoretical writings, is a major influence on Hartman. But the question of revelation as conceived by Blanchot is a linguistic question: can language make available an authentic experience of the real? For Hartman, concerned in *Scars of the Spirit* with the psychological effects of our technologically driven media culture, drenched in simulacra, the question becomes: can one "be a witness, if only to oneself"?

If we consider the spirit of attentiveness in the light of Hartman's own biography, it would seem a response to the long trauma of separation from his mother that I would guess to be the founding experience of his personality. The trauma of separation (John Bowlby) and the difficult process of separation-individuation (Margaret Mahler) are by now much-investigated themes of psychoanalysis. What is remarkable is how Hartman has made his personal trauma the basis of a critique of our contemporary predicament that integrates his intimate experience with the philosophical work of Hegel and Heidegger and more recent figures like Maurice Blanchot, Emmanuel Levinas, Jean Baudrillard, Gianni Vattimo, and Giorgio Agamben, as well as writers like W. G. Sebald and the French novelist Patrick Modiano.

Hartman's discussion of Modiano's novel *Dora Bruder* bears on both his own story and Holocaust testimonies. The novel takes off from the actual occurrence of an ad in the *Paris-Soir* of December 31, 1941, for information about a missing young person. Forty-seven years later the narrator ("I"), who is depicted with "only a spotty autobiographical density," comes upon that ad and initiates a search for what happened to the missing young woman. That search makes up the substance of the novel, in which the author-narrator adopts the role of historian investigating how an actual person became lost and stumbled into the roundup of Parisian Jews and died an early death in a Nazi concentration camp.

Hartman relates this "post" memory of Modiano's fictive narrator to the situation of the generation that came after those who were alive during the years of the Holocaust: "The fullness of the empty center called Dora suggests an incarnation arising from an 'absent memory' that afflicts a postwar generation of Jewish writers." But it may not only be the imaginations of the next generation that are "haunted by absent presences." It may be that the relative eventlessness and solitude of Hartman's years in England created in him a relation to absent memory similar to that of the next generation. Certainly he had suffered profound experiences of loss before those years that were sufficient to leave their traces and shape a life. But being left stranded and alone during what is typically a boy's phase of socialization probably left a huge void, even if he was rescued from despair by the mothering of nature.

So this theorist of Holocaust testimonies is himself a survivor, yet not an eyewitness to the horrors that befell so many of his European Jewish contemporaries. That means Hartman's consciousness does not participate in the "dense" and "unmediated" sense of reality that, in his view, distinguishes great poetry or the richest testimonies. Hence, I think, his sensitivity to the "memory envy" he ascribes to the present generation. If we ask, then, what might induce a literary scholar who has been a great interpreter of Wordsworth to expand his study to embrace the video testimonies of Holocaust survivors, our answer might be that his fascination with the poet's "consciousness of consciousness" might well find a worthy complement in his new interest in the process by which survivor-interviewees awaken and respond to their repressed memories as they tell their stories. It may be that both objects of study speak to "the wish" Hartman describes as latent in most of us "for strong, identity-shaping memories."

5.

Of all the academics involved in the Yale project, probably Lawrence Langer, author of *Holocaust Testimonies: The Ruins of Memory* (1991), has studied more of the videos than anyone else. Hartman probably has not watched as many as Langer, but he has theorized the subject as much as anyone. Hartman has been involved with the archive for over twenty years and recently he has seemed to be advancing and consolidating his ideas. I will take up here what seem to me his most interesting lines of thought, relating those ideas where it seems possible to his earlier writing on Wordsworth.

I must first acknowledge that when I speak of that poet, I am not speaking of something locked away in Hartman's past. There are no fewer than fifteen allusions, some extending for more than a page, to Wordsworth in *Scars of the Spirit*.

In *Scars of the Spirit*, Wordsworth's ubiquity is all the more remarkable given Hartman's emphasis in that book on present-day pop culture. Indeed, *Scars* begins with an allusion to the pop singer Eminem. In what follows I will be quoting Hartman from whatever has come to hand, which includes interviews, my own as well as others', and published essays.

In "Testimony and Authenticity," Hartman distinguishes the Yale project's idea of authenticity from that of professional historians. Thus he writes: "The burden of how to be a witness to the witness—how to attend, interpret, and value the testimonies—clearly falls on all for whom Nazism's 'culture of death' is a frightening riddle. There is a duty of reception." Authenticity for the professional historian depends upon the witness having been present at the event and having recorded her testimony at the time of the events. Memory, so important in Hartman's (and Wordsworth's) idea of what is real, is for the historian synonymous with trouble: the more time that elapses between the event and bearing witness, the more unreliable will be the testimony. Moreover, "reliable" for the historian means there is only one true account: all witnesses to an event must concur in the particulars. Factual precision is central to this notion of what is authentic.

Holocaust survivors often remember the same events differently, and within the individual witness memory often evolves. Should we then think of the video testimonies at Yale as fictions and fantasies? Should they be disallowed as contributions to our understanding of the Holocaust? Hartman shifts the argument to different terrain. He acknowledges the importance of the historian's criteria in assessing the competence of the witnesses but denies to the historian's concept of history its claim to authenticity. That word belongs to another kind of meaning, another kind of experience. Authenticity is a word "at home only in moral philosophy."

Hartman's privileging of Holocaust testimony over evidence like rescued ghetto documents calls to mind Aristotle's privileging of poetry over history—and philosophy as well. Hartman's own moral emphases, which are influenced by a contemporary philosopher, Emmanuel Levinas, have shaped his ideas of how the interviews ought to be structured: "Precisely because Levinas's understanding of moral action is not dialogic in the sense of aiming at a balanced mutual exchange, a potential space is opened for the immediacy, the directness of the witness to others, or to the other in the self."

If the videos are records of "talking heads," the only heads to be seen in the Yale video testimonies are those of the interviewees. The questions come from two interviewers off camera. And those interviewers should exercise self-control so as not to interfere with the flow of the survivor's thought, her memories and possible reactions to those memories. Nor should the interview setting be distracting; a screen behind the interviewee and sometimes a plant suffice. And there is no triumphalism such as characterizes the video testimonies in the Steven Spielberg archive, which has recorded ten times as many hours of testimony in a third as many years, thanks to greater funding and national publicity.[3] In many of those videos the survivor's family is asked to come forward cheerfully at the end of the interview, as if to proclaim, "Behold, she has come through!"

Now, what will the Yale project's self-conscious asceticism unlock? What do we mean by this "flow of thought"? Hartman insists that the essential thing is "the survivors' defining struggle with trauma or loss. We glimpse the flux and reflux of consciousness, as witnesses grapple with what has escaped or overwhelmed memory. Memory itself is remembered." The flow, then, is not an unimpeded flow to the sea, any more than in "Tintern Abbey." Mind responding to itself is not a linear affair.

That is why in the interview the initiative should always be left to the witness. The effect, in the most spontaneous testimonies, is experience as close to being unmediated as in Wordsworth, where the only mediation consists in the poet's style. Yes, the Yale videos call for interviewers, a camera, time restrictions on the session, but these are managed so as to contribute to a single goal: aiding the witness in unlocking memories that until the occasion of the interview may have been unknown to the interviewee's family, that may even have been unknown to

3. The connection between the two Holocaust archives, the Fortunoff at Yale and Steven Spielberg's Survivors of Shoah Visual History Foundation, is a complex and evolving relationship. Here is what Hartman had to say about it in an interview in 2001. "Part of that inevitable movement forward is also seen in the transition from the Yale testimony project to the Spielberg project. The question is raised: when does quantity affect quality? The Spielberg library project is an important one. It has financial resources that we could never have. And it is good that it taped many, many more survivors than we could have, so I support all of that. But then the emphasis shifts to: what you *do* with it, and that is much more difficult to answer. I remain suspicious, but I've seen progress there, too. . . . One always has to remind oneself that Hollywood, with an intelligent person like Spielberg, and resources that are enormous, sooner or later is going to produce something important" ("Witnessing Video Testimony: An Interview with Geoffrey Hartman" by Jennifer R. Ballingee, *The Yale Journal of Criticism* 14, no. 1 [2001]: 217–32). Eds.

the interviewee. The Spielberg staff may have the idea that this coming to awareness of Holocaust-related traumas issues in jubilation. Hartman's title phrase, "scars of the spirit," re*f*lects the Yale project's deeper understanding, that the traces left by such experiences, *re*membered or not, *re*main to give pain. (The *re's* of the verbs in the previous sentence *re*mind one of the degree to which Hartman is absorbed, as in his study of Wordsworth's poetry, with the complex process of the witness's memory of memory.)

The retrievals of memory in *The Prelude* and in Wordsworth's lyrics appear to differ radically in having no comparable historical resonance and in generating not pain but a rejuvenated consciousness. It is true that Wordsworth's "spots of time" are personal, but if we reflect on the context of "Tintern Abbey" and *The Prelude,* we see that history has contributed to the necessity of imaginative restoration. Wordsworth had first visited the ruins of Tintern Abbey on a walking tour in 1793. There had followed his direct experience of the French Revolution, which had led, as he says in *The Prelude,* to the "impairment" of his imagination. Five summers have passed and these have affected the poet like "five long winters" due to that impairment of consciousness.

Moreover, in "Wordsworth, Inscriptions, and Romantic Nature Poetry" (*Beyond Formalism,* 1970), Hartman shows that "Tintern Abbey" is not a simple fable of spiritual renewal. He points out the omnipresence of death as a motif in that poem. He finds the origin of "Tintern Abbey" in the epitaphic mode of an important grouping of poems in the classical Greek anthology. Those Greek inscription poems, or the literary tradition they foster, rely similarly on an elegiac tone and the presence of a monument or ruins. But in Wordsworth "there is no corpse in that vicinity . . . the corpse is in the poet himself, his consciousness of inner decay." Hartman argues that the poet's sense of decline is related to a historical intimation of the decline of English nature feeling in general. Wordsworth's poetry may celebrate the revived sense of continuity with his younger self, but, according to Hartman, he "fears that the very spirit presiding over his poetry" is in decay and identifies his personal crisis with a national decline.

So Hartman's own continuity appears in his phenomenological emphasis on the turns of consciousness both in Wordsworth's poetry and the Holocaust testimonies and in relating individual memory to history and a collective consciousness. But the pain of England's national poet is universal, common to all humanity. The catastrophe of the Holocaust cannot be so easily integrated into the evolution of humanity from the death of Pan and nature feeling to the rise of our present consciousness of consciousness. The Holocaust represents a break in the grand march of spirit that Hegel thought to be devoid of scars.

Hartman is quick to deny that psychoanalysis provides a model for the interview situation. One can see his point that analysis is an audio technique, the "talking cure." The analytic process is open ended, even "interminable" in some instances. The Yale videos, on the other hand, are mostly limited to a single interview. That is a limitation but also potentially a prod to memory. But is it the case that, as Hartman also says, the interviews are not intended as therapeutic?

Dori Laub is a psychoanalyst and child survivor who was cofounder of the original project in New Haven to systematically videotape survivors. His "paradoxical" position, as summarized by Hartman, involves viewing "witnessing as an 'impossible' act, at least in theory—not because the death camps defy description but because the Nazi machine, when it did not murder the victims, tried to make sure the survivors' view of themselves would be so severely injured, their self-image so darkened, that they would be unable to testify." The aim of the project, from Laub's point of view, would, then, appear to be therapeutic to the extent that it "wishes to restore a damaged or deeply buried ability to speak and so to testify."

Hartman's view is similar but stresses "embodiment" as well as what he refers to as the "Philomela project," the restoration of voice to the voiceless. His difference from Laub is minor in that they both emphasize damage, but for Hartman that damage, as in his own boyhood, is associated with unreality, absence. His rationale for the use of video in the interviews is that voice alone is "ghostly." He maintains that "when you just hear the voice, the effect is that of disembodied sound, as if from the dead, from an absence." Video representation may seem antithetical to poetic imagination, but it has the effect as poems do of rendering an absence present: "We feel it essential to add a face to that voice, to reduce the ghostliness, even to re-embody the voice. Embodiment is essential because it was precisely the body . . . that was denied, the full presence of the survivor that was denied in the time of persecution."

6.

Audio and video technology are important, but equally important is the witness's trust, which has also been damaged by her wartime experience. In discussing the immediate addressee of the survivor's story, Hartman imagines a person with the sensitivity of an ideal reader of literature. Survivor testimony "is partly a flashback, an obsessive monologue like that of Coleridge's Ancient Mariner in the poem of that name. But it is also a narrative in search of itself that depends on a voluntary rather than a hypnotized listener, on a caring and careful ear." Care and trust are important because the survivor's recall of what happened has a continuing impact on her psyche. The pervasive presence of the past is revealed in the "afterthoughts [that] often arise in the very moment of giving testimony."

The trained, caring listener differs from the solitary reader in being part of a larger framework. Holocaust testimony, as the Yale archive conceives it, is a public act intended for public understanding. Hartman's conception of what goes on within the survivor while presenting testimony relies on a certain idea of community: "Witness is made possible when representatives of an 'affective community' create a testimonial alliance between survivor and interviewer."

In discussing the growth of Wordsworth's poetic mind, Hartman comments on the belated humanization of that mind but has little to say about "community." Nowadays, however, he frequently alludes to Pierre Nora and Maurice Halbwachs and the question of community and collective memory. Altogether, the idea of community with relation to the Holocaust testimonies now has the place in Hartman's restitutive paradigm that nature has in Wordsworth's poetry.

There is an immense proliferation of theory, his own and that of others, in *Scars of the Spirit*. For example, Hartman is concerned with what will become of the testimonies in the age of instantaneous digital transmission and especially with the emotional impact these testimonies have on the individuals who view them. He writes of "telesuffering," the "secondary traumatization" of those who study these audiovisual stories of primary trauma, and he reflects, also, on "memory envy," which can generate a fantasy like Binjamin Wilkomirski's *Fragments*, his discredited "memoir" of being a child in the concentration camps.

There are lots of theories, but I will limit myself here to Hartman's hypotheses about a "testimonial alliance" and communal memory. Hartman dilates on these topics in the following passages from "Tele-suffering and Testimony."

"The best interviews result from a *testimonial alliance* between interviewer and interviewee; a trust relation forms, in which the search for facts does not displace everything else. Such an alliance, however, is a framing event that lies beyond the scope of the camera. It cannot be made transparent (in the sense of visually readable)," but is crucial nonetheless. It is the product of the "mediation" that Dori Laub has created with the cooperation of all those involved with the project. Hartman goes on: "When I talk of the project's communal frame, a return of trust, a wounded trust, is involved. The interviewers—indeed, all persons associated with the project—form a provisional community and become representative of a larger community, one that . . . recognizes the historical catastrophe and the personal trauma undergone."

"Memory . . . always has a milieu. How do you photograph a memory, how do you give it visibility, when that milieu has been destroyed by Holocaust violence as well as the passage of time?" Hartman offers a psychological basis for the Yale project's solution to that dilemma: "Experiences do remain imprinted on the mind, set off by the very absence of what inhabited the original space." One option for photographed testimony is to restore the survivor to "what is left of their milieu of suffering, as Claude Lanzmann often does in his film *Shoah*." That is clearly not the option the Yale project has chosen. The scene of the camera's work and its mobility in general are severely restricted in the Yale testimonies because, as Hartman argues, the essential element is "the mental space such minimal visuality ('I see a voice!') allows."

That emphasis on inwardness ("mental space") assists the release of memory and contributes to the formation of an emotional bond (a minicommunity) between witness and viewer: "Witnesses can 'see' better into, or listen more effectively to, themselves, and viewers too respond to that intimacy." As for the interviewers, at best "they become more than questioners. They comprise, as Halbwachs said, a new 'affective community.'" In Hartman's view that invisible community "substitutes, however inadequately, for the original and tragically decimated milieu."

The mature scholar who as a boy was torn up from the roots that attached him to his native home now writes over and over about *community*. The boy who was so tragically separated from his mother and lacked a way to *communicate* his most urgent needs has as an adult found the means to communicate his discoveries about Holocaust survivors. Hartman shares a great deal with those survivors, who in presenting testimony are reembodied and recover their lost milieu, often in the act of communicating for the first time what happened to them and rendered them voiceless for so long.

I find Hartman's view—really, his vision—very eloquent, but I fail to find it compelling. For one thing, just what is it precisely that makes for the witness's trust? Hartman has emphasized that the Yale project avoids psychotherapists because, in his experience with them, they were motivated in part by their own professional "agenda." But the kind of trust he wishes to induce in the survivor is likely to be more difficult to elicit than he implies. The mistrust of a victim of Nazi oppression is likely to be greater than that of the typical psychoanalytic patient, and even for the latter the establishment of a positive transference enabling minimal trust often requires considerable work and time.

But Hartman stresses that the role of the Fortunoff archive's interviewers is severely constrained: it is just to assist the survivor's release of memory. How does such a relationship make for a sense of community? Is the idea of the Yale project as affording the interviewee a sense of community more than wishful thinking? Consider that the interviewers are strangers to the witness, and they are likely to be decades younger and the products of very different backgrounds. What is there about this "affective community" to overcome such major differences between interviewers and interviewee? Moreover, is the "framework" Hartman invokes as firm, as actual, a structure as his terms imply? I can well believe that the project staff has built up an atmosphere of good will that eases the way for the visitor, and I find it understandable that the archive context enables many Holocaust survivors to gain access to their memories and open up as never before. But the idea of an "affective community" fits better with an organic rural society and an oral tradition than with our own electronic-media culture. Hartman himself acknowledges as much when he expresses his anxiety that "archives of conscience like ours may not be able to resist being turned into megabytes of information, electronic warehouses of knowledge." That anxiety bears also on this theory of memory envy. The real-life Wilkomirski sounds like a character out of Dostoevsky. But how many Americans are likely to suffer memory envy at a time when memory has become confused with the idea of information and information-memory on every conceivable topic is available in seconds from the servers of search engines like Google? This transformation of memory in the form of video testimonies into knowledge in the form of video-sound bites has already begun to marginalize the values that have guided the Yale project.

I think the contribution of the Yale project toward understanding the effect of the Holocaust has been invaluable. It has been the pioneer in the systematic recording and cataloguing of survivor testimonies; the much more expansive Spielberg archive would not have come into being had it not been for the efforts of Hartman, Dori Laub, and those who have devoted themselves to this great work. But I am writing here not of the testimonies themselves but of Hartman's theorization of them. I find his proliferation of theory attractive as a self-contained intellectual effort. However, despite the mental stimulation these essays provide, they do not significantly increase my sense of what it is like bearing witness for the survivors or what ontological status to accord to their testimony. This, to be sure, is a limited criticism. There is inevitably a void in our understanding of the effect of Nazi brutality on those who survived the experience. It is hardly damning to suggest that Hartman does not fill this void as well as he filled the void in our understanding of difficult individual poems in his early essays in stylistics.

As a substitute "affective milieu," poetry—especially that of Wordsworth—was restitutive for Hartman after, as a child, suffering the abrupt loss of his mother and his early environment. Presumably an orphanage in Frankfurt that had allowed him to see his mother on weekends was more comforting than a foster home in a strange land where he had no mother and was obliged too quickly to learn a new mother tongue. And the Yale project itself has provided Hartman with a new, Jewish community that has undoubtedly been comforting during the past two decades.

That project would seem to have provided a more satisfying affective community than words alone. There had been precedent, apart from his own suffering during the Holocaust, for Hartman's interest in the Jewish past. His grandfather on his mother's side had been a rabbi and teacher in a Jewish school. His grandfather died about the same time that his father left the family, but he has remained enough of an imagined spiritual influence that Hartman recalls him well in conversation and relates him to his own interest in Judaism. Indeed, Hartman's knowledge, though belated, of Hebrew and the rabbinic tradition of biblical commentary have been sufficient to enable him to mediate midrash as a method of textual interpretation to academic literary scholars. In *Midrash and Literature,* a rich collection of essays that he coedited, he brought together contributors as diverse as specialists on ancient biblical exegesis and Jacques Derrida on the poetry of Paul Celan.

Plainly Hartman's particular history and interests are unique and his personal restitutive achievement quite remarkable. It is hard for me to conceive of a single two-hour interview with a Holocaust survivor as having the same grand reintegrative effect. Perhaps Hartman's self-cure might best be understood as the restitutive vision of a man of imagination who has even been a sometime poet.[4] But while admiring his overall achievement as a literary interpreter, I remain conscious of the limitations of that achievement in relation to his childhood trauma: Hartman's later experience of community can hardly have redeemed the loss of the capacity for "strong feelings of attachment to people" that he suffered as a boy. Still, allowing for that limitation, theory as a form of imagination fills in as best it can.

Hartman's theories about the Yale Holocaust testimonies might be regarded as a pale version of that sublime moment in Book Six of *The Prelude* when Wordsworth recalls his great disappointment upon learning that the long-anticipated moment of crossing the Alps is behind him. Unknowingly, he and his companion have already crossed the Simplon Pass and are on the other side. A true Romantic, Wordsworth feels a great letdown upon learning that the "something evermore about to be" now belongs to the past. The void that has opened is then filled by a "vapour," something that arises from within:

> Imagination—here the Power so called
> Through sad incompetence of human speech,
> That awful Power rose from the mind's abyss

4. Geoffrey Hartman, *Akiba's Children* (Emory, VA: Iron Mountain Press, 1978).

> Like an unfathered vapour that enwraps,
> At once, some lonely traveller. . . .

That imaginative or theoretical power is "unfathered" in the poet and the critic, both of them deprived so early of their actual fathers.

Hartman's imagination of the archive as an ideal "affective community" lacks the sublimity of this passage and the poet's ensuing vision of apocalyptic nature. It is just theory, after all, and we have been drowning in theory for some time now. But his vision of restoring the "disembodied" survivor to herself and integrating her into an "affective community" has affinities with other great visions of ingathering. Instances of the latter are Emma Lazarus's vision of Europe's "wretched refuse" welcomed by a tolerant America and the old Zionist dream of Israel in relation to Jews of the Diaspora.

I have been arguing that in Hartman's personal case the Holocaust trauma consists of negation, a void, rather than active violations of selfhood such as were perpetrated by the Nazis in the concentration camps. It is possible, with either kind of wound and with appropriate help, to deal with the trauma. However, Hartman's career, both as poetic interpreter and Holocaust theorist, shows that in his case, where the wound consists of a gap, restitution may be most likely to occur if the victim builds *over* the wound rather than seeks to dig under it. So there is, I believe, continuity between Hartman's interpretation of Wordsworth and his interpretation of the Holocaust testimonies. But this continuity in the work is a response to a discontinuity in the life.

Cynthia Ozick
Embarrassments

Writing about Cynthia Ozick twelve years ago, I thought of her as she had presented herself in the late 1960s and through the '70s, as a Jewish writer with a self-consciously Jewish agenda.[1] She had declared herself a modern-day Litvak Mitnagged, that is, one of the Lithuanian Jews, chiefly from Vilna, who offered rationalistic opposition to what they regarded as the chaotic mysticism of East European Hasidism. For Ozick the equivalent of Jewish pietistic spirituality in modern-day America was the counterculture, and the figure she demonized was Allen Ginsberg, who in her view had turned everything—Judaism, Buddhism, Hinduism—into "allee samee." Another enemy of hers was "idolatry." By idolatry she referred to aestheticism, different versions of which popped up in the '60s. She might have taken Susan Sontag as her target, but perhaps Sontag was not sufficiently identified as a Jewish writer. So she took as her focus Harold Bloom, who incorporated the kaballah into his well-known theory of the anxiety of influence in poetic creativity.

Ozick had a lot of peeves. Yet another object of her polemics was the present state of Jewish American prose fiction. She exempted certain writers, like Malamud and Bellow, from her overall critique, but in general she found this body of fiction to be morally enfeebled and Jewishly ill informed. Instead of naturalistic fiction about poor Jews on the make, like *What Makes Sammy Run?*, Ozick proposed something new:

1. "Cynthia Ozick as the Jewish T. S. Eliot," *Soundings* 74 (Fall–Winter 1991): 351–68.

a "liturgical" Jewish novel. She was vague about this literary program, but at the least it involved a turning to the "Jewish idea," which seemed to involve religious Judaism in one form or another. It also involved a turning away from the sociological emphasis of the immigrant generation.

My present conception of Ozick is quite different from the one she proposed of herself and that I uncritically took over from her. Rather than seeing Ozick as a public and polemical writer chiefly concerned with Jewishness and Judaism, I now think of her as much more personal in her emphases. These personal themes have a Jewish context and implication, but these need teasing out. The explicit concern that I think of now as her main subject has been herself as a woman, chiefly in relation to the life of art on the one hand, and the quest for emotional fulfillment on the other. Related to my changed view of Ozick's true subject, I now think her best writing appears not in her fiction but in her essays, especially in her autobiographical and biographical essays. Oddly for a writer so little concerned with romance in her novels and stories, she is often preoccupied with love and longing in her essays.

I will be approaching Ozick's essays by way of a "representative anecdote" that happens to come from her fiction. The inventive theorist of rhetoric Kenneth Burke originated the idea of a representative anecdote as a point of departure for talking about any large subject. The use of the anecdote for the critical interpreter is to provide a vocabulary and themes adequate to the scope of a discursive field, and at the same time selective enough to screen out most irrelevancies. The discursive field for my purposes is Ozick's literary corpus.

My representative anecdote for describing Ozick's work comes from a particular story, "Puttermesser Paired," which appears in her collection *The Puttermesser Papers*. In that story we meet Ruth Puttermesser, now in her fifties, retired from her job as a lawyer in New York's civil service bureaucracy, and still unmarried. Puttermesser's surname is "butterknife" in Yiddish. Puttermesser calls herself "buttercutter." It is a haimisch name, calling attention both to her physical plainness ("homeliness") and her domesticity ("hominess"). Puttermesser's idea of happiness is to stay at home eating fudge and reading book after book, without having to worry about getting them back to the local library on time. Since I will have some negative things to say about Ozick's fiction, I want to say here that for me Puttermesser is the most lovable of the diverse literary alter egos

of Jewish writers of fiction, a group that includes Nathan Zuckerman
(Philip Roth), Arthur Fidelman (Bernard Malamud), and Faith Darwin
(Grace Paley).

Puttermesser may have quit the world of work, but she is not content to live alone. Bookish as ever, she dreams of a marriage that would
be like the "ideal friendship" of her heroine, George Eliot, and Eliot's
mate, George Henry Lewes. That Victorian couple lived as husband
and wife but not without scandal, because Lewes was already married
and, as Ozick writes, "it was an age of no divorce." Puttermesser dreams
of repeating George Eliot's romantic experience, and by chance she
meets a man twenty years her junior who seems apt for the role of
George Lewes. Rupert Rabeeno is an artist who copies the great masters, insisting all the while that these are in some sense his own paintings: "Reprise invigorated him." He describes his copies rather egotisti-
cally as "Reenactments of the Masters."

Puttermesser can nearly bring herself to see Rupert as he sees himself. In any case, she sees herself as a mirror image of Rupert in her own
habit of reading and reliving the lives of the great writers: "Whatever
had happened once, she conspired through a destiny of purposefulness,
to redraw, redo, replay; to translate into the language of her own respi-
ration." What better description of the respiration/inspiration of the
artist as biographer!

Puttermesser's aim is to relive George Eliot's life with George
Lewes, and she finds Rupert happy to indulge her fantasy. At first they
read *Middlemarch* together, but they move quickly to biographies, by
various hands, of their model couple. Inevitably they move on to fulfill
the implication of their bookish friendship. Puttermesser proposes to
her eccentric companion, hoping he will agree to relive with her George
Eliot's honeymoon trip to Venice. Rupert Rabeeno agrees, but he
dreams of duplicating a far more dramatic honeymoon—which had itself been a copy.

In biographical fact a little more than a year after George Lewes
died at sixty-one, George Eliot married again. Her new husband,
Johnny Cross, was a tall, handsome banker. When he married George
Eliot, she was sixty and he was forty. Cross had been a friend of the
couple, deeply devoted to Lewes, though he was not himself an intellectual. None of the biographies of George Eliot brings Johnny Cross

into clear focus, so Rupert sets about reconstructing this athletic, high-minded Victorian on his own. And what he concludes is that Cross was not so much in love with George Eliot as with George Lewes. Hence Cross's desire to imitate in every particular Lewes's honeymoon experience was a way of getting closer to the older friend he idealized.

But in actuality this second honeymoon turned out to be a grotesque parody of the first. Rupert "does" the Eliot-Cross honeymoon as if it were one of his museum paintings. Puttermesser watches as he remakes George Eliot's life with Johnny Cross, who was "only footnote and anti-climax," as the coup de théâtre. And that of course is what Ozick herself is doing, transforming grand opera into farce. A wary Puttermesser has a good idea where Rupert is heading. "All right," she tells him, "get it over with. You don't have to milk it."

However, in Rupert's version Johnny Cross has gone a full month on the honeymoon without once fulfilling his conjugal duties. But once the couple are established in their Venice hotel, George Eliot begins to feel desire as she had twenty years before, and she is more active in seeking to awaken her new husband to her availability.

Ozick—who gives the credit to Rupert—milks the situation to the extent of infusing it with a spirit of dread and decay that is a parody of *Death in Venice*. When the bride slips into bed, she finds her husband still dressed and cold to the touch. Responding to her entreaty that he let her see his face to determine if he is unwell, Johnny Cross "turned to her then, and showed her his eyes." Here Ozick mixes Thomas Mann, the Henry James of *The Aspern Papers,* and the tradition of Gothic melodrama. Johnny Cross's eyes "were unrecognizable—the rims of the lids as raw and bloody as meat, stretched apart like an animal's freshly slaughtered throat. Only the whites were there—the eyeballs had rolled off under the skin."

George Eliot thinks he must be seriously unwell. Suddenly she is shocked by an "instant cyclone" and the flight of "a projectile of some kind" out the window of their suite. Shortly thereafter she hears "blasts of laughter" from a "raucous party" on the canal, and gondoliers mocking her cry: "Gianni, Gianni!" Johnny is visible in full flight swimming away from the hotel; earlier we have learned that he is a strong swimmer. Only a few pages later Ozick wraps up this tale of duplication and reduplication by having Rupert Rabeeno marry Puttermesser—and then abandon her before the wedding night. After the Johnny Cross story, Ozick's ending to her own story comes across as anticlimactic, a pale repetition.

My main themes are present *in nuce* in the marital farce of George Eliot and Johnny Cross: the story of the sober-minded bookish woman taking a chance on romance; a man who is wholly without empathy or concern for the woman who stakes all on him; the belated artist who copies the great artists rather than suffer the anxiety of influence; and above all the theme of a woman's profound humiliation. This last theme appears in nearly all Ozick's best biographical essays, including those on Virginia Woolf, Edith Wharton, Alfred Chester, T. S. Eliot, and Lionel Trilling.

Humiliation is a central theme in the fiction of Henry James that Ozick most admires. It appears as a theme in *Embarrassments,* the title of a collection of James's short stories that appeared in 1896. That was just a year after James was himself humiliated by hooting and catcalls from angry playgoers at the opening night of *Guy Domville.* Ozick follows James's biographer, Leon Edel, in regarding that public shaming as the turning point in the author's career. And humiliation and shame come up again in the only one of Ozick's several essays on James in which she undertakes a full reading of a single novel. The essay is "What Henry James Knew," and the novel is *The Awkward Age.* Vulnerability and awkwardness are distinguishing traits of James's girl protagonists like Nanda Brookenham *(The Awkward Age)* and Maisie Farange *(What Maisie Knew),* and also characterize slightly older females like Milly Theale *(The Wings of the Dove)* and Maggie Verver *(The Golden Bowl).*

Art and Ardor, Ozick's first collection of essays, appeared in 1983. It was the most provocative book of nonacademic literary essays by an American writer since Susan Sontag's *Against Interpretation,* nearly twenty years earlier. It marked a late beginning—Sontag was born in 1933, Ozick in 1928—but it is arguable that Ozick's essays called for a sensibility that was just as original in the American context as the very different "new sensibility" which Sontag represented. In essays like "Notes on Camp," which appeared in *Partisan Review,* Sontag upset her elders by arguing for an "erotics" of art as an alternative to deep interpretation. Ozick's moralism, on the other hand, made her closer in temper to New York precursors like Lionel Trilling. But she was like Sontag in standing for something quite foreign to the universalist-minded old New York intellectuals. Ozick exemplified a self-consciously traditionalist ardor for an idea of Jewishness that the earlier generation had written off as parochial.

Still, the point needs to be made. *Art and Ardor* not only contained Ozick's important essay "Toward a New Yiddish" and her attack on Harold Bloom as an idolater; it not only featured essays on European Jewish writers who had been touched by the Holocaust, like Bruno Schulz and Gertrud Kolmar; it also contained essays that had little or no Jewish content. Rereading them now, we may feel, as I do, that these essays could have been written by a different person. That person, less shadowed by Jewish concerns, seems to me as much the real Cynthia Ozick as the public, polemical figure who up to now has attracted more commentary. I am thinking of the Ozick who wrote that book's essays on Edith Wharton, Virginia Woolf, E. M. Forster, and Henry James. That author is no less strong minded than the author of "Toward a New Yiddish," but she is also quirkier, more personal. She is as self-conscious about being a woman as being a Jew.

One's reactions to many of Sontag's essays, when they first appeared in the sixties, was to admire the author's brilliance and to hurry out and see for oneself what she was recommending. Since we had not previously been acquainted with Artaud and Claude Lévi-Strauss and the new avant-garde cinema, we were hardly in a position to question Sontag. On the contrary, we were happy to be armed with her introductions to the new arts and ideas. Moreover, she proposed to save us some work by maintaining that moral disputation was irrelevant to aesthetic experience.

Sontag agreed with the newly influential French theorists in her sense of what they referred to as "the problem of the subject." The problem of the subject was, simply, that the old bourgeois-humanist notion of a unified self was exhausted, part of a Western mythology that had not survived the two world wars. So the nineteenth-century life-and-works format of Ozick's biographically oriented essays made her appear old-fashioned and even middlebrow to advanced theorists in university departments of literature.

In fact, Ozick's fiction never achieved the canonical stature on college reading lists once enjoyed by experimental novels like Thomas Pynchon's *The Crying of Lot 49*. But taste has changed since the 1960s, and the rise of Jewish studies and the intensified concern with women writers have insured a place for Ozick's challenging revisions of literary lives. The best of her essays are remarkable in displaying a fiction writer's gift for summing up her biographical subject in a certain image or ruling passion. Altogether, Ozick's gifts as a fiction writer have in my view served her better in her essays than in her fiction.

M rs. Woolf: A Madwoman and Her Nurse" is an early essay that was reprinted in *Art and Ardor*. It is a story of the humiliation of Virginia Woolf by her husband, Leonard. Ozick judges Leonard adversely for not attending sufficiently to Virginia's needs as a woman while acting as her caretaker. Leonard acted as a buffer, and he does appear to have saved Virginia from psychotic episodes. But in Ozick's jaundiced view of him, his most salient trait was his "obtuseness": he misunderstood the relationship between art and madness.

Ozick argues that Woolf was perfectly sane in her writing. Her overall point is that in considering the psychology of the artist we need always to emphasize the healthy part of the otherwise sick mind and not reduce art to symptomatology. In this view, by conceiving his role as the madwoman's protector, Leonard failed to do justice to Virginia as either wife or writer. Ozick's argument for emphasizing the sanity of the artist recalls that of Lionel Trilling's influential essay "Art and Neurosis," a work of the mid-1940s that was reprinted in *The Liberal Imagination*.

In both her essays and fiction, Ozick frequently appears as a defender of beleaguered Jews. Indeed, her Woolf essay begins as an account of the genteel anti-Semitism of Virginia Stephens's social circle, which included a substantial part of England's intellectual aristocracy. One might expect Ozick to be anxious to do justice to Leonard as a Jew who has usually been regarded as a saintly figure because of his total dedication to his wife's well-being. Ozick does acknowledge that, despite all Leonard sacrificed for Virginia, she did not exempt him from occasional flashes of her anti-Semitic disdain. But, given the choice of doing justice to Leonard the selfless Jew or speaking up for Virginia the wife and writer, Ozick finds herself identifying with her writer-sister.

Ozick's essay soon turns to sharp scrutiny of Leonard's motives in marrying Virginia and assuming the burden of her care. In her skeptical view, taking over the care of Virginia and assuming responsibility for her mental health was Leonard's way of gaining permanent access to the world of the Stephenses and their friends, which over time became the world of Bloomsbury. Ozick is unrelenting in her severity toward Leonard. She maintains that such a dully sober-minded fellow would never have been accepted by Virginia but for her vulnerability to mental breakdown, and except as Virginia's "nurse" he would never have been accepted by others in her upper-class circle. It is unclear whether, in Ozick's view, Leonard was conscious of his own motives, but she leaves a distinct impression of him as an opportunist and social climber.

And worse. Leonard is shown as having taken advantage of Virginia's vulnerability to exercise his will to power over her: "Yet Leonard Woolf dominated Virginia Woolf overwhelmingly . . . because he possessed her in the manner of—it must be said again—a strong-minded nurse with obsessive jurisdiction over a willful patient." This leads Ozick to the most intimate areas of Virginia's existence as a woman. We learn that Virginia was not roused sexually by Leonard, as she appears to have been by her aggressively lesbian friend Vita Sackville-West. If that is correct, it strikes me that one reason is that Virginia may have been predominantly lesbian in her sexual makeup. But Ozick finds Leonard at fault for his wife's sexual indifference to him; it might have been different had Leonard not so easily accommodated himself to that indifference.

As nurse, Leonard's chief motive was to arrange Virginia's life so as to protect her sanity. That was his reason for siding with her wish not to have children. Ozick criticizes him for not overruling her; in her interpretation he becomes guilty of depriving his wife of the gratifications of the marital bed and the pleasures of attending at the children's bed. (Beds, as we will also see in Ozick's essay on Edith Wharton, play a large role in her thinking about the women authors who interest her.) Ozick thinks that raising children would not have been so difficult because the Woolfs always had several servants. But that does not take account of the physicalness of pregnancy and childbirth and some aspects of the mother-child relationship that cannot be laid off on strangers. Physicalness made this psychically unstable woman queasy.

Sometimes in Ozick's essay we feel as if we are in the world of Foucault and his prisons. She depicts Leonard as exercising near-total surveillance over his charge so as to make it impossible for her to achieve any autonomy or authority in her domestic life. The Woolfs' home in Sussex was called Monk's House. For Ozick that name symbolizes the extreme asceticism that the Jewish nurse imposed—as revenge?—on his highborn Gentile wife. And in the inevitable conclusion, as Ozick imagines it, to this narrative of imprisonment, Virginia lies down in the River Ouse. Taking her own life becomes her only means of freeing herself from the frustrations, losses, and miseries that afflict her due to her husband's jail-guard treatment of her.

There seems to me a large element of barely controlled fantasy in Ozick's story of the conditions that afflicted Virginia Woolf and made it so hard for her to have both a life as a writer and a full life (as Ozick defines it) as a woman. In her early essays Ozick presents herself as a mitnagged, as a hyperrationalist suspicious of mysticism and even of fantasy. But there is a good deal of fantasy in her early short stories *(The Pagan Rabbi)* and in her portrait of Leonard Woolf as the Jewish nurse-husband. One can only wonder how Ozick seized upon a person so devoted to the pre–World War I idea of progress through reason, and turned him into a villain of Gothic melodrama, along the lines of Charlotte Bronte's Rochester or the Svengali of George du Maurier's *Trilby*. In this story, of course, the madwoman is not locked up in the attic. She is welcome to the tea party on the lawn at Monk's House, but her nurse continues to watch over every one of her moves. Ozick's account of this marriage seems to me unlikely. Still, this essay has the makings of a fictional narrative more compelling than all but a few of the fictions Ozick actually wrote.

The other important biographical essay in *Art and Ardor* is "Justice (Again) to Edith Wharton." The "again" in her title refers to Edmund Wilson's essay on Wharton in *The Wound and the Bow*. In that essay Wilson portrayed Wharton as a neurasthenic-female victim of the upper-class New York society in which she was reared. Wilson's idea is that Wharton, like so many women writers, turned to writing as compensation for emotional difficulties. Unlike her friend Henry James and other great male writers, she had no true métier: art was not a self-transcending vocation for her as it was for the men.

Ozick stands that argument on its head. She presents Wharton as an example of a woman writer as obsessed with her work as any man. Moreover, Wharton comes across as a ruthless person, a victimizer; she appears as an example of what Ozick calls in another essay "the artist as a bad character." Ozick's main point is that for Wharton the writing always came first. Her biographers have not concentrated on the writing self because she so effectively obscured it behind the persona of the society lady. The writer hardly appears in the biographies because in her actual life Wharton as writer was "very nearly invisible."

It is Ozick's way of foregrounding Wharton's writing self that makes her essay so effective. She once wrote in an essay on diaries that Virginia Woolf's success in her literary portraits derived from her ability to condense a life in a moment of illumination. That gift made her the great "English Essayist." Ozick appears to have modeled her own portraits on that principle. Discussing R. W. B. Lewis's long biography, she finds the key to Wharton's obsessive self, which was her real self, in a ten-line passage on page 353. As in the essay on Woolf, a bed is at the center of things.

On a tour of Europe's great cities and museums with Bernard Berenson, they check into their separate rooms in a hotel in Berlin, and Berenson, the great connoisseur of art, hears Wharton raging about the placement of her bed. It had not been situated so as to face the window and receive the morning light: "She worked in bed every morning. . . . It had been her practice for more than twenty years; and for a woman . . . who clung so tenaciously to her daily stint, the need was a serious one."

Not even her marriage, in an era when an upper-class person risked expulsion from respectable society for divorcing, was allowed to get in the way of Wharton's writing life. When her feckless and increasingly unreliable husband, Teddy, got out of line, he found himself permanently "replaced in bed by a writing board." Teddy had become an obstacle, and Wharton was ruthless in dealing with him.

Ozick says Wharton's great fear was "writer's death." She removed everything from her path that might compromise her writing life. Ozick is horrified by her selfishness but also awed by it. Wharton "did nothing to spare her husband the humiliation of his madness. It is one thing to go mad [as Teddy had], it is another to be humiliated for it." So it was not a case, as Edmund Wilson argued, of this woman being stimulated to write by "some exceptional emotional strain." Ozick turns that formulation inside out in order to present a view of Wharton that emphasizes not neurasthenia but strength of will: "If anything made the novelist possible, it was the sloughing off of the sources of emotional strain and personal maladjustment."

Ozick writes enough about the selfishness of the artist to suggest considerable ambivalence about the working out of self-insistence in her own career. But it is always the hyperscrupulous who are most prone to guilt. Whatever the cost to others of her absorption in her life as a writer, it seems small compared to the price of the megalomania of various male writers she admires and whose lives she does not call into question. Saul Bellow, for example, appears in James Atlas's recent biography as a man nearly as self-absorbed as some of his heroes, but Bellow has written no essays with titles like "The Artist as a Bad Character" and "The Selfishness of Art." On the contrary, he seems to have felt little of the sense of obligation to serve others that is part of the socialization of women. Rather, he has struggled to free himself from external obligations in order to pursue his own spiritual salvation. With regard to Bellow's women characters in particular, his fictional alter egos have registered mainly resentment and self-pity. The curious thing is that Bellow's commentators, including Ozick herself, have regarded his "metaphysical quest" as an unqualified positive, ignoring its unhappy side effects on the lives of nonmetaphysical wives and lovers.

The figure of the humiliated woman sometimes appears frankly in Ozick's essays as a figure for herself. She is a vivid presence in her study of Alfred Chester, a college friend who became a minor celebrity in Greenwich Village in the 1950s, when Ozick herself was writing on a regular basis but had not yet discovered either her voice or her true subject. "Alfred Chester's Wig" is my favorite among her longer biographical essays. It tells a familiar story of literary precocity transformed into despondency, madness, and early death. Ozick's adolescent friend descended into a chaos of homosexuality, drug addiction, and loneliness that ended with his suicide at age forty. Ozick makes her depiction of his shame and humiliation compelling by weaving it into her own story of humiliation. It will help to deal with the portraitist and her sitter separately, beginning with the latter.

From the beginning, Chester—Ozick then and now never thinks of him as "Alfred"—is a writer who delights in making a rumpus. We first meet him in a freshman composition class he takes with the young Cynthia at the Washington Square branch of New York University. In a class taught by a Professor Emerson, the two Jewish youngsters, Cynthia from the Bronx and Chester from Brooklyn, compete with one another in writing exercises, papers, and short stories. Professor Emerson is happy to egg them on. The year is 1946, and veterans in the class on the G.I. Bill are the dullish audience for this agon fought out between teenagers inspired by literary passion and ambition. Ozick says bluntly of their rivalry: "I wanted more than anything to beat him; I was afraid he would beat me."

Chester has the advantage from the start. His excitement about writing is matched by a flair for publicity. Ozick, the "puritan and bluestocking," becomes an unhappy observer of Chester's early success in getting his reviews and stories published in quality magazines. His exhibitionistic brilliance also makes him the center of a student cult. But Chester's love life is not as successful as his literary life. Popular as he is for his iconoclasm, Chester has a physical defect that repels the girls he cares about. (Cynthia herself is the exception, but I'll come to that later.) As a consequence of a childhood disease, Chester does not have a single hair on his body: no eyebrows, no eyelashes, nothing.

He wears a yellow wig to conceal his perfect baldness, and that wig is the organizing device of this essay. Ozick presents Chester's wig at the center of his secret life as she had placed the beds of Woolf and Wharton at the center of their secret lives. She quotes from a long, confessional passage of Chester's, written near the end of his life. In it he describes being fitted for his first wig, at age fourteen, as the decisive moment of his life. Forever after he will appear as different, freakish, monstrous to himself. "It was like having an ax driven straight down the middle of my body. . . . Hacked in two with one blow like a dry little tree. Like a sad little New York tree." Chester is writing to account for his later life as a homosexual and embittered isolate. He writes about the wig as another homosexual writer, Jean Genet, writes about having his destiny determined early by being named a thief. Similarly, the wig denominates Chester as a criminal because of the deception it entails. His life now is divided between "hat people and wig people. Wig people at school. Hat people at home. . . . The terror of encountering one side in the camp of the other. Of the wig people catching me without the wig. Of the hat people catching me with it."

Ozick's view of Chester is very different. At the start, as a fellow student, she is awed by his passion for literature and his fluency as a writer. Then, after they graduate, though they never meet again in person, Ozick continues to be awed by Chester, although now it is by his worldly success. Overseas he becomes one of the *Paris Review* circle, a fiction editor for the fashionable journal *Botteghe Oscure,* and, Ozick says, a writer "well into the beginnings of an international reputation."

As a student in Washington Square, Chester had fancied an exotic-looking poet named Diana. But while she and the other conspicuously arty girls reject Chester, Ozick is infatuated with him. And when Chester makes it obvious that he does not take her seriously as a woman, she is deeply hurt. All through the 1950s, as Chester's star rises and Ozick's is totally invisible in the literary firmament, he finds occasions to hurt her again. The pain of unrequited affection is intensified for Ozick by their continuing literary competitiveness, in which she is unambiguously the loser. These experiences cause Chester to be firmly associated with humiliation in Ozick's thoughts and feelings.

The 1950s were Ozick's years of apprenticeship; they were also years of self-doubt as she wandered in the wilderness searching for her own voice. She devoted the better part of that decade to a philosophical novel she never completed. The experience was all the more humiliating because Chester seemed to be doing so well. Many of Ozick's best essays have the period of her apprenticeship as their context, although they were written much later. These include her long essays on Trilling and T. S. Eliot, who were her most important literary-cultural guides as she started out; her brief memoir, "The Lesson of the Master," about her early years as an epigone of Henry James; and her oddly candid personal essay, "Lovesickness," in addition to the portrait of Chester.

The essay on Eliot includes the story of how this revered hero of culture threw over two women, one an American and the other British, who had waited for decades in the hope that in the end he might marry them. Eliot did in the end remarry, but to neither of these women, and he was brutal in the way he let them down. As regards Ozick's essay on Trilling, for the most part she sings his virtues as a latter-day Victorian sage. But there remains a sense of hurt when she writes of his indifference toward all but a few of his favorite students, of whom she was never one. Trilling seems to have been typical of his literary generation in his incapacity to take younger women writers seriously.

If the primary aim of the Chester essay is to remember him and lament his fall, its secondary theme is Ozick's experience of defeat and humiliation and quest for vindication. This is a highly personal confession on Ozick's part about her hunger for literary honor. Although she does not conceive the literary life as Norman Mailer used to, as a series of prize fights, she is quite open about how much she felt motivated to reverse her defeats in the 1950s. And clearly she did win out in the end in her competition with Chester. It is hard to imagine a decline and fall, in literary and personal terms, more total than that of the boy who had once taken such pleasure in patronizing her.

Ozick's desire for vindication takes the form of a will to power that expresses itself in a zeal for renaming. Chester's parents had damaged their son by causing him to wear his yellow wig, in effect bestowing on him an identification as abnormal and, in his own mind, as obscene. Ozick's intervention, her naming, seems more benign. She insists to Chester, in a letter she wrote him in the 1950s, that he is not really homosexual. She develops that argument in the present essay. Ozick reminds Chester that he had cared for girls as a younger man and especially yearned after Diana, and she insists he only became homosexual because he was rejected by the straight community. As Ozick makes the case to Chester, he found himself accepted by the homosexual society of Paris and Tangier, where he kept an Arab lover, as he had not been by the community of heterosexual "normals." If he had been accepted by the heterosexual community, he would have been straight.

She makes the same case in this essay. Chester plainly needed friends and an audience—Ozick writes that his life finally fell apart only when he "stumbled into a private loneliness so absolute that he was beginning to populate it with phantom voices." That is why, she thinks, he settled on a community that did not treat him as a pariah. In Ozick's view, Chester's life of gay decadence was a mask. It had nothing to do with his real self, which she locates in the little yeshiva boy from Brooklyn or in

the teenage literary genius she had loved as a freshman. Ozick is eloquent in her denial of Chester's homosexuality: "He was not what he
seemed; he was an injured boy absurdly compelled to wear a yellow wig.
Shame gave him the power of sham—an outrageously idiosyncratic, if
illusional, negation of his heart's truth."

Myself, I can only understand Ozick's counterintuitive insistence on
Chester's heterosexuality in terms of her own continuing affection for
him. The underlying idea seems to be that no one to whom she had
once felt so close can have been gay. Chester's portraitist gives the impression of needing to repudiate the notion of his being deviant so that
she need not repudiate her cherished memories of him.

The problem may be that of the portraitist. Ozick's idea of homosexuality appears as a nightmarish fantasy from which anyone dear to
her—including Virginia Woolf—has to be protected. I do not think the
important thing is whether she is right or wrong. Who can know? It is
that she rejects Chester's self-understanding in favor of her own. To the
extent that she refuses to see him as monstrous, that is all to the good.
But her resistance to accepting his actual existence as a homosexual puts
her at odds with Chester in a less attractive way. She is "naming" him
anew, as his parents had when he was a boy. Ozick's relationship to him
becomes a dangerous kind of nurturing such as Henry James dramatizes
in *The Turn of the Screw*. A morally impassioned Ozick thinks to "save"
Chester by her revisionary interpretation as the governess tries to save
the endangered children in James's story. The little children in that
story may be in jeopardy only because the governess projects her turbid
sexual fantasies onto them. That Ozick projected what appears to be
pure fantasy about Chester's sexual normalcy may not have been as innocent and nurturing as she now makes it appear. Like the governess's
fantasy in *The Turn of the Screw*, Ozick's act of interpretation may have
been an act of violence, as it appeared to Chester himself when she first
broached it in a letter to him.

Violence, and even perhaps a revenge of sorts. I am reminded of
Ozick's indictment of Leonard Woolf's "overwhelming domination" of
Virginia. Is there not in Ozick's literary takeover of Chester's life an
echo of the "possessiveness" she attributes to Leonard, who acted in the
manner of "a strong-minded nurse with obsessive jurisdiction over a
willful patient." In the last part of her essay, she reminds us on nearly

every page how famous Chester had become in the 1950s and how she had failed. Her consciousness of their rivalry never leaves her. But gradually, as Chester's life falls apart on account of his increasing reliance on drugs and booze, the tone of this portrait settles into a calmly confident judgment that in her slow and sober way Ozick has won this particular race. She can afford to be wistful: "He lives in my mind, a brilliant boy in a wig." But that affection is only personal, and Ozick is seldom merely personal. Actually she turns out to be quite severe in her comments on his writing, and wraps up her opinions in this summarizing judgment: "If [Chester] was in a gladiatorial contest, and not only from the perspective of Mr. Emerson's adolescent amphitheater, but with all of his literary generation, then it is clear Chester has lost."

That is three paragraphs from the end, but Ozick cannot leave things with herself the unambiguous winner, vindicated in terms of character and achievement. It proves hard for her unambivalently to assert her victory over a boy she once loved and who so completely failed to live up to his youthful promise as a writer. That leads her to a kind of compromise. So at the very, very end she imagines how things might have turned out had Chester been able to overcome his self-destructiveness and to achieve the public celebrity he craved, perhaps as a literary panelist on television. Then the grown-up Cynthia, still a homebody, might have been happy to sit before the "bright tube" watching him and thinking: *"You've won, Chester, you've won."*

What a complicated portrait! I would set these three portraits alongside each other with an eye to comparing the experience and attitudes of the woman in each. Virginia Woolf appears as a victim pure and simple of her husband the jailer-nurse. Edith Wharton is her antithesis, a writer who triumphs over every obstacle to her art—above all, the prejudices of her social class and the burden of a psychotic husband—by the amoral strength of her will. There is a slight suggestion that Wharton took things a little too far in that direction, but Ozick's general attitude toward her is one of respect and approval.

Ozick herself is more directly involved in the story of Chester. She plays the role of unrequited lover as American college student; fierce literary competitor; the woman writer as a tortoise who began slowly but who in the end achieves a decisive triumph over the male hare Chester (and by implication over many literary male hares in their generation);

but then as slightly guilty about her victory and willing to play therapist-counselor toward the wounded brothers-sons. Ozick, so often described as if she were an ideological dogmatist, turns out to be emotionally quite complex. What has this complexity to do with her self-conscious Jewishness?

Much might be said of Ozick's attitude toward Henry James. He is her favorite writer: the subject of her MA thesis (1950), when she was twenty-two, and a key point of reference ever after, playing the key role in her literary consciousness that Wordsworth has played in that of Geoffrey Hartman. James is the only writer to whom she devotes at least one essay in every one of her four collections. He has been, for over a half-century, an object for her, as she says, of "adoration, ecstasy and awe." But James has also been associated for her with error, embarrassment, and humiliation. In "The Selfishness of Art," her most recent exercise in Jamesiana, the Master is shown to be as opportunistic in relation to a woman writer, Constance Fenimore Woolson, as T. S. Eliot was in dealing with the self-sacrificing ladies who hoped one day to marry him.

In another long essay, "What Henry James Knew," Ozick provides a clue to why she has always been able to forgive James. As "Selfishness" was about the shame he caused a woman who looked to him for love and approbation, "What Henry James Knew" is about a public shaming and humiliation he himself endured. If Ozick might identify with poor Fenimore Woolson in the first case, in the latter she identifies with James himself. The humiliation came about in 1895, when James was hooted off a London stage on the opening night of *Guy Domville*, the drama he hoped would launch him on a new career as a popular writer. The event plunged James into a nervous breakdown, from which he emerged with a more agonized sense of the relations between social surfaces and what went on beneath them, and of course with a new, more difficult style.

In his post-1895 fiction James increasingly projected his uncertainty and embarrassment through the consciousness of young females. One of these is a prepubescent girl, Maisie Farange, in *What Maisie Knew*, from which Ozick borrowed the title of her own essay about what Maisie's creator himself knew. James was able to project himself into the vulnerable situation of a young woman of marrying age in a subsequent novel, *The Awkward Age*, which Ozick interprets at the end of "What Henry James Knew." From 1895 to the end of James's career every one of his "fine central consciousnesses" appears to be going through an awkward age, including Milly Theale in *The Wings of the Dove* and Maggie Verver in *The Golden Bowl*. James's sympathy for female suffering may be one reason, among others, why Ozick has remained so loyal to him.

Of all her essays on James, "The Lesson of the Master," her first and most personal, still appeals to me most. Ozick's title comes from one of the many tales of writers and artists that James wrote in his later years. Her essay is brief, the kind of anecdote James referred to as a "germ" and that he took as a point of departure for a short story that often expanded to the length of a short novel. Ozick's "Lesson" is a portrait of the artist as a young woman so overtaken by the influence of a great literary model that she can say, almost without exaggerating, that she "became" Henry James. A further complication is that the James Ozick sought to become was not the straightforward author of *The Americans* and *The Europeans* but rather the Master of the late, baroque style.

The quintessential classical critic, T. S. Eliot, concurs with his Romantic opponent, Harold Bloom, in urging that a new poet must engage with strong precursors. She must engage with the tradition, however we define that term. It is no good for the beginning artist to rely solely on her own inspiration, because some day that inspiration will give out and she will need something outside herself to nourish her gift. So what is wrong with what Ozick did in setting out to be a novelist in her early twenties? The answer is that, in worshiping James himself worshiping at the altar of art, she took her veneration too far, losing herself in the process. She spent the 1950s, when she was in her twenties, modeling her own writing on the work of a high priest of the religion of art. She tried to write in her twenties as James had in his sixties. So this young woman "carried on the Jamesian idea," but along the way she sacrificed her youth. Ozick describes the lost decade as a huge error: "a stupidity, a misunderstanding, a great Jamesian life-mistake: an embarrassment and a life-shame."

"Lovesickness," another superb and strange personal essay of Ozick, is about two instances in her earlier life of passionate but unexpressed love for a man who was off limits to her. This essay will lead me to the question of the larger significance, in Ozick's career and in modern

Jewish American writing, of the personal themes I have been tracing. In "Lovesickness" an already married Cynthia falls in love with the groom at the wedding of a girlfriend. This infatuation is more rapturous than any she has ever known, but for obvious reasons it cannot be communicated. So, like some rapt kabbalist, she repeatedly copies in pencil the burning letters on the postcard the groom had written to her during the newlyweds' honeymoon.

The most striking aspect of Ozick's strange passion is something we have seen before in her writing, the duplication of a classic original, what Ozick refers to as her "mimicry." I mentioned this literal-minded conception of art as imitation (mimesis) in connection with Rupert Rabeeno in "Puttermesser Paired." In that story Rupert's art of duplication is judged to be a kind of "duplicity." In "Lovesickness" Ozick refers to her copying of the groom's handwriting as "forgery."

One does not bring about a literary revolution by copying great predecessors. And I think Ozick's habit of veneration and her impulse to duplicate older works, even as parody, has too often got in her way as a writer of fiction. She has been too conscientious a student, too good a Jewish girl, in dealing with the awkwardness of literary invention. Some voices she has used to muffle her own are those of: Henry James *(Trust),* Bernard Malamud ("Usurpation"), and Bruno Schulz *(The Messiah of Stockholm).* Sometimes this strategy has worked for her, as in her replay of the George Eliot/George Lewes relationship in *The Puttermesser Papers.* And then there is the very best of her fictions, "Envy; or, Yiddish in America." Ozick manages in that story to sound alternately like the poet Jacob Glatshtein (Edelshtein) and the triumphant fantasist Isaac Bashevis Singer (Ostrovsky).

"Envy" is a story that will last, but the strategy works in that instance because of Ozick's intimate knowledge of the little-known Yiddish literary subculture she portrayed. It is a fascinating, tragicomic world that she evokes in a style worthy of the great East European Yiddish masters. Elsewhere, as in *Cannibal Galaxy,* which is about a Jewish day school and its "dual curriculum," she writes about a mother and a daughter concerned with educational matters. Unfortunately, the Anglo-Hebraic curricular politics of a Jewish day school and the involvement of mother and daughter are too narrow to engage most readers for long. Literary posterity operates according to a different standard from that of the classroom. What will last through time is not usually what gets an A in class.

I have been suggesting a link between Ozick's modesty and humility as a writer and the recurrent theme of embarrassment in her work. We can see how her habit of veneration has handicapped her as a fiction writer by comparing her career with that of her near-contemporary Philip Roth. Roth has become famous by being disrespectful, outraging the middle class and thereby proving wrong all the critics who insist readers can no longer be shocked. Ozick, on the other hand, has won her readers by her consistent excellence in writing essays in appreciation.

But if the art of fiction requires a break, at least to some degree, with honored precursors, the art of the essay often profits from a writer's capacity for veneration. Just see the affinities in this respect that link Ozick to another gifted essayist with whom I earlier contrasted her. I am thinking again of Susan Sontag in early books like *Against Interpretation* and *Under the Sign of Saturn.* To be sure Sontag's heroes—Roland Barthes, Walter Benjamin, Antonin Artaud, Elias Canetti, and others—are quite different from Ozick's. But there is a shared schoolgirl veneration-complex at work in Sontag's lengthy *hommages* and Ozick's biographical portraits.

It has not been easy for Jewish writers of the 1950s generation to find a way that is decisively different from the sociologically oriented way of the *Partisan Review* generation of the 1930s and forties. Roth did it, as he said in *Portnoy's Complaint,* by putting "the id back in Yid." It is clear that somewhere along the way Roth determined, by an act of will, to overcome the decorum not only of Henry James but of literary-critical fathers of his like Howe and Trilling. At the start Sontag polemicized "against interpretation," by which she had in mind the Freudian–Marxian search for concealed meaning, which was the method in both political and literary analysis of the old radicals. But with age she has taken on a good deal of the high moral seriousness that she once so self-consciously fled.

Ozick took a different course. She was frankly concerned with women's issues notwithstanding her resistance to the new feminism, with its affirmation of a specifically female tradition in Anglo-American writing. She wrote about women writers and the embarrassments they suffered due to the incompatibility of their aspirations as writers and their aspirations as women, but she detested what she saw as the ghettoizing of her sex whether promoted by practical-minded American feminists like Gloria Steinem or new French theorists like Hélène Cixous.

So she was part of a movement among women in the direction of a self-conscious assertion of their interests. Curiously, this was an issue that Sontag tried to avoid. But when it came to other political-cultural issues, Sontag was way out ahead of Ozick. Unlike the *Partisan Review* intellectuals, who had failed miserably to stand up against the Vietnam War, Sontag spoke out boldly. Ozick, for her part, has avoided politics of general concern, largely limiting herself to Jewish issues. With respect to Israeli-Palestinian matters she was bluntly pro-Israel. And when she wrote about Jews and blacks in the Crown Heights section of Brooklyn, she sounded like one of the many American Jews who had been traumatized from afar by Jewish history. Her conservatism at times sounded as if it had less to do with principle than with terror that the Cossacks were coming yet again. And her horror of those who brought about the Holocaust has not diminished with time. The two fictions in her thin book, *The Shawl*, are probably her most widely known.

In fact, however, there was principle undergirding her defense of the Jews. She was one of many who took as their lesson from the Holocaust that the cosmopolitanism and universalism of the older Jewish intellectuals had failed and that Jews ought to recover a sense of their particularity. This argument formed a basis of her consistent support of the Israeli right wing in the propaganda war against the Palestinians. I have not gone on about this aspect of Ozick's work, the *Commentary* magazine side of it, because other critics, who share Ozick's political sentiments more than I do, have done justice to it. In any case, I think it is possible to overstate the importance of Ozick's politics. She is, above all, a literary person rather than a political partisan. Her recent essay "She: Portrait of the Essay as a Warm Body" makes clear the degree to which she identifies with the broadly moral focus of the great English essayists. That is an emphasis that allows for disinterestedness as the unrelenting tendentiousness of *Commentary* does not. It allows Ozick to include in "She" a long quotation from the radical William Hazlitt as well as from Matthew Arnold, who was always trying to keep things in balance.

Still, I do not wish to fudge Ozick's fundamental conservatism. She articulated better than any writer a major shift of emphasis in Jewish American politics and culture as a whole. And we ought not to minimize her concern with "the riddle of the ordinary." Undeniably she was preceded to some extent by Trilling in appealing to the habitual and commonplace, but she carried his incipient conservatism much further by combining it with religious orthodoxy.

There are other aspects of her conservatism that are not so obvious. I have said that Ozick does not represent a new literary departure but that she is a belated member of the New York group, along with Sontag the most intensely devoted and literature-soaked student among them. But coming late to the scene, in a new political-literary situation, she had to make it in her own way. Partly owing to her politics, she did not find *Partisan Review* or the *New York Review of Books* open to her. So she had to find her voice in different media, writing book reviews and short essays in more popular periodicals for a broader public. It is not easy to be as wonderful as she has been, injecting splendid aperçus in relatively short essays with the knowledge that an editor will be thinking: Look, keep in mind that the people reading you will not all be intellectuals or professors of English. Will our readers understand your references? Is there any way you can say that less elliptically, in plainer language?

Her personal essays—including "A Drugstore in Winter" *(Art and Ardor)* and "A Drugstore Eden" *(Quarrel and Quandary)*, as well as others I have mentioned—are among the best by any writer of her generation. And her biographical pieces rise to the standard of the best life-and-works essays of the nineteenth century, before literary talk became professionalized. But Ozick's portraits have not been free of the influence of modernism. We might have another go at characterizing her distinctive method—which to a degree is the characteristic method of the classical modernists like Proust, Joyce, and Mann.

Ozick did with individual historical figures what the great modernists did with entire worlds. I can imagine her living a little like Puttermesser, except with a husband—actually he is the lawyer in the family—and a daughter now grown up and married. Unless her doctor has warned her against it, she sits with a box of truffles on her desk, still the desk she used when she was a girl at Hunter College High School studying elocution. She is surrounded by the materials she will need to bring some dead writer alive: biographies, diaries, memoirs, letters, and of course the writer's poems or fiction. The writer will be someone she has lived with over time, someone she has already ingested to some degree. She is nothing like the literary scholar who has no more reason for working on one writer than another except, perhaps, that less has been done on one.

Unlike Rupert Rabeeno, her art has not been one of simple copying. Rupert's art reduced his subjects, turning them into fetish objects, little four-by-six postcards. Ozick *swallows* her subjects. She takes them inside her, with all the impedimenta she has assembled. And then she spits them out, all changed, with her signature on the "life," the portrait. What comes out is indelibly hers, in a way we hardly ever see in standard literary biography. That is because Ozick has infused her dead subjects with a vitality we are only used to finding in first-rate fiction.

The biographical essay is an extraordinary art form as Ozick has practiced it. Her fiction has not raised her to the level of Henry James — she remains, as she has always insisted, a minor writer. Still, her "copies" have been the basis of her originality and have created for her a permanent place in literary history.

I imagine Ozick as a solitary figure filling up some of the big spaces in her life by gathering her imaginary friends about her. To some extent her minibiographies are like gossip. They are guesses about famous people. Although she wins more and more honors and is invited to present distinguished lectures and is admitted to elite organizations like the American Academy of Arts and Letters, I do not envision her presence at many glamorous Manhattan dinner parties. She is not a Jewish Emily Dickinson, to be sure, but neither is she one of Manhattan's Dark Ladies. Mary McCarthy, Elizabeth Hardwick, and Susan Sontag, all of whom got their start at *Partisan Review,* have all been big-ticket items in New York's literary bazaar. Ozick's career could not have been more different.

Someday someone will have access to Ozick's personal writings, like letters and diaries, and that person, probably a woman, will write a biographical sketch of Ozick influenced by her own biographical portraits. Yes, you admirers of Hardwick's elliptical essays or Sontag's pious tributes to one or another Continental avant-gardist, Ozick has been a conservative continuator of what she ponderously refers to as "the tradition of the 'English Essay.'" In that horribly named "She: Portrait of the Essay as a Warm Body," Ozick is eloquent about that form. Forget about her off-putting title. That essay is worth reading because Ozick is as eloquent there as the classic essayists—Montaigne, Hazlitt, Lamb, Emerson, Arnold, Stevenson—she quotes as examples. That is quite a lot to say of a minor figure.

II

LIONEL TRILLING AND THE ORDEAL OF CIVILITY

Lionel Trilling and the Deep Places of the Imagination

1. Imagination and Mind

It was Lionel Trilling, of the New York intellectuals of his generation, who wrote in the 1940s of "the deep places of the imagination." He did so in the course of contrasting the great literature of European modernism—that of Proust, Joyce, Mann, and others—with what he regarded as the drearily unimaginative American writing of the forepart of the twentieth century. In "The Function of the Little Magazine" (1946), Trilling did not offer the names of the American writers he thought most representative of the American lack of imagination. But from his other essays in *The Liberal Imagination* (1950), it is clear that he had in mind older figures like Theodore Dreiser and Sherwood Anderson, especially their writing in the 1930s, and younger socially oriented novelists like John Steinbeck, especially the latter's Pulitzer Prize–winning bestseller, *The Grapes of Wrath* (1939). He was especially interested in the appeal of these writers to a group he referred to as the "liberal educated class."

Any study of Trilling is obliged to gloss, as he does not, the contents and implications of his key terms. A great deal might be said of his idea of the liberal educated class, or his alternative version of the same idea,

An early version of this essay, titled "Jewish Intellectuals and the Deep Places of the Imagination," appeared in *Shofar: An Interdisciplinary Journal of Jewish Studies* 21, no. 3 (Spring 2003): 29–47.

the "educated class." Trilling derived the idea from Matthew Arnold, the subject of his first book and Trilling's model of the literary and cultural critic. But there is an immense difference between the liberalism of the cultivated wing of the middle class as Arnold saw it, or the liberalism of the Schlegel sisters in E. M. Forster's *Howards End,* and the "liberal" politics of the educated class of early twentieth-century America. The latter group could hardly be thought of as a saving remnant; rather, it was a largish public whose aesthetic taste and political attitudes Trilling sought to refine and correct. His educated class, considered as his own contemporaries, was the generation influenced by the great movement of the liberal Left that had gained momentum in the 1920s and become dominant in some areas of American culture in the thirties.

The educated class may seem a euphemism because, in Trilling's use of the phrase, it included many left-liberals who had become sympathetic to Soviet Russia, communist fellow travelers, as they were called at the time. In general, however, Trilling was probably being shrewd as well as cautious in lumping everybody together as "liberals." That way he would not seem to be writing polemically as an enemy of the educated class; he could project an image of himself as a liberal critic of liberalism. And he could imply a larger argument. The problem with America's educated class was not merely its perversion of liberalism but the effect on the imagination and the spirit of its exclusive absorption in ideological politics. Trilling insisted that, in the end, he, too, thought of politics as determining human destiny. But he defined "politics" so broadly, as involving the "sentiments" and "quality of life," that when, in later years, he turned against all kinds of political activism, it should not have surprised anyone who had been following his career. At any rate, in "The Function of the Little Magazine" he seemed quite convinced that "no connection exists between our educated class and the best of the literary minds of our time."

In that assertion he invoked "mind," another of his key terms. But in the sentence that followed, which appears syntactically only as an elaboration of the preceding, he added: "And this is to say that there is no connection between the political ideas of our educated class and the deep places of the imagination." Well, are we talking about the literary "mind" or the literary "imagination"? Freud stated as an aim of psychoanalytic therapy that where there had been the id, or the unbridled dominance of fantasy, there shall be the ego, what analysts call "reality testing." Was Trilling reversing or deconstructing the Freudian hierarchy, such that "imagination" now has priority? If that is the case, a cultural critic ought to direct his rhetoric toward replacing "mind" with "imagination," indeed its "deep places." That critical effort might be conceived, like psychoanalysis, as a kind of therapy, but for the educated class and the culture as a whole.

I do not think that Trilling ever intended to deprecate "mind," except as that honorific term might have been appropriated by left-wing utilitarians whose dry rationalism prevented them from seeing or feeling beyond the necessity for social legislation and bureaucratic organization (see the preface to *The Liberal Imagination*), or as "mind" had been associated with the humanly deficient scientism of researchers like Alfred Kinsey (see Trilling's essay "The Kinsey Report" in the same volume). To take a different tack, did Trilling perhaps believe mind and imagination to be the same? I think that is closer to the truth, even if, in the process, he was opposing the major current of critical thinking of his time, in which literature was seen as the product of the "symbolic" or "mythopoeic" imagination, which stands in opposition to logical, discursive thought (see "The Meaning of a Literary Idea," also in *The Liberal Imagination*).

He never did fully elaborate on his understanding of the relations between mind and imagination. But he provides us with a start, in the preface to which I have already referred, in the course of discussing the way in which John Stuart Mill was rescued from the ill effects of his father's utilitarian liberalism by poetry, ideas of poetry in Coleridge and actual poems by Wordsworth. Trilling writes that "the principles of Mill's upbringing very nearly destroyed him." It was the desiccated rationalism of his father's home tutoring that brought on the crisis that Mill recounts in his *Autobiography* and about which Trilling reminded his readers: "And nothing is more touching than the passionate gratitude which Mill gave to poetry for having restored to him the possibility of an emotional life after he had lived in a despairing apathy which brought him to the verge of suicide." Trilling makes his chief point, that contemporary liberalism's exclusive concern with the rationalized organization of life—by way of delegation to agencies and bureaus and technocrats— "drifts toward a denial of the emotions and the imagination." And here

he draws this lesson from Mill's born-again experience: "The imagination [is] properly the joint possession of the emotions and the intellect,
that it [is] fed by the emotions, and that without it the intellect withers
and dies, that without it the mind cannot work and cannot properly
conceive itself."

So, I would argue that Trilling's conception of mind was not only
more complex than that of the dominant liberalism of his day; it was
also more complex than is usually allowed by recent critics and admirers. Leon Wieseltier, the longtime literary editor of the *New Republic,*
has brought together a substantial selection of Trilling's essays in *The
Moral Obligation to Be Intelligent.* It is obvious from this title and Wieseltier's preface and choices—he omits "The Function of the Little
Magazine"—that the Trilling he wishes to honor is the Trilling most
like himself: a polemical writer engaged in contemporary issues in the
politics of culture. Previous writing about Trilling has tended to approach him from the same angle, in terms of the politics of culture. I
even did so myself, although taking greater account of his personal
psychology, in my 1986 book about Trilling. This time I want to displace
that focus. I continue to think of Trilling as best understood in terms
of his ideas, but now I am interested less in his ideas about political-
cultural attitudes than in his ideas about the imagination. These emphases are obviously not totally separable, because the question of the
imagination so frequently arises in Trilling's essays in the context of his
reflections on our cultural attitudes. Still, I would urge that a book
about Trilling might well take as its subject "the moral obligation to be
imaginative."

Speaking in 1974 about the political-cultural situation to which the
essays of *The Liberal Imagination* were a response, Trilling alluded to
"the Stalinist intellectuals of the West." But he had good reasons in the
forties, when he was writing these essays, for using the phrase the "educated middle class" rather than referring, in the French manner, to *les
intellectuels.* He was referring in those years not to full-time intellectuals
and not to a professional intellectual class employed in great academic
institutions. On the contrary, many of the politically engaged people
Trilling had in mind were educated middle-class Jews like himself except that most of them were not professors. But that does not mean
they did not engage the leading political-cultural issues of the time.

They simply had to do so minus the special privileges of academics. This made for lives very different from those of us who launched our careers in the universities in the second half of the twentieth century.

The Jews of the educated class represented a greater range of persons than in our own culture of specialists. Worrying many of the same issues as Trilling himself were lawyers and doctors, high school teachers and civil servants, journalists and editors, as well as the broad nonspecialist class that read magazines of civic opinion like the *New Republic* and the *Nation.*

Many of these liberals were also supportive of what they believed to be the social goals of Russia under Stalin. In the early thirties, in America as well as Germany, the Communists set themselves apart from and in opposition to other groups on the Left, including the Socialists. In America they promoted an agenda that emphasized class conflict and political revolution, and in their John Reed Clubs they encouraged largely uneducated workingmen to write "proletarian" novels. In the later thirties, when Stalin felt the need for allies as Hitler went to war, the appeal to workingmen and to the exclusive spirit of revolutionism was summarily withdrawn. The commissars on the American cultural front launched a new agenda, which involved a blurring of class lines and an effort to win over the educated class. Communism in this new guise became "100 percent Americanism." This was the period of the Popular Front. The work of older American writers—like Tom Paine, Walt Whitman, and Carl Sandburg—was reinterpreted so as to make them spokesmen for this new public version of Stalinism. They were seen as tribunes of the common man. The influence of Popular Front attitudes became so pervasive in these years that it made its way even into the better writing of the time, like Hemingway's *For Whom the Bell Tolls* (1940). To the extent that *The Liberal Imagination* sets out to attack "liberalism," it is the Popular Front and its sentimentality and simplifications that most irritated its author.

Trilling summed up his case against the popular literature of the common man in his essay on the little magazines, the original home of the difficult, little-read modernist writers. That essay had first appeared as the introduction to *The Partisan Reader: Ten Years of Partisan Review, 1933–1944: An Anthology* (1946), edited by the magazine's cofounders, William Phillips and Philip Rahv. *PR* had begun with the blessing and financial support of the American Communist Party, but almost from the start the founders were chafing from the constraints of the party on what they might publish. They were Marxists, but their literary taste disposed them to a body of writing very different from that promoted by the Communist Party. In 1937 they broke with the party and started *PR* all over, this time as a magazine of the independent Left, opposed to Stalinism in its politics and disposed to publish work by and about the literary modernists.

Trilling's own progress was a paler version of that of someone like Rahv. He had never been fully engaged in communist politics, and when he found his critical voice in the late thirties it was as a critic concerned with the middle class and not as any kind of Marxist. Still, of all the little magazines, it was *PR*, and its concern for *ideas* of politics and culture, that most spoke to his own concerns and where he published many of his most influential early essays. Soon after going independent, that magazine would publish one of T. S. Eliot's *Four Quartets* and critical essays on Kafka, Mann, and other moderns. The shared interest in cultural modernism continued to maintain the tie between Trilling and the editors of *Partisan Review* even when his politics departed from theirs.

Trilling's idea of the deep places of the imagination is usually associated in his writing with literary modernism, and his idea of the latter ought to be easier to sum up than his idea of imagination. Surprisingly, that is not the case. He does not offer an overall interpretation of modernism as a literary-cultural movement until fairly late in his career, in the essay "On the Teaching of Modern Literature" (1961). And nowhere does he write a full-length essay on any particular modernist author or modernist text—except in the one case to which I shall return.

Trilling wrote no fewer than three major essays on Jane Austen, and he wrote at length about other Anglo-American nineteenth-century writers like Wordsworth, Keats, Hawthorne, Dickens, Howells, and Henry James (the last in his most Victorian mode, in *The Princess Casamassima* and *The Bostonians*). But "modernism" he merely invoked as if we all know what the word meant for him. In "The Function of the Little Magazine," he did at least assist his readers by offering a list of the writers who counted: "Proust, Joyce, Lawrence, Eliot, Yeats, Mann (in his creative work), Kafka, Rilke, and Gide." This list corresponds fairly closely to the modernist writers most discussed in *Partisan Review*.

2. Isaac Babel and the Cossacks

If Trilling never devoted as full an essay to any of the modernists above as he did to Keats or Austen or Henry James, he did write at length, and without his frequent tentativeness, about one modernist figure. I refer to his essay on the Jewish Russian writer Isaac Babel, whose body of work is small but whose stories have the verbal authority of Flaubert and the concision of Maupassant, as well as a knack for the precise image and the mot juste he learned from the French symbolist poets. Trilling's essay originally appeared in 1955 as an introduction to a collection of Babel's stories and was reprinted in *Beyond Culture* (1965). It is notable for its expansive and freewheeling affect and remarkable for its own energy and joyfulness in the course of celebrating these features in Babel's art.

Babel was one of many Jewish writers murdered by Soviet Russia's secret police during the long reign of Stalin. He died in 1940 at age forty-four. The entire corpus of his surviving work, which recently appeared in translation with an introduction by his daughter Nathalie, fits into a single volume of just over a thousand pages. In the midfifties, Babel was hardly a household name, even among readers knowledgeable about other still-obscure modernist writers. That Trilling, who evaded writing at length about other modernists, should have singled out Babel provokes questions about the nature of that writer's special appeal for him.

The fact that Babel was a Jew was certainly part of his appeal. (Proust, a half-Jew, did not write as a Jew, and remarks in Trilling's essays show he was always uneasy about Kafka.) One reason, I believe, is his personal identification with Babel. The autobiographical aspect of Trilling's felt affinity with his subject accounts in great part for the success of this particular critical performance in drawing upon the deep places of his own imagination. What follows is an account of Trilling's reading of Babel, a specific example that we can unpack to make some broader generalizations about Trilling's idea of the imagination.

To readers whose conception of East European Jewish life comes from writers like Sholom Aleichem, Babel must appear an unusual type. Born in 1896, he grew up in Odessa, where his successful businessman father made sure he studied the Bible and the Talmud in Hebrew.

But he went to school at Tsar Nicholas II Commercial College, where his classmates were, as he later wrote, "the sons of foreign merchants, the children of Jewish brokers, Poles from noble families, Old Believers." Between classes this multilingual cohort reveled in the pleasures of their cosmopolitan city. They went down to the port to Greek coffee houses and to "drink cheap Bessarabian wine in the taverns." Odessa was more like Marseilles than like the shtetlach in the Russian Pale of Settlement. It was here, in his commercial college, that Babel studied French literature and got the idea of modeling himself on Maupassant. Indeed, his first stories, written when he was fifteen, were in French.

At the same time, Babel was reading widely in Tolstoy, whom he revered throughout his life. One reason has to do with Babel's literary economy. He was endlessly revising his very short stories and went for years at a time producing little new work. It is not surprising that this younger man should look with awe upon the plenitude of a Tolstoy, whose fiction fills ninety volumes in the Soviet edition of his work. But there was more to Babel's awe in relation to Tolstoy. It was through reading him, Babel said, that he "came to understand the sublime virtue of the Russian people." His father, indifferent to his son's literary passion as he was to his idealism, sent him after secondary school to complete his education at the Institute of Financial and Business Studies in Kiev. However, after graduating in 1915, Babel broke free from his father's control and the prospect of a life in commerce. He moved to Petersburg, where he met Maxim Gorky, who promptly published some of his stories. In his early twenties, he was already being noticed by advanced literary figures like the formalist critic Victor Shklovsky.

Babel's Tolstoy-inspired idealism became manifest in his sympathy with the Revolution. He enlisted in the Red Army and served on the Rumanian front. After a short spell in Odessa recovering from malaria contracted in the army, Babel returned to Petersburg to resume his apprenticeship to Gorky. The older writer urged him to abandon the ivory tower of some of the Frenchmen who had earlier influenced him and to move about the vast nation and become acquainted with its people. Babel worked at a variety of jobs during this period, frequently as a journalist, including a job working for Gorky's own paper. In 1920 he received the call that would transform his life as a writer. He was assigned as a war correspondent to accompany General Budyonny's Cossack cavalry regiments. After the Revolution, civil war had broken out between the Bolsheviks (the Reds) and their reactionary opponents (the Whites). By 1920 that war had spread to Poland, where Budyonny's army was posted.

For the divisional newspaper, *The Red Cavalryman,* Babel wrote up-beat campaign stories sounding as if they were pitched to the tastes of his superiors. But in his diaries and short stories he wrote very differently. He saw how brutally both Cossack and Polish armies destroyed Jews and their villages. He particularly noted the murderous violence of the Cossacks, but at the same time he acknowledged their physical grace and their adherence to their own codes of honor, however much they stood in contrast to the ethical precepts of the Jews. It was here, in Babel's ambivalence about these traditional enemies of the Jews and all the Jews stood for, that Trilling located the interest of that writer's work. He praised Babel as he had other artists he admired—Keats, James, Yeats, Scott Fitzgerald—to the degree that his writing contained the suggestion "that one might live in doubt, that one might live by means of a question."

The word "ambivalence" seldom appears in Trilling, despite his commitment to Freud. The reason is that ambivalence suggests feelings over which we have no control. He did, however, seem to be acknowledging ambivalence in saying that "in Babel's heart there was a kind of fighting—he was captivated by the vision of two ways of being, the way of violence and the way of peace, and he was torn between them." But at the same time that the critic presents to us a writer "captivated" and "torn," he also describes Babel's mind and imagination as creative forces. Babel was one "who *makes* [my italics] his heart a battleground for conflicting tendencies of culture. . . . The conflict between the two ways of being was an essential element of his mode of thought." So, instinct and emotion ("heart") become identified with mind and will ("mode of thought"). And the whole thing is not regarded as a mish-mash of irresolution and confusion but as an ideal, indeed as the ideal to which Trilling himself aspired. He represented this tolerance for inner contradiction as the characteristic mode of great art, and he praised this mode of being as an alternative to the failure of much of the "liberal class" in falling for the simplifications of communist ideology.

Babel was a Jew and thus, as Trilling understood him, one who "conceived his ideal character to consist in his being intellectual, pacific, humane." On the other hand, he was powerfully drawn to the Cossacks even though to the Jews "the Cossack was physical, violent, without mind or manners." In the Jewish imagination, the Cossack stood for "animal violence" and "aimless destructiveness." There was a potential political dimension to the detestation of the Cossack. If the Jew "thought beyond his own ethnic and religious group, he knew that the Cossack was the enemy not only of the Jew—although him especially—but of all men who thought of freedom; he was the natural and appropriate instrument of ruthless oppression."

The Cossacks were not regarded with such disdain—and dread—by all Russians. Non-Jewish Slavophile intellectuals idealized the Russian peasant and nationalities that maintained their archaic ways in eluding Western modernity. Trilling said of Tolstoy, for example, that he "had represented the Cossack as having a primitive energy, passion, and virtue. He was the man untrammeled by civilization, direct, immediate, fierce. He was the man of enviable simplicity, the man of the body—and of the horse, the man who moved with speed and grace." Trilling follows up this description by invoking a theme that is pervasive in his own later writing, as the theme of the divided self was central to his earlier writing. That is the theme of regret. The Cossack as noble savage "stands for our sense of something unhappily surrendered, the truth of the body, the truth of full sexuality, the truth of open aggressiveness." And the great paradox was that "Babel's view of the Cossack was more consonant with that of Tolstoy than with the traditional view of his own people."

For Trilling, Babel's sometime idealization of the Cossack had to do with the "grace" and "joy" (Trilling's words) he discovered in their unfettered instinctual life. In other words, the Cossack inspired his art by representing a life that, however barbarous, might be seen in aesthetic terms. We can begin to dilate on the components that coexisted in Trilling's view of the deep places of imagination.

3. Instinct and Emotion

Trilling's reference to "full sexuality" and "open aggressiveness" point to Freud as his major influence. Of course, he might have invoked Nietzsche, who had a much greater influence than did Freud on Russian intellectuals at that time. Nietzsche might be seen as the model for

Babel's aestheticizing amoralism, evident in his willingness at times to overlook the Cossack's murderousness. Babel was, of course, not Nietzschean in his narrative strategy of reserving judgment. Aesthetic ambiguity, rather, was as much a moral code as a literary strategy.

But it is Freud on the instinctual life and on "civilization and its discontents" that engaged Trilling more. The close association in his thinking between imagination and instinct is evident in his essay on "The Function of the Little Magazine," in which the sentence about the disconnection between the educated class and "the deep places of the imagination" is followed by this one: "The same fatal separation is to be seen in the tendency of our educated liberal class to reject the tough, complex psychology of Freud for the easy rationalistic optimism of Horney and Fromm." Freud's "toughness" lay in his view that the demands of the superego and society can never be easily squared with the drive of the instincts toward gratification. For Freud, as Trilling read him, the instinct-life is biological, and changing the social environment cannot alter the conflict between civilization and what is biologically given in the individual psyche. Liberals of Fromm's type were only carrying over utopian dreams from the left-wing politics of the thirties in conceiving a psychology in which the tragic effects of emotional conflict and repression might be resolved.

However much Trilling perceived his own self-dividedness as similar to that of Babel, he actually stood in relation to Babel in a way that was similar to Babel's stance in relation to the Cossacks. That is, he admired Babel's original imagination and genius as Babel admired the uninhibited instinct-life and premodern authenticity of the Cossacks. The suffocatingly respectable middle-class society in which Trilling was raised was as far as could be from what Babel remembered as the "gay, rowdy, noisy and multilingual" world of his Odessa. Babel's stories about Benya Krik and other raucous Jewish gangsters indicate that he had witnessed a great deal of brutality even before he met up with the Cossack cavalry.

Trilling was less disposed to invoke the word "instincts," however, than "emotions." I wrote earlier about the important role he granted to the life of feeling in his preface to *The Liberal Imagination*. The question of the emotions comes up also in his essay on the little magazine, in which he dismissed the progressive literature of his moment as a literature of "piety and charm," designed to confirm its audience in its politically correct sentiments. This writing was devoid of the "real emotions" that were to be found in the literature of modernism. Trilling located in the modernist elements of Isaac Babel's art a moral neutrality and an energy untrammeled by a culture that by the end of the nineteenth century had begun to be exposed as the enemy of "life." The idea was to strip away the veneer of middle-class respectability in order to restore access to the springs of our being. Diving deep into the springs of man's being might be made possible by recovery of the most archaic and primitive instincts and feelings.

Freud figures importantly in that fin-de-siècle movement to get at what lay beneath the rationalizations of civilized society. And he made use of categories akin to Trilling's. But Trilling spoke of instincts, emotions, and imagination, as against Freud's "drives," "affects," and "fantasy." The difference was that Freud thought of himself as a scientist and of his work as a project for a new scientific psychology, and Trilling, though clearly influenced by Freud, remained a traditional humanist. Fantasy, in particular, might for Trilling have been associated with Hollywood B movies or erotic daydreams. Imagination was more dignified. It is too bad Trilling was shy about the fantasies. Had he been less uneasy about his own, he might also have been on better terms with his own imagination.

In any case, the relation between the hidden places of the instinctual life and the deep places of imagination is made visible in Babel's story "Di Grasso: A Tale of Odessa," for which Trilling appended a brief commentary in his jumbo textbook-anthology *The Experience of Literature* (1967). In that story the actor Di Grasso enacts on stage the vengeful passion of a wronged suitor. Babel describes his crime of passion. The actor "gave a smile, soared into the air, sailed across the stage, plunged down on [the villain's] shoulders, and having bitten through the latter's throat, began growling and squinting, to suck blood from the wound." To which Babel adds this gloss: "There is more justice in outbursts of noble passion than in all the joyless rules that run the world." Babel is plainly thrilled by this display of spontaneous feeling. And Trilling, who undertook his doctoral dissertation on Matthew Arnold because he wanted to understand the reasons for the melancholy that pervades Arnold's poetry, is able in his response to Babel to overcome his own melancholy, which might have had its origin in his own compliance with "the joyless rules that run the world."

But Trilling would not be Trilling if he were simply recommending "outbursts of noble passion." His larger purpose becomes evident in his ruminations on Babel's "lyric joy in the midst of violence." For him the deep places of emotion are allied with the deep places of imagination. By way of analogy to Di Grasso's great leap, Trilling adduces the great leaps of the dancer Nijinsky, whose seeming ability to fly across the stage gave his audience a precious "intimation of freedom from the bondage of our human condition." And that is one of the potentials of great art: to carry us "beyond culture," or what Trilling frequently characterized as "the conditions." Babel is concerned not with whether an act like Di Grasso's conforms to the traditional norms of morality but with the manner and style of the act. In this sense Di Grasso's leap is akin to the violence of the Cossack. It inspires aesthetic emotions—awe before its sublime transcendence of earthbound ordinariness and lyric joy by its sheer animal grace. Babel has plumbed the deep places of imagination and in the process liberated the reader. In the preface to *The Opposing Self* (1955), Trilling credited Hegel with first affirming the moral primacy of the aesthetic: "For Hegel, art is the activity of man in which spirit expresses itself not only as utility, not only according to law, but as grace, as transcendence, as manner and style. He did this not in the old way of making morality the criterion of the aesthetic: on the contrary, he made the aesthetic the criterion of the moral."

4. The Primacy of the Aesthetic

The implications of this emphasis on the aesthetic are manifold in the case of writers and also of critics like Trilling whom they influenced. First, there is the influence on the politics of the literary modernists. In "The Function of the Little Magazine," Trilling says of the modernists he has listed that "all have their love of justice and the good life, but in not one of them does it take the form of a love of the ideas and emotions which liberal democracy, as known by our educated class, has declared respectable." This is a gross understatement. Not only were several major writers bored with bourgeois-democratic politics; several were powerfully drawn to fascism. That attraction was latent in Yeats's love of "the old disturbed exalted life, the old splendor," a phrase Trilling quotes in his essay on Isaac Babel. The disdain of writers like Lawrence and Yeats for ordinary middle-class life led them to seek out alternative cultures in which order, energy, and beauty reigned, but at the cost of authoritarian leadership. These writers, and T. S. Eliot as well, only flirted with fascism; Ezra Pound, who lived in Italy during World War II, lent his active support. Pound was nearly imprisoned in America for having broadcast speeches on Italian radio in 1940–43 hailing Mussolini's rule. What can have led him to such a stupid mistake? Possibly Pound's was only the most extreme instance of a writer applying aesthetic values to a realm of human experience where they had no proper relevance. Many modernists went astray in advocating an ideal society that would have the qualities they sought to encourage in their personal imaginative creations.

The reactionary politics of many modernists created a problem for Trilling in thinking about the imagination. He had no truck with fascism himself, but the literature he admired was at odds with his liberal political sympathies. He followed Hazlitt, another critic with liberal sympathies, in believing that the imagination was in its essence allied to elitist politics. On more than one occasion, Trilling cited Hazlitt's essay "Coriolanus" on that theme. He might also have mentioned Hazlitt's "On the Spirit of Monarchy," which starts with a passage from *Shenstone's Letters:* "As for politics, I think poets are Tories by nature, supposing them to be by nature poets. The love of an individual person or family, that has worn a crown for many successions, is an inclination greatly adapted to the fanciful tribe. On the other hand, mathematicians, abstract reasoners, of no manner of attachment to persons, at least to the visible part of them, but prodigiously devoted to the ideas of virtue, liberty, and so forth, are generally Whigs."

A taste for the literary modernists did not always translate into right-wing politics. In the 1960s, students transformed some of the subversive ideas of modernism into an activist counterculture. Trilling denounced that "adversary culture" for having institutionalized and dumbed-down what had been for his own generation a difficult new literature for a select few. He wrote of the sixties counterculture as "modernism in the streets." For Trilling the deep places of the imagination produced aesthetic objects that existed for contemplation, not as guide-books to practical action, but the professor's teachings may well have served as a spur to his students. His repeated emphasis on morally neu-tral values—spontaneity and energy, manner and style—as alternatives to a joyless world of rules must have had some impact on how his fol-lowers fantasized about their lives. The decisive factor for the young is that they were coming of age at a time in which Trilling's kind of subli-mation gave way to a new ideal, of desublimation. It appears to me in retrospect that Trilling stands to this generation much as Walter Pater stood to Oscar Wilde's generation. The students took the professor's theoretical preferences literally, thereby contributing to a cultural revo-lution, however different from the sexual scandal involving Wilde.

But the aspect of Trilling's advocacy of the aesthetic mode of judg-ment that interests me most is the biographical. Why had the idea of the primacy of art so appealed to him? In Trilling's occasional com-ments about himself in his criticism, he is never direct about his own moods and motives. He reveals far more in his ostensibly impersonal statements about "culture." One of the most interesting of these occurs in the preface to *The Opposing Self,* as he moves from a discussion of Hegel's philosophy of art to a particular poem of Matthew Arnold's, "The Scholar Gypsy."

Trilling alludes to Arnold the elementary school inspector, the Vic-torian Arnold who affirmed the importance of duty and morality, "and the pain and suffering that the moral life entails." "But," he goes on, "in 'The Scholar Gypsy' we have an Arnold who . . . speaks of the 'patience' which the life in culture requires as 'too-near neighbor to despair.'" We have already heard, in the preface to *The Liberal Imagination,* of John Stuart Mill's despair that brought him close to suicide. In Mill's case the cause was the emotionally destructive educational regime his father had imposed on him. "In Arnold's case it is the despair of those who, having committed themselves to culture, have surrendered the life of surprise and elevation, of impulse, pleasure, and imagination. 'The Scholar Gypsy' *is* imagination, impulse, and pleasure."

"Our habitual life in culture," as Trilling calls it, exacts as its price the life of imagination. "Elevation" is the one quality of imagination we have not seen referred to before and might seem to pose a problem inas-much as I have up to now maintained that for Trilling imagination was a principle of depth. When he referred to imagination's deep places, he had in mind what Arnold called the "buried life" and Freud the unconscious. But tapping into the depths, where lie the springs of our being, precisely enables the elevation, the sublimity, of Di Grasso's leap. Elevation is the effect, the creative act, enabled by the imagination's plumbing of its own depths. But "we" ought not to think about "our" habitual life in culture. What matters here is Trilling's own life in culture, and that of his intellectual contemporaries, first-generation American sons of Jewish immigrants.

5. Creative Imagination and Criticism

Up to now I have been discussing Trilling's *ideas* about the imagination. Now it is time to assess how effectively he was able to draw upon imagination in his own writing. Does the Babel essay represent an exception in his writing? It may seem strange to consider a critic's career in terms of the degree to which he embodied in his own work ideas about imagination that he devised to interpret and evaluate the writing of poets and novelists. Although I will begin this section with an account of Trilling's own major attempt at fiction, I want to make plain now that I regard his essays in criticism as belonging to a mode of writing in which imagination can play an important part. Just consider the case of Harold Bloom, who was coeditor with Trilling of an excellent anthology of nineteenth-century British literature but who jibbed at Trilling's critical influence, although not as much as he objected to that of T. S. Eliot. Trilling was an Arnoldian moralist and Eliot a classicist, whereas Bloom is a High Romantic committed to aesthetic values. In his critical writing, Bloom exercises his imagination in a unique way, creating a critical method in which fantasy was central, blending such disparate influences as kabbalah, ideas of the Romantic Sublime, psychoanalysis (which he understood differently than Trilling did), and Kenneth Burke's version of rhetorical criticism. Bloom exemplifies variousness more than did Trilling, although it was among the latter's most emphasized values. Bloom's broad range of interests is suggested by his books on the Hebrew Bible, Shakespeare, Romantic poetry in English, and nonmainline sects in American religion. Most importantly, he argues, along with other advanced theorists of his generation, on behalf of the idea that critical commentary can be as original as the text that provides its occasion. May not criticism, then, be read as an act of creative imagination?

But, first, as I said, I will start not with Trilling's work in criticism but with his fiction. When he began writing for publication in his twenties, his dream was not to become a literary critic and public intellectual. His ambition was to become a novelist. The chances are that if he had gone on to realize that ambition, he would have written novels of society like those of Balzac, Stendhal, and James that he admired, in which young men are made to endure an initiation, a rite of passage. The one novel he did write, *The Middle of the Journey* (1947), is about such an ordeal, although it is not in its form a nineteenth-century novel about the sentimental education of a young man from the provinces like Stendhal's Julien Sorel or James's Hyacinth Robinson. Trilling's eloquent essay on Hyacinth and *The Princess Casamassima* appeared about the same time as his own singleton novel.

John Laskell stands in for the author of *The Middle of the Journey*. The novel is set in the midthirties, when Trilling had entered his own thirties and was thinking his way out of his earlier sympathy with communism. Laskell is around thirty and thinks of himself as a "well-loved young man of the middle class," which the novel offers as a reason for his orientation toward the future and his affinity with left-wing utopianism. Laskell, like the liberal class in relation to communism, has been "brought up on promises." But an event has occurred that has shaken his convictions: an illness has brought him to the brink of death. Now convalescing, Laskell faces an ordeal of belief. In the course of the novel he undergoes no dramatic change of heart, but the new tendency of his being is toward a rejection of absolutes, whether political or religious.

Laskell's relation to communism has merely been one of ideas. "Communism" as an organized party appropriately is spelled with a capital *C*, whereas "communism" as idea or even as a movement is usually spelled lowercase. Another of the novel's characters, also a communist sympathizer, has carried his ideas into action, as a spy in the service of the Communist Party. The ex-spy, Gifford Maxim, has also broken with communism, but unlike Laskell, whose commitment has been only notional, Maxim has risked his life in defecting from the party. Also unlike Laskell, who remains a centrist liberal after leaving behind his dream of an ideal socialist future, his extremist friend retains his will to believe in absolutes. So, in repudiating the principles of Communist orthodoxy, Maxim has found a new orthodoxy in Christian dogma. His Christianity serves as his rationale for a markedly irrationalist right-wing politics. Laskell judges the new Maxim to be "no disaffected revolutionary. He was the blackest of reactionaries."

The other characters who matter are Arthur and Nancy Croom, liberals and, like Laskell in his precrisis time, sympathetic to what they take to be the goals of communism. Unlike their friend Maxim, they have taken no risks in entertaining ideas favorable to a postcapitalist social order. That makes all the more striking their anger about Maxim's defection from the party. Although their own relation to communism has not involved them in political action, much less espionage, they prove to be quite as rigid as Maxim himself. And even more than Maxim, they show themselves to be impervious to experience.

Laskell has come to their Connecticut country home to recover his strength. He brings with him a sense of hauntedness that is the effect of his brush with death. He is no longer the privileged middle-class child brought up to look forward to a perfect future; the changed Laskell, in the middle of his journey, finds himself preoccupied by the past and reflections on death. It would seem that Trilling, in fixing on death (and communism) as his subject, has chosen the topic most likely to call forth the boldest acts of imagination. But the novel itself is disappointing. And that is because it does not take on death directly or by way of dream, symbol, or myth. Rather, Trilling turns his novel into an abstract reflection on the disconnection between communism as ideology and a proper appreciation of the implications of death. He limits himself to the philosophical ideas, the political attitudes, and the particular opinions of his characters. For a Freudian, he appears surprisingly averse to guessing at the unconscious motives underlying their different positions or the emotions that move them.

Thus the Crooms are shown as uneasy with Laskell, as if he still carries the germs that nearly ended his life. Their reasons have to do with the emotional incapacity fostered by communism as a culture. For his part, Laskell's near-death experience has caused him to become absorbed in "questions of being, in questions of his own existence." This interest of Laskell's will echo a few years later in Trilling's comments on

Wordsworth and "the sentiment of being." But the Crooms are fixed on becoming, and whatever threatens that stance threatens them. Laskell has been speaking of the death of his former love, Elizabeth, and a "claim" that Gifford Maxim had made on him in showing Laskell a photo of her that he always carries in his wallet. But Nancy Croom will have none of that. She shows by her manners as well as her words that to her "'claims' were of the past, the dead were of the past. They had no place in Nancy's bright, shining future, and he, Laskell, by giving them place in his thought, had committed what amounted to an obscenity."

Trilling shows Nancy Croom as sympathetic to the communist dream of the future but totally incapable of sympathetic identification with Laskell in the present due to his association with death. Trilling puts it this way in his introduction to the new edition of *The Middle of the Journey*, which appeared in 1975: "The Crooms might be said to pass a *political* judgment upon Laskell for the excessive attention he pays to the fact that he had approached death and hadn't died. If Laskell's preoccupation were looked at closely and objectively, they seem to be saying, might it not be understood as actually an affirmation of death, which is, in its practical outcome, a negation of the future and the hope it holds out for a society of reason and virtue? Was there not a sense in which death might be called reactionary?"

To say the least, as a novel of ideas *The Middle of the Journey* does not achieve the originality of Thomas Mann's *Magic Mountain*, one of the influences on his own book, and as a novel of manners it does not achieve the dramatic force of *Howards End*, another model for Trilling in which death figures importantly. Most important of all, in electing to write a novelistic version of the argument put forward in *The Liberal Imagination*, Trilling failed the test he had himself devised. His abstractly intellectual handling of the death theme offers no sign that Trilling had plumbed the depths of his imagination. *The Middle of the Journey* attracted little critical attention when it first appeared, but it did elicit one very intelligent review. Robert Warshow, a junior editor at *Commentary*, was an acquaintance of Trilling whose own writing on mass culture showed the impact of the older man's work. But Warshow was devastating in his critique of the novel. He faulted Trilling for glossing over the historical particularities of the intellectual crisis he was depicting. It is certainly true that in making all his characters Gentile and removing the drama from its appropriate New York City setting to John Cheever country, Trilling introduced a genteel "Episcopalian aroma"—the phrase is John Bayley's—that was altogether alien to the political debates of the thirties.

The effect of the book's critical failure was his turn away from writing fiction; there is no evidence that he ever again attempted another story or novel. After his death Diana Trilling, in her memoir *The Beginning of the Journey,* wrote of the reasons for her husband's retreat from fiction in slightly different terms: "It was to decency that Lionel felt that he had sacrificed his hope of being a writer of fiction—conscience had not made a coward of him, it had made him a critic." But, as Mrs. Trilling continued, he never came to terms with that renunciation. "Did his friends and colleagues have no hint of how deeply he scorned the very qualities of character—his quiet, his moderation, his gentle reasonableness—for which he was most admired in his lifetime and which have been most celebrated since his death?" It may be that his contemporaries never penetrated Trilling's mask, but my own emphasis is on the appeal to Trilling of the "untrammeled" life of instinct and emotion that he associated with imagination's deep places.

But, as I have said, I do not think that the decision to stick to criticism had to spell the end of Trilling's opportunities to be imaginative. We have seen, for example, how Isaac Babel's imagination liberated his own. Literary criticism need not be prosaic. Necessity did not dictate that his critical writing was condemned to share his failed novel's unimaginative sobriety. What in fact did Trilling do after 1947?

Trilling in his critical writing did not have to renounce the attempt to scale the heights and plumb the depths of the imagination. But, apart from isolated moments, that is exactly what he did. Indeed, the most striking feature of his essays of the early fifties, which were collected in *The Opposing Self,* was his highly self-conscious affirmation of the counterimaginative principle in literature. These essays find a variety of reasons for recommending a lowering of stimulation and a tamping down of the instincts, the emotions, and the life of fantasy. Examples are close to hand. In "Wordsworth and the Rabbis," he speaks up for the Stoic virtue of apatheia, or not-feeling, and in his essay on *Mansfield Park,* he praises Jane Austen's least vivacious heroine, Fanny Price, for her habit of Christian self-abnegation and for her unfailing sense of duty. In his comments on "The Scholar Gypsy," Trilling had seemed to join Arnold in striking out against such renunciations on account of the price they exacted in the surrender of happiness. But in Austen's novel, as Trilling points out, Fanny is both unglamorous and happily at one with herself. In the case of Fanny and the works he singles out for praise, passivity is among the highest virtues.

Trilling paid tribute to George Orwell for his old-fashioned decency. "Old-fashioned" takes on honorific value in these essays; the critic means to underline his reaction against the histrionics, the apocalypticism, the moral extremism of the new-fashioned and influential modernists. He even praised the feeling for the commonplace in William Dean Howells's *Hazard of New Fortunes.* Trilling celebrating Howells! His culturally radical students were shocked that he was speaking not only on behalf of the commonplace, as in Wordsworth's poetry, but on behalf of mere social convention. What had happened to their modernist-minded mentor? No doubt Trilling was suffering from fatigue. Part of it, I would guess, resulted from letdown after the large amount of writing he had done in the forties and the great acclaim that greeted *The Liberal Imagination.* But it represented a letdown, too, amidst the intensity of ideological debate in the immediate postwar years. Certainly the phenomenon of McCarthyism and the red scare in general meant that politics had not vanished as a focus of debate. But Trilling opted for a separate peace. He was hardly alone among his contemporaries in his retreat in the early fifties from left-wing politics, but he went about it in a different way from other liberal anticommunists. His writing reinforced the status quo by indirection, by calling attention to the virtues of contemplation and moral quietism.

In a review-essay on *The Liberal Imagination,* R. P. Blackmur referred to Trilling as "an administrator of the affairs of the mind." It is not an attractive designation, but it does fit the Trilling of essays like "Freud: With and Beyond Culture" and the three essays on higher education in *Beyond Culture.* He gave himself over, not without frequent signs of inner protest, to his public intellectual role. He busied himself correcting tendencies he deplored in American psychoanalysis and the social sciences; he gave reasons why modernism did not belong in the streets and ought to be restored to the classroom; and he intervened in the debate between C. P. Snow and F. R. Leavis on the natural sciences versus the humanities. In Trilling's decision to write on the latter debate we can see the opposing priorities that never ceased to pull at him.

Stanley Burnshaw, a prominent New York book editor, was a long-time acquaintance of Trilling. It was Burnshaw who persuaded Trilling to take on the job of compiling selections and writing commentaries for the ambitious textbook-anthology *The Experience of Literature*. That anthology was a long time in the making but finally appeared in 1967. During the long period that book was in gestation, Burnshaw tried to persuade Trilling to get back to writing fiction.[1] Burnshaw himself wrote poetry, plays for the radio, and memoirs and experimented in other genres as well. He had good reason for thinking Trilling might be amenable to his encouragement. In the late fifties, Trilling had seemed to lose focus in his critical writing. His old argument about the weaknesses of liberalism had lost most of its relevance in a cultural situation dominated by business-minded conservatism. And the argument for moral passivity had revealed itself to Trilling as potentially an apology for a "morality of inertia," which he deplored in a perceptive essay on Edith Wharton's *Ethan Frome*.

But about this time the Snow-Leavis controversy became a favorite topic of campus debate, a topic resident tutors would raise when they joined undergraduates in college dining halls. The current debate was a replay of a major intellectual controversy of the Victorian era, and Trilling may well have believed it would have broad ramifications for our moment as its precursor had in Matthew Arnold's England. As it turned out, attention to the controversy faded quickly. I am not interested in the debate—from the start the positions were crudely stated and the argument quickly got bogged down in personalities. My point is that for the sake of making his contribution to this transient cultural episode, Trilling sacrificed a good opportunity to try out his imagination. That pattern of sacrifice became a near constant from Trilling's middle years on.

Trilling paid a large price for his life in culture. The "culture" for

---

1. Burnshaw and I exchanged letters when I was working up my book on Trilling. I owe him for the encouragement he gave me at the time and for the story of Trilling's near return to writing fiction that I relate here.

which he surrendered so much was high cosmopolitan culture, to which he turned, and never looked back, once he had become convinced that Jewishness, at least in America, was a narrow, parochial affair. But it exacted a price, his self-invention as a Columbia University humanist who became a better example of what is best in that tradition than did his senior colleagues, who had at the start looked askance at him as a "Freudian, a Marxist, and a Jew." Trilling had his own particular Freud. His Freud was not the author of "The Uncanny" and "Beyond the Pleasure Principle," the Freud of recent critics influenced by poststructuralist theory. Rather, Trilling's Freud was both a moralist and a philosopher of culture. He attended most closely to the pessimistic author of "Civilization and Its Discontents," who provided him with a rationale for his rueful acceptance of his own self-created public burden. That burden was the consequence of Trilling's lifelong ordeal of civility. The "discontents" in Freud's argument had to do in Trilling's case with the sacrifice of instinctual life that Babel (and Trilling after him) associated with the uncivilized Cossack.

He paid a price, too, in having to repress any impulse to waywardness. He had to edit out any conduct or personality traits that might detract from his self-imposed role as a model for students, especially the young Jews among them, whom he was helping to launch on the difficult process of acculturation. And private person that he was, he paid a price in maintaining his stance as a public intellectual who felt an obligation to speak up on cultural issues of the day, like the science-humanities controversy. It was a great price to pay, "the life of impulse, pleasure, and imagination," and a note of regret and wistfulness is frequently audible in Trilling's later essays. An example is his excellent essay on Keats, in which he attempts to arouse in the reader envy of the childhood that enabled that poet's imagination of sensuous delight.

Although Trilling may have suffered more from the discontents of civilization than other New York intellectuals, he was not alone in paying greatly for the assimilation he achieved. But he alone conceived of his role as being that of a sacrificial figure whose purpose in life was to bear the contradictions, the opposing principles, of his culture. He made it sound at times as if the culture-hero existed to bear the cross for everyone else.

6. The Man in the Middle

An early short story serves to illustrate the question of the imagination in relation to other themes I have been discussing. "Of This Time, Of That Place" (1943) is the best known of Trilling's stories, mainly because it has frequently been thought to draw on his own experience as one of Allen Ginsberg's professors at Columbia. It is a story of initiation, about a young English teacher fairly new to his role at Dwight College. The instructor, a thoughtful, outwardly composed person of middle-class background, has his composure shaken by a new student, Ferdinand Tertan, who strikes us at first as the teacher's antithesis in every respect. The most important thing about Tertan is that he is undergoing a process of psychotic breakdown. The instructor is squeamish about the young man's anguish, but also about his lower-class city ways. For Tertan brings with him "the stuffy sordid strictness of some crowded, metropolitan high school." The student happens also to be a person of imagination: a "rich-hair'd Youth of Morn" such as appears in late eighteenth-century poetry. But then we recall how many poets of England's Age of Sensibility were themselves mad.

The teacher's problem, and the test that he faces, involves what to do about Tertan. His obvious choice is to bring Tertan's perilous condition to the attention of the college's dean. But he is not only a fastidious product of middle-class privilege. He is also young enough not to want to conform to the "official way," which would mean an end to Tertan's career at the college and possibly his being dispatched to a very different kind of institution, for the mentally ill. Something else causes the teacher to hesitate. Like Tertan, he too is a poet and knows what it is to feel an alien among the college's philistines. A recent collection of his poems has been attacked for its "precious subjectivism" by a middlebrow reviewer much admired by his English department colleagues.

Oddly, Ferdinand Tertan, notwithstanding his eccentric ways, is the secret sharer of his teacher. There is something locked up in this cautious, slightly anxious academic that can respond to the wildness in a person who might seem to stand for an opposite principle of being, the teacher's cool rationality the antithesis of Tertan's anarchical madness. The mainly unconscious identification of the instructor with Tertan may explain a little why Trilling did so much to protect Ginsberg when, as a student, the young poet's recklessness got him in trouble with the authorities. And it helps to account for Trilling's friendship with Norman Mailer, another writer with a sensibility far more extreme than that of Trilling.

The instructor's intuition of their bond makes it more difficult for him to act on Tertan's case. But in the end he bows to Necessity, or the reality principle, and tells the dean. The decision, however difficult for the teacher, is the mature one. The student is falling apart, and college is not the right place for him. But the decision is shown to be tragic for Tertan, who, in a final graduation-ceremony tableau, appears by himself, removed from the festivities. He is outside the magic circle in which the dean stands in an avuncular posture at the instructor's side. In turning the student over to the dean, the instructor has earned points. He has acted as the agent of the Law, conforming to "the joyless rules that run the world." He reaps a reward, promotion to assistant professor, for playing society's game, but he feels guilty not jubilant. Spirit, in the form of the mad poet, has been overthrown, but the event is tragic also for the teacher-poet who has here allied himself not with Spirit but with the Law.

I have borrowed these capitalized abstractions—Necessity, Law, Spirit—from Gifford Maxim's madly reactionary interpretation of Herman Melville's "Billy Budd" in *The Middle of the Journey*. There can be no question but that Trilling approves of the instructor's decision to turn over Tertan just as Maxim approves of Captain Vere's decision to execute Billy for killing Claggart. That does not mean Trilling's story is also politically reactionary. Considered as moral initiation, the young instructor has passed from innocence to experience, from his earlier illusions to an acceptance of reality. In the end he has learned to accept that some tragedies are irreversible, that some evil in the world is not subject to amelioration. That is the interpretation of his own story that Trilling proposes in *The Experience of Literature,* in which he included and glossed the story "Of This Time, Of That Place."

But we do better, I think, to trust the tale and not the teller. The teacher, by accommodating himself to the "official way," has achieved success: his promotion and the dean's support. But he will pay a price for his decision, even though that decision was the realistic one. His last gesture is to reach out to Tertan. Leaving the dean's side, he looks for

Tertan but finds his former student has already left. By his decision the instructor has abandoned his secret sharer, but he remains the story's man in the middle, as John Laskell remains the man in the middle of his personal journey. The instructor's middleness is a matter of inner conflict. Outwardly he has identified himself with the dean and the "official way" at Dwight College. Inwardly, he continues to long for Tertan, who represents for him a principle of being that is precious, however mixed up with insanity.

The instructor's way of occupying his middling position will cost him dearly. Unlike in Conrad's "Secret Sharer," the teacher has failed to integrate the enlivening traits of his anarchical double. He has, in symbolic terms, let slip away Tertan's intensity of affect, instinct, and fantasy, and his resulting incompleteness signals that his poetry may never get beyond "precious subjectivism." His desire to be accepted by the authorities has caused him to rely on prudence and caution. These are clearly desirable qualities in dealing with the worldly world, but they militate against access to the deep places of imagination.

What is curious about Trilling, then, is his own stance as a man in the middle—I am borrowing Geoffrey Hartman's characterization of him—who accepted that his sacrifices cost him much that he valued, but who continued to yearn for what he had surrendered and thus dreamed of having things both ways. It is easy for Jewish intellectuals coming after Trilling to fault him for the effect on his writing of his compromises. But the fact is that Trilling, in managing as he did, was able to open a new career path that had not previously existed. Academics, especially Jewish academics, who came after him did not have to make the same sacrifices, although every life requires some compromises. It would betray a lack of grace—a word that in Trilling's writing points to both an aesthetic value and a moral value—not to recognize this surrogate father of so many of us for his achievement.

The Trillings
A Marriage of True Minds?

The tension between analytic reason and imagination was not exclusively a function of Lionel Trilling's inward life. It figured importantly in his domestic life as well. His wife, Diana, suffered as much as he from this disjunction. In this essay I will be emphasizing the disjunction in their mental lives and between them as husband and wife, as revealed in her late memoir, *The Beginning of the Journey: The Marriage of Diana and Lionel Trilling* (1993). But first I want to discuss Mrs. Trilling by herself.

Born in 1905, she was the same age as Lionel. They were both unlike other early contributors to *Partisan Review* in having been raised in respectably middle-class families engaged in the garment trade. Mrs. Trilling took the unusual course of enrolling at Radcliffe, where she concentrated in the fine arts. She later regretted her education because, unlike her husband, who studied the Great Books at Columbia, she learned little of classic Western literature and had to assimilate what she did on the fly from Lionel.

This review-essay originated as a review of Diana Trilling, *The Beginning of the Journey: The Marriage of Diana and Lionel Trilling* (New York: Harcourt Brace, 1993), for *Salmagundi*, where it appeared in 1994. Mark indicated in the last months of his life that he was planning to revise that essay, and this one was found on his computer, dated March 23, 2003, just six days before his death. It is only a slight exaggeration to say that he rewrote this essay with his last breath. Mark's animus toward Diana Trilling, who had placed numerous obstacles in his path while working on *Lionel Trilling and the Fate of Cultural Criticism*, is very much in evidence in this draft, and some of the backgrounds to that are taken up at the end of Mark Shechner's afterword. Eds.

However, she did not set out to be a controversialist in the old left tradition. As a young woman she appears to have been more interested in the arts of performance than in those of moral and logical argument. Her early, aborted ambition was to be a concert singer. Her most notable frustration lay in having been too emotionally inhibited to become the diva she aspired to be.

She once lamented: "I regard the whole of my life as having been lived in an anxious world." Another person subjected to her fears and frustrations, when she finally became capable of expression, might have become noted for kindness. Mrs. Trilling, however, having become a literary-cultural critic, became a specialist in moral denunciation. She entered upon "a life of significant contention."

At the center of Diana Trilling's self-understanding, as she conveys it in her memoir, was her frustrated desire for attention. She describes herself as a little girl shamed by her puritanical businessman father out of her normal instinct for exhibiting herself. It was made clear that she was not to outshine her considerably less talented older brother. Later in life that patriarchal injunction against self-display led to the failure of her grand ambition to be a concert singer. It seems to me that having to play second fiddle to a privileged near-contemporary male prepared her for the frustrations of her adult life as a faculty wife.

Fortunately, she married an academic who showed considerable patience and compassion. Diana and Lionel met in their early twenties and married at twenty-four. Soon afterwards she was behaving like a psychological invalid. As a little girl, she had been fearful of the dark and burglars. As a young wife, she was soon suffering from hyperthyroidism and agoraphobia. She was terrified of being alone and of venturing out of their apartment.

It is hard to imagine the extent of the duress Lionel Trilling suffered on account of his wife's poor health and neuroticism. In the same years in which he stood by her, he was also obliged to support his parents, whose fortunes had collapsed with those of the nation's economy. Lionel's father, who had previously been a tailor, had taken to making fur coats for chauffeurs. His timing could not have been worse. As a consequence, Lionel, who had never known economic adversity, now was obliged to support an extended family that included his parents at the very moment that he was under pressure to complete his Columbia doctoral dissertation and establish himself academically.

As we know, he survived the hard times and even the suspicions of his colleagues that as a Freudian, Marxist, and Jew he might prove subversive. It is hard to conceive that there was once a time when literary academics could have been so provincial and shortsighted and understood Trilling so little. At the start of the 1930s, his future at Columbia was dubious; by the end of that decade, his dissertation-turned-book on Matthew Arnold guaranteed his future in that department.

Lionel's success provided a leg up for Diana, as she gradually overcame her need to hide. She tells the story of overhearing a phone call in 1941 from Margaret Marshall, the literary editor of the *Nation,* to her husband. Marshall was asking if Lionel could recommend a regular reviewer for the magazine to which Trilling was himself a frequent contributor. As soon as the call was over, Mrs. Trilling asked her husband to put her forward. The result was that from 1941, when she was thirty-six, to 1947, when she gave birth to their son, James, the Trillings' only child, Diana Trilling read a novel a day for the *Nation* and wrote a review every week.

During the 1940s and '50s she also wrote essays, mostly for *Partisan Review,* on ideas of politics and culture, above all attacking what remained of Stalinism among the intellectuals. But she did not limit herself to politics of the Cold War. She also had a flair for the politics of sex. She edited a hefty *Viking Portable D. H. Lawrence* and in 1963 wrote a provocative essay on John Profumo, the high Tory minister of war in Harold Macmillan's government. Profumo had engaged in an affair with Christine Keeler, a London prostitute who simultaneously was involved with the naval attaché to the Soviet embassy, a man suspected of being a Soviet intelligence officer. This story had in common with the Jean Harris–Herman Tarnower case, to which Mrs. Trilling would years later devote an entire book, that it was a huge scandal at the time. She never became a diva, but she was able to register her fascination with sex.

Just how much blunter Mrs. Trilling's sensibility was than her husband's can be measured by the fact that his only comparable essay focuses on Henry James's *The Bostonians.* In that essay Trilling concentrates, for the first and only time, on the war between the sexes. Trilling on *The Bostonians* is far less successful than he is on *The Princess Casa-massima,* his other James essay, published five years earlier. And it is a measure of Lionel Trilling's evasion of direct issues of his personal life that he should have had so little to say about sexual conflict, which we now know figured so largely in his marriage.

Not until Lionel Trilling's death in 1975, at the age of seventy, did Mrs. Trilling come into her own as a writer. The Trillings were unlike other couples among the New York intellectuals in remaining steadfast in their marriage; they had been together forty-six years when Lionel died. But the Trilling family story was far from over in 1975. Mrs. Trilling, sickly at the start, now proved to be a strong finisher. She lived twenty-one more years, writing every day, even after she had lost her sight. No writer from the 1930s had more staying power. One is tempted to suggest William Phillips, the cofounder with Philip Rahv of *Partisan Review,* who was born three years later than Mrs. Trilling and lived into the twenty-first century. But apart from Phillips's autobiography, he barely wrote at all.

The important thing about Mrs. Trilling is not only the sheer quantity of her output. It is the invention of a new style and self that she undertook in her seventies, after Lionel's death. What a strong will! *Claremont Essays,* her collection of essays from the previous two decades, had borne the stamp of her intellectual collaboration with Lionel, but Mrs. Trilling's 1981 book on Jean Harris, the spurned lover and murderer of the Scarsdale Diet doctor, was clearly not the kind of project Lionel Trilling would have pursued.

In *The Beginning of the Journey,* Mrs. Trilling presents herself as being very different from the high-culture essayist who published in *Partisan Review* and *Commentary* in the 1950s and '60s. In dealing candidly with the intimate lives of public persons, notably Lionel and herself, Mrs. Trilling has written a book as sensationalist in its way as her book about Mrs. Harris and the diet doctor. The most surprising part of this memoir is Mrs. Trilling's unsparingly deflationary portrait of her husband. She is intent on replacing a common idealized image of Lionel Trilling the intellectual with one that takes account of his shortcomings as a person. Although they are mainly limited to the first part (1929–50) of the Trillings' marriage, the complaints carry on nearly up to Lionel's death.

The particulars in this bill of complaint are of unequal gravity. We learn that Lionel was incompetent or merely comical at swimming, dancing, and driving a car. Mrs. Trilling also adduces his ineffectiveness in handling money and dealing with his publisher. She does not tell these stories in a spirit of generosity or sentimentality. Rather, her tone is mean and reductive. Her apparent intention is to peel away her husband's familiar image of poise and gentility to reveal a man feckless and inept. We read of a young husband insufficiently dominating in relation to his wife and of an older husband who disappoints her by failing to exercise the leadership that might have been his during the student demonstrations at Columbia in 1968. The complaint is basically the same from start to finish: Lionel was not much of a man.

The most intimate of Mrs. Trilling's revelations concern her husband's lifelong pattern of depressive illness. She writes that Lionel's depressions were punctuated five or six times a year by irrational rages, during which he blamed her for all of his unhappiness. Again in the spirit of exposing secrets, she reveals that some four decades of intermittent psychoanalysis did little to mitigate the problem. Mrs. Trilling exposes what she describes as her husband's deep sense of failure, his occasionally excessive drinking, and his periodic cycles of gloom and abusiveness.

These revelations are startling, because Mrs. Trilling had previously been a fierce defender of her husband's posthumous reputation. After his death she devoted herself to editing the twelve-volume Uniform Edition of his work. These volumes brought together previously published essays, but also essays and reviews published for the first time. Her revelations are surprising also because, as Mrs. Trilling says, her husband was the most private of men and went to great lengths to conceal his emotional difficulties and his involvement with psychoanalysts from even his closest friends.

Lionel Trilling's reticence about his emotional problems was the focus of a quarrel between husband and wife during his lifetime. The quarrel surfaced in the late 1940s, when Mrs. Trilling was pregnant with James and had temporarily put aside her career as a writer. In those years Lionel's reputation was growing as a consequence of the essays he had published, mainly in *Partisan Review,* and was to bring together in 1950 in *The Liberal Imagination.* Mrs. Trilling describes her "fury" of resentment at that time about her husband's public image: "I very much disliked the image of Lionel as someone immune to profanation."

Mrs. Trilling remembers feeling that the image of the infallible Lionel "lessened" him. She has now gone far in the direction of righting the balance. But why has she elected to present him in so unflattering a light? It is possible that she was led to say more than she might have intended because of the way this memoir was composed. Because her sight was badly impaired in her last years, she was obliged to dictate the book. Inevitably, talking about the past encourages confidences that might have been edited out had she been working at a typewriter and been able to see what she was saying. Also, the speech situation, involving a silent amanuensis, mimics that of psychoanalysis, with its encouragement to say all that comes to mind. But these are only speculations, and the highly organized and focused quality of the book argues against them.

Mrs. Trilling's portrait of her husband is all the more mysterious in view of her wholly credible affirmations of love and admiration for him. There is also the biographical fact, which she acknowledges, of Lionel's unwavering loyalty and service to his young wife all through the 1930s, when she was more a patient than a helpmate on account of her harrowing phobias and nearly fatal hyperthyroidism.

Mrs. Trilling has always been more a political-cultural writer than a person of literary sensibility. She has been drawn to the world of telegrams and anger that Lionel largely avoided. Oddly, she emerged as controversialist, even of her own intimate life. The impulse to externalize, to find the causes of one's misery outside the self, is all the more striking in view of Mrs. Trilling's long experience of psychoanalysis. She reveals that, like Lionel, she was a psychoanalytic patient during the greater part of their life together. She had analyses with seven doctors, all of whom she describes as having served her poorly. The horror stories she tells about her analysts, one of whom was hooked on drugs, another of whom took both Trillings along on his summer vacation with his family, are adduced to support her judgment that at best her doctors helped her little and at worst did considerable damage.

Mrs. Trilling's severe rationalism disposed her to a harshly judgmental view of others. Her harshness is cognitive as well as moral. I cannot think of many occasions when she has acknowledged being wrong or has changed her mind about an important idea. The epithet "cold war critic" has been bandied about too freely in our time, but it does fit Mrs. Trilling in relation to both her substantive politics and her ideological inflexibility.

In a review of Mrs. Trilling's memoir in the *New Criterion* (October 1993), Hilton Kramer writes that she disparages Lionel Trilling out of a misguided, leftish psychoanalytic ideology that demands the stripping away of bourgeois appearances, even those that protect the privacy of one's own closest intimates. On the contrary, I would say that Mrs. Trilling held herself together, from at least the 1940s on, by a nearly dogmatic insistence on middle-class values. Far from having transferred her allegiance from antibourgeois Marxism in the 1930s to antibourgeois Freudianism afterward, Mrs. Trilling turned to ideas of order when she left communism behind. She was as rigid in her middle-class tastes and in her anticommunism as she had been as a communist fellow traveler. She never wrote against herself or took her own doubts as an intellectual point of departure, as did Lionel. This is not to say that she lacked doubts. It's more the case that she suppressed them in the service of her well-known stance of unassailability.

Any number of texts might be cited as evidence of Mrs. Trilling's solidly middle-class social and moral preferences. Her essays on the famous cold war treason cases, involving Alger Hiss and J. Robert Oppenheimer in this country and Profumo in England, are among her most directly political writings, but they are less to the point than her essays on literary and cultural subjects. The most revealing of these is her essay on a reading by Allen Ginsberg and other beat poets at Columbia University, titled "The Other Night at Columbia: A Report from the Academy." This is Mrs. Trilling's favorite among her essays and Lionel's favorite as well.

In her "report," Mrs. Trilling patronizes Ginsberg and his friends on a variety of fronts. She finds these 1950s bohemian rebels less authentic than the 1930 proletarians. Whereas F. W. Dupee, a board member of *Partisan Review* in its early years and English department moderator of this campus event, is described as exhibiting "dignity and self-assurance," Ginsberg and his companions are only "panic-stricken kids in blue jeans." For Mrs. Trilling, Ginsberg is a "case"; his former teachers, on the other hand, stand for respectability to which the waif-poet inevitably but helplessly aspires. As if it were not enough to discredit the poets, Mrs. Trilling goes on to categorize the audience: "so many young girls, so few of them pretty, and so many blackest black stockings; so many young men, so few of them—despite the many black beards—without any promise of masculinity." To which one can only respond: How could you tell?

According to Mrs. Trilling's new memoir, readers misunderstood her intention—which, she now says, was to call into question what would seem to be her report's smug sense of superiority. That intention, almost universally unperceived by readers at the time, is signaled, we now can see, by the last paragraph, in which Mrs. Trilling describes herself as returning from the reading to find "a meeting going on at home of the pleasant professional sort which, like the comfortable living room in which it usually takes place, at a certain point in a successful modern literary career confirms the writer in his sense of disciplined achievement and well-earned reward." Mrs. Trilling's irony here is of the most glancing kind, almost indistinguishable from the complacency it so gently chides.

Mrs. Trilling had gone to the Ginsberg reading in the company of two other English department wives. None of Columbia's professors of English had attended except Dupee, whose presence seems to have been intended to defuse the event, to keep what Mrs. Trilling calls the "vast barbarian hordes" from erupting. At McMillin Theater, Mrs. Trilling, the faculty wife, had felt self-important in relation to the hapless barbarians on stage. But at home she adopts, very briefly, a different role, coyly mocking the establishment respectability of her guests. She interrupts the grownups, the successful men in suits, to say: "Allen Ginsberg read a love-poem to you, Lionel. I liked it very much."

We learn from the 1993 memoir that the meeting Mrs. Trilling interrupted involved the staff of the Readers' Subscription, the upper-middlebrow book club that Lionel served, along with W. H. Auden and Jacques Barzun, as editor and consultant. Recent scholarship has discussed the role of book clubs like this one in providing guidance to a culturally anxious, newly enlarged educated middle class in the 1950s. Had Mrs. Trilling said in her original report what those writers with their "modern successful literary careers" were doing in her living room, it is possible that the irony she cites in her memoir thirty-five years later would not have been so widely missed at the time. "It was in the ironic contrast between the stage capers of Ginsberg and his friends and the comfortable scene to which I returned when I came home that I found much of the meaning which the evening had for me and which I wrote about. For me, perhaps no less than for Ginsberg, it had been an evening of ambiguities. As I weighed the choice between rebelliousness and acceptance, the beats held their own on many scores."

Both Trillings were drawn to this kind of situation: the unresolved opposition. The capacity to live with contradictions was for Lionel the mark of the mature as well as the tragic character. But sometimes it took some doing to contrive such a situation. In the case of Diana Trilling's report, the later authorial explanation is at odds with the manifest tone and tendency of the original report, in which the ragtag bohemian poets do not hold their own on any score at all. Ambivalent she may have been at the time, but in the essay Mrs. Trilling actually wrote in 1959, self-righteousness and status-consciousness overwhelm the small voice of self-doubt. The slight identification of English department faculty wife with self-consciously gay, bohemian poet does not amount to much.

That is not to say that the report might not have been cast in different terms. A deeper, more inward, more truly psychoanalytic relation to herself might have suggested to Mrs. Trilling a bond between herself and the outrageous homosexual poet. This would have been a bond founded not on a shared antibourgeois ideology but on a shared condition of exclusion and narcissistic hurt. And how shocking it might have been for Mrs. Trilling to suspect that the faculty wife might have something really in common with the outsider-poet.

There are moments in the original report in which Mrs. Trilling comes close to acknowledging the bond, but then she retreats into the familiar "great lady" pose and insistence on "seniority" that Robert Lowell once remarked upon, in connection with her essay of 1968 in *Commentary* on the student disturbances at Columbia. She seems never to have been able to resist one-upping Ginsberg. She is still doing it in this memoir. She describes a dinner party, some years after her report on the poetry reading at Columbia, at which Ginsberg explodes in anger at her. She is upset by his anger and works it over in her mind, finally deciding that it is owing to Ginsberg's guilt over her disapproval of his involvement with drugs. But what if it was not guilt but Ginsberg's reaction to years of being patronized and bullied? Mrs. Trilling doesn't

entertain explanations other than the one she offers, and she demonstrates its correctness, Q.E.D., by noting that Ginsberg's last communication with her was by way of a postcard written on Yom Kippur, the
Jewish Day of Atonement.

Mrs. Trilling does not herself go in for atonement, even when she is
clearly in the wrong. An interview with her in the *New Yorker* (September 13, 1993) includes the interviewer's mention that she tried to find the
love poem to Lionel Trilling in Allen Ginsberg's collected works. Not
finding it, she contacted Ginsberg himself, who told her that the poem
Mrs. Trilling refers to was not in fact about her husband. Indeed, Ginsberg's poem, "The Lion for Real," is not a love poem for anyone. As
Ginsberg remembers, "I guess she misheard it. I visited them for years
afterward, but I never brought it up; I thought it was better just to let
it go."

Among the things she holds onto from the past are her fixed ideas.
So when the *New Yorker* interviewer tells her what Ginsberg has said
about the love poem that was not, she is unfazed: "Ah, was I wrong? He
should have told me I was wrong. But in any case . . ." If Mrs. Trilling
were a novelist, Henry James, say, we might remark of her 1993 account:
She seized a fragment, a "germ," and worked up her own version of
the events, which is so much more interesting than the anecdote that
set her into motion. And if the novelist's version is shown to diverge
from the actuality that inspired it, so much the worse for actuality. The
only problem is that Mrs. Trilling is presenting her memoir not as fiction but as fact.

The question of what is perception and what fantasy is central in any
memoir. It is all the more exigent in New York intellectual memoirs,
which seem so often to be mainly concerned with setting the record
straight. As one of the relatively few persons about whom Mrs. Trilling
pronounces in her memoir who is still alive to defend himself, I want to
correct an interpretation of hers that bears on me and is presented as a
fact.

Mrs. Trilling comments on a review that I wrote of a 1971 book that
Lionel Trilling edited, entitled *Literary Criticism: An Introductory
Reader:* "Featured in [*Modern Occasions*] first issue was an extended attack upon Lionel by a then-unknown teacher of English, Mark Krupnick. Like 'The Duchess' Red Shoes,' Delmore Schwartz's attack on

Lionel in *Partisan Review*, Krupnick's piece was of course solicited and predesigned." Mrs. Trilling's remarks on my piece occur in the context of a hostile portrait of Philip Rahv, the supposed solicitor and designer of my review. Rahv had been a friend of the Trillings in the early years of *Partisan Review* and had later turned cool. He had resigned his editorship at *PR* and had launched a new quarterly, *Modern Occasions*, of which I was an associate editor.

What Mrs. Trilling calls my "extended attack" on Lionel took up five-and-a-half pages in all and appeared in the journal's second, not its first, issue. The date is winter 1971. But clearly the important point is Mrs. Trilling's contention that the review was "solicited and predesigned." What she intends to convey is that Rahv put me up to it, as — again, according to her — he had put Delmore Schwartz up to similar mischief in 1953. The facts of the case are that Rahv had been asked to review the book for the *Boston Globe*. He wasn't interested in doing it but, knowing my interest in Trilling, asked me if I wanted to. The piece grew under my hand, and I asked Rahv if he might want to use it in *Modern Occasions*. The main thing is that Rahv made no suggestions before or after I wrote the review about what it should say. Nor did he in my two years with him at *Modern Occasions* express much concern about Trilling. The writer who obsessed him was Norman Mailer. Rahv was only seriously interested, as a polemicist, in writers whose stock was high in the current literary marketplace. For him Lionel Trilling was a back number.

Perhaps it is inconceivable to Mrs. Trilling that Lionel should not have been at the center of Rahv's thoughts as he was at the center of her own. In any case, I was the one who was concerned with Trilling in 1971, not Rahv. In the book I later wrote on Lionel Trilling, I explained how my initial enthusiasm for him when I was an undergraduate in the late '50s had turned to disillusion over the course of the next decade as a consequence of his long silence on the Vietnam War. My thoughts about Trilling continued to change over the years I was writing about him, so that the view I presented in my book of 1986 is much more positive than the review of 1971. But Mrs. Trilling finds it hard to believe that the "then-unknown" assistant professor was doing his own thinking about her husband. She not only presumes to know how this piece came to be written. For her it's obvious, a matter "of course."

Others who have been the objects of pronouncements by Mrs. Trilling must have wondered, as I do, how she can be so self-assured and yet so mistaken about events of the past. Most of those upon whom she animadverts are in no position to talk back. That is a great virtue of long life. Is it not possible that Mrs. Trilling is as wrong about the origins of Delmore Schwartz's essay as she is about mine? Neither Schwartz nor Sidney Hook nor Mary McCarthy nor Hannah Arendt nor many others about whom Mrs. Trilling writes are around to tell their side of the story. Who knows if she didn't get them wrong, too? And is it not possible she has misrepresented her husband as well?

Mrs. Trilling mentions several times that she never had a workroom of her own until Lionel died and she took over his study. It's not a criticism of Lionel as a person that his wife's writing life only really got underway after his death, by which time she was already seventy. It was in the structure of things—the genteel patriarchal conventions of literary academic life and the Trillings' own fear of violating the suffocating conventions they inherited from no less fearful parents—that Diana and Lionel should both have felt baffled, deprived of an easy relation to pleasure, self-assertion, and their own large ambitions.

As a younger woman, Mrs. Trilling felt mainly anger at Lionel's "conspiring" in his students' idealization of him. This memoir makes clear that she is still exasperated by her husband's public image. But idealization is inescapable as an aspect of students' identification with great teachers and as the engine of many kinds of positive development—moral, emotional, social—in young people. Earlier in her career, as a faculty wife and contributor to magazines of opinion, Mrs. Trilling was respected but rarely idealized. She was always too blunt and practical for that. With this new book, however, she has become something of a heroine for younger women reviewers for whom she is a survivor, a woman-warrior who would not be crushed by the Church Fathers of *Partisan Review*. She has come a very long way from the panicky, inexperienced young woman she was fifty years ago.

The Beginning of the Journey, with all its flaws, is still Mrs. Trilling's best book, the book in which she seems most herself: not the high-culture intellectual of the 1950s with large ideas of culture and society, but a shrewd social observer with a nineteenth-century novelist's eye for manners and motives. This memoir is surely one of the best of the many published in the past twenty years by aging New York intellectuals, and that is because it goes beyond the stale repetition of political pieties to help us see the connections between public discourse, such as Lionel Trilling's, and the private life of that time and place that went into that discourse.

Best of all for Diana Trilling, it represents an overcoming of her baffled impulse to self-display. Still the good wife, she shares its pages with Lionel. But it is her story. The Lionel that appears in it is a character in her life (or, rather, in her fantasy of what that life was about). But renown is not a zero-sum game or a hydraulic system in which, as in Henry James's *The Sacred Fount*, one party must be sucked dry so that the other is pumped up. It should not have been necessary to make Lionel Trilling smaller so that his widow might be bigger. In any case, this memoir is not likely to damage Lionel's reputation, because most readers will recognize that Mrs. Trilling's account of their life together remains a specimen of autobiography. Everything she says about Lionel is a revelation about her as much as it is a fact about him. She will not have the last word about his character or the larger meaning of his life. I expect that biographers, in relation to their subject, will be more struck by Lionel's fortitude and finesse than by his ineptitude and fecklessness.

What we have, then, is a revelation of a strong-minded woman, admirable in many ways, who didn't get all she wanted out of her marriage or her life. Would she have liked more time for her own writing and a room of her own? She might have had both if she had been born in 1955 rather than 1905, and therefore been in a position to reap the benefits of the feminist revolution. Also, no small matter, she might with luck have been treated by psychoanalysts informed by more enlightened ideas. As it was, she had the great good luck, which she acknowledges, to enjoy the company and conversation in their prime of New York's most gifted intellectuals, including, of course, for half a century, Lionel Trilling.

Lionel Trilling and the Politics of Style

During the heyday of Stalinist influence on America's liberal intellectuals, Lionel Trilling repeatedly recommended "complexity" and "variousness" as correctives to the Left's tendency to oversimplify issues. But Trilling was not himself "various" in the sense of moving about quickly in his writing from one topic to another as a means of holding his audience's attention. Rather, Trilling achieved his eminence by returning, from decade to decade, to a few favorite authors and a few overriding preoccupations. Of these preoccupations, one of the most nourishing for Trilling's thought was the relation of literature and politics.

He was always trying to reconcile the great formative influences of his own early career: the influence of literary modernism of the 1920s, when he was an undergraduate at Columbia, and that of Marxist politics of the 1930s. So these words "politics" and "literature" have a specific meaning in Trilling's writing. "Politics" for him usually refers to the politics of the Left. Stalinism had been the overwhelming political fact in the experience of his intellectual circle, and it appears to have

This essay appeared in 1988 in *American Literary Landscapes: The Fiction and the Fact*, edited by Ian Bell and D. K. Adams. It was not on Mark's original list for publication, and we are very grateful that Eric Homberger brought it to our attention. It strikes us as a powerful and original essay on Trilling and the dilemma of style in modern life, and it contains ideas nowhere touched upon in either *Lionel Trilling and the Fate of Cultural Criticism* or the "Deep Places" essay in this book. It appeared originally in an anthology in England, where few American scholars are likely to come across it, making its inclusion here imperative. Eds.

left little room for anything else in the way of political concern. For the intellectuals of *Partisan Review,* fascism was a terrible actuality but not an intellectual one. There was nothing the New York liberal mind could do with fascism, at least not until Hannah Arendt's *Origins of Totalitarianism* in the early 1950s and Susan Sontag's essay on fascist aesthetics twenty years later. But Arendt was a fringe member of this intellectual group and Sontag a member of a later generation. This neglect of fascism is one reason the old New York intellectuals seem provincial when compared with their counterparts, like Theodor Adorno and Walter Benjamin, among the intellectuals associated with the Frankfurt School.

If Trilling ignored fascism, so did he ignore the nonfascist Right in America. He took the view that the intellectual expressions of American conservatism amounted to no more than the reflexive philistinism of Main Street. In a much-quoted passage from the preface to *The Liberal Imagination* in 1950, Trilling said that "the conservative impulse and the reactionary impulse do not, with some isolated and some ecclesiastical exceptions, express themselves in ideas but only in action or in irritable mental gestures which seek to resemble ideas." There was no need therefore to argue with exponents of the conservative mind—conservatives in America had no minds.

What Trilling meant by "the literary imagination" was the modernist imagination. He found a central statement of the modernist position in Nietzsche's statement in *The Birth of Tragedy* that "art rather than ethics constitutes the essential metaphysical activity of man." Trilling accepted the dictum in an oddly unproblematic way, not seeming to perceive that if existence and the world may be justified only as an aesthetic phenomenon, it may be because life is terrible and not because art is wonderful. But for the young Trilling, trying to work his way free of Marxism, the notion of art as the central human activity was notably liberating. He was much drawn to an aestheticized form of morality about which I will have more to say and for which he found sanction in modernist writing and thought. In arguing this position he cited Hegel as well as Nietzsche. In the preface to *The Opposing Self* he attributed to Hegel the idea that "art is the activity of man in which spirit expresses itself not only as utility, not only according to law, but as grace, as transcendence, as manner and style."

Trilling's reference to "utility" provides the clue we need to get underway. Left politics, whether Marxism or the liberalism derived from John Stuart Mill, is founded on the ethics of utility. Reason is to be exercised to bring about human happiness, of the individual and of the greatest number. In Trilling's view, modernism was indifferent to the welfare of the masses, and its aim for the happy few might be summed up in the demand not for happiness but for "more life" ("The Fate of Pleasure" in *Beyond Culture*). The claim that he had "more life" in him than his happier contemporaries had is of course the claim of one of modernism's most miserable and alienated antiheroes, the Underground Man of Dostoevsky. What is valued is not happiness construed as material comfort, power, and pleasure as the worldly world understands these concepts but, rather, in Yeats's phrase, "control over the sources of life." That last phrase is from Yeats, and what it refers to, as Trilling glosses it, is the maximum "fullness, freedom, and potency of life." Modernism, on this account, has as its aim self-renewal, self-transcendence. Yeats would have agreed with Nietzsche that it was not man as such who seeks material happiness, it was only Englishmen.

Thus as Trilling and his intellectual contemporaries understood these two key terms, literature and politics, were at odds. In many instances great modernists were also political reactionaries, and in none of these writers did the ideals of American progressivism loom large. The strategy of Trilling's best essays is well known. In his best writing, which appeared between the late 1930s and the early 1950s, Trilling used literature as the standard by which to correct the errors and refine the dullness of that liberal-progressive mind. Literary values—wit, surprise, complexity, irony—were invoked as a criticism of the positivism and drab materialism of the liberals.

But the day would arrive when Trilling would come to distrust modernist literature and the application of aesthetic values to social-cultural life. The inner debate in his writing focused on the question of style. In this paper I take up some discussions of style in essays Trilling wrote between 1938 and 1965. My main concern is with Trilling's changing ideas about literary style and, by implication, about styles of selfhood. But I will also be looking at Trilling's own style and trying to show how that style sometimes seems to undermine his ideas about style.

In his essay of 1938 on John Dos Passos, Trilling is discussing the morality informing *U.S.A.*, the novel-trilogy Dos Passos had published in installments in the 1920s and 1930s. That morality, Trilling says, "is concerned not so much with the utility of an action as with the quality of the person who performs it." Dos Passos looks to what Trilling calls the "quality of personality" rather than to "the rightness of the end." That is, he cares less about outcomes than about the quality of being revealed in conduct. Trilling offers these examples from *U.S.A. "What* [Dos Passos's] people do is not so important as how they do it, or what they become by doing it. We despise J. Ward Morehouse not so much for his creation of the labor-relations board, his support of the war, his advertising of patent-medicines, though these are despicable enough; we despise him rather for the words he uses as he does these things, for his self-deception, the tone and style he generates. . . . But we do not despise the palpable fraud, Doc Bingham, because though he lies to everyone else, he does not lie to himself."

Thirty years after this essay Trilling would be using the word "authenticity" to characterize Doc Bingham's special kind of integrity, an integrity compatible with the most loathsome conduct. In *Sincerity and Authenticity*, Trilling would express grave doubts about the implications of such a morality, but in 1938 he is all for it. He argues strongly for the intimation of value by way of style and tone, praising this mode of judgment because it is subversive of what he calls the "dominant morality of his moment."

That dominant morality was the morality of intellectual Stalinists and middle-class liberals sympathetic to the aims of the Communists. What the right-thinking intellectuals of the Left had in common was their assumption that the collective aspects of life are more important than the individual aspects, and their hatred of the idea of individual moral responsibility. What is mysterious about Trilling's argument is why, if he wants to advocate individual moral responsibility, he needs to put so much emphasis on style and tone. The question becomes more mysterious when Trilling cites John Dewey as the exponent of the morality of style that Dos Passos is said to exemplify. For the philosophical rationale of his position, Trilling cites a passage from Dewey's *Ethics*, a work that had first appeared in 1908 and had been reprinted in 1932:

The moral assumption on which Dos Passos seems to work was expressed by John Dewey some thirty years ago; there are certain moral situations, Dewey says, where we cannot decide between the ends; we are forced to make our moral choice in terms of our preference for one kind of character or another: "What sort of an agent, of a person shall he be? This is the question finally at stake in any genuinely moral situation: What shall the agent *be?* What sort of character shall he assume? On its face, the question is what shall he do, shall he act for this or that end. But the incompatibility of the ends forces the issue back into the questions of the kind of selfhood, of agency, involved in the respective ends."

It is understandable that Trilling might have wished to propose his position as authorized by Dewey, for in 1938 Dewey was the leading philosopher in America of the non–Marxist Left. He had been the major figure in a delegation of American intellectuals who had taken it upon themselves to investigate Stalin's charges that Trotsky had betrayed the Russian Revolution. This delegation, which traveled to Mexico City to interview the exiled Trotsky and take testimony, included several members of Trilling's New York intellectual circle, and Trilling himself was a member of a committee of Trotsky's defenders.

Dewey's prominence in 1938 may explain Trilling's appeal to him in the essay on Dos Passos. But the argument in terms of style and tone is Trilling's own. Trilling's idea of the self involves an implicit appeal to the work of art as model. As in the emergent New Critical idea of the poem, a self ought not mean but be. Dewey's morality, in contrast, is not an aestheticized morality. Dewey remained, as he had always been, a practical-minded, action-oriented thinker. His idea that moral choice involves the choice of a kind of selfhood has nothing to do with styles of selfhood in Trilling's sense. Trilling's argument against the Stalinists derives its aesthetic coloration not from Dewey's pragmatism but from Trilling's experience of modernist literature. As Trilling puts it later in the same essay on Dos Passos: "The novelist goes where the law cannot go; he tells the truth where the formulations of even the subtlest ethical theorist cannot." And what he reveals is that there is nothing within that passeth show, that whatever we do or whatever our pious protestations, we will be revealed by our tone and style.

It would seem that Trilling had found a way to put (Stalinist) politics in its place by arguing for manner and manners, for style and tone, as more important and more revelatory than virtuous principles and right-minded action. A morality of qualities of being might be opposed to the left-wing morality of action. Just as Matthew Arnold had tried to displace religion by poetry, Trilling displaces politics by style. But Trilling's own style is very canny. It would appear that Trilling is moving in the direction that was common among the major literary critics of his generation, by proposing a privileged and autonomous realm of the aesthetic in opposition to the vulgar world of politics. But he never goes this far—it remains only an implication. For Trilling is not willing to cede the realm of the political. By an adroit redefinition of the word "politics," he claims in fact to be more political than his activist opponents. For, as Trilling asks rhetorically at the end of his Dos Passos essay, "In the long run is not the political choice fundamentally a choice of personal quality?"

To which we may be disposed to reply, Well, yes and no, and depending on how long a run. But Trilling's rhetoric is so reasonable-minded that we find ourselves, assenting: Well, all right, so political choice is ultimately a choice of what kinds of persons we wish to be. But as we assent we are not likely to be considering the implications of our Yes.

There is a problem that Trilling's formulation raises but does not resolve. That is the relation between a morality founded on choices and on the idea of self-responsible individuals, and a morality in which judgments are founded on style. Or, to put it differently, Trilling presents contradictory notions of the relation of self to style. On the one hand, we choose attractive qualities of being that we manifest in our tone and style. In this account of self-invention or what we more recently have come to call self-fashioning, we consciously control and determine our styles. At the same time, however, Trilling suggests that style is something we cannot control; it differs in this respect from our conscious beliefs and actions. On this account, style is the external manifestation of a spiritual condition, something like a state of grace for those who are among the authentic few. We know who has that "more life" to which we as moderns aspire by paying close attention to external signs. "A true relation to the sources of life does not refer to rational criteria; it is expressed not in doctrine, not in systems, ethics, and creeds, but in manner and style. We know whether or not a person is in touch with the sources of life not by what he says, by its doctrinal correctness, but by the way he says it, by the tone of his voice, the look in his eye, by his manner and style."

There is a real conflict between these two notions of the relation of self to style. Once we become attuned to this central ambiguity in Trilling's idea of self-formation, a whole series of oppositions begin to unravel. Is there really any such clear-cut opposition as Trilling posits between a morality of action and a morality of being, between the social world and the individual, between politics and literature? These are problems, however, that only reveal their implications as Trilling's career unwinds. I have remarked on what I take to be fundamental contradictions in Trilling's text. But it is possible to be effective without being self-consistent or self-identical, and Trilling's essays in the 1940s were very effective. For the most part, I would say, Trilling's influence in the ten years following his Dos Passos essay was a good one. He helped an entire generation of politically oriented humanistic intellectuals to escape from the simplifications of a Left liberalism of the most muddled kind, a politics and a culture that was corrupted at its roots by its inability to speak out against Stalinism. Even if one regards Trilling's later work as a falling off, as I do, it should still be possible to regard his achievement in the '40s as liberating. For an entire generation he made literature again possible, and he helped to relegate a once-powerful group of intellectual commissars to oblivion.

Trilling's influence became less salutary as the strength of Stalinism declined at the end of the '40s and as nearly all dissident positions became nearly mute in the '50s. When the radical Left collapsed, Trilling shifted his attention from the dangers of Stalinist politics to the dangers of mass culture. I say this knowing that the notion of a sharp break, in which Trilling moves from questions of politics to questions of culture, has to be qualified somewhat in that left-wing politics in the late '30s and early '40s was itself a form of mass culture; the political philistinism of the *Nation* and the *New Republic* in the period of the Popular Front is not discontinuous with the culture of togetherness and domesticity of the '50s. Perhaps the salient difference, for my purpose here, is that in the '50s Trilling's position became the majority position; his "opposing self" became the very voice of Establishment liberalism. The herd of independent minds was now lined up behind Trilling, not against him. He was no longer a lonely dissident among a small group of anti-Stalinist pariahs, as he had been in the late '30s.

Trilling's position as a critic of mass culture is summed up in the preface to *The Opposing Self,* the collection of essays he published in 1955. In the preface to that book Trilling leaves John Dewey behind and cites Hegel instead, but the argument is very like the argument presented seventeen years earlier in the essay on Dos Passos. Trilling now is worrying not about Stalinism but about the dullness and conformity of habitual life in culture in the pleasantly tranquilized America of Dwight Eisenhower. The corrective, which he derives from Hegel, is "the experience of art projected into the actuality and totality of life as the ideal form of the moral life." In other words, the ideal self invents itself as if it were an artwork, and the ideal society has the qualities—orderliness, intensity, surprise, and amenity—of art. This is the lesson Trilling had learned from modernism, the answer to the lack of tension, the lack of beauty and dignity, in the postwar culture of consumption.

The 1950s were Trilling's years of fame. He may well have been the most influential literary intellectual in America, in the years just before the apotheosis of Northrop Frye and the academicization and professionalization of criticism. But if we look at the essays Trilling actually wrote in the '50s, it is remarkable how few important ideas appear. Instead of rational argument, he relies mainly on certain tonalities. Trilling's manner is often that of the urbane bookman, a latter-day equivalent of the Victorian and Edwardian belletristic critic putting in his hours in the library. That tone especially marks the short essays Trilling wrote to introduce the selections of two middle-to-highbrow book clubs he served in those years, the Readers' Subscription and the Mid-Century. The style projects the persona of the gentleman critic in a mass democracy, amiable but a little exasperated as he strives to maintain standards against the flood of the imitative and second-rate.

But here, too, Trilling was caught up in a contradiction. For the democratization and the rise of the culture industry that he made possible were themselves the reason for Trilling's prestige. They made for the culture-anxiety to which he responded with his tone of gentlemanly authority. He could not have become so important as an arbiter of taste in a culture less bent on leaving behind the crudities of the period of radical politics that had just ended. Trilling's message perfectly fits the needs of a middle-class intelligentsia eager to have its ideas and feelings refined. Trilling was too intelligent and too self-conscious not to be aware of these contradictions. So we find two Trillings in the '50s, the elegant bookman, the colleague of Barzun and Auden at the book clubs, and another Trilling in the longer essays who wonders about whether this reliance on amenity and style is really desirable.

Style could not by itself be a "position" for a critic so intensely moralistic in outlook. As with Matthew Arnold himself, Trilling found himself working his way back to the once repudiated world of his fathers, back from Hellenism to Hebraism, from modernity to tradition. Arnold wrote explicitly on religion in his last years, whereas Trilling only moved in that direction. But in both cases the critic as moralist largely expunged the aestheticism of an earlier phase. In Trilling's career the collapse of politics had left him high and dry, and morality as the choice of qualities of personal being, morality as style of selfhood, was by no means able to fill the void.

In the '50s Trilling was still divided between morality as style and the older categorical morality. The crucial text for this period is his essay on Jane Austen's *Mansfield Park* in *The Opposing Self*. What is so odd about this essay, with its qualms about the aesthetic mode of morality, is that it was written at about the same time as the preface to *The Opposing Self*. The preface moves in a direction almost diametrically opposed to the tendency of the essay on Austen. It is striking that this critic who argues so powerfully for a concept of the shaped, unified, centered, perdurable self should yet so differ from himself from one essay to the next and even within individual essays. The concept of style enables the creation of the self as organic totality; at the same time it undoes the self, revealing it as a linguistic construct.

In the '40s Trilling had praised the energy of art as a way of lightening the fanatical temper of ideological politics. Now, in "Mansfield Park" he worries about that lightness. He argues in this essay for the advantages of a direct profession of principle as against the intimation of value by manner and style. He argues against the modern displacement of character by personality, of integrity by charm, of principles by style. The danger, he argues, is not only to society but also to the self itself, which becomes volatile and is revealed as a void when personality is placed at the center of the moral life.

Mansfield Park is partly about ordination. One of the characters, Edmund Bertram, is trying to decide whether to become a clergyman. And it is partly about play-acting; the young people in the novel are putting on an amateur theatrical to entertain themselves while the master of the house is away on business. Both the theater and the church involve role-playing, but the difference is that Bertram's choice of the clergy would involve the "open avowal of principles and beliefs." Moreover, although he would assume a role, the role would be permanent. The mask of the clergy becomes his face; it cannot be traded in for another role. It is altogether different with the actor, in whom there is no such singleness of being.

Sir Thomas's absence means that the decorous Bertram home will be plunged into disorder. The centrifugal force comes from outside; modernity comes to Mansfield Park by way of the Crawfords of London. Reflecting on *Mansfield Park* in *Sincerity and Authenticity,* Trilling wrote that these city cousins of the Bertrams appear as perverse embodiments of the idea of art projected into the actuality and totality of daily life. For their vivacity and playacting make for confusion and sophisticate the simple virtues of their country cousins. Their elaborate charm is the outer sign not of grace but of spiritual nullity. As Trilling says of Mary Crawford, "We are led to expect that her vivaciousness and audacity will constitute the beneficent counter-principle of the stodginess of . . . Mansfield Park." But the effect of her playacting "is regressive—its depreciation of Mansfield Park is not an effort of liberation but an acquiescence in bondage, a cynical commitment to the way of the world."

Trilling is surprised to find himself admiring poor Fanny Price, the novel's creep-mouse heroine. Anything is better than the lightness of the Crawfords, which is the lightness of being that a conscious commitment to modernity brings with it. From this point on in Trilling's writing metaphors of heaviness and hardness become the rhetorical means to anchor and lend gravity to a culture without stable traditions, a culture floating off into a condition of terminal frivolity. These metaphors clearly have a relation to Trilling's later conservatism, his last-ditch effort to rescue a failing metaphysical world view, together with the notion of the perdurable, dense, impenetrable, unified self that such a metaphysical world view implies.

By the 1950s, then, Trilling was already suspicious of the modernist morality of style that he himself had promoted and still advocated in the preface to *The Opposing Self.* But it was only in the 1960s that he sharply broke with that position. His famous essay of 1961, "On the Teaching of Modern Literature," marks his repudiation of what, in his view, the new generation had made of his old positives. In that essay he marks the transition from the proud, isolated "opposing self" of the early modernists to the gregarious, vulgar "adversary culture" of the present. The "adversary culture" turns out to be a consumer society parody version of the older modernist ethos.

Trilling's target in his 1961 essay "On the Teaching of Modern Literature" (in *Beyond Culture*) is the institutionalization of the modern within academic literary studies. He looks out upon his undergraduate students at Columbia and is horrified by the parodic mirror image they present to him. He engages in a kind of reception aesthetics in remarking their spiritless response to the classical modernist texts, by Conrad, Mann, Freud, Eliot, and others, he is teaching. In a frequently quoted passage he notes "the readiness of the students to engage in the process we might call the socialization of the antisocial, or the acculturation of the anti-cultural, or the legitimation of the subversive." It is only 1961 but Trilling is already anticipating a certain neoconservative polemic against the student Left of the latter part of that decade.

But if Trilling became godfather to the neoconservatives, he was never one of them. He largely avoided the polemical debates of the 1960s, sticking mainly to questions of pedagogy. I want for my last text to take up another essay Trilling wrote in the '60s on the question of teaching. This essay, which deserves to be as well known as "On the Teaching of Modern Literature" is entitled "The Two Environments: Reflections on the Study of English," and it was first presented in 1965 as the Sidgwick Memorial Lecture at Newnham College, Cambridge. In this essay Trilling discusses the establishment a century ago of modern literature in English as a subject of formal university study. His purpose is to show how the original rationale for English studies has become outmoded in our time.

Trilling says that the original purpose of training in modern literature had been to strengthen the students' city to stand apart from the philistine environment from which, presumably, they had come and in which they would be obliged to make their way. Trilling observes, "The theory of literary education as it was first formulated supposed that literature carried the self beyond the culture." The trouble in 1965, as it seemed to Trilling, is that it had not worked out that way. One reason is that modern literature in the universities has turned out not to mean the whole range of English and American literature but mainly the literature of our own century.

This literature of modernity, Trilling says, has been indifferent to the morality of the Victorian theoreticians of English studies, who had been deeply concerned with the conflict between interest and duty. In contrast to that Victorian morality, Trilling says, modernist morality is concerned with obtaining "control of the sources of life." For modernism, virtue as the Victorians conceived it is beside the point because there is no longer any external, objective standard against which the self may measure itself. Similarly, the establishment of truth through rational discourse is beside the point, because we cannot hope to come into contact with the sources of life, cannot hope to command the "fullness, freedom, and potency of life," through reason.

But now Trilling assigns this modernist morality an opposite valence from that he has previously assigned it. The morality of style has become an idol of the tribe. First came early modernists like Yeats and Lawrence, assuring their readers that there was nothing within that passeth show; then came the modern critical movement, which mediated the difficult new literature to the educated middle class. And now, some thirty years later, thanks to the absorption of this elite culture by the mass arts of advertising and television, the morality of style has largely lost its critical edge in relation to the dominant culture. This is how Trilling puts it:

> The economy itself is deeply involved with matters of style and with the conditions of the spirit or psyche. Our commodities are not only mere things but states of mind: joy, freedom, self-definition, and self-esteem. One industry after another is benefited by our overgrowing need to choose a fashion or dress, or decor, or locomotion, which will serve to signalize some spiritual or psychic grace. Advertising joins forces with literature in agitating the question of who one is, of what kind of person one should want to be, a choice in which one's possessions and appearance, one's tastes, are as important as one's feelings and behavior.

If politics comes down to choices about styles of selfhood, so obviously does advertising. Every ad shows us how to participate in the great status competition of our historical moment, about who has "more life" in him or her. In this way the intimation of value by style had passed from the proud and isolated early modernists to the new philistines of our own moment. Examples of that new, more glossy philistinism come readily to hand. Thus a recent ad in the *New Yorker* shows a prosperous looking middle-aged man being served a lavish breakfast in his hotel room by a bellman in impeccable livery. The hotel guest has a phone in one hand, the *Wall Street Journal* in the other, and a look on his face of immense self-satisfaction. The message of the ad—it is communicated both in its images and in writing—is this: "Success is a style." At the bottom of the ad are these words: "The Westin Hotel is the ultimate expression of your style." Salvation manifests itself in wondrous ways.

Trilling was of course right in seeing that his own earlier position had ceased to provide an alternative to the dominant morality, had ceased to provide a road for moving "beyond culture." But his response to this impasse itself constitutes a dead end. Disappointed that the modernist morality of authenticity had proved vulnerable to cooptation and exploitation, Trilling tried to go beyond culture in an escape from history. It was possible to withstand culture, he argued, because the self is at bottom a biological fact inaccessible to cultural determination. In his essay "Freud: Within and Beyond Culture" in *Beyond Culture,* Trilling says: "Somewhere in the child, somewhere in the adult, there is a hard, irreducible, stubborn core of biological urgency, and biological necessity, and biological *reason,* that culture cannot reach and that reserves the right, which sooner or later it will exercise, to judge the culture and resist and revise it."

Trilling falls back here from a modernist position to an affirmation of nineteenth-century absolutes, absolutes without God. The chief instances he cites of the biologically founded "sentiment of being" are Wordsworthian solitaries like the Leech-Gatherer of "Resolution and Independence." Trilling found his chief absolute, then, in the notion of the unified, indivisible, unmovable self, a self more rocklike, perhaps, than plantlike, but in any case wholly self-identical. The emphasis on the biological shows the extent to which this critic of culture was willing to go in affirming the self as a natural fact, organic and thereby beyond culture.

Attempting to escape from history, Trilling arrived at a position that is itself subject to historical criticism. Fredric Jameson provides the means for approaching from a different angle than Trilling's the historical mutation that Trilling's writing manifests but fails to explain. Jameson says that nowadays we take style for granted as "an essential and constitutive component of the literary work of art." But the modern notion of style is "a relatively recent phenomenon and comes into being with the middle-class world itself." It was rhetoric, not style, that dominated literary study from the classical period up through the *eighteenth century*, and the difference between rhetoric and style is that rhetoric was the means by which a writer or speaker was able to achieve an impersonal excellence of expression, "conceived of as a relatively fixed class standard." Style, on the other hand, belongs to our world, the world of self-fashioning, and the world of personalities. What's really at stake in this change is middle-class individuality. Style, as Jameson says, "is the very element of individuality itself, that mode through which the individual consciousness seeks to distinguish itself, to affirm its incomparable originality" (*Marxism and Form* [Princeton: Princeton University Press, 1971], 333–34).

Personal distinction, "incomparable originality," whatever might separate the critic from his students, from other New York liberals, from the members of the book clubs for which he wrote introductions, these made up a large part of what Lionel Trilling's career was about. He had ideas, good ideas, but originative thought and sustained rational argument always mattered less than a certain tone and style, the special difference that sometimes amounted to no more than the narcissism of small differences.

In his later phase, up to his death in 1975, Trilling argued for the unified, masterful, executive capacity of the self as it appears in American ego-psychology of the 1950s and more recently in the self psychology of Heinz Kohut. It seems to me that, without knowing the new French theory at first hand, Trilling fully intuited the threat of that theory to humanist notions of individual autonomy and freedom and self-invention and, by implication, to traditional liberal politics. For if the self is a mere linguistic function, as subject to displacement as any other signifier, it follows that nearly any strategy we devise to weaken the hold of the consumer culture on the self can itself be transformed into a consumer item and become the means of confirming the power of that consumer culture.

As Trilling says, in our culture, for the educated classes, the privileged commodity is not the thing, as it was for the nineteenth-century philistines of Flaubert and Ibsen. Our favorite commodities have become styles of selfhood, "lifestyles" as we say. The philistine has become harder to recognize. The enemy now is not the absolutely other; it is within ourselves, in our will to think ourselves more in touch with the "sources of life" than everyone else. It is a new kind of status competition, a kind of culture snobbery, different than in Veblen's time, to which literary intellectuals are especially prone.

Trilling wanted to oppose the modernist morality by which we intimate superiority by style. But he wound up simply urging one style at the expense of another. More and more in his later writing the word "archaic" appears as an honorific, and in his last book he praises what he calls "sincerity" as against a more recent, extreme style of selfhood that exalts "authenticity." But sincere or authentic, both are only styles, preferences, choices among a repertoire of modes of being available in the great department store of contemporary culture. In any case, picking and choosing qualities of being this way, Trilling could not in his writing manifest the Victorian density of being that he celebrates. Rather, in "The Two Environments," he gives us a performance in which he puts on the manners and tone of Victorian Cambridge. Aimed at an audience gathered at Newnham College, Cambridge, Trilling's performance places him somewhere between America and England, between the present age of the "adversary culture" and the more dignified world of the Victorian educators who first formulated the rationale of English studies. In this curious essay an American critic takes up problems that in 1965 were still mainly American, while taking his examples and arguments from nineteenth-century British moral philosophers, in the course of addressing an audience of twentieth-century Cambridge dons.

"The Two Environments" is not the only performance of Trilling in which different self-image and identifications bump up against each other. John Bayley has noted that Trilling's novel, *The Middle of the*

Journey, is a "composite of different voices, in an intertextual pastiche" ("Middle-Class Futures," *Times Literary Supplement,* April 11, 1975, 399). We have, Bayley says, "the Episcopalian aroma of Forster and T. S. Eliot, but also a sense of outdoor passion lifted from Lawrence." To this we might add echoes also of Dante, Blake, Melville, Mann, and several others. Trilling, as Bayley says, is never completely himself in his fiction. I have been trying to show that Trilling is never completely himself in his criticism either. How could he be, given his notion of gratuitously choosing qualities of being?

If Trilling is right and we do fashion ourselves by gratuitously choosing what seem to us desirable qualities of being, it follows that there can be no such hardness, density, and weight in the self as he admired. Density is not achieved by putting on and taking off styles of being. That is precisely the mode of self-invention fostered by the modern culture of consumption and the source of that lightness of being that Trilling laments. In other words, Trilling's solution is itself part of the problem, the modern problem of the subject.

Trilling had an important role in post–World War II American culture. He was a major arbiter of taste in a philistine but culturally eager mass democracy from which he distinguished himself by way of a carefully modulated, highly mannered prose. But was not this role and this style only an upscale version of what Trilling would later lament in our vulgar consumer culture, in which, as he said, "our commodities are not merely things" but styles of personality? Trilling's own critical style itself appears as an instance of a manner chosen "to signalize some spiritual or psychic grace." I say this while at the same time wanting not to detract from the actual grace and nobility of mind that coexisted in Trilling with the factitiousness I am pointing to. So far, I have been commenting on Trilling's style while providing few instances of that style at its most characteristic. Let me conclude with a passage that seems to me typical of his later work. I cite the passage because, to my ear, Trilling is making a special effort here "to signalize some spiritual or psychic grace." I quote the first paragraph of his essay of 1964, "Hawthorne in Our Time" in *Beyond Culture:*

> Henry James's monograph on Hawthorne must always have a special place in American letters if only because . . . it is the first extended study ever to be made of an American writer. But of course it is kept in

the forefront of our interest by more things than its priority. We respond to its lively sense of the American cultural existence and the American cultural destiny, to the vivacity, which arises from James's happy certitude that, in describing the career of the first fully developed American artist, he celebrates the founder of a line in which he himself is to stand pre-eminent. And we can scarcely fail to be captivated by the tone of James's critical discourse, of a mind informed and enlightened, delighting in itself and in all comely and civilized things; it is the tone of the center, far removed from the parochialism which (together with strength) James imputes to Poe as a critic. For the student of American literature in general the little book is indispensable.

Graciousness is rare enough that perhaps we ought to welcome it wherever we find it, but in this passage the graciousness and amenity seem self-conscious. The effect, in the context of the rest of the essay, is of tendentiousness. Trilling wants to speak out against modernism. He wants by his own gentleness and benignity to dissociate himself, as he said Hawthorne did, "from the fierce aggressions and self-assertions of the literary life." By affecting the elaborate cordiality of Henry James in his letters and literary essays Trilling wants to signalize an alternative to the "Waste Land mystique," and its impulse to regard as real only evil and extremity, and its contempt for quietness and civility. But Trilling's style, relaxed and urbane as it is, has the effect of suggesting not spontaneous good nature but ideological will. There is a force of intention in this amenity.

In the end Trilling is right: there is nothing within that passeth show. And what Trilling's own writing shows is that he knew his preferred style of selfhood was as little natural, as little organic, as any other. His very preoccupation with selfhood as style, as well as the presence in his writing of contradictory voices and self-images, suggest a consciousness on his part that the solid, shaped, unified, single-minded, perdurable self could only be a literary idea, an enabling myth.

The obsessive preoccupation with issues of personhood in Trilling's last essays bears out one of his recurrent themes, that what presents itself as politics in American writing often has less to do with society as such than with cultural debates about preferred modes of selfhood. The ultimate implication of Trilling's revisionary reading of John Dewey in 1938 was a body of criticism that would be concerned not with politics as the 1930s understood it but with a politics of the self.

III

CRITICS AND POLEMICS

Philip Rahv
"He Never Learned to Swim"

The summer of 1970 was the best time for *Modern Occasions*. I had come up from Cambridge in August to take a cabin in New Hampshire near Rahv and Alan Lelchuk, the other associate editor. We lived in separate houses about ten miles apart from each other and got together a few times a week for dinner to plan the first issue, which was to come out in the fall. Lelchuk had met Philip Roth at a writer's colony and was now his protégé. Alan treated Roth like the king of the mountain, and, in return, when Alan's first novel, *American Mischief,* was about to appear, Roth puffed it in print as "the greatest New England love story since *The Scarlet Letter.*" On this weekend Roth arrived with his girlfriend of the moment and we all gathered for dinner.

Frances Fitzgerald, who was then living with Alan and finishing her book on Vietnam, *Fire in the Lake,* did the cooking. There we were, like a scene out of Updike's *Bech: A Book,* four Jewish literary types and our four Gentile women. None of us was married, although Rahv was to marry Betty McIlvain soon after. Roth's friend was silent and beautiful the whole time, and except for a little mugging and a big brother–little

This essay dates back to 1976, when it was first published, but in a way it is new. Mark wrote it in 1975, not long after he had started teaching at the University of Wisconsin–Milwaukee. However, as he describes, he was unable to place it with a journal in the United States. It was turned down by Ted Solotaroff at the *New American Review,* by *TriQuarterly,* by *Atlantic,* and by the *New York Review of Books.* Mark finally took it to Ian Hamilton at the *New Review,* who published it in January 1976. Twenty-nine years after its publication in England, this is the essay's first publication in America. Eds.

brother routine Roth and Lelchuk had worked up, the two Philips did almost all the talking as the rest of us sat in attendance. The incongruities were wonderful in the meeting of the quick and voluble laureate of masturbation with the heavy-lidded, somnolent-looking old Trotskyite. It was like Lenny Bruce meeting Doctor Johnson.

Roth was in his post-*Portnoy* phase. He had come up from New York with a batch of Times Square stroke magazines with titles like *Suck, Scum,* and *Semen,* and discoursed with a slightly hysterical comic eloquence on the photographs and personals as a revelation of the night-world of American erotic fantasy. But at dinner he was the good Jewish son deferring to the old man, clearly conscious of the line of cultural succession. And he was very generous, for all the differences of age and cultural style. "Philip Roth" sounds a good deal like "Philip Rahv," and so Roth was able to tell the story of being greeted and lionized in London some years before by A. Alvarez as the great critic of the thirties. Now, Philip Roth was born in 1933 and doesn't much look like a thirties intellectual. The story seems fairly unlikely, but Rahv was flattered by it. He had a strong sense of values in the literary marketplace and knew that Roth was far more famous than he was and that his own name counted for less than it had twenty-five years before, at the height of his influence as a critic and editor of *Partisan Review.*

We were the academics and Roth was having a good time outraging us. Who, after all, he wanted to know, was going to read *Modern Occasions* when they could get their hands on *Scum?* But he had himself come of age in the great period of the *Kenyon* and the *Hudson* and the *Sewanee* and respected our project even though he had moved into the big business of million-dollar best-sellers. Also, he had taken the success of *Portnoy* hard and kept muttering about his lost "dignity." The rabbis and the Jewish magazines were cursing him, and cab drivers and other strangers were accosting him on the streets of New York: "Hey, Portnoy. Your fly's open." Besides that, he was fairly well isolated from other writers and, apparently, from society generally. So he had proposed to Rahv, I don't know how seriously, that he would like to help him in editing the magazine.

Rahv was happy to publish Roth's "Salad Days" in our first issue and then later a section from Roth's Nixon book, *Our Gang.* It was good for circulation, and Roth, out of deference or a desire for academic respectability or whatever motive, was willing to be paid at the rate of four cents a word, which is probably about one-tenth of what he would have received from *Esquire* or *Playboy*. But making editorial decisions was another matter. Rahv had a comically suspicious attitude toward writers, which is not so odd since he knew so many of them so well. In his view the poets were worse than novelists, but they were all monsters of self-promotion, logrollers, puffers, morally retarded. So Roth, he was certain, would use his editorial power to advance his friends, who were always minor talents and therefore no threat, and to suppress the serious competition.

The dinner was a good time. Most of our good times occurred before the magazine got going; once we had begun it was downhill all the way. Indeed, what I want to suggest in this memoir is how a man and a magazine, starting with the greatest hopefulness, ran down and into the ground, how a kind of psychic dead-end overcame the project and the man who went down with it. For the magazine was in every sense a reflection of the man; its glories and contradictions and final failure were his.

Since much of what I shall have to say is critical, I should say right at the start that in my view Rahv was one of the most distinguished critics of his generation. The sadness and frustration of his last years do not alter that. He exerted far more influence as the editor for thirty years of the *Partisan Review,* but as a critic he belongs in the company of Trilling, Tate, Winters, and Blackmur. His best essays—on Dostoevsky, Tolstoy, and Kafka, and on Hawthorne, Henry James, and "The Cult of Experience in American Writing"—are among the most rereadable essays of our time.

Rahv's criticism is of a special kind having little in common with the technicist preoccupations of the New Critics. For him the essay was a position paper, a tactical exercise in a continuing war of ideas, usually between Christians and Communists. He was always preoccupied with ideological tendency, sniffing it out in the apparently most innocent places the way Freudians always manage to discover sex. Like other Marxist critics of his time, he was concerned above all with reconciling his revolutionary politics with an admiration for decidedly illiberal modernist writers. The solution was to minimize the professed beliefs of the reactionary writers he liked and to adapt them for his own cause.

An example is his review of *Murder in the Cathedral,* in which the play's "desiccated pattern" of original sin and theological salvation is detached from Eliot's "radical" critique of a dying civilization. Or, as Rahv makes the distinction in an essay on Dostoevsky: "Reactionary in its abstract content, in its aspect of a system of ideas, his art is radical in sensibility and subversive in performance." As I hope to show, the "creative contradictions" Rahv noted in modernist writing were central to his own makeup. His general view of the modern imagination is summarized in one of the essays on Henry James: "In modern literature . . . it is above all the creativity, the depth and quality of the contradictions that a writer unites within himself, that gives us the truest measure of his achievement. And this is not primarily a matter of the solutions . . . but of his force and integrity in reproducing these contradictions as felt experience."

His greatest contribution to American literary opinion may have been his insistence on the importance of historical consciousness, Nietzsche's "sixth sense," at a time when it was unfashionable. So, irritated by neo-Christian critics of Hawthorne in the forties, Rahv argued that the American writer's religious imagination could not legitimately be compared with Dostoevsky's, because the Russian writer's consciousness of sin and evil "flows from a mighty effort to regain a metaphysical and religious consciousness" in a disintegrating society suffering from a chaos of experience and derangement of values. The problem for the America of Emerson and Hawthorne was not a chaos but a poverty of experience; the pre–Civil War culture of New England was still semiclerical and therefore no breeding ground for a Dickens or Dostoevsky, for whom secular experience is taken for granted. Hawthorne, like James after him, was still playing peekaboo with life.

There is a danger of misrepresenting Rahv's talent in focusing on his long, synoptic essays. Above all, he was an occasional writer and a Marxist polemicist. The Marxism in his criticism was never of the vulgar variety and sometimes little more than a materialist preoccupation with underlying social forces, but it gave his writing an edge, a discipline and focus almost uniformly lacking in contemporary criticism. And from the thirties apprenticeship, Rahv retained also an undiminished zest for literary combat. It is hard to think of another American critic who equaled him in exposing fools, opportunists, and faddists.

The attack might be *ad hominem,* but the object was always an idea or tendency. The style is closer to that of *Les Temps Modernes* than that of Anglo-American intellectual quarterlies.

Rahv was one of the last of the unattached men of letters in America. Allen Tate, R. P. Blackmur, and he were not professors until their later years, and they distrusted the university and despised academic critics, as did Yvor Winters, who wrote scathingly about "Professor X" and his secondhand mind. The money that supported *Modern Occasions* was not university money, it was Rahv's own, and when the magazine ran into financial trouble he never thought of asking for university or foundation support. The point about being independent was that you did not have to kowtow to anyone. Most importantly, Rahv did not want to be hampered in the expression of his political views. The American universities today are probably more tolerant of radical ideology than they had been in the thirties, but in this instance—unlike others I shall mention—I admired Rahv's stubbornness. He was serious in his convictions and, if his manners in literary controversy were sometimes rough, he never trimmed his sails to suit the prevailing breeze.

In the summer of 1970, at the age of sixty-two, Rahv was starting a new life. His wife, Theo, had died a couple of years before in a freak fire at their house in Boston, and Rahv himself had been very sick after that. He had recently quit *Partisan Review,* which he had founded thirty-five years before, and was beginning again, with a new magazine and new wife.

Just like starting out in the thirties. In the old photographs of Rahv and the original *Partisan* crowd of the late thirties—F. W. Dupee, Dwight Macdonald, Delmore Schwartz, William Phillips—he is strikingly handsome. He's also strikingly young. When Rahv started *Partisan Review* in 1934 he was only twenty-six. He had come to Providence, Rhode Island, in 1922; his parents, early Zionists, had remained in Palestine, to which they had emigrated from the Ukraine after the Russian Revolution and Civil War. In America Rahv went to work young. Somehow he managed to get to Oregon, where he worked as a junior advertising copywriter, and he returned east to New York during the Depression. He never went to college, but, like the New York Jewish intellectuals of his generation, he had read everything—not only Marx, Lenin, Trotsky, but also Joyce, Conrad, Proust, Mann.

In 1970 Rahv looked older than his age. I have a photograph of him in New Hampshire. He is looking into the camera with some suspicion, which is the way he looked at life generally. He appears confused and withdrawn, vaguely depressed; his eyes seem dull above large, puffy bags; his heavy frame is carrying too much weight. But there remains the panache — a green-and-yellow striped shirt open at the throat. He dressed conservatively — often a blue blazer and grey flannel trousers — but then there were the bright red socks, just a touch of the dandy about the old Marxist polemicist.

Rahv and his coeditor William Phillips had broken with the Communist Party over the Moscow purge trials in 1936, and the new *Partisan Review* emerged in 1937, free of its affiliation with the John Reed Club, to champion the modern sensibility in literature and the arts against the proletcult and to rescue socialism from the Stalinists. As with *Partisan Review, Modern Occasions* came into being chiefly as a response to a political situation. The magazine would be radical in its politics while reserving the right to criticize the New Left and those, like Louis Kampf, who wanted to politicize literature in the manner of the old-time commissars. It was not serving the revolution to put down Marcel Proust as a yenta, as the graffiti had it.

It was pretty clear by the summer of 1970 that the New Left had little future as a political movement, but it was the only game in town, and Rahv was hoping that the increasing domestic chaos would lead to total social collapse. The New Deal had rescued American capitalism in the thirties; maybe the scenario would work out differently this time. So Rahv watched the students with hope as well as skepticism.

Every revolutionist is in a sense time's fool; he must wait on history to provide the "revolutionary situation," much as the Christian waits on providence. Rahv had been a long time in the wilderness waiting on events. All through the 1950s he had written little, experiencing the internal exile of a political man in a society without politics. He had written a valuable essay for the *Kenyon Review* on the criticism of fiction, attacking the flight from historicism of critics who read novels as if they were poems, as purely an affair of language, but his polemical wrath was chiefly directed against critics like Northrop Frye, who had found in myth a substitute religion and an opiate for intellectuals tired of politics.

Rahv was politically astute, and he never saw more than a glimmer of hope for a revolution in the protests against the Vietnam War. He was unlike Noam Chomsky in not being primarily motivated by moral indignation against an unjust war. For Rahv the fighting in Vietnam was primarily an occasion, a cause of fighting at home and a first step toward social chaos and bringing down the system. He was not a revolutionary saint; he was a Leninist, and though he acknowledged them as allies, he was privately scornful of what he took to be the naive idealism of Chomsky and the Catholic priest Daniel Berrigan.

But he was a fearfully disillusioned Leninist. He often complained how dreary it was to live in a country where the politics were so infantile and the quality of ideological debate so poor. Rahv wasn't any happier with "the kids," his name for the young militants, than he was with the hacks of the Democratic and Republican parties. As early as in his editorial introduction to the second issue ("What and Where Is the New Left?" Winter 1971), he was attacking the Weathermen and lecturing "the kids" in the accents of a disappointed Bolshevik: "So far," he wrote, the New Left has "shown no understanding whatsoever of the first rule of revolutionary strategy, which is the education, build-up, and preservation of its leading cadres."

It wasn't just the tactics of the students that Rahv disliked; neither did he care for their neo-Romantic "counter-cultural" style. The free and easy ways of the urban guerrillas offended a certain socialist prudishness that had marked the generation of 1917 but was passé in 1968. He dissociated himself from the disillusioned old leftists, like Lewis Feuer, who in these years carried out filicidal attacks on the young disguised as "objective" analyses of their parricidal neuroticism. Philip wasn't that kind of old lefty, but he was still an old man in a country of the young. Caught in that sensual music, he could only look on disapprovingly as "Revolution, / drugging her terrible pre-menstrual cramps, / marches with unbra'd breasts to storm the city." The lines are from one of Robert Lowell's skeptical sonnets on "The Revolution," which we published in the first issue.

If Rahv offered himself as elder statesman to the young militants, it was not that he really expected to see a revolution in his own time. He acted, rather, out of a temperamental need to feel involved in history and the public world, but he wound up seeming merely grumpy and censorious to the young activists who had trouble distinguishing his negativism from that of explicitly conservative cold war intellectuals like Feuer and Irving Kristol. They were wrong about Rahv's politics—his revolutionism was sincere—but right about his mood, which was very close to that of Saul Bellow's *Mr. Sammler's Planet,* which came out at this time. The revulsion against the pornographers, the "swingers," the black militants, the patrons of pop, the publicists of apocalypse—the revulsion was total. And how could you be against all the characteristic features of the emergent culture and continue to call yourself a radical?

As an editor Rahv was not free from an essentially conservative nostalgia. Not of course the nostalgia of a Robert Lowell, who had an aristocratic New England tradition to be nostalgic about—"We, the Romanoffs with much to lose"—but the nostalgia of a type Philip Rieff has called "the Jew of culture." The Jewishness of the Jew of culture often seems to consist only in his refusal to disavow it: Rahv himself was entirely secular in outlook and profoundly skeptical of all pieties, including the Zionism of his parents. Yet at the end, possibly disenchanted with the deceiving promises of American life, more probably merely determined that his wife shouldn't get it, he willed his money to the State of Israel.

Rahv identified himself as a Jew of culture in the very choice of his name, which is Hebrew for "rabbi." He had changed it from the family's Greenberg. He was a revolutionist and a "culture rabbi," and sometimes the opposing selves made for contradictions in the magazine. What line, for example, were we going to take on the university disorders?

Rahv's conservative side was represented in the first issue by Robert Brustein's "The Decline of Professionalism." As dean of the Yale Drama School, Brustein had been traumatized by the bizarre antics of his students, and in this essay he argued that the students' (and some of the faculty's) revolt against the university was simply bad theater, second-rate costume drama. Rahv was himself entirely unsympathetic to university reform. Still, it was embarrassing for a Left magazine to be publishing an Establishment heavy who invoked Plato's *Republic* as an ideal and probably would have welcomed Napoleon had he come to New Haven on horseback, and who was so obviously more concerned with institutional continuity and hierarchy than with changing the society and ending the war.

Rahv was uneasy about Brustein and knew very well that his tone and substance derived from Lionel Trilling, the image of the Jew of culture as social conservative. In the same issue Rahv's other side—one of his other sides—was expressed in Noam Chomsky's "Revolt in the Academy," which firmly refused to repudiate the campus militants despite the excesses of ultra-Left splinter groups and individual psychotic acts. In decrying the insurrectionaries at Yale and Columbia and Berkeley, Brustein was forgetting about the greater violence of the American war against Southeast Asia.

Sometimes the magazine's balancing act became impossible, as when I published a piece in the second issue directly criticizing Trilling's politics: usually the Arnoldian sweetness and light had been mystified as if it were purely "literary," having nothing to do with social attitudes. Hilton Kramer, the daily art critic of the *New York Times* and a staunch Trillingite, had written an article on the New York art scene for our first issue. He was among those scandalized by my article and angrily withdrew from the magazine. Rahv probably could have sacrificed me and attempted to mollify Kramer, but he let him go with a delighted snort and some choice remarks about petite-bourgeois fetishists of culture.

Rahv's own dedication to the highest standards in culture had attracted a number of Trilling groupies to the magazine, but in this minor crisis he responded not as a culture rabbi himself but in the spirit of his master Trotsky when he complained that Maxim Gorky had greeted the October Revolution "in the manner of a director of a museum of culture," supporting the revolution, "but only if it was free from disorder." Observers and biographers have frequently commented on Trotsky's arrogance: it was certainly a conspicuous aspect of Rahv's attitude to his fellow intellectuals. In part it was the revolutionist's impatience with the softness and caution of the order-loving, self-protective bourgeois intellectual. But there was something else, related to his lifelong devotion to the antiliberal modernist writers he had first read as a youth. A Marxist in his deepest convictions, Rahv had nevertheless during the misery of the Depression years absorbed many of the seignorial values of the artists—James, Conrad, Yeats, Eliot—whom he had loved no less than the revolution.

Most academics, he would complain, have the souls of dentists and accountants. He himself, having come late to university life—accepting

a professorship at Brandeis University in 1957—belonged to a generation that regarded professors as genteel time-servers and unfrocked
clergymen. What he would have wished of his academic colleagues is
probably a blending of Plekhanov and Major Robert Gregory; what he
saw was timidity and self-seeking. He disliked in the culture rabbis not
their devotion to high standards—he was no defender of mass culture—
but their smug exploitation of culture to defend their recently achieved
position within the American mainstream. Culture had been an avenue
of assimilation and advancement, and some of the once-liberal intellectuals were protecting their new status with all the tenacity of a recently
arrived group.

Rahv's large capacity for aristocratic disdain was only partly literary
in origin. It had to do also with his own social ambitions and large ap-
petites. As with other Marxists of his generation and since, Rahv took
an immense pleasure in beautiful and expensive things—women, paintings, wines—which disposed him to enjoy the company of the wealthy
and well born. A revolutionist he may have been, but his taste in friends
and wives ran to blue blood; he was a terrific snob who used to advise
his wife about what "people of our class" did and didn't do. In his cultural style Rahv was a nineteenth-century Russian intellectual, but his
social aspirations were as American as a Dreiser hero's.

The best writers *Modern Occasions* attracted were like Rahv in being
culturally conservative, not to say negative in disposition. In this respect
it clashed with its chief rival, *Partisan Review,* which took the threat seriously enough to devote a substantial part of its Summer 1972 issue to a
"Symposium on the New Cultural Conservatism." The gap between
Rahv and *Partisan Review* had opened up in the fifties, when he had left
New York and moved to Boston and the job at Brandeis. The gap wid-
ened all through the sixties. *Partisan Review* had remained nominally
radical, but in practice it had jettisoned its old Marxism as a new generation took over.

The new *Partisan Review* was indifferent to ideological debate and
the refinements of Marxist theory. Its interests lay elsewhere, in what
the journalists at the time were calling the "new sensibility." The "sixth
sense" of Rahv's collection of essays, *Literature and the Sixth Sense,* was
the sense of history; *Partisan Review* in the late sixties was preoccupied
with the present and the immediate. It was a time of pornography,

science fiction, rock, film, happenings, and of course direct political action. It wasn't a time, so even intellectuals believed, for high seriousness and measured theorizing. Susan Sontag's *Against Interpretation* was directed against the humanist intellectuals of the thirties who were the pleasure-denying father figures. Her book became the manifesto of the "new sensibility."

If twenty years earlier the *Kenyon Review* delivered the news, now it was *Rolling Stone,* and *Partisan Review* read more like a pop magazine with each issue, with features on William Burroughs, camp, McLuhan's media, the Beatles, the New Mutants (Leslie Fiedler's term), and Protean Man. The editors weren't buying Charles Reich's "greening of America," but they weren't going to miss the train either. Good writing appeared fitfully, but there was no center, no focus, and no commitment. *Partisan* spoke for unpartisan middle-aged professors nattering on about having their minds blown and wanting above all to keep up with their students and make up for the years they had wasted reading books.

Sometimes it seemed then as if the intellectual world was divided between the avatars of Peter Pan and Timon of Athens. There were pink-cheeked old satyrs maundering on about red Indians and "the death of literature," and there were other old men hissing and spitting in exasperation over a world getting away from them. Rahv detested the new fashions and the hustler-intellectuals. His talents and sensibility disposed him to rage against the "trendies" and the "swingers," and *Modern Occasions* soon turned away from politics to its primary task: cultural hatchet-work.

In the second issue we published a polemic by Saul Bellow that set the tone for the remaining issues. The essay was about the treason of the go-go "publicity intellectuals," and Bellow was happy to name names. The essay deserves to be reprinted as a contemporary *Dunciad.* What Bellow talked about was the rise to prominence of the pop intellectuals— Leslie Fiedler is the chief object of attack—who tarted up the familiar themes of modernism for a mass audience and to make a fast buck, not as literary men but as prophets to the newly bohemianized masses.

The essay was angrily eloquent in defense of a lost cause, the cause not of Bellow but of a whole generation of liberal intellectuals, which included Rahv, Trilling, and Irving Howe, and who bore a resemblance in the disillusion and crotchetiness that had overtaken them. (The mood was not at all limited to the Jewish intellectuals: they were merely the most articulate when it came to lamentation and complaint.) The cause was classical modernism, an older humanism and idea of art, perhaps above all a sense of the past and of the continuity of human achievement. According to Bellow, the new guru-intellectuals were schismatic: for them "whatever is not contemporaneous is worthless." Their nihilism was opportunistic: "*It*—civilization—is a failure, but *they*—the publicity intellectuals—are doing extremely well."

I quote Bellow's jeremiad at some length because, without sharing Bellow's conservative politics, Rahv was in total sympathy with his exasperation. Whoever set up as a guru in this situation of cultural crisis, whether Norman O. Brown or Marshall McLuhan or Leslie Fiedler or R. D. Laing or Herbert Marcuse, their politics didn't matter. Rahv was instinctively against them, as he was instinctively against anything new. His conservatism could not take refuge like Bellow's in piety toward the dead, as in *Humboldt's Gift:* He was too committed to quarreling with the follies of the present. But in the process his skepticism turned into dogmatism; he became attached to an orthodoxy of negation. In her eulogy Mary McCarthy wrote of Rahv's negativism that he had always been "grumblingly out of sorts with fashion." Toward the end it was more than that: he was a wrathful, disappointed old man entirely given over to destructiveness.

The trouble with sheer destructiveness in cultural criticism is that the negatives tend to cancel each other out. In the third issue, for example, Rahv had a go at Charles Reich and the counterculture. In effect that piece was another skirmish in the elders' war on the young. Reich himself wasn't important enough for all that polemical wrath expended on him; he was more a symptom than anything else. The symptom that disturbed me more was Rahv's unrelieved negativism. At bottom I had some skepticism about the whole business of ideological warfare. Did it really matter? Was the quarrel between "trendies" and "old humanists" any more interesting than the quarrel between anticommunist liberals and anti-anticommunists in the fifties? Didn't it make more sense to get on with one's proper business—providing that one could decide what that was?

But in the meanwhile I had some negativism of my own to release. My ideological stance in this comedy of ideas was to be a negative antinegativist. *Commentary* magazine, under Norman Podhoretz, the *Making It* man, had converted to a defense of Nixon-Agnewism. Here the assimilation, the Americanization, of a section of the old New York liberal intelligentsia was complete. The "alienation" of the thirties had become "making it" in the boom years of the sixties, and these latecomers to the American mainstream were writing like Rotary Club businessmen with investments to protect. The positions were different, but in attacking the political backsliding of the once-liberal *Commentary* I had also in mind the reflexive negativism of our own positions on culture. Rahv was committed to keeping open "the wound of the negative," an attitude of Kierkegaard he much admired. But now there was nothing heroic in that position, only a generalized disenchantment with everything. In the editorial criticizing *Commentary* I urged that its contributors liberate themselves "from an increasingly sterile and curmudgeonly conservatism characterized by a spirit of lamentation, rancorousness, meanness of spirit, and mourning for a lost world." I hoped also that my captain would sometime relent.

That never happened. Rahv increasingly wanted not literary criticism but literary assassinations. He contracted with America's number one cultural hit-man, the movie critic John Simon, to "do a job" on Vladimir Nabokov; he was being taken too seriously. Simon didn't come through; neither did Gore Vidal. In the absence of these more practiced and professional critics, Rahv took what he could get. And so we had Flora Natapoff taking off after Clement Greenberg and Robert Manners attacking Claude Lévi-Strauss, Francis Coleman dismissing film as a low art and Emile Capouya dismissing George Steiner as a low critic, Bernard Elevitch exposing R. D. Laing and Pearl Bell lashing Fiedler, and so on and on. There was never anything—person, idea, or movement—the magazine wholeheartedly supported.

I was continually being pushed to perform demolition jobs on new books of literary criticism, but it was demoralizing to be used as an extension of another man's anger, the hammer in his hand. So I found excuses, gradually detaching myself from Rahv's vendettas. Above all he wanted somebody to denounce Norman Mailer. Juliet Mitchell had written on *The Prisoner of Sex* but disappointed Rahv by taking the book seriously. Arthur Edelstein, in a review of Robert Langbaum's *The Modern Spirit*, had pointed out the flaws in *An American Dream* and *Why Are We in Vietnam?* But Rahv remained unsatisfied. Mailer was his obsession, eating away at his entrails, the white whale of a monomaniacal hatred. "All that most maddens and torments" was symbolized to Rahv in Mailer's high reputation among the critics. I was in England in 1973; Rahv's last letter to me, in the summer of that year, was still another appeal that I cut down Mailer. His stock was too high.

To every suggestion for an article he responded with a grunt and a rejection. He sometimes dismissed article ideas that he might have been expected to greet enthusiastically. In 1971 Georg Lukács's *History and Class Consciousness,* which had originally been published in 1922, appeared in English for the first time. This should have been a major occasion for a Left magazine, but instead of having it reviewed Rahv proceeded to dig out an old essay by Isaac Deutscher attacking Lukács and reprinted it in our "Past and Present" department.

The "Past and Present" section featured reprints of old articles, such as Ernst Curtius on Balzac and Lev Vygotsky on Bunin. In his happier days Rahv had discovered or encouraged young writers like Bellow, Randall Jarrell, John Berryman, Bernard Malamud, William Styron. Now he was indifferent to the younger writers, falling back on old friends—Mary McCarthy, Robert Lowell, Roman Jakobson, Elizabeth Hardwick, William Styron—and reprinting old critical classics. The younger writers he published were often those who wrote him the most gushingly flattering mash notes.

The neglect of Lukács and the susceptibility to flattery were signs of Rahv's increasing sense that he had failed. Lukács had created a massive body of work; Rahv's essays needed only a single volume. He was essentially a magazine editor and not a Marxist aesthetician, but his gifts as a critic were awesome, and it is sad that he didn't leave behind a more substantial body of work to fix his place in literary history.

But Rahv was primarily a talker and not a writer, and he missed his Boswell. Saul Bellow has brought back the splendor of Delmore Schwartz's conversation in *Humboldt's Gift,* but Rahv appears in fiction only as a caricature. He is Will Taub in Mary McCarthy's *Oasis,* a roman à clef of 1949. McCarthy's satire was never intended to be fair; neither did she recreate Rahv's talk very well. His sheer joy in speech does not come across in his reviews and essays either; when he sat down to write, he composed in a neutral style modeled to some extent on T. S. Eliot's prose.

At his death Rahv was working on two books, one on Trotsky for the Viking Modern Masters series and another on Dostoevsky, a subject that had occupied him off and on for thirty years. It always seemed unlikely that he would ever finish these books. He was too impatient to sit alone in a room for long stretches; he craved companionship and talk. He was immensely private about personal things, hardly ever talking about feelings or about his past, but he delighted in sharing opinions.

Toward the end, when he felt increasingly out of things and unsympathetic to everything happening around him, he would summon friends over to his house to regale them with pronouncements on the state of the nation, or, more happily, to gossip about the intellectual greats he had known and about mutual friends. Rahv had a special delight in talking about the vagaries of very intelligent people, many of whom had been his friends. He loved to talk about the book of gossip he wanted to write about the literary celebrities he had known.

Rahv wanted above all else to be in the thick of ideological struggle and needed always a cultural occasion to get him going. But America is no country for literary intellectuals who want to participate in a public existence unless, like Mailer, they have a penchant for the clownish. It was possible for Harvard professors to transfer themselves to John Kennedy's Camelot, but Rahv's model was not the pragmatic action intellectual like Arthur Schlesinger or Daniel Patrick Moynihan but more like the publicists of mid-nineteenth-century Russia who provide the context of Dostoevsky's early work. America in the sixties had no use for a Belinsky or Herzen or Chernyshevsky.

The thirties were the last such time in America. After that time Rahv's sensibility was disastrously unsuited to the historical moment. Unlike the Protean ideal advocated by Robert Lifton, he was monumental and blocklike in his resistance to change. Mary McCarthy captured this stolidity (and perhaps his weakness as well) very well in her eulogy: "He never learned to swim. This metaphorically summed up his situation: he would immerse his body in the alien element (I have nice pictures of him in bathing trunks by the waterside) but declined, or perhaps feared to move with it. His resistance to swimming with the tide, his mistrust of currents, were his strength."

Toward the end, as the magazine fell on evil days, Rahv gave in more and more to his rages. Joan Friebely, who had been secretary-proofreader-advertising manager and the presence who assured the magazine's continuity, finally quit, after one of Rahv's scenes. All of us wanted to stand by him, but he drove us away, as if humiliated by his defeat. In the end the magazine came to a stop, after six issues.

In his Timon-like rages Rahv was the wreck of a still-dominating personality, but his health was deteriorating as well as his hope. He seemed always to be taking a different pill for one of his innumerable symptoms. In addition, he was drinking too much and acting alternately violent and depressed with Betty; finally they separated and waged war through their lawyers. By 1972 the magazine had discontinued publishing and the new beginning had fizzled.

I was surprised to learn, at Rahv's death in 1973, that he had been only sixty-five. He had seemed that old when I knew him as a student at Brandeis in 1962. He had seemed oddly detached from the university setting then, and he seemed wholly out of things by the end. The "kids" had let him down; so had America; and so had history. The new world presented an opaque wall to his understanding. "It was a sad way to go," Rahv had said about Edmund Wilson's death in 1972. Like Wilson he was a massive intellect and presence from an age that was intellectually heroic—but that had ended before he did.

Afterword: 2003

The preceding memoir appeared in the English literary magazine the *New Review* in January 1976. That magazine was edited by Ian Hamilton, who had risen to prominence in the early 1960s as guiding spirit of its predecessor, the *Review*. I had met Hamilton in Soho during a two-year sojourn of mine, from 1972 to 1974, in England; he thought the piece right for his magazine, which was then publishing a series on editors of little magazines.

Rahv's name, however, was little known in England, and I would have preferred that my memoir appear in America. But when I submitted it to two respected New York editors, I received only their scorn. These editors agreed that, instead of my cavils, I should have been expressing gratitude for Rahv's help and my memoir should have been an unambivalent tribute.

In retrospect, I think I was, if anything, too respectful. As regards Rahv as critic, he was not, as I had said in 1975, one of the great critics of his generation, comparable to Tate, Winters, Blackmur, and Trilling. For one thing, he just did not write enough. Like some other minor writers—Oscar Wilde comes to mind among dramatists—his oral pronouncements far exceeded his written output; he was a better talker than he was a writer. By the time of the publication in 1949 of *Image and Idea: Fourteen Essays on Literary Themes,* his first collection of essays, his critical oeuvre was half complete. Most of his best essays had already been written: "Dostoevsky in *The Possessed*" and "The Paleface and Redskin," his most cited piece of writing although it was only five pages long. Rahv was a great enthusiast of James. In 1944 he also edited an eight-hundred-page anthology, *The Great Short Novels of Henry James,* many of them about naive American heiresses caught up in the coils of cunning European men. A favorite Rahv essay of mine, "Tolstoy: The Green Twig and the Black Trunk," also appeared in *Image and Idea.* Subsequent collections of his essays, like *The Myth and the Powerhouse* and *Literature and the Sixth Sense,* reprinted many essays that had already appeared in that first collection.

On the personal side, there were good reasons for my not feeling the gratitude that my elders thought would be more becoming. My years at *Modern Occasions* coincided with the domestic upheaval over the Vietnam War, and the latter Kulturkampf unfortunately coincided with a crisis in my own academic career. In short, I came up for tenure at Boston University at a time when my involvement in the antiwar movement, at least as my senior colleagues measured it, counted as much as my teaching and publications. In fact, that involvement had been minimal, but I did come from a different generation and had different attitudes. In truth, I detested the gentility of the department chair and many of the veteran professors he had recruited. As things turned out, I received the support of the majority of the promotions and tenure committee, but was blocked by the most influential persons in the department on grounds that were personal and political. And with the notorious John Silber serving as the newly installed president of BU, my fate at that university was sealed. Silber was at that time the most outspoken opponent of the student antiwar movement among American university presidents. Many who stayed on at BU later wrote about Silber's career as the enemy of the BU faculty.

It is unlikely that Rahv could have done much to swing opinion in my favor. However, despite my entreaties, the one sure thing is that he did not try, even in the form of a strong letter recommending me. Considering how much time I had devoted to *Modern Occasion* that I might otherwise have spent attending to my career in academe, Rahv's failure to come forward was a blow to my vanity as well as my professional standing. Inevitably I cooled toward him in the aftermath of that drama. In any case, I had moved from the Boston area to Marblehead on the North Shore in 1971–72, the year in which I was up for tenure. I kept visiting the magazine's office in the first semester, but as things looked bleaker at BU my visits became less frequent.

Rahv was a strong-minded editor during the whole of his career, and he inspired diverse responses. Some of the old-timers to whom I told my story about Rahv and the final days of *Modern Occasions* smiled in recognition, correcting me only in pointing out that Rahv's negativism was not a function of old age; he had always been that way. On the other hand, he had also always had a keen eye for fresh talent; and when he started *Modern Occasions,* now-famous writers he had discovered in the early days of *Partisan Review* stepped up and contributed something to the new quarterly.

Old friends Mary McCarthy and Elizabeth Hardwick responded by mail to his typically broad questions. Those exercises in give-and-take appeared as "Interviews." Robert Lowell, who married Hardwick and later wrote a well-known poem about "drinking with the Rahvs," contributed six sonnets under the rubric *Revolution* that had been inspired by the recent political turmoil. Also represented in *Modern Occasions* by an interview was William Styron, an early favorite of Rahv's.

Perhaps the most fun of all these pieces was a polemic by Saul Bellow entitled "Culture Now: Some Animadversions, Some Laughs." Bellow felt personally insulted by the conversion of old comrades to the counterculture of the 1960s, which he located in the newly hip *Partisan Review.* He ridiculed Leslie Fiedler, who had turned himself into a connoisseur of comic strips and other aspects of American pop culture; he exposed *PR's* founding editor William Phillips as a moral weakling in trying to argue for the Francophile aesthetics of Susan Sontag, that magazine's hottest new acquisition; and he directed his greatest wrath at Richard Poirier, the new moving spirit at *PR*, who had been one of the few major critics to denounce Bellow's prize-winning novel *Herzog*. It was easy to see why Rahv was delighted to receive such a jeremiad. He himself shared Bellow's attitudes about the "new sensibility" of the 1960s, but he lacked the ease and flexibility with English to have written anything like it.

The intellectuals most devoted to Rahv, who looked to him as a spiritual father, were those who had founded and were now editing the *New York Review of Books*. When I was visiting Rahv at his New Hampshire place one summer, Robert Silvers, the editor of *NYR*, came up from New York to try out some ideas. I was struck by Silvers's deference; after all, his paper, launched almost ten years earlier, was already enjoying considerable influence, and, though only forty years old, Silvers was well connected. He asked what Rahv thought of the new controversy about education that had been stirred up by *Deschooling Society*, the most recent book by Ivan Illich, one of the counterculture gurus of the 1960s.

Not surprisingly to me, Rahv dismissed Illich and educational policy as a topic for *NYR*. In general, he was indifferent to all the social issues that affected ordinary American citizens. That was partly because he shared so few of their concerns. He could afford to be complacent about schooling because he had no children, and he could afford to be indifferent to pensions or tax policy because he had no worries about money. At the time of Silvers's visit, Rahv was living off his inheritance from his recently deceased wife, Nathalie Swan, who had herself inherited one of the great American fortunes.

Rahv once explained to me that it was important that radicals have sturdy financial backing to support them when assailed, as they would assuredly be, by right-wing pressure groups. Otherwise, they might be disposed to sell out to protect their jobs and families. The fact is, however, that, rich or not, Rahv was very cautious in the early 1950s, the heyday of anticommunist ideologues in Congress. Whatever his reasons may have been, he wrote very little all through that decade, whether on politics or literature. It is not likely that he was ever in great danger; the

House Committee on Un-American Activities was made up of opportunists who wanted to expose and destroy—as they did—Hollywood celebrities like John Garfield, not the left-wing editor of a cultural journal
that had about five thousand subscribers. But, looking always to Russian
history for his examples and to set a framework for his expectations,
Rahv may have thought there were precedents that suggested caution.

On another occasion, when Rahv had been invited to present a guest
lecture to a Harvard Summer School audience, Elizabeth Hardwick
came up from New York to see him. Hardwick had known Rahv con-
tinuously since 1945. However, despite that long friendship, when he
died toward the end of 1973, she was at a bit of a loss as what to say
about him at a funeral service held in his honor in the chapel at Brandeis University.[1] She began tentatively: "I don't know that I am the
proper person to speak here at the time of the death of Philip Rahv, and
I am not confident that I can speak properly." Hardwick is a most articulate person and has been a loyal friend to many; I attribute her uneasi-
ness to what she remarked on in her eulogy: "We must respect the fact
that Philip was not especially autobiographical." Rahv's guardedness
about his personal history and his general reluctance to be known had
the effect of keeping even his most intimate friends at a distance. Nobody knew just who he was.

I remarked in my memoir on Rahv's obsession with cutting cultural
celebrities down to size. I recently came upon an article in the *New Criterion* in which John Simon writes amusingly of the pressure Rahv applied to get him to perform "radical surgery" on the reputation of Vladimir Nabokov. Simon had his doubts about Nabokov, but not knowing
Russian or enough about Nabokov's oeuvre, he declined the assignment.
Hardwick acknowledged the Sweeney Todd element in Rahv's literary
personality but described it in general, positive terms. She spoke of his
ruling passion as "contempt for provincialism, the tendency to inflate
local and fleeting cultural accomplishments." But Hardwick did not
feign total sympathy with Rahv's project as a critic. "This slashing away

---

1. Hardwick's eulogy appeared in the January 24, 1974, issue of the *New York Review
of Books*. Mary McCarthy adopted a very different tone in her memoir, "Philip Rahv,
1908-1973," which appeared on the front page of the *New York Times Book Review* on
February 17, 1974.

at . . . small achievements passing as masterly, permanent monuments was a crusade some more bending souls might have grown weary of." She was herself one of those "more bending souls," as she also had occasion to acknowledge when implicitly comparing herself with Mary McCarthy.

Rahv was strong willed in a way that made him appear awesome at some times, but merely comical at others. Will Barrett provides the best over-all portrait of Rahv in his book *The Truants*, a memoir of life at *Partisan Review* in the 1940s. Rahv hardly comes across as an epic figure in Barrett's pages. Rather, he is remembered as a devious comic figure who spoke ill of all the people he knew when they were not present, and guarded his own secrets as if they were chunks of gold at Fort Knox. Rahv's proclivity for negative gossip, especially about his long-suffering partner, William Phillips, created embarrassment for others but hardly seems to have ruffled his own surface.

I think now that Rahv had some very good years, especially from the late 1930s into the early '40s. Rahv was able successfully to model himself on the radical journalist-intellectual Vissarion Belinsky, who in the 1840s had greatly influenced the young Dostoevsky. However, that role required a culture in which politics had a high intellectual component. Inevitably, in later years Rahv found himself frustrated by what passed for politics in America. The Depression years constituted a once-only opportunity for Marxist ideology. When politics largely disappeared from literary-cultural discourse, as it did in the 1950s, Rahv was reduced to silence. Although Rahv fancied at first that the student movement of the 1960s had revolutionary potential, he was soon disillusioned. It did not make him feel a part of things, and he judged the student movement by anachronistic criteria derived from the Bolshevik Revolution. Ideas like "participatory democracy," which were indigenous to the new movement, were unreal to him. Rahv never became as involved in the intergenerational debate as Irving Howe, but he was twelve years older than Howe and had less to fall back on. His disappointment over the movement, over *Modern Occasions,* over his personal life, was all encompassing. There seemed nothing left for him to live for.

Alfred Kazin and
Irving Howe

1. Alfred Kazin

Lionel Trilling's critical contemporaries were not more successful than he in penetrating to the "deep places." Like most of the older Jewish intellectuals, the two I have chosen as examples did not start out as academics and did not hold doctorates. Trilling was exceptional—in a group that included Lionel Abel, Clement Greenberg, Harold Rosenberg, and Philip Rahv—in belonging to both the world of public intellectuals and that of university professors.

If Trilling attended more to abstract ideas than to imagination, Alfred Kazin failed to achieve the distinction of the finest critic-theorists of his time precisely because he had few compelling general ideas. But if I had written about Kazin in the years when I myself was starting out, I would have not have judged him as having "failed" in any respect. On the contrary, it was Kazin, more than any other critic, who in my teenage years guided me in thinking about American literature and showed me by his own example how one might write about books. As an undergraduate in the late 1950s, I used to read Kazin in the Sunday *New York*

Mark wrote about Kazin and Howe elsewhere. He wrote about Kazin up to *New York Jew* in the light of his agonized self-identity in "Alfred Kazin: An American Life," *Salmagundi* 44–45 (Spring–Summer 1979). He also wrote a detailed summary and critique of Howe for *Dictionary of Literary Biography: Modern American Critics*. Since the agenda behind it is largely scholarly and instructional, rather than personal and reflective, it has not been included in this volume. Eds.

Times Book Review and especially in the *Reporter,* a glossy liberal anti-communist magazine that had been founded in 1949 by Max Ascoli, an antifascist Italian Jew.

In later years I was not as enthusiastic about Kazin's writing, which I now came across most frequently in the *New York Review of Books.* He had been a friend and guide to an eager boy who had grown up in a home without books, but now I was ready for a stiffer challenge. As I grew older, I paid less attention to Kazin than to critic-theorists who were new to me, like Frank Kermode. I came upon Kermode early in the 1960s in a collection of his own reviews, *Puzzles and Epiphanies,* a Joycean title that implied a formalist commitment to literary modernism absent in Kazin. As with many members of his New York generation, Kazin's influence waned in the 1960s with the surge in new theories of textuality. Indeed, it was hard to believe that Kermode, with his French-influenced interest in narratology, was only four years younger than Kazin (b. 1915).

Apart from modernism, the other commitment Kazin never made—and here he followed Trilling—was to literary theory. Trilling was able during his life to escape the oblivion that is the fate of the critic who does not adapt to the fashion of his day. Indeed, Trilling's last book, *Sincerity and Authenticity,* was greeted with more positive reviews than he had received since the 1950s. Those reviews were written mainly by literature-department conservatives, especially in England, who were grateful because Trilling summarized in cogent terms his case against the "adversary culture." The Oxford English faculty, represented by John Bayley and others, expressed its regard by offering Trilling a permanent appointment. Flattered as he must have been—an appointment at Oxford for her son had been the ultimate dream of Trilling's mother, who had herself been raised in London's East End—Trilling turned down the offer. He could not see the point in his late sixties of leaving New York and Columbia, where he was by then a University Professor. A couple of years later, in 1975, Trilling died. Literary theory was then at its peak, but Trilling exited the scene before his influence had sunk correspondingly.

Kazin was not as fortunate in that respect. He had been born ten years after Trilling and lived almost a quarter century past Trilling's death. During the whole of that time, he continued to write at a furious pace. "Writing was everything," according to the title of one of his later books. But no single one of his subsequent books earned him the prestige of his very first, *On Native Grounds* (1942). That extraordinary book was a 540-page tour de force, the product of five years of twelve-hour days reading and writing at the New York Public Library. Kazin was twenty-seven when it was published.

However, even that exciting account of the rise of American literary realism from Howells and Dreiser through the new currents of the 1930s reveals flaws that did not secure Kazin a critical following such as Trilling and other New York critics enjoyed. Kazin had briefly studied with Trilling at Columbia after receiving his bachelor's degree from City College. That is a curious detail. *On Native Grounds* is a passionate historical celebration of the liberal-minded movement of American letters from 1900 to 1940, Trilling's chief focus of attack in *The Liberal Imagination*. Kazin's pageant of historical progress manifested a generous spirit of enthusiasm, but less in the way of close analysis and argument. His excited identification with his subject outstripped his capacity to make important distinctions of style and value. Thus his wrong-headed devaluation of William Faulkner.

Kazin's analysis of Faulkner partakes of the qualities he finds in him: "extraordinary intensity" and "profligate rhetoric." His chief objection is that Faulkner's rhetoric floats free of any larger purpose or social vision. His "monstrous overwriting" demonstrates "a need to invest everything he wrote with a wild, exhilarated, and disproportionate intensity—an intensity that was brilliant and devastatingly inclusive in its energy, but seemed to come from nowhere." If you are going to get your author wrong, at least Kazin's responsiveness to the "sullen, screaming intensity" of Faulkner's characters shows that, however wrongheaded in his overall judgment, Kazin was not miles away from a proper appreciation. And, in fact, not too many years later Kazin decided that he had been wrong about Faulkner and wrote one of his very best essays, in praise of *Light in August*.

Kazin emerged as a leading spokesman for literary nationalism in the final chapter, "America! America!" of *On Native Grounds*. Once, in Kazin's company, the poet-critic Randall Jarrell mocked the typical academic critic for being incapable of writing even a line of original verse. Kazin was stung by Jarrell's disdain, but of all the New York critics he was probably the one who tried hardest to write in the accessible, vernacular style that made Jarrell's essays on his fellow poets so attractive. That is not to say Kazin sounded at all like the witty author of "The Age of Criticism"; irony was not Kazin's line. Rather, as critics go he was a rhapsode. "America! America!" brings to a crescendo an account of national self-discovery that is also the record of the author's self-making. Kazin's excitement in his signature work plainly grew out of his identification with "the new writer coming up in the Thirties who really was of the people — who lived between dread and a wild new hope that with a book he would create his own life at last." That autobiographical hope distinguishes Kazin's prose style from that of Jarrell, who wrote about poetry out of his own experience as a poet, not as someone determined to build an identity out of his nation's literary history.

American studies, which did not fully emerge as a new academic field until after World War II, is latent in Kazin's wide-ranging acquaintance with the non-high-culture forms that dominated the 1930s. By "the documentation of America in the depression," Kazin is referring to the vogue of documentary reportage and photography, which he himself documents in detail. Whereas Trilling's prose is full of abstractions, Kazin's is full of titles of books and people's names: Edmund Wilson and *The American Jitters,* Margaret Bourke-White, James Agee, Walker Evans, *Let Us Now Praise Famous Men,* and many more. There were documentary productions other than journalistic accounts of labor strikes like Wilson's or works of photography by Bourke-White and Evans; there were also guides to the states of the nation commissioned by the Federal Writers' Project. The "thunderous climax" in which "the American people" drove toward "national inventory" to reclaim the "national inheritance" sounds like pure rhetoric, but it has a reference, too, ranging from collections of folklore to the vogue of American biography and historiography as the decade ended.

It is thrilling to think of the attachment to America that made it possible for this historian/observer, a child of Yiddish-speaking immigrants still in his midtwenties, to write with such intimate knowledge and enthusiasm about so many diverse topics. If there is no discussion of works of poetry or prose fiction in this chapter, that is because the American experience of social crisis did not allow for the polish of aesthetic completion. Kazin proved to be as adept at the description of fragmentation as at suggesting broad historical outlines.

He is not supposed to have been sensitive to aesthetic matters. But consider this analysis of the aesthetic of the camera in relation to "so stupendous and humiliating a disorder as the depression scene provided." Once again, it is the objective realism that engages his critical eye: "The camera did not fake or gloss over . . . it was at once so aggressive and uncertain that it highlighted an awakened, ironic, militant, yet fundamentally baffled self-consciousness. Most important, the camera reproduced endless *fractions* of reality. . . . And if the accumulation of visual scenes seemed only a collection of 'mutually repellant particles,' as Emerson said of his sentences, was not *that* discontinuity, that havoc of pictorial sensations, just the truth of what the documentary mind saw before it in the thirties?"

Kazin was a man of his moment in that what he, and the camera, saw before it was a vision of society in disorder. He strongly identified with what he took to be the chief tradition in American criticism, from Emerson to the Van Wyck Brooks of *America's Coming of Age*. In that early polemic, Brooks had written that literary criticism "is always impelled sooner or later to become social criticism . . . because the future of our literature and art depends upon the wholesale reconstruction of a social life all the elements of which are as if united in a sort of conspiracy against the growth and freedom of the spirit." The notion that literary criticism should be allied with a vision of "wholesale reconstruction" of society might seem to link Kazin to Philip Rahv, the dominant voice at *Partisan Review*. The difference was that Rahv's vision was European, Marxist, and materialist, whereas Kazin's was American, Emersonian, and idealist.

Apart from Edmund Wilson, Brooks was probably the living literary critic who most influenced Kazin. Brooks had been an original and penetrating critic of the national culture in the late teens and early 1920s. Then, after suffering a breakdown, he transformed himself into a kind of impressionist painter of important periods and scenes in American literary history. Perhaps the best of Brooks's pen-portraits is *The Flowering of New England, 1815–1865*. Whereas academic New Critics were writing forty-page essays devoted to the explication of a single poem by Donne or another metaphysical poet, Brooks's group portraits included minor as well as major figures and ignored texts in favor of reproducing the atmosphere of the scenes he depicted. Kazin was a more muscular writer and set up his authors in opposition (e.g., Dreiser vs. Edith Wharton), but, like Brooks, his attempt to evoke the temper of a historical moment took the place of close analysis of individual texts.

It must have been Kazin's curiosity about America life, a trait not common among his New York contemporaries, that attracted me to him when I was young. I had been a solitary "walker in the city" as he had been, although slightly older, during the year and a half I spent in Manhattan on a leave of absence from college, and, eager to see more of the country, I had spent the summer of 1958, when I was nineteen, driving over the Rockies and, starting in San Francisco, picking up odd jobs down the California coast. I identified with Kazin's Whitmanesque effort to absorb American culture into himself and assume an American voice. That he had actually achieved this leap, this son of a barely literate immigrant house painter, gave me hope. When I arrived at college, I chose to concentrate in American history and literature.

The critics Kazin wanted to be most like were not his Jewish contemporaries but American-born figures of the 1920s like Wilson, Brooks, and Randolph Bourne, who were all, he said, "concerned with the continuity of progress in American life and were not afraid to attack social and political evil." When, from the late 1930s on, the revelation of Stalin's crimes and his pact with Hitler caused Kazin's radical contemporaries to cast their nets wide in search of a new post-Marxist orientation, he followed a characteristically different course. Never as passionate about ideological politics as they and largely indifferent to Marxism—he described himself as a "*literary* radical"—he turned in on himself and started keeping a journal, which he was to raid in subsequent years for successive volumes of memoirs.

If Kazin was not wholeheartedly a critical intellectual in the New York style, what constitutes his interest? The answer, for me, has to do with the emotional and spiritual elements in his writing. Let me start with the emotions. As we have seen, in Trilling's conception emotion is always an element of the great creative imagination. But then another question arises. What was he feeling? Kazin's readers no doubt looked forward, as I did, to reading his reviews because of their high quotient of personal engagement. But searching for the most successful representation of emotions in Kazin, one finds that the best place to look is not his literary work but his large body of autobiographical writing. He was as much a memoirist as a literary critic, although it is hard to draw a sharp distinction between the two, inasmuch as many of his finest critical observations appear as one-liners in his memoirs and journals.

Kazin's emotionalism as an element in his writing is an uneven affair. His first memoir, *A Walker in the City* (1951), written in his mid-thirties, is about the prevailing sense of wonder in a boy growing up in a poor Jewish immigrant family in the Williamsburg section of Brooklyn. Kazin plainly was striving for a lyric effect. But his lyricism does not always make for joy, as in Isaac Babel, because it frequently spills over into nostalgic sentimentality. Where it does work is in remembering his anxiety-ridden mother, who appears as the representative of Jewish suffering through all the ages. The son recalls the decisive mark of her character as "an unrelenting remembrance of our powerlessness, of every hurt, betrayal and sorrow, unquestioning obedience to the dark god, a fearful pledge of grim solidarity with all the forces that had ever molded her and all the people she had ever met."

His other major memoir, *New York Jew* (1978), offered profiles of many of the famous people Kazin came to know during his own years of relative fame. If *A Walker in the City* is flawed at times by the excessive nostalgia of the author, this later study is limited by the fact that Kazin himself is more an absence than a presence in his own story. He writes about figures like Robert Frost, Edmund Wilson, and Saul Bellow in such a way as to suggest that their confident sense of themselves had the effect of making them more actual to him than he was to himself: "The outside world was still more real to me than I was."

Notwithstanding my cavils, Kazin's trilogy of memoirs—he also wrote another, shorter memoir, *Starting Out in the Thirties* (1965)—includes some of his best writing. Still, he did not fully come into his own as an autobiographer until he reached his seventies, when his true subject, a religious yearning for faith, made itself explicit for the first time.

Writing Was Everything (1995) is more about Kazin's reading than his writing. It is organized about the author's search for grace in the books he was reading during the years of the Holocaust and directly after. He had been dispatched to Europe as a journalist after the war. Just turned thirty, he found himself hailed in literary circles in Paris and Rome for his pioneering work on the new American fiction that was now attracting European writers. But he himself "wanted fiercely to learn Europe," which he proceeded to do in contemplating the thought of metaphysical and mystical writers such as Simone Weil, the French Jewess who had turned against Judaism and been claimed by many Catholics who found inspiration in her writing. But the quarrel over whether Weil truly became a Catholic was less important to Kazin than his sense of her as an unchurched clairvoyant who intuited the "urgent connection between the death of Europe in the second world war and the eclipse of a God embodying the absolute good."

Kazin's spirituality was deeply inflected by his sense of himself as a Jew, but his significant relation was not to Judaism, especially in its institutional form, but to Jewish culture. His son, Michael, himself a distinguished historian of the American labor movement, summed it up: "Everything that he wrote, everything that he was, came out of his being Jewish." Kazin himself said in *New York Jew* that "the Jews are my unconscious."

However, that positive commitment was compatible with his sense of being separated from a positive faith that he craved. Kazin's unchurched spirituality consisted chiefly in an agonized allegiance to his own "inability to believe." That inability and the will to overcome it pervade the pages of Kazin's next-to-last book, *A Lifetime Burning in Every Moment* (1996). (The last book published during his lifetime, *God and the American Writer* [1997], is a set of twelve new essays, on Lincoln and William James as well as classic American poets and novelists. The binding theme is those figures' diverse struggles with God.) *A Lifetime Burning* seems to me the best of Kazin's autobiographical works. In that book we can track his journey from the spiritual-ecstatic, which was implicit in his very early edition of William Blake's poems, to the quasi mystical.

A Lifetime Burning does not suffer, as does Kazin's literary criticism, from a deficiency of general ideas because it is in its form a selection of snippets—cultural observations, prayers, outbursts of feelings—that were culled from the personal journals he conscientiously maintained from 1938 to 1995. The reporter's sharp eye is in as much evidence as the religious yearning, but it is the latter that I want to emphasize because it is the basis of his intensity.

Kazin reveals himself in the journals as a writer painfully sensitive to the divine silence, but also open to the possibility of revelation. Ultimately, he is not as concerned with "mind" as is Trilling, because he is placing his bets elsewhere. In one of the many prayerlike reflections that dot the pages of his last two books, Kazin appeals once again to Blake, uttering this readerly plea that sums up his longing for divine illumination: "But where—how—is the writer to be found who will have the inner certainty to see our life with the eyes of faith, and so make the world shine again?"

However, the core of his spirituality did not derive from Europeans like Blake, Weil, and Czeslaw Milosz, another favorite of his. Neither did it come from the tradition of Jewish sacred writing, although it is possible to think of Kazin as an ecstatic Hasid whose historical connections to the Torah and ritual have been lost. But it is safest to think of him as a writer who went native on his native grounds. The writers who most influenced his spirituality—his "being interested in religion without being religious"—were figures who are generally accepted as central figures in the making of a distinctively American high culture, from Emerson and Whitman to Emily Dickinson to William James. Their writing would always represent a rebuke to media-culture triviality and the tendency of other New York intellectuals to get caught up in transient issues in the politics of culture.

2. Irving Howe

Irving Howe, another near-contemporary of Trilling, had in common with Kazin that for at least two decades they dominated the Sunday *New York Times Book Review* when it came to writing on new American and European fiction and Jewish-related books. I cannot think of any critic since them who has appeared as regularly. Their presence was almost as predictable as that of the weekly reviewers in the Sunday papers in London, Philip Toynbee in the *Observer* and Cyril Connolly in the *Times*. Nowadays, it is commonplace to find British literary-political journalists dominating American magazines and Web sites. Kazin and Howe were rare among American journalist-critics in their immense lucidity. Cynthia Ozick has been their worthy successor among later Jewish essayists writing in the New York intellectual tradition.

Howe did not figure as importantly as Kazin in my own education as a critic. As a critic, I usually found him to be dry, uninspiring, and in his assumptions and interests tangential to my own. I had missed him by a year at Brandeis, where I wound up with Philip Rahv, another New York old-timer, as my dissertation advisor. Howe was like Rahv in aspiring to an overall perspective on literature-and-society and in being absorbed in practical politics in a way that neither Trilling nor Kazin was. His life, as he recorded it in his "intellectual autobiography," *A Margin of Hope* (1982), consisted of a series of public controversies in which opinion was everything.

Howe was the anti-Kazin in that he seldom registered feelings and appeared to have experienced few shining moments. In his polemical writing, the range of affect was narrow; he manifested mainly what he described as "corrosion and distrust." Those feelings owed much to his particular family background, but they were reinforced by the sorry fate in America of democratic socialism, on which he had pinned his hopes from youth. Despite Howe's spirit of exasperation, however, his socialist idealism inspired the loyalty of gifted younger intellectuals. At *Dissent*, his political quarterly, he contributed to the intellectual development of prize-winning younger colleagues like the political theorist Michael Walzer, the literary academic David Bromwich, and the novelist Brian Morton.

Before I discuss what seem to me to be Howe's limitations, I want to pay homage to one of his special qualities. No one of the old left intellectuals was more sheerly *competent*. He wrote valuable full-length critical studies of Sherwood Anderson, William Faulkner, and Thomas Hardy; other books on the history of the Communist Party and Walter Reuther; collections of his own essays in political and literary criticism; and he edited innumerable volumes, including a selection of Trotsky's writings and works of translation from Yiddish poetry and fiction. A full Howe bibliography would probably come to more than a hundred titles, and these books are ably done, at least the many I have read through or of which I have read parts.

Howe was like Trilling in leaving an important intellectual legacy, but not, I think, as a critic who was able to guide readers to the imaginative and emotional depths of the literary works he discussed. Rather, in my view Howe's chief gift to future readers and scholars consists in having introduced them to the riches of *Yiddishkeit*, in the books of translations he edited and in his most famous work, *World of Our Fathers*.

The latter book is a compendium of fascinating information about the lost world of union-organizing, socialist-inclined *Yiddishkeit* on New York's Lower East Side. His dedication to doing justice to that world may have been all the greater because the middle-aged Howe was expiating his youthful rebellion against his parents. As a youth he had fled the parochial world of the Jewish immigrants in favor of cosmopolitan Marxism; just so, in his later years he returned in a rush. His profound disillusionment with the New Left in the 1960s added greater urgency to his effort at retrieving his Jewish past.

Like Kazin, Howe also tried his hand at self-writing. However, his affectless intellectual memoir, *A Margin of Hope*, illustrates Trilling's point that political consciousness can be antithetical to imaginative depth. Howe's kind of absorption in ideological politics is likely to lead an intellectual away from the intimate self-knowledge that Trilling had to such a high degree, and which is necessary for plumbing the deep parts of imagination. Near the end of this 350-page book, Howe devotes a few pages to his father. His avoidance of the personal elsewhere in his autobiography contrasts with Kazin's candor in registering his hurt about his father's muteness in his company. That muteness was a function of the uncrossable gap between many uneducated and emotionally stricken immigrant fathers and their American-born intellectual sons. Although frequently muddled about his emotional life, Kazin was aware of the origins of his yearning for "You the Everlasting." That spiritual longing plainly had its source in his traumatic experience of silence as a very young boy: "Speak, Father, speak!"

It happens that I visited New York shortly after Lionel Trilling's death in 1975, because I had been thinking, even before Trilling died, of writing a book about him and wanted to hear the recollections and opinions of his contemporaries. I met with Jacques Barzun, Clement Greenberg, Will Barrett, Kazin, Howe, and a few others. In general, Howe commented appreciatively about Trilling, but at a certain distance, as he did in *A Margin of Hope* and in various reviews he wrote of Trilling's books. Howe had a complicated relationship with Trilling, though plainly not an adversarial one, as Kazin had. Then, toward the end of our time together, he mentioned in passing that his own father was sick and that he would be going up to the Bronx to see him later that day. It was hard to identify Howe's attitude or emotion in relation to his planned visit. He simply seemed grim and slightly depressed. But I would not have guessed that his father was dying and that this was causing a moral-psychological crisis for the son.

That I learned from the few pages on his father in *A Margin of Hope*. The relevant passage begins: "The day my father died I felt almost nothing." But that blankness itself points to emotional crisis. If Howe had felt more at the time, no doubt he would have devoted more pages to his lifelong ambivalence toward his father than, as he did, to his quarrels in the sixties with the SDS leader Tom Hayden. It is the relationship between the son's frozen affect and the father's inveterately disapproving attitude toward him that Howe's profile both exposes and half-conceals. These are unusually moving pages amidst Howe's huge body of work and make a reader wonder what this autobiography might have been like had the author not insisted, in the rest of it, on being so intellectual and remote. I think he might have been freed up in his literary writing had he plumbed the depths of that early, damaging relationship. As it is, much of his criticism comes across as an addendum to Trilling's writing. Howe reacted against Trilling's tendency toward intellectual abstraction, and he filled in historical contexts where Trilling was frequently moralistic in an ahistorical way. Howe's historicist revisions also brought with them a more overtly political stance.

The consequences for Howe of his father's lifelong disdain for him were complex. He understands, and clearly identifies with, the old man's "gift for discrimination," while at the same time he is crippled because he has internalized the father's conviction that he is not a good and loving person. The son's ambivalence causes him to be evasive at the end; he takes three hours to get to and from his father's hospital but spends only twenty minutes there. He "could not look at his [father's] wasted body, for I knew myself to be unworthy, a son with a chilled heart."

That a person of Howe's integrity and selfless loyalty to the lost cause in America of democratic socialism, that such a person should feel himself at root "unworthy" may shock the reader. But just maybe his internalized sense of self-disdain was itself a major element in his later attachment to so ideal a political goal. But that is impossible to know because Howe makes no connection between his utopian politics and his most intimate emotions. He says, "Even before my father died, I had made him into a myth." And "myth" for Howe, trained in the arts of demystfication, is hardly a positive term, a conduit for imaginative expression. Rather, "Myths are wonderfully convenient for blocking the passage between yourself and your feelings."

It seems that Howe was not directly in touch with the hatred and rage that are inevitably a consequence of such pain as his father had visited on him. His father spent wearying years as a presser in a garment factory. In *World of Our Fathers,* the wounded son turned this weak, abrasive father into the myth of a community that was vital, even if not totally united by shared values. Howe expiated his seemingly suppressed anger toward his father by creating an idealized portrait of a world he once sought only to repudiate. *World of Our Fathers* is a valuable introduction to that world and proved to be Howe's commercially most successful book. But that is because it became a coffee-table icon for assimilated, middle-class Jews, who, like Howe himself, were forever removed from it. That is, notwithstanding the author's intention, *World of Our Fathers* was greeted as a work of cultural piety.

A qualification of my criticism is in order. Howe wrote with affection about that lost world, but he was never uncritical, never schmaltzy, as Kazin was at times in *A Walker in the City.* Indeed, one of his intentions was to supersede the sentimental portrayals of *Yiddishkeit* by Harry Golden and the Broadway musical *Fiddler on the Roof.*

In *A Margin of Hope,* Howe's habit of emotional repression continues to muffle his account of his relationship with his father even though, as he says, it is "the only story I had to tell." Still, the few pages that he gives to this tragic parent-child misunderstanding make me wish he had opened himself more to personal emotion and self-reflection. Instead, as autobiographer he offers us a life in which he rehearses stale opinions about once-controversial, now largely forgotten, figures.

By the end—Howe died in 1993 at seventy-three—he had changed so that his general attitude was closer to Trilling's than at any time before. That is, his taste for left-wing polemics and activism had lessened, and he had come closer to being a familiar enough figure, a liberal humanist. Howe had spent a lifetime fighting over the correct position on this or that, and now he was happy to find some ease. He developed an enthusiasm for George Balanchine's dance company and took time out to reread Rudyard Kipling's *Kim*—and not in the spirit of Edward Said's interpretation of novels and operas in terms of imperialism. Trilling had himself written on *Kim* in the 1940s, and with a similar motive, an attempt to achieve respite from the moral urgencies of the moment.

Howe's series of unsuccessful marriages came to an end; he was married, happily, to Ilana Wiener, an Israeli-born woman with whom he edited a playful anthology of very short fictions, *Short Shorts*. Alienated from American culture, he made friendships with left-leaning Israeli Zionists and found much to engage him in Israeli affairs. One hopes that he came to have a higher view of himself and his lifetime achievement. Howe was not scintillatingly original, but everything he did was solid. I recall teaching one of his edited books, a collection of ten classic modern short fictions by Tolstoy, Kafka, Mann, Forster, and others. I marveled over the usefulness of Howe's introductions to each story and felt sorry that he had left Brandeis too soon for me to derive the benefits of his teaching. If he was a little sour for my taste and rarely addressed my own interests, he was heroic in his capacity for sustained quality work and in his faithfulness to his vocation as a critical intellectual.

The Two Worlds of Cultural Criticism

I.

Why is it that American literary academics interested in a generally left-wing critique of culture are so indifferent nowadays to America's native tradition of radical criticism? More particularly, what happened to induce would-be oppositional critics in this country to look for direction to Frankfurt intellectuals such as Theodor Adorno and Herbert Marcuse rather than to American contemporaries of the Frankfurt

Mark did not select this essay for the collection, and we came upon it, actually on the two essays from which this is cobbled together, in the course of research. But those essays strike us as important statements at a certain time of Mark's life of his ongoing commitment to the New York intellectual ethos, after publishing *Displacement: Derrida and After,* and also his own desire to resurrect the New York intellectual tradition by seeing Edward Said, whom he would later reject on other grounds, and Susan Sontag as carrying on the legacy. Mark wrestled with the New York intellectuals and their bewildering legacy throughout his career, and no account of his career and its trajectory can be complete without at least some of this.

The essay as it appears here is an amalgam of two others, written at about the same time and more or less about the same issue: the need for American critics and their students to rediscover native radical and intellectual roots. Parts 1–3 appeared as "The Two Worlds of Cultural Criticism," in *Criticism in the University,* ed. Gerald Graff and Reginald Gibbons (1985). It was the first volume of the *TriQuarterly* Series on Criticism and Culture. The section on Susan Sontag and the neoconservatives is excerpted from "Criticism as an Institution," in *Crisis of Modernity: Recent Critical Theories of Culture and Society in the United States and West Germany,* ed. Gunther H. Lenz and Kurt L. Shell (1986). The rest of that essay is similar to the one that appeared in Graff and Gibbons. Eds.

School critics such as Lionel Trilling, Philip Rahv, and Harold Rosenberg? It seems odd, on the face of it, that academic critics well informed about the debates centered on Antonio Gramsci, Walter Benjamin, and Mikhail Bakhtin should know next to nothing of the early Van Wyck Brooks and Edmund Wilson or of the New York intellectuals associated with *Partisan Review* in the thirties and forties.

One obvious explanation is that the present generation of literature-and-society academics is, however vaguely, "Marxist," and the New York intellectuals were not. Trilling and Sidney Hook and Clement Greenberg may have started out as Marxists, but they gradually turned away not only from Marxism but also from political radicalism altogether. More recently the New York critics' liberal anticommunism of the 1950s has modulated into neoconservative antiradicalism in the intellectual monthlies edited by Norman Podhoretz *(Commentary)* and Hilton Kramer *(New Criterion)*. It seems to become easier every day for New York writers to overcome the radical piety of their progenitors.

But the conservative mood of some of the New York intellectuals doesn't by itself explain the neglect of Trilling, Rosenberg, et al. in academic literary circles. There is nothing to stop left-wing academic critics from retrieving New York criticism in its more vigorous, more radical phase, between, say, 1935 and the beginnings of the Cold War. Critics have shown themselves able to distinguish between the John Dos Passos of the radical trilogy *U.S.A.* and the later, more conservative Dos Passos. Why, then, the neglect?

The main reason, I think, has to do not with the specific positions of the New York critics but with their intellectual style. Many elements of that style distinguish it from contemporary academic criticism. Above all, the New York style in criticism is unabashedly secular and worldly in outlook, alert to the movements of opinion and aggressive in staking out positions. The pressures of politics make themselves visible in the texture of this writing, which more closely resembles the work of Wilson and George Orwell, say, than R. P. Blackmur and Roland Barthes. New York–style criticism is freewheeling and speculative and gets bored easily. It is bored by the close reading of texts; sometimes it is too easily bored with sustained argument altogether. It relies for its authority on the critic's own voice, not on impersonal method or system. It avoids the fetishism of technique in academic criticism and at its best it also avoids the sometime gentility and mandarinism of the professors.

One of the most important distinctions between criticism in the universities and the older New York criticism is the latter's relative indifference to technical philosophy. In the thirties the Marxism of the American left literary intellectuals was a rough-and-ready affair, philosophically thin and based on a skimpy knowledge of the socialist intellectual tradition. Nowadays, the emphasis in academic Marxist theory is on "theory" as much as on "Marxism," and the new academic Marxism, like the Marxism of the Frankfurt School, is very much a philosophical critique. It is the relative indifference of the *Partisan Review* circle to technical philosophy that separates them from their Frankfurt contemporaries.

Of the most important New York intellectuals only Sidney Hook was a philosopher, and Hook came to Marxism by way of John Dewey rather than by way of Hegel. The German philosophical tradition, as it runs from Kant and Hegel to Nietzsche and Heidegger, was the core of the Frankfurt intellectuals' culture. For Hook, on the other hand, much of that tradition represented simply a collapse into obscurantism and irrationalism. To say that German philosophy was central to the work of the Frankfurt critical theorists is not, of course, to say that they endorsed the tradition without qualification. One has only to think of Adorno's detestation of the post–World War II cult of Heidegger, whom he attacked in his late book *The Jargon of Authenticity* (1964). But Adorno thought it necessary to deal with Heidegger; the New York intellectuals, with the exception of William Barrett, hardly mention him.

One way of measuring the distance between the intellectual styles of Frankfurt and New York is to compare Adorno's philosophical treatment of authenticity with Lionel Trilling's much more literary approach to the question in *Sincerity and Authenticity* (1972). Trilling's book deals with Rousseau, Hegel, Nietzsche, and Sartre, but it is "philosophic" only in the discursive way of the English-speaking man of letters. It's symptomatic that Trilling doesn't even cite Heidegger or Adorno's book on him. Sartre is more to Trilling's point than Heidegger because, like Trilling himself, Sartre was as much a man of letters, a *politique et moraliste*, as a metaphysician.

Enthusiasm for philosophy among the New York intellectuals probably reached its peak in the thirties, when Hook emerged as the leading
American exponent of Marxism and, only a few years later, as its most
formidable philosophical adversary, in his attack on the idea of the
Marxist dialectic. William Barrett, Hook's successor in the philosophy
department at New York University and as resident philosopher at *Partisan Review*, became better known as a popularizer of existentialism
and as a man of letters than as a technical philosopher. The best known
of the New York critics were not philosophers at all but full-time literary
men, and practical critics at that, rather than aestheticians. Nowadays
academic theoreticians celebrate Kenneth Burke, the most dauntingly
philosophical literary man of the thirties. Meanwhile, once-popular
critics like Trilling are discounted because of their lucidity.

The irony is that the New York critics prided themselves on their
zeal for ideas, in contrast with what they thought of as the intellectual
vacuity of genteel academic scholarship. Neither did they subscribe to
the theorized anti-intellectualism of their chief rivals, the New Critics.
Those critics, the progeny of John Crowe Ransom, took their stand in
opposition to generalizing intellect and "abstraction" (which they associated with science and technology), in favor of "imagination" and "sensibility." The New York intellectuals were like the New Critics in being
drawn to concreteness, but they were not shy about abstract ideas and
the inevitable connection of ideas with ideology. Despite their interest in
general ideas, however, by comparison with philosophical academic critics of a later generation, the New York intellectuals seem in retrospect to
have always had about them a touch of the journalist. "Journalist" is a
term of opprobrium in academic literary circles. But after twenty years
of floating about the skies of philosophical abstraction, criticism would
do well to touch down and recover contact with the concrete, ground
level virtues of the older literary journalism. Criticism has forgotten recently that, like literature itself, it must ultimately derive its strength
from contact with the earth.

In the 1970s the Frankfurt intellectuals became a substantial presence in American academic literary theory. The rise of the new academic Marxism, championed by younger critics like Fredric Jameson,
helped to put Adorno and Benjamin on graduate school reading lists.

At the same time the rise of the Frankfurt School was matched by the falling influence of the New York intellectuals. The decline of the New Yorkers' prestige in academic circles was not totally a surprise. Rahv and Howe had always been rather neglected, and Trilling, the most respected of the New York group in the universities, had never been a model for advanced academic criticism. The reason is probably that Trilling had no critical method that could be easily imitated. He had, instead, a certain style, tone, quality of intelligence. Such gifts are not transferable. Many critics have thought to inherit Trilling's mantle, but it has been with him as with F. R. Leavis in England: there have been no true successors.

It was hardly to be expected that Trilling's Arnoldian gracefulness would make him central in a specialist academic culture of professionals and technicians. But there was something new in the seventies. There had always been a small number of academic critics, like W. K. Wimsatt, Eliseo Vivas, and Murray Krieger, who were almost exclusively devoted to theoretical issues. But in the seventies "theory" took on a broader implication and became the focus of advanced criticism. Every academic critic who wanted to be taken seriously was obliged to be concerned with ideas at the highest level of philosophical abstraction.

The change was devastating for the old New York intellectuals, whose general ideas were rarely presented in the language of formal philosophy, and who were more often concerned with practical questions of culture and society than with abstract questions of method and interpretation. These intellectuals were more disposed to deal with large ideas in a glancing way than to engage in sustained theoretical argument. Irving Howe, in his famous essay "The New York Intellectuals," in *Decline of the New,* has described the New York idea of the intellectual life as "freelance dash, peacock strut, daring hypothesis, knockabout synthesis." That seems to me a caricature of the New York critical style, but it does suggest the influence on the New York critics of writing for nonspecialist magazines of opinion. The important thing at *Partisan Review* was to be lucid, lively and "brilliant." It was left for professors to be scholarly, thorough, and (presumably) dull.

The New York intellectuals have sometimes described themselves as if they had been born out of the Depression and the radical movement of the thirties. In fact, they were carrying on the central tradition in

American criticism, which has always been more or less culturally oriented and journalistic. As Geoffrey Hartman has recently observed of the literary situation in the twenties and thirties, which the New York intellectuals inherited: "It was not the universities at all but the journals and magazines that spread what literary culture there was." The result, as Hartman adds, is that what grew up between the world wars was "a culture of journalism, not yet a culture of criticism" (See Hartmann's "The Culture of Criticism," *PMLA* 99 (May 1984)].

Hartman means to point out the limitations of that culture. His point about the American journalist-critics is something like Matthew Arnold's about the English Romantic poets: they did not know enough. Hartman's point seems to me valid. No one is likely to argue that Stuart Sherman and Ludwig Lewisohn possessed the learning or critical acumen of Paul de Man or Hartman himself. Still, that old journalistic criticism has its own virtues. One thinks especially of the passionate sense of nationality and the feeling for the textures of American life that are to be found in the journalistic criticism of successive waves of New York literary intellectuals since the time of Van Wyck Brooks and the young Edmund Wilson.

The question at present, when academic criticism seems to be moving toward the left, is whether "theory" can be adapted to the cultural concerns of that older American tradition of literary-intellectual journalism. We won't know until it's been tried, but we may get a better idea of the difficulties faced by contemporary criticism if we consider what has been happening since the sixties, when "theory" first began to dominate academic literary studies.

2.

The situation of cultural criticism today may be illuminated if we compare it with the situation twenty years ago. For my contrast of then and now, I mean to take as my representative figures Lionel Trilling and Edward Said. For all their marked political and cultural differences, Trilling and Said do share a distinctive New York intellectual style. And it's convenient for the contrast I wish to show that Said is now the leading literary intellectual at Columbia University, as Trilling was up to the time of his death in 1975.

Trilling was born in 1905 and formed his characteristic stance as a critic during the ideological battles over Marxism in the 1930s. Although Trilling was teaching at Columbia in the thirties, the university was not his whole world. In that decade the avant-garde was still a minority culture and a genuine alternative to the official culture of the universities. There were the true producers of art and culture, and opposed to them were the professors of literature, fuddy-duddies such as hardly exist anymore in a pure form. The professors of old were gentlemen scholars piously defending "civilization" against barbarism. By the mid-sixties, all this had changed. The decorous spokesmen for "traditional values" were more likely in the sixties to be found among the contributors and editors of nonacademic middlebrow magazines than among the ranks of influential academic critics. And professors of literature who wanted to think of themselves as "radical" or "advanced" no longer were obliged to look beyond their own campuses. Everything—creative writing, continental theory, and radical politics—was taking place within the university. Demographic shifts, together with capitalism's success in diffusing and diluting the styles of modernism, had brought about a mass youth culture. In this great democratic nation the young were all in the universities, and the most fractiously antinomian of them seemed to be taking Lionel Trilling's course in modern literature at Columbia.

Suddenly the university had become the world. The introduction to *The Liberal Imagination* (1950) shows that Trilling had been concerned in the late forties about the bureaucratization and Stalinization of the liberal mind. As the cold war got underway, politics was something more than the politics of one or another theory of interpretation, which is what politics often means in recent academic criticism. Trilling's major essays after 1948 were written in the shadow of great spy trials like that of Alger Hiss, which was hardly an academic affair. His singleton novel, *The Middle of the Journey* (1947), had uncannily prophesied just such an ideological confrontation as was later exposed by the Hiss case and the split within the intellectual community that was a consequence of that case.

Compare Trilling's introduction of 1950 with his introduction to *Beyond Culture* (1965), where he speaks of the chancellor of the University of California system and his grandiose vision of the super-university to come. In 1965 Trilling was worried not about Stalinism but about the cultural imperialism of the new American multiuniversity, where everything, including the old culture of subversion, was being institutionalized and legitimized. Trilling wrote uneasily of "the new circumstances in which the adversary culture of art and thought now exists." His anxiety about the university as the new focus of intellectual life only increased after 1965.

Trilling spent fifty years of his life at Columbia, with very few breaks from his freshman year in 1921 to his death in 1975. Yet up to the sixties he never wrote about teaching or about the academic context of literary studies. Nothing seemed duller to *Partisan Review* intellectuals than problems of pedagogy. They were "intellectuals" in their self-conception, not schoolteachers. But in the sixties Trilling was able to overcome his embarrassment about taking seriously the academic context of criticism. Half the essays in *Beyond Culture* are about problems of teaching and learning, and there is a similar preoccupation with the humanities and the problems of teaching literature in the essays published posthumously in *The Last Decade: Essays and Reviews, 1965–75.*

It may also suggest Trilling's shift of focus that he published no fewer than four textbooks for the college classroom between 1967 and 1973. These include two anthologies jointly edited with Harold Bloom: *Romantic Poetry and Prose* and *Victorian Prose and Poetry;* another anthology, *Literary Criticism: An Introductory Reader,* and, most importantly, *The Experience of Literature,* a thirteen-hundred-page reader with longish commentaries by Trilling on many of the selections. This textbook, which had been over ten years in the making, sums up in canonical form Trilling's taste and the taste of an entire generation of New York critics. Now that the politics of canon-formation has become a popular subject of criticism, Trilling's reader is worth another look. It is indispensable for anyone concerned with how modernism was transformed from a genuinely adversary culture into an academic tradition.

What happens when the university becomes the whole world? I think the case can be made that Trilling's turn to pedagogy was not a flight from the great world to the ivory tower. For the university in the sixties was no longer a sanctuary from the worldly world and its corruptions. It was the decisive context of intellectual life, as the Communist Party had been in New York thirty years before. Still, the university is not really the whole world, and Trilling's writing in the sixties revealed a certain abandonment of the large political-cultural issues he had discussed in the forties. More and more Trilling's literary criticism forfeited its grip on contemporary society in shifting its focus to "the self." His writing suffered a corresponding loss of concreteness and vividness as it came to be haunted by Hegelian abstractions. There was a price to be paid for the academicization of criticism.

One might suggest that price by referring not to any literary theorist of the sixties but to a novelist, John Barth, and his most representative fiction, *Giles Goat-Boy* (1966). This is a comic novel about the university as world, which, not coincidentally, is also a novel about narcissism, solipsism, and the price of living exclusively in your own head. Barth was typical of the new academic culture in that his brilliant inventiveness, his proliferation of fictions, was not deflected to the slightest degree by the resistance of politics, history, or social actuality. Confined within itself, whether as fun house or prison house, the mind can enjoy the fantasied omnipotence inseparable from its actual impotence. Literary theory, inspired by renewed interest in the great Romantic mythmakers, showed a similar preoccupation with the gap between art and life and a similar turn to pure subjectivity. Blake and Shelley had by no means been indifferent to the situation of English society, but their North American academic expositors took over the High Romantic faith in imagination as redemptive without adequately acknowledging the historical world that needed to be redeemed. Harold Bloom's postmodern gnosticism shared with T. S. Eliot's incarnationist Christianity a profound revulsion against history and nature alike.

3.

One difference between the generation of critics influenced by T. S. Eliot and the generation of critics influenced by Harold Bloom is summed up in the word "theory." In speaking of the present generation of critics, I have in mind a group of men and women born between 1930 and 1950 whom we can associate with two major tendencies of the sixties: the emergence of continental theory in university departments of literature and the revival of radical politics. Edward Said is a senior member of this group and came to the new theory largely on his own. His first book, a phenomenological study of Joseph Conrad, appeared

in 1967, only a few years after Geoffrey Hartman's important phenomenological study of Wordsworth. And *Beginnings: Intention and Method*
in 1975 established Said as a pioneering figure among American critics
mediating the new French theory.

Said the literary critic has frequently been dealt with severely by
critics distrustful of his specific political aims. There is reason for caution. Said has shown himself to be a tough and provocative spokesman
on behalf of Palestinian nationalism. It's probably true to say that at
some level all of Said's writing promotes that cause. I think, however,
that his literary work exists at a different level than his political pamph-
leteering and deserves to be treated on its own terms.

What we see when we approach Said without prejudice is that his
early work emerges from the hypertheoretical context of sixties academic literary studies. His Conrad book, originally written as a doctoral dissertation in comparative literature at Harvard, is markedly different in its theoretical assumptions from the criticism of Harry Levin,
Harvard's chief comparatist in those years. But the book is not really
very threatening. It is marked by an apolitical, sixtiesish academic concern with personal identity summed up in its title: *The Fiction of Autobiography*. It largely stays away from politics.

Neither is Said's next book, *Beginnings*, directly polemical in the
manner of his more recent writing. The book is full of virtuoso readings
of nonliterary figures like Freud as well as canonical figures such as
Milton and Dickens and Hopkins, but the strongest impression the
book leaves is of an ingenious mind as much drawn to problems of theory as to literature itself. The problem for such a mind is going to be
how to free itself from the trammels of its own impulse to abstraction.
Putting forward a politically minded theorist like Michel Foucault in
opposition to an unrelievedly ironizing theorist like Jacques Derrida, as
Said does in *Beginnings,* is not going to solve his problem. That problem is to overcome the critical heritage of the sixties and find a language for talking about politics and the common world. The problem,
as I would put it, is how to reconcile the theoretical sophistication of
academic criticism with the political-cultural savvy of the old New York
intellectuals.

Orientalism (1978), which is Said's best book so far, is one approach
to such a reconciliation. This book is an ambitious critique of Western

scholarship on Islam since the time of Napoleon. Apart from its interest as a revelation of European stereotypes about the Arabs, it has been very influential in directing critical attention to the history and ideology of literary studies as an institution. As advanced academic critics in English and comparative literature grow more and more self-conscious about the circumstances of their own profession, the book's influence can only become more pervasive.

When the book appeared, Said's relentless attention to the "discourse" of Orientalism caused him to be widely regarded as an American epigone of Foucault. In fact, however, Said's study may be less close in spirit to Foucault than to the classic humanism of German literary philologists such as Erich Auerbach and Georg Curtius, and to the American variant of that humanism in the work of such New York writers as Trilling. Said turns out to be a traditional humanist in denying that impersonal systems of language and power can explain Orientalism as a discursive system. His final appeal is always to human agency and efficacy. Also, whereas Foucault relies on a philosophy of language that stresses difference, Said's chief objection to Western scholarship on Islam is that it makes the Arabs out to be too different and thereby denies their common humanity.

Said's "humanism" mixes oddly with his Nietzchean-Foucauldian emphasis on power and may be thought evidence of his lack of philosophical rigor. It can also be seen as an attempt to rescue the foundation of a positive politics. For if language does all the work, it's hard to see how men and women can bring about historical change. Whatever the reasons may be, the effect in Said's writing is a new methodological eclecticism, wholly unlike the rigor of theoreticians such as Foucault, Derrida, and de Man. Like Trilling in his best essays, Said now uses whatever helps him deal with the job at hand: New Critical close reading, Frankfurt-type ideology critique, psychobiography, cultural anthropology, old-fashioned history of ideas.

Said's collection of essays entitled *The World, the Text, and the Critic* shows where he may be coming out. These essays don't achieve the concision and pointedness of Trilling's essays in *The Liberal Imagination*. Nor would Trilling much care for Said's political attitudes. But the books have a great deal in common. Said's struggle to bring his philosophical interests to bear on immediate cultural issues is bringing him ever closer in method and tone to New York–style cultural criticism and setting him apart from an increasingly ghostly theoreticism, including Marxist theoreticism, in the university. (See Said's "Reflections on American 'Left' Literary Criticism," in *The World, the Text, and the Critic* [Cambridge, Mass.: Harvard University Press, 1983].)

What Said seems to be working toward is suggested in his complaints about recent criticism on Jonathan Swift:

> My impression is that too many claims are made for Swift as a moralist and thinker who peddled one or another final view of human nature, whereas not enough claims are made for Swift as a kind of local activist, a columnist, a pamphleteer, a caricaturist. . . . It is as if critics assume that Swift really wanted to be a John Locke or a Thomas Hobbes, but somehow couldn't: therefore it becomes a critic's job to help Swift fulfill his ambition, turning him from a kind of marginal, sporty political fighter into a pipesmoking armchair philosopher.

Now, the fact is that Said himself is some way from achieving the "sportiness" he praises in Swift. Rather, his collected essays reflect the difficulty for academic critics of our moment to get out from under the burden of theory and method: Once the social-historical world is lost to criticism, it's not so easy to recover it.

That's why "world" appears so frequently in these essays. The thesis statement appears early and often: "Texts have ways of existing that even in their most rarefied form are always enmeshed in circumstances: time, place, and society, in short, they are in the world, and hence worldly." It's a measure of academic criticism's loss of the world that such a truism needs to be repeated so many times. Said complains of contemporary criticism that "it has achieved its methodological independence by forfeiting an active situation in the world." A few pages later, he says that "contemporary critical discourse is worldless."

But what is this "world" to which criticism is being recalled? It is striking that a critic whose life has been shaped by the traumas of international politics should be so abstract in setting out his agenda for a politically and culturally oriented criticism. Nothing appears more difficult, in the present age of theory, than the recovery of the old, un-self-conscious conviction of the world's actuality. In his abstractness Said is representative of the situation of contemporary criticism. Even in moving toward the flexible, worldly style of the old New York intellectuals, he carries the burden of academic theoreticism. He is abstract in arguing against abstraction and theoretical in decrying the excesses of theory.

Certainly criticism needs to move worldward. The danger is that when American literary intellectuals get involved with politics they often betray their vocation as intellectuals in their zeal to be tough-mindedly practical. The record of radical criticism in America is marred by excursions into simple-minded progressivism and American-style Stalinism. Despite misgivings, however, one welcomes the new, world-lier criticism. It has been forty years since the New York intellectuals provided America with its last important body of social-cultural criticism written from the point of view of unspecialized men and women of letters. During the past two decades the dominant forms of literary criticism have offered very little encouragement to anyone concerned with the material circumstances of art. With the exhaustion of the recent wave of aesthetic formalism, academic critics have the opportunity now to retrieve the mainline American tradition of cultural criticism. Inevitably, in an academic milieu, the older style of criticism will be to some degree academicized and subjected to theoretical elaboration. It's hard to imagine any contemporary academic critic saying again what T. S. Eliot once said, that the best method for the critic is simply to be very intelligent. But there is at least the possibility that American academic intellectuals may be able to restore criticism to a larger, more confident role in the general life of the culture.

4. The New Sensibility and Neoconservatism

Susan Sontag's career has great symbolic importance in the transformation of the New York scene in the '60s. Her position in *Against Interpretation* (1966), her first and most influential book, can be summed up quickly by saying that she puts forward the aestheticizing tradition of Oscar Wilde and Roland Barthes in opposition to the dominant Freudian-Marxist tradition of the New York School. The New York intellectuals were mostly secular Jewish moralists who took their inspiration from these earlier German-speaking moralists, "non-Jewish Jews," as Isaac Deutscher has called them. Sontag sought to replace the drive toward hidden meanings of the great Jewish moralists with the surface satisfactions of camp aestheticism and irony. In her "Notes on 'Camp'" in 1964, Sontag tries to make the case for the cultivated unseriousness of pop art as antidote to the moralizing, historicist consciousness of the ruling patriarchs of New York. There was a large measure of naughtiness in Sontag's defiance of the Jewish intellectual fathers. But there was also considerable prudence. Sontag was writing for *Partisan Review* in the early '60s, and she made what appears to be an effort not to give offense. Thus, despite her generally polemical tone in *Against Interpretation,* she never mentions by name any of the dominant figures associated with that magazine. All the same, Trilling might well have considered himself the particular target of Sontag's attack on what she called "the Matthew Arnold notion of culture," which she dismisses as "historically and humanly obsolescent." The Jewish fathers she singles out for cavil are all European Marxists: Lukacs, Benjamin, Adorno, and Lucien Goldmann, who are said to fail to appreciate art as art rather than as documents for sociological, cultural, moral, and political discussion.

A decade later, Sontag reversed herself on Adorno and Benjamin. In her book *On Photography* (1977), without acknowledging the shift in position, she is quite as moralistic and historicizing in outlook as any of the European Marxists she had attacked in the years of her celebration of mere surfaces. The reversal is nearly total. Freedom from moralism had made the visual arts seem so liberating in the mid-1960s, but now Sontag perceives that freedom as their most dangerous and enslaving feature: "Whatever the moral claims made on behalf of photography, its main effect is to convert the world into a department store or museum without walls, in which every subject is depreciated into an article of consumption, promoted into an item for aesthetic consumption. Through the camera people become customers or tourists of reality."

Art for art's sake had taken a terrible fall. High culture now needed to be defended because pop culture had triumphed all too completely. As Trilling had lived to be horrified by the transformation of cultural modernism, which he championed, into "modernism in the streets," which he deplored, so Sontag came to see cinema and photography increasingly absorbed into the culture of consumption. A serious critic despite her celebration in the '60s of the arts of unseriousness, Sontag saw in the '70s that her praise of pop culture at the expense of the traditional literary arts simply confirmed the general direction of modern mass society. She had helped to put herself and her fellow New York intellectuals out of business. Who needs critics in a culture of hype? Thus Sontag's reconciliation in the '70s with the high-culture intellectuals she had defied ten years before.

But it isn't this older, more mature Sontag that I am concerned with here but the Sontag of the '60s, the age of Marshall McLuhan and *Understanding Media.* That Sontag frightened older New York male writers and intellectuals, who interpreted her aesthetic polemic as an attempt to write their death notice. Even those, like Irving Howe, who conceded that the earlier movement of New York writing had exhausted itself, wanted to see their generation die in its own way, not pushed over the side but buried with solemn obsequies. In an essay of 1968, Howe lashes out against a whole new generation, symbolized by Sontag, that wants "works of literature—though literature may be the wrong word—that will be as absolute as the sun, as unarguable as orgasm, and as delicious as a lollipop." What offended Howe was Sontag's indifference to the historical experience of the older generation, for most of whom Marxism, the Depression, and the Holocaust had been the major formative events and influences.

Sontag's insurgency has been valuable because it has irritated older, more conservatively disposed writers to articulate their own conception of what, ideally, it had once meant to be a New York intellectual. Howe himself has been a socialist through the whole of his career, but his position on "the adversary culture" was not very different from that of the neoconservatives, against whom he was also polemicizing about the same time. Howe's attack on Sontag was recently taken up in a new neoconservative magazine, the *New Criterion.* That magazine, founded in 1982, has dedicated itself mainly to fighting the battles that originated twenty years earlier. Susan Sontag has herself implicitly disavowed much of what she said twenty years ago, but the *New Criterion* needs to keep that younger Sontag alive as its chief reason for being. In a position paper in the *New Criterion's* first issue, its editor, Hilton Kramer, was still worrying about Sontag's "Notes on 'Camp,'" which first appeared in 1964. Kramer's comments on Sontag are worth quoting at length, because they sum up the cultural neoconservatism that aims to represent the legacy of the older New York writers.

This important essay ["Notes on 'Camp'"] can now be seen to have performed for critical discourse a service very much akin to that which Pop Art performed for the fine arts. It severed the link between high culture and high seriousness that had been a fundamental tenet of the modernist ethos. It released high culture from its obligation to be entirely serious, to insist on difficult standards, to sustain an attitude of unassailable rectitude. It relaxed the tension that had always existed between the fierce moral imperative of modernism—its critical conscience—and its appetite for novel aesthetic gratifications. "The whole point of Camp," Miss Sontag wrote, "is to dethrone the serious," thereby defining the special temper of postmodernist culture.

"Entirely serious . . . difficult standards . . . unassailable rectitude": these were integral to the style and attitude of the older New York intellectuals. Irving Howe's 1968 essay mainly takes that high seriousness for granted. In characterizing the intellectual style of the older generation of New York writers, Howe speaks, instead, of "a style of brilliance," a style marked above all by a certain exhibitionism: "A kind of writing highly self-conscious in mode, with an unashamed vibration of bravura and display. Nervous, strewn with knotty or flashy phrases, impatient with transitions and other concessions to dullness, willfully calling attention to itself . . . fond of rapid twists, taking pleasure in dispute, dialectic, dazzle—such, at its best or most noticeable, was the essay cultivated by the New York writers."

This has to be taken with a grain of salt, like Howe's similarly flamboyant description of the New York idea of the intellectual life as "freelance dash, peacock strut, daring hypothesis, knockabout synthesis." Such epithets make good copy, but they apply only to a very few in the group, Dwight Macdonald perhaps or the art critic Harold Rosenberg. The style of the New York intellectuals, including Irving Howe's own style most of the time, was plainspoken, lucid, and above all "serious." Their prose was generally closer to the plainness and modesty of George Orwell, say, than the preening of R. P. Blackmur. The rather Victorian upbringing of these children of East European immigrants and their detestation of totalitarianism both fascist and communist disposed them to what I would call a style of decency. None, perhaps, was as self-conscious in vaunting his plainness as Orwell, an old Etonian who by his style as much as his arguments devoted himself to opposing other old Etonians who had gone on to Oxford and become Stalinists, early examples of radical chic. But the New Yorkers have in common with Orwell a remarkably sustained, explicit concern with goodness, humaneness, and compassion. It's odd that Howe doesn't call attention to this quality of their style and this moral preoccupation, especially given his own often-reiterated appeal to a vague ideal he calls Menschlichkeit.

A strong feeling about what is becoming to man as man—the male chauvinism in that formulation is intrinsic to New York writing—appears in Trilling's modernist will to absolute freedom; in Meyer Schapiro's insistence on the humanity, not just the formal features, of abstract painting, and in Delmore Schwartz's "Russian" feeling for saintliness. It appears also in polemics, such as Philip Rahv's dissent on Jean Genet and Howe's attack on the cult of "unobstructed need" of the '60s. Of course, to speak of the humanism of the New York intellectuals is not to say that they were individually nicer or kinder than other writers, such as those who affirm a postmodernist antihumanism. Certainly Delmore Schwartz was anything but saintly himself, and Irving Howe has not always been menschlich in his polemics. And a Frankfurt Marxist might well consider the New York intellectuals' humanism a form of false consciousness, moralism in the service of social and political conformism.

Edmund Wilson and Gentile Philo-Semitism

Inquiry into Edmund Wilson's ideas about the Jews has led me to believe that Wilson's statements about Jews tell as much about him as about their ostensible subject. Turning to ancient Jewish history was a way for this old-stock American, who had been reared as a Presbyterian, to affirm his links to his ancestral tradition without affirming his ancestors' theology. Wilson wound up identifying with the Jews as had his New England Calvinist forebears. Thinking of himself as a kind of Jew gave him a dignified alternative to what seemed to him the cheapness and light-mindedness of twentieth-century American culture.

Matthew Arnold's opposition of Hebraism and Hellenism remains a central topos of Western civilization. The opposition of Athens and Jerusalem appears also in the writings of Heinrich Heine, from whom it came down to Arnold. Heine was concerned with real Hebrews, including himself insofar as he was torn between his Jewish origins and his ambition to be accepted as a European poet. But the "Hebraism" Arnold had in mind was that of the English Nonconformists who were his contemporaries. For Arnold, Hebraism stood for strict observance of divine law, as embodied in the English Puritan moral tradition. "Hellenism," its opposite, stood for "culture" in what was for Arnold its most positive sense, as the free play of the mind.

This essay was first published in *Edmund Wilson: Centennial Reflections*, edited by Lewis M. Dabney.

Wilson himself was an inheritor of the old Christian way of thinking about Jews, that is, thinking typologically, figuratively, or in any other way that satisfied the needs of Christian supersessionist apologetics. Like Arnold, he had a Hebraism of his own. He started out in the 1920s with many of the social prejudices characteristic of his upper-middle-class WASP background. But Wilson transcended the limits of that culture in the course of his lifetime. Unlike Arnold, he had the chance to know many Jews. Most striking, in view of the conventional prejudices of his social class and his generation, Wilson usually liked the Jewish literary intellectuals, academics, and publishers with whom he rubbed elbows. Among the friends whose company he most enjoyed were Isaiah Berlin, Daniel Aaron, Leon Edel, Alfred Kazin, and Jason Epstein. What makes the congeniality surprising is that Wilson's heyday, the period 1920–50, is often thought of as the age of T. S. Eliot, who made Christian orthodoxy fashionable in literary studies and who famously thought too many freethinking Jews undesirable in an ideal Christian society. The Jewish writers for whom Wilson served as a model or mentor or just plain friend were usually deeply devoted. And with reason. It's hard to think of another Anglo-American literary person of Wilson's time who was as philo-Semitic as he.

That doesn't mean Wilson liked every Jew he met. What he celebrated was a certain idea of the Jews. To understand that idea we need to turn to Wilson's view of his American Calvinist inheritance and his conscious effort, in the post–World War II period, to retrieve his American spiritual legacy. We have to start with his state of mind in the 1940s. Wilson had spent most of the Depression years researching and writing *To the Finland Station*, but by the time he reached the end of that book he had decisively turned against Marxism and lost most of his interest in socialism. Like many other former leftists, he responded to his loss by turning inward. The evidence of that turning is *The Wound and the Bow* (1941), a loosely "Freudian" book that brings together seven essays on writers who had experienced emotional turmoil yet, like Sophocles' Philoctetes, found a compensating strength.

At the end of the war, Wilson toured a devastated Europe and wrote a travel report, *Europe without Baedeker* (1947), which is remarkable for its Schadenfreude over the drab, depressing, postwar scene. In addition to reaffirming his distaste for the British establishment, he was announcing the cultural bankruptcy of Europe. The effect of two world wars was to persuade him that the Old World was quite as unregenerate as his American forebears had believed. Wilson wrote much less about European subjects after 1945. Although he continued to travel abroad, the last three decades of his literary life mark a coming home. The literary historian who had written pioneering studies of Proust and Joyce turned now to the writing of Ambrose Bierce and Mary Chesnut. The socialist who had admired Marx and Lenin in *To the Finland Station* devoted the 1950s to such national heroes as Ulysses S. Grant and Robert E. Lee. Even when Wilson did write about non-American topics, his mood was retrospective. Typical of his last collection of essays, *The Bit between My Teeth* (1965), are the eccentric and "oldfogeyish" (Wilson's word for himself in these years) reconsiderations of minor, distinctly nonmodernist figures who had been popular in his youth. During his last two decades, he also explored Western societies that were dissident in relation to mainline culture and centralized governments. The travel book *Red, Black, Blond and Olive* (1956), which succeeds *Europe without Baedeker*, contains substantial sections on Haiti and the Zuni Indians of the American Southwest. Wilson subsequently wrote entire books on marginalized groups, like the Iroquois, who used to roam the region around his upstate New York family home and the French Canadians of Quebec. These are the years in which he was most engaged with the Jews, who also appear in his writing as a minority culture crushed by successive imperial powers, down to the Nazis in our time. Wilson studied the Jews partly to learn what had enabled them to survive.

In *Patriotic Gore* he is the historian of the fate of American Calvinism in the developments leading up to the Civil War and in its aftermath. The question to which he kept returning was this: How did old stock Americans, people like himself who had been brought up on an older creed, adjust to the plutocratic America that followed the Civil War? His Civil War book occupied him on and off for about fifteen years. Wilson shows a certain sympathy for the Old South, which appears as yet another minority culture victimized by the central state, but his major focus is on the North, including the abolitionists, who provided what he considered an ideological cover for the North's drive for expansion. The sections on northern writers like Harriet Beecher Stowe allowed him to consider the role of Calvinism in the abolitionist crusade and, by a curious route, take up the ancient Israelite component in New England Calvinism and in his own family's tradition.

This would seem to be an unusual way by which to come to philo-Semitism. But of all the proud, dissenting groups Wilson praised in the postwar period, it was the Jews who appear from his writing to have mattered most. There are many threads in his romance with the Jews. He writes in *Patriotic Gore* about the Old Testament scholar Calvin Ellis Stowe, the husband of Harriet Beecher, who so identified with the ancient Israelites that Harriet sometimes referred to him as "my poor rabbi." Wilson himself was descended from the first New England Puritans; Cotton Mather, like Calvin Stowe in wearing a skullcap in his study, was a collateral ancestor. These early Americans, as Wilson frequently pointed out, had thought of themselves as latter-day Israelites who had come to the New World as to Canaan. "The Puritanism of New England," he writes, "was a kind of new Judaism, a Judaism transposed into Anglo-Saxon terms. These Protestants, in returning to the text of the Bible, had concentrated on the Old Testament, and some had tried to take it as literally as any Orthodox Jews." Believing themselves to have been chosen by God for their "errand into the wilderness," the Puritans conceived their leaving England as a latter-day Exodus from Egyptian enslavement. In the New World, they felt themselves, like Abraham, to be bound in a covenant with God, and conducted themselves as if charged with being a light unto the nations.

One theme never explicitly spelled out but implicit in Wilson's autobiographical essays and in his biographical portraits is that of chosenness. Although Wilson had no use for Calvinist theology, he retained, in a secularized form, a sense of having been marked for a special destiny. David Castronovo has pointed out that "Bible study and the pride of being set apart from less serious people were very definite features of [Wilson's] early life." He may have disliked his grandmother's religious lessons when he was a boy, but his memoirs make clear his pride in a tradition that included successive generations of doctors and lawyers, including his own father, Edmund Wilson Sr., who was attorney general of New Jersey when Woodrow Wilson was its governor. That long line of ministers and professional men on both sides of the family had been deeply marked by their Calvinist inheritance. Edmund Wilson Jr. identified with that heritage, of which he was a nonbelieving continuator.

Jews and Judaism have a long and various history, intermixed during the Diaspora with most of the peoples of the world, but Wilson's philo-Semitism was selective, even when it came to Jewish intellectuals. He respected Trilling and encouraged Kazin. On the other hand, he was always slightly snobbish about Philip Rahv, William Phillips, and *Partisan Review*, which in the '30s he sometimes referred to as "Partisansky Review." Neither did he often write on the Jewish authors discovered by *PR*, such as Saul Bellow, Bernard Malamud, and Delmore Schwartz. He was interested in kinds of Jewishness that connected with his understanding of his Calvinist inheritance. For example, there is no evidence of his having been much interested in the Eastern European culture of *Yiddishkeit,* the New York immigrant variant of which Irving Howe studied in *World of Our Fathers.* In his essay on S. Y. Agnon, Wilson refers in passing to the "Yiddish humorists." But it is ancient Jewish writing in Hebrew that he mainly cared about, not modern writing in Hebrew or Yiddish. Nor did he make a special study of Sephardic Jewry. Most important, Wilson had almost nothing to say about the Holocaust, and when he did declare himself on the topic, he could seem chillingly detached. Alfred Kazin wrote me (July 21, 1995) that Wilson once remarked to him during World War II that it was useless for the Jews to try to fight Hitler, since so many of them "had already been exterminated."

We see, then, that much of what Jews consider Jewish is not dreamt of in Wilson's philosophy. What then does he honor? The answer is: everything that has points of contact with his post-Protestant commitment, especially that which may be derived from the Old Testament. Wilson's idea of the Jews is continuous with that of his Puritan forebears. For example, he responded powerfully to the people of modern-day Israel, seeing them, rather romantically, as in the same mold as the Hebrews of the Bible. Thus the appeal to him of Yigael Yadin, an archaeologist who did major work on the Dead Sea Scrolls and was later his nation's military chief of staff. One corollary of Wilson's attraction to the epical biblical Jew is that he was not much amused by the figure, so common in Jewish American writing, of the *pintele yid,* the "little Jew." An exception is his pleasure in the comedy sketches of Elaine May and Mike Nichols. Another exception is Agnon, who wrote about the lost world of the shtetl, in which the schlemiel was a familiar type.

More typical is Wilson's famous "Dissenting Opinion on Kafka" of 1947. To Wilson, Kafka was too intent on being defeated to be the great writer of the modern age; Wilson thought him "unfortifying." But he took to Agnon, whose fiction had the warmth and human interest and reflected the faith that Kafka quite lacked. His way of praising Agnon is to link him to the Bible—he declares himself ready to accept Agnon as a "true representative of that great line of Jewish writers that begins with the authors of Genesis."

Genesis marks the beginning of the Bible and also of Wilson's significant relationship with Judaism and the Jews. His superb essay "On First Reading Genesis" (1954) echoes in its title Keats's poem "On First Looking into Chapman's Homer." Both essay and poem are about the excitements of language. But whereas Keats had read Homer in Chapman's Elizabethan English, Wilson believed that no one really knows Genesis who has not read it in the original. From the very first sentence, his emphasis is on the Hebrew language: "I discovered a few years ago, in going through the attic of my mother's house, an old Hebrew Bible that had belonged to my grandfather, a Presbyterian minister, as well as a Hebrew dictionary and a Hebrew grammar." In 1952, well before he had thought of going to Israel to report on the Dead Sea Scrolls, he was studying Hebrew at the Princeton Theological Seminary, where a century earlier his paternal grandfather, Thaddeus Wilson, had matriculated before becoming a Presbyterian minister.

His most interesting observations on reading Genesis concern the lack of conventional verb tenses in Hebrew. He compares the Hebrew time sense with that in Russian, another language he had taught himself, and concludes that what has allowed the Jews to survive is their "sense of persistent values." The language itself conveys the "dimension of eternity." Wilson also discovers "the perdurable" in the characters of the Hebrew alphabet, which have "the look of having been once cut in stone." His fascination with even the mass and shape of Hebrew characters links him to the Jewish kabbalists, with whom he otherwise has little in common. Altogether, his unqualified enthusiasm makes it possible to understand how his Anglo-Jewish friend Isaiah Berlin can have remembered Wilson as taking "more interest . . . in Hebrew [than] anyone I have ever known who was not himself a Jew."

Wilson is not the first instance of a Protestant scholar's coming to a greater appreciation of the Jews through a fascination with their language. The Israeli historian David S. Katz has written of the Jews' return to England in 1655. England's Jews had been expelled by King Edward I in 1290 and were readmitted during the Puritan protectorate of Oliver Cromwell. Katz writes that sympathy for actual, living Jews grew out of the Reformation-inspired zeal to read the Word of God in the language in which His Book had been written: "Christians after the Reformation were left alone with the Word, and in order to understand it without priestly intermediaries they were forced to arm themselves with the proper tools, including a basic knowledge of Hebrew. As was the case everywhere that Hebrew studies flourished, Christian interest in the Old Testament inevitably created a climate of theological opinion which attracted Jews, converted or otherwise." It wasn't only that Jews were needed to gain philological competence in dealing with the biblical text. It was believed by some Christian scholars that "God created the universe by speaking Hebrew: 'Let there be light,' He said, and suddenly all of existence came into being." It was thought that Hebrew held within itself the secrets of the cosmos, and thus the Jews held the keys to unlock these mysteries. I don't wish to suggest that Wilson himself entertained any such mystical conceptions of language — no one is likely to confuse him with his near contemporary, Walter Benjamin. Neither do I attribute to Wilson a religious belief he clearly didn't have, as a skeptic about all religions. But what may appear idiosyncratic in Wilson's ideas of the Jews and Judaism appears much less strange when we understand it in the context of Calvinism's high valuation of the Old Testament and its emphasis on the importance of Hebrew in studying God's word.

It will be obvious, then, that in arguing for Wilson's self-conscious affiliation with his New England Puritan ancestors, I am not saying that he sympathized with their theology or their supernaturalism. Indeed, it has seemed to me at times that one reason Wilson praised the Jews as much as he did was his defiant identification with a people who refused, as he did, to accept Jesus as the Messiah. Jason Epstein had his doubts about the relation of Wilson's idea of the Jews to reality, doubts Wilson recorded in his journals of *The Sixties:* "Jason out of tune and grumbling, thought I overrated the Jews, on account of the New England identification with them; [in Jason's view] they were really awful people." Many Jews have expressed themselves as Epstein does about other Jews, as have blacks about other blacks, and so on. More important for my present purpose than Epstein's "grumble" is his seeing that Wilson's idea of the Jews was romantic and literary, though we ought to add that it was much more realistic than that of Cromwell's British contemporaries, most of whom had never met a real-life Jew.

One is aware, on reading what Wilson has to say about Israelis, both in his book on the Dead Sea Scrolls and in his travel writing, that he was always looking at this country through the lens of his reading, not only of the Bible but of everything else he could find about ancient Jewish history. The scholar James Sanders believes that Wilson's careful reading of Pliny, Philo, and Josephus about the ancient Essenes still "commands respect as a general account of the topic." What he responds to in the Israelis is their heroic fealty to the past. According to Wilson, they refer everything they do to events that happened on the same terrain four thousand years before. He is clear-eyed enough to see that at times this confusion of present and past has negative implications. Thus Wilson registers his disapproval of a certain Israeli "moral fanaticism" and "narrowness" that have their origins in the Bible. Apropos the Israelis' treatment of the Palestinian Arabs, he notes "signs of returning to the callous intolerance of the Israelites in relation to the people they dispossessed." Sometimes, however, he is himself as indifferent to the suffering of the Arabs as any modern-day Israeli settler on the West Bank.

Nothing in Wilson's background disposed him to concern for the Arabs. It was the Israelis he admired, and curiously, in view of his own militant atheism, he admired them most for their faith. "It is the faith that keeps Israel going and that has allowed her to take all these problems on, the faith of the Jewish prophets from Moses to Aaron David Gordon [an important early Zionist who argued the dignity of manual labor], and the loyalty of contemporary Israelis to this." It should be kept in mind in reading such an endorsement (for Wilson, uncharacteristically warm) that he was responding to the Israel of 1955, when the state was only seven years old and still animated by the idealism of the pioneering Zionist generations. Yet Wilson appears to be seeing what he wants to see: a people who are able to turn the wilderness into fit habitation because of an idea in their hearts. He contrasts the Israeli freshness with "European discouragement and cultural staleness, the running down and falling apart."

Wilson's response to Israel incorporates his own ego ideal, his dream of a selfhood sufficiently strong to carry on despite the adversity of circumstance, and it suggests a displaced version of the old Calvinist sense of the Jews as a witness people crucial in the fulfillment of God's design. For many evangelical Christians, it will only be with the conversion of the Jews in their own land that Christian history will be completed. There is no need to claim that Wilson subscribed to this theology if we point out a comparable, unusual evangelical fervor in his writing about Israel. Thus toward the end of the 1969 edition of his book on the scrolls he writes: "This millennia-spanning mixture in Israel of ancient and modern history makes it, in my opinion, a place of unique interest and of heartening inspiration. . . . To visit the modern Israel and to see what is going on there is to feel oneself partly released from the narrow constructions of today's and yesterday's newspaper and to find oneself, thus rising above the years, with their catastrophes and their comings and goings, in touch with one of the greatest human forces for the tenacity and authority of our race."

It is hard not to be awed by Wilson's own tenacity and authority, his industriousness and professionalism. No one should think that everything came easily to him. It's clear that he was vulnerable to periodic fits of discouragement—depression may be too strong a term, though his distaste for writers who are not "tonic" or "fortifying" points to a fear that an author's gloom may be contagious. And parts of *A Piece of My Mind* and the oft-discussed introduction to *Patriotic Gore* reveal a bleak pessimism that was the other side of the affirmation of the spirit in Wilson's writings about Israel and the Jews. Many of his writer friends from the '20s had not fulfilled their promise, fizzling out instead or dying young. He was determined to stay the course, and in later years repeatedly looked to Jewish history and his own ancestral tradition in reminding himself of the importance of moral courage and strength, of dedication and endurance. He had a plaque placed over the oxygen tank in his bedroom-study that said: "Be strong." This watchword, the longer version of which appears on his tombstone, "Be strong and of good courage," was that of the early rabbis, who invoked it when they had completed one book of the Pentateuch and were summoning their resources to begin the next.

Wilson's sympathy with the Jews was imperfect in that he preferred an idealization — the modern Jew as intellectual hero, following on the Old Testament Jew as hero of faith — to the Jewish actualities all about him. Still, he showed himself to be more truly cosmopolitan than his American precursors, men like James Russell Lowell, Barrett Wendell, John Jay Chapman, and Henry Adams, all of whom knew the great world outside of New England but could never fully emancipate themselves from the anti-Semitic stereotypes of their class. The chapter called "The Jews" in *A Piece of My Mind* shows he was quite aware that his own consistent philo-Semitism marked a break with the American tradition of the upper-class WASP as man of letters to which he belonged. In a recent interview, Saul Bellow recalls Max Weber's idea that "the Jews are aristocratic pariahs, pariahs with a patrician streak." Whether or not that self-consciousness is endemic among Jews, it showed itself at times in Wilson. It won't do to overstate his conception of himself as a pariah, inasmuch as he thought himself to be the rightful heir to an American cultural legacy. But in identifying, during the '30s, with the artist-outsider and with the Jew as champion of oppressed groups and radical new ideas, he located himself outside the existing class system. Still, he remained an upper-class radical. He liked his communists and Jews best when they acted like spiritual aristocrats.

The central theme of the American gentleman-intellectual, beginning with James Fenimore Cooper, is the decline of the Republic. Wilson's career offers the familiar spectacle of the old-stock American of cultivation and goodwill lamenting the manifold changes that have brought his world close to dissolution. The question for such patrician intellectuals — Cooper, Holmes, Henry Adams, Robert Lowell — is how to respond to that decline. It's easier to see now than it was in Wilson's own time that, for all the jeremiads of his last decades, he came to terms with the loss of the WASPs' exclusive dominance better than most. We need only think of the anti-Semitism of twentieth-century writers of comparable ancestry, like Edith Wharton, T. S. Eliot, and Ezra Pound, to appreciate his uniqueness in identifying with the Jews rather than blaming them for the changes that had brought about the loss of his class's primacy. It's not simply that, unlike Pound and Eliot, he was able to resist the impulse to load onto the Jews responsibility for everything he hated about modern life. Much more than that, he positively affirmed a bond with the Jews. But what kind of alliance was it that included in its embrace an Englishman like Isaiah Berlin, an Israeli like David Flusser, a number of American literary critics, and book publishers Jason Epstein and Roger Straus?

Whatever its content or aims, it was an alliance that continued beyond his death. He designated Leon Edel as general editor of his papers, which included his private journals. Daniel Aaron also helped to keep Wilson's work before the public with his excellent introduction to Wilson's *Letters on Literature and Politics: 1912–1972*, edited by Wilson's wife, Elena, and published in 1977. That his posthumous literary life was largely entrusted to Jewish scholars confirms the trend. It's true that, in absolute numbers, Jews probably made up only a small percentage of Wilson's regular readers. It's also true that his most vocal admirers have included writers and critics who are not Jewish, like John Updike and Lewis Dabney. But if we ask who has most effectively carried on his central work as a literary critic and historian, the answer would include the aforementioned Jewish scholars, as well as others like Irving Howe. The philosopher John Dewey inspired a similar loyalty among a different group of Jews who were more concerned than the tribe of Wilson with social policy issues. The allegiance to Dewey of his disciple Sidney Hook, in the '30s and after, is paralleled by Alfred Kazin's continuing attachment to Wilson over more than half a century. Both Wilson and Dewey were unchurched, liberal-minded WASP intellectuals who were thought by second-generation Jewish Americans to be worthy of the considerable idealism they brought to their study of American literature and society. Wilson, like Dewey, figured as more than one thinker among many, seeming to his younger Jewish admirers and imitators to stand for America itself.

It becomes harder and harder to remember that there was once a time when writers dreamed of swallowing America whole. That ambition, evident in the young Kazin, was by no means limited to Jews, but it was more conspicuous among writers who were to some degree outsiders, such as Theodore Dreiser, than among writers who felt themselves to be America's rightful heirs. The crucial decade in the history of these intellectuals is still the '30s, when most belonged to the radical opposition. The Depression had the effect of discrediting the Protestant cultural establishment as well as the existing economic order. Many of the writers and intellectuals waiting in the wings for their turn were Jewish. By the '50s these men and women of letters had themselves become something of an establishment and found themselves supervising the cultural tradition rather than trying to subvert it. It may be that they had never been quite as alienated as they thought, for once American society acted more hospitably toward them, they were ready not to be outsiders. They can be accused of opportunism, but from the start the Jews were more open to acculturation than any other group in the great wave of immigration from southern and eastern Europe. They eagerly learned basic American values as children in big-city public schools and libraries and settlement houses, all staffed by teachers and social workers ready to inculcate "Americanism" in these most willing pupils.

The WASP-Jewish alliance has been above all an alliance of like-minded Americans in the culture-and-society tradition of Arnold. Marginalized WASP intellectuals like Wilson might more easily find supporters among culture-hungry, assimilating Jews than in the world of Gentile country clubs and corporate boardrooms. Wilson could enjoy drinking with old Princeton classmates, but except for the most eccentric and independent-minded, these would have been men who had made their peace with the new America, as he never did. And however much Jewish intellectuals retreated from their earlier radicalism during the years of the cold war, they never gave in to the boosterism of the group Wilson wrote off collectively as "bond salesmen."

Since the '60s, we have entered a third stage of immigration, and the label of multiculturalism is used to reject most of the Western heritage in the name of the equality of non-European peoples of color. Meanwhile, many Jews have become part of the American establishment. At the moment, the presidents of most of the Ivy League universities are Jews, or, as in the case of Harvard's president, Neil Rudenstine, partly Jewish. And here is the irony. As professors and administrators, these Jews, now obliged to exercise power, must deal with new minorities, which resist them, having a very different idea of their own relation to the majority culture. Nowadays most Jewish scholars are vocal supporters of the white, Western culture that only sixty or seventy years ago inclined to treat them like pariahs. In that distant time, identification with Edmund Wilson became one way Jewish insurgents, raised in a culture that was in truth centuries distant from the European world in which their immigrant parents had grown up, adopted Western humanism on American terms. Having enjoyed for less than a half century the pleasure of taking their place in the tradition, which Wilson symbolized, they find themselves in the strange (to them) position of being resented as part of a white, male, Euro-American establishment.

Success in America is a complex fate, and one of its names is failure. Jewish intellectuals may still have something to learn from Wilson. They can learn an idiom once thought to be the exclusive property of the WASPs, the idiom of the culturally disinherited upper-class American.

IV

PORTRAITS AND OBITS

Listmania in *Humboldt's Gift*

Saul Bellow's *Humboldt's Gift* is a wonderful novel, but no one is likely to celebrate it for unity of form. It is divided between two stories, that of the ill-fated poet Von Humboldt Fleisher and that of his onetime friend Charlie Citrine, the narrator of the novel. The Charlie part is basically a static meditation on death. It is highly discursive, consisting of an exposition of metaphysical ideas, many of them derived from the Austrian-born theosophist Rudolph Steiner, plus Charlie's personal speculations on the "higher soul." These reflections on death and the afterlife are not lugubrious, as they might be, but they are slow going. And most readers are not as likely to be as interested in Charlie's meta-physical "deposition," as he calls it, as Charlie (and Bellow) is.

But *Humboldt's Gift* also contains the story of its eponymous hero, a funny, exuberant account that is Dickensian in its variety of characters and settings. This is the Humboldt story, a pastoral-satirical-farcical memoir. Bellow's portrait of Humboldt is surely one of the best in a ca-reer remarkable for portraiture. The only flaw is that Citrine interrupts the Humboldt story so frequently to point to a moral, either cultural or metaphysical. *Humboldt's Gift* preaches against the mere appearances of the great world—money, glamorous women, fame, politics—while causing them to be so much more "there" than the neo-Platonic radi-ance to which Charlie aspires.

The Bellow who appears in this novel as the comic observer, incor-porating all that he sees and exuberantly accepting (if not affirming) so

This essay first appeared in *Literary Imagination: The Review of the Association of Literary Scholars and Critics* 4.1 (Winter 2002): 60–67.

large a part of it, this Bellow is a good deal closer to Walt Whitman than to Rudolph Steiner. Citrine explicitly cites Whitman on the "death question," but I am more interested here in a well-known feature of Whitman's style that also appears in *Humboldt's Gift:* lists, catalogues, and a paratactic syntax that is American and democratic in refusing to reduce any phrase to relative status.

Where Bellow differs from his American precursor is in his intellectualism. So the lists by which Citrine makes Humboldt known to the reader are lists of authors and movements and ideas. One artistic problem for Bellow is how to convey the feel of Humboldt's manic conversation without quoting whole speeches with their syntactical links. He succeeds brilliantly in inventing a style that is remarkable for its speed and lightness and epigrammatic concision. Humboldt's favorite texts and topics do not entirely coincide with Bellow's, but the fictional creature shares with his authorial creator a style that allows for the coexistence of allusions to literary high culture and the particulars of American pop culture. It is a remarkable style that lets them juxtapose Plato's dialogues and the banter of street-smart urban Americans, Miltonic cadences and Yiddish inflections.

But enough of general remarks. Let me call the reader's attention to some passages from the book. In characterizing the genre(s) of *Humboldt's Gift*, I have suggested that, among other things, it is an exercise in pastoral. On the first page of the novel, Charlie describes his Greyhound bus trip from Appleton, Wisconsin, his hometown, to New York City. He has set out on a pilgrimage to pay homage to Humboldt, the avant-garde poet who has already established himself on the literary scene. Charlie appears as an excited innocent from the heartland: "The bus windows were open. I had never seen real mountains before. Trees were budding. It was like Beethoven's *Pastorale*. I felt showered by the green, within."

Ten years later Humboldt is well on his way to madness and ruin. Charlie now visits him in the broken-down house in rural New Jersey, where the poet has set up housekeeping with a new wife. The "girls" still believe in Humboldt, though he has already begun his descent into self-doubt and paranoia. But with Charlie's arrival Humboldt pulls out all the conversational stops: "When I visited them [Humboldt] was all earth, trees, flowers, oranges, the sun, Paradise, Atlantis, Rhadamanthus.

He talked about William Blake at Felpham and Milton's Eden, and he ran down the city. . . . To follow his intricate conversation you had to know his basic texts. I knew what they were: Plato's *Timaeus,* Proust on Combray, Virgil on farming, Marvell on gardens, Wallace Stevens' Caribbean poetry, and so on. One reason why Humboldt and I were so close was that I was willing to take the complete course." It is a measure of Humboldt's genius that even amidst the wreckage of his life he can still hold in mind his personal canon of great pastoral writing. But the discrepancy between Humboldt's texts and his life calls to mind these lines from Wordsworth, another great pastoralist: "We Poets in our youth begin in gladness; / But thereof come in the end despondency and madness."

Depression, madness, and the plunge to an ignominious death. I turn now to a brief section of *Humboldt's Gift* in which Citrine composes a bitter obituary of his friend. First, he describes the death notice that had appeared in the *New York Times.* Instead of quoting directly from the *Times* obituary, he sums up for us the attitude that informs it. Citrine is irritated by what he takes to be the paper's collusion in a certain vulgar myth about the artist in America. Citrine finds evidence here that "America is proud of its dead poets," finding in their ruin evidence that the poet can't stand up to the material powers of this society. To make his point Citrine composes a list of American *poètes maudits.* He contends that the "successful bitter hard-faced and cannibalistic people," the survivors, exult whenever a poet—he names Edgar Allen Poe, Hart Crane, Randall Jarrell, John Berryman, and now Humboldt—comes to a terrible end: "The weakness of the spiritual powers is proved in the childishness, madness, drunkenness, and despair of these martyrs."

Whitman usually invokes the catalogue form when he wants to celebrate something, as, for example, in "Salut au Monde!" Bellow, in contrast, is often energized by anger, and that anger generates lists just as surely as the American scene inspired Whitman's. See, for example, Citrine's response to the photograph of Humboldt in the *Times:* "It was one of those mad-rotten-majesty pictures—spooky, humorless, glaring furiously with tight lips, mumpish or scrofulous cheeks, a scarred forehead, and a look of enraged, ravaged childishness. This was the Humboldt of conspiracies, putsches, accusations, tantrums, the Bellevue Hospital Humboldt, the Humboldt of litigation." In short, the *Times* has bought into the American myth by which our culture simultaneously romanticizes its visionaries and glories in their inevitable downfall.

At this point Citrine gets off his green sofa, where he has been meditating on his personal past, and composes his own, tougher-minded interpretation of Humboldt's career. An obituary at best can discern a figure in the carpet of the dead person's life. Or the life can be made to illustrate an idea. It turns out that Citrine is not only angry about American philistinism; he is also angry that Humboldt conspired with that philistine culture. In Charlie's view, his old friend failed because he wanted to have things both ways: he wanted both the Orphic Radiance and American Success. But Bellow's generalizations, in capital letters, about the Poet in America are less compelling than his prose evocation of Humboldt's talk. And once again that evocation takes the form of a list: "Orpheus, the Son of Greenhorn, turned up in Greenwich Village with his ballads. He loved literature and intellectual conversation and argument, loved the history of thought. A big gentle handsome boy he put together his own combination of symbolism and street language. Into this mixture went Yeats, Apollinaire, Lenin, Freud, Morris R. Cohen, Gertrude Stein, baseball statistics, and Hollywood gossip. He brought Coney Island into the Aegean and united Buffalo Bill with Rasputin." There is, to be sure, considerable irony in Charlie's memory of Humboldt's favorite topics, but the passionate fidelity of Charlie's recall is a measure also of the love he had once felt. Citrine feels that love again on learning of his friend's death. It is also, of course, a love of his own younger self as it flowered in Humboldt's company.

Nothing, though, is sentimental about Charlie's vision of his friend. Here, as he comes to the end of his alternative obituary, he modulates into a darker tone and yet another list of sorts. He hammers out one short sentence after another until he arrives at a longer, summarizing sentence at the end: Humboldt "swallowed more pills, he drank more gin. Mania and depression drove him to the looney bin. He was in and out. He became a professor of English in the boondocks. There he was a grand literary figure. Elsewhere, in one of his own words, he was zilch. But then he died and got good notices. He had always valued prominence, and the *Times* was tops. Having lost his talent, his mind, fallen apart, died in ruin, he rose again on the cultural Dow-Jones and enjoyed briefly the prestige of significant failure." This is a version of Humboldt's life that knows what it is about. It has the stylistic authority lacking in the *Times* notice, which Citrine mocks as having been written in a "tinkertoy style of knobs and sticks."

Citrine's reference to the paper's obituary-section style is of a piece with his self-consciousness about style throughout his narrative. As Bellow wrote to an admirer: "I *heard* the words as I wrote *Humboldt*. And towards the end I dictated it from beginning to end—a typist took it all down. What couldn't be spoken was dropped from the text" (quoted in James Atlas, *Bellow: A Biography*). The choice of the fast-talking Humboldt as a subject seems finally to have determined Bellow's move, in the course of several drafts, to a freewheeling oral style. The oral style creates the effect of spontaneity, manic energy, prodigality. That effect, however, is the result of the self-conscious choice of certain stylistic devices.

At the start of the novel, Citrine recalls the earliest phase of his initiation as an acolyte of Humboldt. They are on a ferryboat that is taking them from Christopher Street in the Village across the Hudson River to Hoboken when Humboldt launches into one of his arias. There is something operatic about his verbal performances, as there is about Whitman's "Crossing Brooklyn Ferry." Once underway, Humboldt is unstoppable: "He was off. His spiel took in Freud, Heine, Wagner, Goethe in Italy, Lenin's dead brother, Wild Bill Hickok's costumes, the New York Giants, Ring Lardner on grand opera, Swinburne on flagellation, and John D. Rockefeller on religion." Humboldt hardly stops to catch his breath, but Citrine interrupts to comment on the dizzying effect of this flood of talk: "Humboldt spoke wonderfully of the wonderful, abominable rich. You had to view them in the shield of art. His monologue was an oratorio in which he sang and played all parts."

Later in the novel Charlie evokes Humboldt's verbal style during a less happy phase of his career, when his days were mostly taken up by litigation and madness. His chief audience now consists not of apprentice writers like Charlie but of lawyers and psychiatrists, men and women who make their living in the worldly world. Curiously enough, he is able to enchant these professional people even though he throws away their bills: "As for the lawyers and shrinkers, they were delighted with him not because he represented the real world but because he was a poet." For them Humboldt represents culture, imagination, genius.

Bored with their usual clients and patients, "dreary Long Island pota-toes," they are delighted by him. "He was no potato. He was a papaya a citron a passion fruit. He was a beautiful deep eloquent fragrant origi-nal. . . . And what a repertory he had, what changes of style and tempo." Again Bellow leaves out the serial commas to create an effect of speed and amplitude. And Humboldt's appeal to the ear (as music) and palate (as exotic fruit) outlasts his appeal to reason.

Sitting in lawyers' offices, Humboldt "worked in Milton on divorce and John Stuart Mill on women." And then Citrine offers up new lists, to convey the energy not of intellectual plenitude but of genius sub-verted by madness: "He accused, fulminated, stammered, blazed, cried out. He crossed the universe like light. He struck off X-ray films of the true facts. Weakness, lies, treason, shameful perversion, crazy lust, the viciousness, of certain billionaires (names were named). The truth!" The energy of passages like this is all the more striking, given that Cit-rine, when his thoughts move to the "death question," can slow down to the speed of an old milk-horse.

A passage near the start shows how much, using his catalogue style, Citrine can pack into a single paragraph. It begins: "[Humboldt] was a wonderful talker, a hectic nonstop monologuist and improvisator, a champion detractor." Then Charlie slides into a discussion of Hum-boldt on the rich: "Brought up on New York tabloids, he often men-tioned the golden scandals of yesteryear, Peaches and Daddy Browning, Harry Thaw and Evelyn Nesbitt," whereupon Charlie juxtaposes these popular scandals with Humboldt's appetite for first-class fiction about the rich, "plus the Jazz Age, Scott Fitzgerald, and the Super-Rich. The heiresses of Henry James he knew cold." One effect of such juxtaposi-tions is to show that Humboldt was blurring the line between high and low culture long before critics like Susan Sontag.

Charlie goes on to say that Humboldt "himself schemed comically to make a fortune. But his real wealth was literary." This frees the narrator for yet another list, this time of the "thick books—Marx and Sombart, Toynbee, Rostovtzeff, Freud"—that Humboldt read during his sleepless nights. And the paragraph finishes nicely, as Charlie reveals just how de-voted an acolyte he has been: "When [Humboldt] spoke of wealth he was in a position to compare Roman luxus with American Protestant riches. He generally got around to the Jews—Joyce's silk-hatted Jews outside the Bourse. And he wound up with the gold-plated skull or death mask of Agamemnon, dug up by Schliemann. Humboldt could really talk." It is hard not to feel about Charlie's friendship with Humboldt that he did, as he says, take "the complete course." And Charlie, a biographer and journalist, has learned enough of the poet's art to use the list as a device for loading every rift with ore.

There is one brief section in which Citrine does provide direct dialogue. It is a scene in which the increasingly antiradical Citrine runs into Huggins, an aging playboy of the Left who is now administrator of Humboldt's estate. Huggins is unforgiving with regard to Citrine's political defection, but Citrine has a rapid-fire rejoinder. He tells Huggins: "Most political views are like old newspapers chewed up by wasps—faded clichés and buzzing." And then Citrine launches into a list: "Humboldt brought me around in the Forties, but I never became part of your gang. When everybody was on Burnham or on Koestler I was somewhere else. The same for the *Encyclopedia of Unified Science,* Trotsky's Law of Combined Development, or Chiaramonte's views on Plato or Lionel Abel on theater or Paul Goodman on Proudhon, or almost everybody on Kafka or Kierkegaard." Here, unlike in the reports on Humboldt's conversation, the purpose is not to associate a character with a canon but to dissociate him from it. Citrine is engaged in negative self-definition. He describes himself as having really been "somewhere else" when he was in the physical company of the left intellectuals during the forties. He expresses himself by means of metaphor, making use here of a surprising analogy: "It was like poor old Humboldt's complaint about girls. He wanted to do them good but they wouldn't hold still for it. I wouldn't hold still for it either. Instead of being grateful for my opportunity to get into the cultural life of the Village at its best—" Huggins cuts him off. No slouch as a talker, he won't hold still for Citrine's monologue.

Charlie uses his list as a kind of shorthand to distinguish himself from the political intellectuals who were his conversation partners before he left New York for Chicago. In retrospect he perceives himself as having always been an internal exile. Not without the pride of an assumed spiritual superiority, he is asserting his difference from other intellectuals who came of age in the thirties. Although Citrine can't very well talk about his spiritual intimations with someone like Huggins, that's what is at stake in his rejoinder. However, from my own point of view, as someone deaf to the appeal of Rudolph Steiner's anthroposophy, it is precisely Charlie's witty recall of Humboldt's decidedly nonspiritual monologues that constitutes the wonder of this garrulous novel.

The reader who is grateful for being given access, through Humboldt, to the talk of the great Village talkers should nevertheless keep in mind that we are given very little direct quotation of Humboldt. And it is Humboldt, not his biographer Citrine, who is the great talker of this novel. Bellow makes us feel that we are present in the room as Humboldt repeatedly goes off on one of his "spiels," but the author does it without transcripts or CDs. The sense we have of hearing Humboldt talk is an illusion made possible by style. For Bellow, unlike his fellow Chicagoan Studs Terkel, is not an oral historian. He is an artist, creating the sense of a time and place and people's talk with an artist's cunning. In *Humboldt's Gift* he does it with smoke and mirrors—and lists.

Assimilation in
Recent Jewish American
Autobiographies

It is a constant refrain, emanating from temple pulpits, the Jewish press, and community leaders: the number of Jews marrying non-Jews has passed 50 percent; attendance at Jewish day schools is dropping; temple members are living high but skimping on their contributions. The rabbis' one, all-purpose word for this Jewish American disaster-in-the-making is "assimilation."

We may be seeing evidence of assimilation, but it is American-style assimilation, which is very different from what it was in old Europe. In Germany, the world center of assimilated Jewry before Hitler, Jews frequently ceased being Jews. They converted, were baptized, changed their names, repressed the traces of Jewish ethnicity. If you want to understand the outlook of pre-Nazi, assimilated German Jewry, a place to start is Hannah Arendt's early book *Rahel Varnhagen: The Life of a Jewish Woman*. Varnhagen, the daughter of a prosperous German Jewish family, created about her a circle of intellectuals and aristocrats during the early nineteenth century. For a time she was able to organize a salon in which aristocrat and bourgeois, Christian and Jew were able to meet outside the conventions and customs of polite society. Respectable society in Germany excluded Jews, but in Rahel Varnhagen's garret room the rules were temporarily in abeyance.

This essay was first published in *Contemporary Literature* 34 (Fall 1993): 451–74.

It was Rahel's misfortune, however, to be a Jew, and as such to have no secure place in the world. She struggled to become part of respectable society, but her Jewishness meant she was always vulnerable in the face of pervasive German anti-Semitism. The only cure for Rahel's Jewish problem, as she saw it, was to stop being a Jew. Often drawing on Varnhagen's own words, from her letters and diary, Arendt makes the reader feel, almost physically, the deep and bitter frustrations of this gifted, vivacious woman whose great ambition was to become a countess and leave Judaism behind for good. Arendt says it was "as though [Varnhagen] longed only to be taken away from what and where she was."

For Rahel Varnhagen, to cease being a Jew was the only way to assimilate. Hannah Arendt's study in Jewish frustration and failure raises many of the issues she returned to in her later, better-known books on politics and society, but it is a difficult book for a Jewish American reader to comprehend. Assimilation in Germany circa 1800, or in 1930, for that matter, was vastly different from what we have been calling Jewish assimilation in America since World War II.

Goethe, whose cult Varnhagen promoted, once said, "Amerika, du hast es besser." Certainly, in making their way in the larger non-Jewish world, American Jews have had it easier than their counterparts in Europe. Up to now, however, we have had to make do with words— "assimilation," "Jewish self-hatred," and so forth—that received their classic definitions in very different circumstances from our own. We have needed a new made-in-America idiom to clarify the sense so many of us have that Jews in America are not in exile, not part of the *galut,* as these categories came to be understood in relation to centuries of European Diaspora experience.

In a recent book, *Saving Remnants: Feeling Jewish in America,* Sara Bershtel and Allen Graubard describe a new kind of Jew, who is fully acculturated in America yet continues an "episodic but intense involvement with Jewishness and Jewish identification." The new American Jews do not live in Jewish neighborhoods, the "gilded ghettos" of their parents; they share the secular modernist outlook of non-Jewish Americans; and they especially value their right to free choice in lifestyle and personal identity. Yet they persist in "feeling Jewish," even if their Jewishness does not lead to their living day to day much differently from other Americans.

Bershtel and Graubard describe the Jewishness of the current generation in terms of "gestures, episodes, enhancements"—"pinches of spice," as they put it, "in the melting pot," rather than the main ingredients. They look on this new episodic, intermittent sense of Jewish identity as something new in Jewish history. It is clearly very different from the anguished Jewish self-identity of Rahel Varnhagen, who wanted only to leave her Jewishness behind. Varnhagen's conviction that Jewishness could only be a terrible disadvantage, a burden to be disposed of, distinguishes the older style of assimilation from the new American "post-assimilation culture." It is clear that the post-assimilated generation in America feels no need to repeat the German-Jewish experience of the total rejection of religious and ethnic expression and connection. If anything, this new social type is contemptuous of the inauthenticity of Jews who try to conceal their Jewishness. But what, in positive terms, does the new American Jewishness amount to? Is this new mode of Jewish self-consciousness, and the sometimes quixotic gestures that express it, to be seen only as "an enhancement of integrated American lives"?

Let's consider another possibility. Perhaps we are seeing, in the autobiographical vignettes of *Saving Remnants,* a new kind of self-identity that is postmodern as well as post-assimilationist. "Episodic" and "intermittent" would also describe the new, disunified identity of many non-Jewish Americans experiencing the dislocations of postindustrial society. I think myself that the Jewishness of many of the unaffiliated is something more than "a pinch of spice." In many ways it is one element, but an important one, of a new, nontotalizing, decentered self-identity in which no element—whether Jewish, American, modernist, or other—is clearly dominant.

The best parts of *Saving Remnants* are interviews with representative American Jews, mostly in their forties and early fifties. The authors have changed the names of some of their interviewees to protect their privacy. A typical case is that of "Michael Stone," who deals with his sense of something missing in his life by isolated, symbolic "Jewish actions [such as] occasionally giving money to Israel [or] choosing a wedding ceremony that is not only Jewish but Orthodox," which Bershtel and Graubard characterize as "discrete moments that add up to no pattern." The familiar metaphor for the retrieval of roots is the spiritual "odyssey," recalling the yearning of Homer's Odysseus to get back home to Penelope and Telemachus. But for the typical unaffiliated, self-fashioning Jew, the intermittent gestures of Jewish identity and solidarity represent no true *nostoi,* or return, but something more like an occasional holiday, a trip to nostalgia land.

It would be easy to decry the "superficiality" of this intermittent Jewish consciousness, to associate it with Disney theme parks, which also offer a postmodern excursion into an ersatz past. But what if this new way of being Jewish in America is a local version of a new mode of self-consciousness that has become pervasive among many ethnic groups in America, indeed in all the advanced nations of the West? Is this, perhaps, the local, Jewish version of "the end of man"? It may be that the modern history of the Jews—the Holocaust followed by the precarious survival of Israel in the years since—has given Jews an especially vivid existential sense of this transformed human condition.

As a small gesture of my own toward complicating our understanding of old words like "assimilation," I will be looking at two recent Jewish autobiographies in which the work of self-invention is especially marked. I have chosen two very different instances of life-writing. The first is Eva Hoffman's *Lost in Translation: A Life in a New Language* (1989), which is a variant of the familiar story of an immigrant's Americanization. The genre to which Hoffman's story belongs, however ambivalently, is that of the acculturation of the Jewish greenhorn. The other autobiography, Paul Cowan's *Orphan in History: Retrieving a Jewish Legacy* (1982), is a "roots" story, a "personal odyssey," according to the blurb on the cover. Cowan's book is a story of disassimilation, a relinquishment of the trappings and consciousness associated with a privileged American upbringing for the sake of an older Jewish religious and cultural tradition.

But why my appeal to recent autobiographies in considering the fate of Jewish assimilation in America? The answer, simply, is that preoccupation with the autobiographical has been the distinguishing mark of Jewish writing of recent years, as it has been during the whole of this century. There is a clear continuity from Ludwig Lewisohn's *Up Stream*

(1922) to Alfred Kazin's *A Walker in the City* (1951) to Paul Cowan's *Orphan in History*. The preoccupation has remained the same: What is it to be both a Jew and an American?

I would include within "the autobiographical" a substantial part, also, of Jewish American fiction. Think of Anzia Yezierska's novels or Grace Paley's stories or Philip Roth in his fictions that draw so heavily on "the facts." (It ought to be added that Roth's ostensibly "true" stories make considerable use of the techniques of fiction. There is no sharp line separating Roth's novels from his memoirs.) Of course there are exceptions, like Cynthia Ozick. But the impersonality of Ozick's fiction is balanced by the personal voice of her essays and her marvelous short memoirs, "The Lesson of the Master" and "A Drugstore in Winter."

The continuous Jewish involvement with the autobiographical shouldn't cause us to overlook changes in emphasis over time. In the thirties and forties Jewish writers often drew on their own life stories because that was all they knew. As long as Jews were excluded from mainstream American life, they were driven back on their own narrow experience. That confinement did not keep Henry Roth from writing *Call It Sleep*, which is surely one of the classic achievements of Jewish American fiction. But more often it produced second- and third-rate narratives of breaking out, of brash young provincials crowing over their conquest of Babylon. *What Makes Sammy Run?* is more typical of that fiction than *Call It Sleep*. What one finds in this writing is defiant self-celebration just barely concealing self-distrust and even self-loathing. Writing in 1944, Clement Greenberg thought that what the Jewish writer needed was "a greater feeling of integration with society, which will by the inevitable antithesis make him less dependent upon its approbation." Only if the social situation of the Jew in America improved would the Jewish writer come to have a more impersonal, that is, a more genuinely aesthetic, relationship to his material.

Recent years have seemed to bring about that "greater feeling of integration with society." Yet Jewish writing remains as autobiographical as ever. If the generation of the thirties and forties was bent on escape from a Jewishness felt to be narrow and provincial, recent Jewish autobiographies and fiction have been about coming home. A new anthology, *Writing Our Lives: Autobiographies of American Jews, 1890–1990*, edited by Steven J. Rubin, traces "a return to Jewish tradition." And the return is as carefully recorded, in memoir and autobiographical fiction, as the escape from Jewish tradition was recorded a half-century ago.

What should we make of this persistence of the autobiographical mode? The situation is quite complex. We see the integration that Bershtel and Graubard describe, but we see also that social acceptance has itself fostered the Jewish return to roots. The post–World War II experience of acceptance and integration has provided the psychological margin that has allowed many American Jews to come home, in their differing ways, to Jewishness. Less insecure, less dependent on the larger society for approval, some Jews have become simultaneously more American and more distinctively Jewish.

The evidence of this new Jewish cultural self-confidence is everywhere. Consider, for example, the two big anthologies edited by the poet-translator David Rosenberg: *Congregation: Contemporary Writers Read the Jewish Bible* and *Testimony: Contemporary Writers Make the Holocaust Personal*. Rosenberg invited Jewish writers, most in their forties and fifties, to reflect on a single favorite book of the Jewish Bible, and in the subsequent anthology on their relationship as Americans to the Holocaust. That these middle-generation Jewish writers were willing to write so personally about Jewish concerns distinguishes them from the older generation, which prided itself, at least in its early years, on its cosmopolitanism and universalism.

Just as Rosenberg provided a forum for Jewish poets and writers, so other projects are providing places for Jewish academic intellectuals. Several collections are underway in which Jewish professors write about the relationship between their Jewishness and the course of their professional careers. It's clear, then, that autobiography has been the mode of choice not only for anxious arrivistes celebrating their escape from the narrowness of Brooklyn and the Bronx but also for culturally self-confident, assimilated American Jews searching for the way back.

Autobiographers often make a gesture toward the public realm, but inevitably the form they have chosen encourages greater emphasis on questions of personal identity and self-presentation. However much recent Jewish writers affirm their return to "tradition," they often seem less preoccupied with the long Jewish past than with their own selves as searchers. These autobiographies worry the question of Jewishness while seeming very American in their preoccupation with the drama of personal destiny. Jewish American writers seem like many non-Jewish Americans in worrying about how to locate themselves in a culture, American culture, that provides few landmarks. Jewish particularism mirrors the complex fate of many non-Jewish Americans insofar as it disposes these writers to be constantly taking their own spiritual temperature, gauging their morale, measuring their progress in the business of self-making. But, again, the Americanness of this recovery of Jewishness shouldn't dispose us to posit some illusory essence, generically American or Jewish American. These new achievements in the autobiographical mode are indeed new. They are expressions of a new moment, of a different social history, to which I now turn.

We know from the first pages of *Lost in Translation* that it is not going to be a conventional immigrant autobiography. The paradigm for such autobiographies was set early, with Mary Antin's *The Promised Land* (1912), in which the movement is from the narrowness and hardship of the Eastern European shtetl to the freedom and wonders of America. The pattern story, which is very self-conscious in Antin, is the biblical Exodus, with czarist Russia as Egypt and America as "the promised land." The tone, more bouncy perhaps than in subsequent immigrant autobiographies, is enthusiastic and excited. The emphasis, as Antin says, is on "noble dreams and high ideals," in which a joy in one's own newly discovered powers mingles with "pride and delight" in the new homeland.

Eva Hoffman lets us know from the start that unlike Antin she will not depreciate her European beginnings. The title of the first of her book's three sections is "Paradise," which refers not to America but to her life, up to the age of thirteen, in Poland. The notion of a cheerful evocation of Poland by a Jew may seem a contradiction in terms, but it is very much to the point that Hoffman grew up in post-Holocaust Poland. The country she comes to know is run by the Communist Party, and the few Jews who remain are despised nearly as much as in prewar Poland. But for the child Eva life is a romance. Imaginatively she lives in the nation of Chopin and the national poet Mickiewicz. She tries to be "cool" in the old Polish way, as she strives for "panache," "flair," "gallantry." She is not a Jewish girl in the shtetl, trying always to be upright, but a Pole in Cracow enamored of "spontaneity, daring, a bit of recklessness."

If Mary Antin's model is the Exodus, Eva Hoffman's is *Paradise Lost*. The titles of the three parts of her triptych are "Paradise," "Exile," and "The New World." The last of these, the American part, is experienced as the postlapsarian world of our first parents, with its confusing mixture of good and evil and bliss and bale. It is not at all like Antin's "promised land." Even at the end, when Hoffman reports herself as dreaming now in English, she continues to experience herself as exiled from her childhood Eden. She complicates the paradigm further by shifting emphasis from civic values and virtues, Antin's focus, to questions of language. *Lost in Translation* has as its subtitle *Life in a New Language*. Hoffman conveys, with linguistic and emotional precision, the displacement that affects the immigrant at the deepest level of self-identity as a consequence of having to find new words for old thoughts and feelings attached at a preconscious level to her mother tongue.

I want here to discuss not Hoffman's ideas about language but her revision of the exhausted form of the immigrant autobiography. I think myself that her compositional recourse to the pattern of paradise lost, exile, and the quest for a new paradise within is as constraining as the Exodus pattern of enslavement and liberation in Antin. It may be, for example, that the young Eva's life, up to 1959, when she left Cracow for North America and the start of a new life in English, was not in actuality as idyllic as she makes it appear in retrospect. But her idea of the Fall as the loss of linguistic un-self-consciousness requires that there be a time before the Fall. So Poland, unlikely candidate though it might seem, becomes the name for the unalienated condition that Hoffman, in other moods, would probably acknowledge can never have existed. Certainly the poststructuralist theories of language that underwrite this memoir argue against the idea of a primal unity of being such as Hoffman attributes to her younger self.

The main feature of Hoffman's New World, lived among graduate students in English at Harvard and among journalists and publishing people in New York, is its abstractness. She is describing what Milan Kundera has made familiar as "the unbearable lightness of being." But for Hoffman that lightness is produced not by communist kitsch, as in post–World War II Czechoslovakia or Poland, but by the near-total collapse of legitimating authority in the American 1960s and since. Hoffman's Poland is barely recognizable as a communist society at all. It appears, instead, as the great good place, outside of time. The first part of *Lost in Translation,* the Polish childhood, is given over to sensuous evocations of un-self-conscious being: young love, summers in the countryside, the ecstasies of music. In the last part, the American adulthood, Hoffman presents a very different self. She is now that most familiar of visitors to these shores—the European critic of American superficiality and utopianism, the satirist of liberal self-deception. In "The New World" Hoffman ceases to be a poet of everyday life, as she is in the section on Poland, and becomes an essayist. Someone like me who attempts a discursive account of Hoffman's book probably should be grateful for her lucid and witty summarizing formulations. But the ending of this book is rather more conventional, as an exercise in cultural criticism, than the first part. Still, we understand that the writer's distance from her new self is the condition of her appreciation of her earlier self, who could not have written about herself as the older, wiser Eva has done.

Sometimes the Americanizing Eva kicks against the domination of conventional American opinion: "My sense of reality, powerful and vulnerable, is in danger of coming under native domination. . . . The mass of shared conviction is so thick as to constitute an absoluteness." At these times she asks herself, in a rage, Why do I have to adapt to America? Why shouldn't America adapt to me? She makes one feel the injustice of the "always already" quality of the place or people or world view or language that was there before she arrived, and to which, in order to survive, she is obliged to adjust. To a degree, of course, this is the shared human condition, not the problem of the immigrant alone.

At other times, the object of Hoffman's complaint is very different. American culture, felt as monolithic at one moment, can be felt as weightless and diffuse in the next. She complains then about the unreality of reality in America. There is no shared reality to which she could assimilate even if she wanted to: "Insofar as I'm an outsider wishing to be taken in, I've come at the wrong moment, for in the midst of all this swirling and fragmenting movement, the very notion of outside and inside is as quaint as the Neoplatonic model of the universe. I do not experience the pain of earlier immigrants, who were kept out of exclusive clubs or decent neighborhoods. Within the limits of my abilities and ambitions, I can go anywhere at all, and be accepted there. The only joke is that there's no there there."

What if everyone is in the same fix, all looking to be taken in, all candidates for adoption in a condition of spiritual exile? In that case, no one would have a privileged relation. There would be no one to do the adopting if we were all orphans. And of course that means there would be nothing special about the Jewish situation.

One of the curious features of Eva Hoffman's book is her relative unconcern with her Jewishness. We know that in the old, communist Soviet Union generations of Jews came of age with a minimal sense of themselves as Jews. Something like this appears to be true also of Hoffman. She describes herself as aware of the anti-Semitism all around her in Poland, but she seems only rarely touched by it. As for the Holocaust, which has so completely marked the lives of her survivor parents, her attitude is that it is better not to cultivate remembrance. Some survivors say, "Never forget." Hoffman has taken to heart a different injunction, from her parents, who tell her again and again, "Be happy."

That counsel, seemingly so simple, sums up the idea that after the Holocaust it is necessary to make a new beginning, cultivating not the memory of horrors but the "prospect of a normal life resuming after the horror." With her characteristic sensitivity to signs and significance, Hoffman speculates that to her parents her birth in 1946 was a signifier of that possibility. Like little American girls assigned by sometimes depressive parents to be their "sunshine," the child Eva sets out in life under the sign of normalcy. But what a fate to live out in a time of the breaking up of all traditions and conventions that were once thought to represent the norm.

In the last part of her book, Hoffman tries on different identities. That of the Jew seems the least compelling, perhaps partly because being Jewish in New York intellectual circles hardly sets one apart. Eva Hoffman is consistent in not blaming the difficulties of Americanization on her Jewishness. She has a completely different attitude from that of Rahel Varnhagen two hundred years earlier. Rather, as Hoffman understands her American life, what is decisive is not race or religion but one's generation. She believes that all Americans who were young in the 1960s struggle with the need to invent themselves and their relation to America: "In a splintered society, what does one assimilate to? Perhaps the very splintering itself. . . . I share with my American generation an acute sense of dislocation and the equally acute challenge of having to invent a place and an identity for myself without the traditional supports. It could be said that the generation I belong to has been characterized by its prolonged refusal to assimilate — and it is in my very uprootedness that I'm its member."

If indeed the exilic consciousness of apartness no longer sharply distinguishes Gentile from Jew, native born from immigrant, assimilation becomes an empty category. Or, as is sometimes said, nowadays we are all Jews. Hoffman sums up a condition that distinguishes her world very sharply from that of Antin: "It could indeed be said that exile is the archetypal condition of contemporary lives."

Perhaps "assimilation" was always the wrong word in the American context. What Mary Antin describes in *The Promised Land* is more like being born again, a sudden and radical self-transformation, than the gradual process of adjustment suggested by "assimilation" or "acculturation." The Israelites needed forty years in the wilderness before they were sufficiently purged of their slavish habits to be worthy of the land God promised them. For Antin about two weeks seems to have been enough. It's shocking to consider the speed, indeed the ruthlessness, with which she and her family divest themselves of their "despised immigrant clothing" and their "impossible Hebrew names" and their "hindering [Old World] prejudices," in making themselves over into Americans.

Eva Hoffman mentions Antin's book and wonders about the contrast between herself and her precursor. Groping for an explanation, she invokes the Zeitgeist to explain the difference. In accord with the poststructuralist conceptions of language she espouses, Hoffman speaks of "the story my time tells me to tell." And rather than urging her own personal uniqueness, she presents herself as a child of her time, just as Antin was a child of hers: "The America of her time gave her certain categories within which to see herself — a belief in self-improvement, in perfectibility of the species, in moral uplift." But that time is past. Flying from Canada to Texas in 1963 to begin college, Hoffman enters modernity, which she characterizes as "the blessings and the terrors of multiplicity." "I step into a culture that splinters, fragments, and re-forms itself as if it were a jigsaw puzzle dancing in a quantum space. If I want to assimilate into my generation, my time, I have to assimilate the multiple perspectives and their constant shifting."

It's clear, then, that Hoffman offers a stark contrast with earlier Jewish immigrant autobiographies. But is the contrast with the past so complete? For if her categories differ strikingly from Mary Antin's, they do resemble those of another American, who was writing his autobiography at about the same time that Antin was writing hers. I think of Henry Adams and his contrast in *The Education of Henry Adams* between an earlier wholeness and modern "multiplicity." Perhaps it is a measure of Jewish success in America that Eva Hoffman's lamentation should so resemble that of Adams, the old-family American patrician who notoriously despised the Yiddish-speaking Eastern European immigrants of New York. Eva Hoffman is right to be proud of her modern consciousness of multiplicity. She has intuited the Adams formula, which has worked for others, too: In America there's no success like failure. Or, as Hoffman puts it, "Perhaps it is . . . my cherishing of uncertainty as the only truth that is, after all, the best measure of my assimilation; perhaps it is in my misfittings that I fit."

Paul Cowan's autobiography, *An Orphan in History*, offers an explosive contrast with Eva Hoffman's. Hoffman was removed from her childhood paradise to make her way in a New World exile. She propelled herself to what others might consider to be America's center, at the *New York Times*, but her book testifies to her discovery that in America, now, there is no center. The immigrant is obliged to assimilate to a culture in which "assimilation" itself is an outmoded concept. The story Hoffman tells is not so much a Jewish story as it is a story about a crisis of language and the self.

An Orphan in History is little concerned with such issues. It is a self-consciously Jewish book about the search for "roots," a central motif in American popular culture during the past three decades. Inevitably that quest takes for granted the possibility and desirability of a centered self, anchored in a firm attachment to the past. And in part Cowan's book is structured as a traditional genealogical account of the progress of the generations. The recounting of family stories, and the faith in the possibility of continuity, gives to this autobiography a heroic, if old-fashioned, cast.

The tone and theme are established in the opening paragraph: *"An Orphan in History* is my story as an American Jew. I have spent years retrieving the religious and cultural legacy, which had evaporated, in my family, under the pressure of assimilation. But, with only slight variations in personal and cultural details, it could be the story of Frankie Ruggio, whose grandfather spoke Italian and was named Dante."

The Frank Ruggio allusion—slightly kitschy this multiculturalism—tells us that this Jewish story is also an American story, a story that is plainly meant to inspire. I want to discuss this book against the grain, because it seems to me more moving and interesting not in its representative aspects—as the story of a generation—but in its uniqueness. I am especially interested in how the terror of discontinuity in the relationship between Paul and his father, Louis, was translated into a massive effort of retrieval that eventuated in this book. And since Cowan was always as much an activist as a writer, that led also to the creation and reconstruction of several Jewish institutions on New York's Upper West Side, where Cowan lived with his wife and children up to the time of his death, in 1988, from leukemia.

I should acknowledge, at the start, that this story has engaged me partly because Paul Cowan was a friend of mine, in college and after. And because, like Paul, I have found myself moved, after the death of my own father, to learn more about the Jewish past.

Cowan writes about the search for the Jewish past. But different American Jews have different pasts. His own, partially suppressed though it was by his father, was extraordinarily rich and crowded. Genealogical work enabled a retrieval of the stories of several generations, going back to their origins in Europe. And what wonderful people they were, like minor characters in Saul Bellow's Chicago novels. Cowan's mother, Polly, was the daughter of Modey Spiegel, the founder of Spiegel's, the great mail-order empire. Without renouncing Judaism, Modey became a Christian Scientist and found pleasure in denouncing recently arrived Eastern European Jews as "kikes."

But the most important discovery of this project of retrieval was Paul's paternal grandfather, Jake Cohen. I have said that Paul's book reminds me of Bellow. In many ways the plot is even better than most of Bellow's. It recalls Dickens and other Victorian novels that are organized about the discovery of a legacy and include a family scandal and a deep secret. As in Dickens, the young initiate is unable to determine his identity until he solves the mystery of his origins. The mystery in this book has to do with Louis Cowan's carefully repressed Jewish background. Those origins are summed up and symbolized in the grotesque figure of old Jake Cohen.

Louis Cowan never denied being a Jew, but his whole life was devoted to being successful in the American way, and that seemed to him to require being ethnically indistinguishable. His own father, back in Chicago, had been all too distinguishable, and so Louis Cowan, the respected television producer and president of CBS, deleted Jake from the record. For all practical purposes, Paul Cowan's grandfather, though still alive, didn't exist. What complicates all this is that Lou and Polly provided enough clues to the part of their past that was left out to encourage their oldest son, Paul, to undertake a search that ended not only with revelations about the Chicago world they had come from, but with a renewed sense of participation in five thousand years of Jewish history and religion.

Jake Cohen was the kind of charming ne'er-do-well whom it is more fun to read about than to have for a near relative. As the eldest of Moses Cohen's ten children, Jake started out as his father's partner in a Chicago scrap-iron yard. But Jake was a restless sort who would leave work without telling anybody to go to ball games and vaudeville shows. His most unsettling trait was his eccentric philanthropy. In the words of a relative, Jake was a "Jewish Robin Hood." He was a regular at the synagogue, where he frequently provided, gratis, the cakes and wine for the Kiddush after the religious service. In addition, he often brought home poor Jews and gave money to them and to needy members among the extended family. He was, as Paul Cowan writes, "the mitzvah man, the bestower of good deeds."

The problem was that the money that underwrote Jake's philanthropy was not his own. He was continually borrowing substantial amounts from relatives and friends. He made the rounds of the synagogues, hospitals, and old-age homes like a Jewish Walt Whitman, but without the great sanity that was part of Whitman's generosity. Perhaps there is a connection between Jake's restless generosity and the life of his grandson Paul, who spent the 1960s searching without success for a cause in which he could believe and who in later years built a struggling Jewish community not only for his own family but for all those he lived among. Quixotic idealism may have come down to my college friend as much from this

Eastern European mitzvah man as from the more sober "secular messianism" he regarded as his legacy from his mother, an ardent and courageous volunteer in the civil rights movement. I don't mean, however, to associate Paul with the fecklessness of his forebear. Paul often seemed disorganized, but he was uncommonly effective in practical matters.

In any case, it's clear that for Jake Cohen the price of living in fantasy was high. He caused the bankruptcy of the scrap-iron business, and later he ran into the ground his own business in used cement bags. The cost of his flightiness is not to be estimated in dollars alone, however. For he fatally alienated his German Jewish wife, Hetty, and forfeited the love of his only child, Lou, who went with his mother when she walked out on Jake in 1930. As Paul Cowan reconstructs the events, Lou Cohen decided then, around the age of twenty-one, to change his name. Lou Cohen became Louis G. Cowan and forever after refused to see his father (although he sent him a substantial allowance for many years). Nor did he allow the old man to see his grandchildren. For the rest of his life, Louis Cowan lived with this secret in his past. When Paul asked if it might be true that the Cohens had been distinguished persons in the old country, their name being that of rabbis, Lou Cowan made a joke of the suggestion, saying that they took the name Cohen at Ellis Island to give themselves some social status among Jews in America.

In Paul Cowan's view, Lou's repudiation of Jake Cohen carried along with it a rejection of a certain kind of Jewishness. A lot of this had to do with the enmity of the assimilated German Jewish Smitzes (the family of Lou's mother) toward the more devout, more emotionally expressive, more uncouth Cohens, who used the "jargon" (Yiddish) and came from backward Eastern Europe. Paul Cowan's researches determined that the Cohens were far from being backward. Contrary to what his father had told him, the Cohens did indeed trace their line back to a distinguished rabbi of Lidvinova in Lithuania. They were genuine Cohens.

If Eva Hoffman's book can be described as an essay on assimilation, no matter how decentered, Paul Cowan's can be seen as a study in disassimilation. Considered in its positive aspects, it is about recovering an ancient religious and cultural legacy. But that recovery implied certain refusals, a shedding of certain attitudes that had earlier gone unquestioned. Thus the Judaism Paul Cowan recovers is the joyful Hasidic spirituality of Eastern Europe, but along with that recovery goes the repudiation of the German Jewish way of the Spiegels and the Smitzes. That way Paul Cowan came to see as too accommodating in relation to American WASP business culture. It was precisely just such an accommodation that was the central thread in Louis Cowan's career.

It seems that Lou Cowan was concealing certain facts about himself even before he changed his name at twenty-one. Paul tells the story of how his father tried to keep his bar mitzvah a secret from his assimilated Jewish friends in Chicago. But the "clandestine" bar mitzvah is used by Paul not to raise questions about his father's overall credibility but quite positively, as proof that Lou knew Hebrew and had real ties to the world of *Yiddishkeit* which he later felt compelled to hide. According to the idea of his father's life presented here by the son, it was this Cohen/Eastern European side of Lou Cowan that emerged in his last fifteen years, after his break with the WASP corporate world.

The structure of a book like this would seem to require repudiation of the father whose concealment of important parts of his past made his oldest son's job of finding his own identity much more difficult. But that doesn't happen. Paul does everything he can to protect his father's reputation in his own mind and that of his reader. Paul becomes a latter-day version of his grandfather, "the mitzvah man." He makes us feel that Lou Cowan's concealments hurt himself more than anyone else.

Considering the effort of research that Paul Cowan invested in learning about the Cohens of Lidvinova, he shows little investigative zeal in tracking down matters closer to hand. One would want to know more, for example, about Lou Cowan's career in business. Paul suggests that one reason Lou had to distance himself from his scapegrace father is that Lou was just starting out as a public relations man in Chicago, with Gentile clients like the Methodist Church and Chicago's Christmas Seal drive. Lou's background also included racier elements, like his publicity work for the old Aragon and Trianon ballrooms and the bandleaders who played there. He was half-owner, too, of a roller-skating rink. There was nothing about the later Louis Cowan of the Damon Runyon Broadway type, but he had enough sense of himself as different from them to resist the pressure of his German Jewish relatives, who hoped he would attend law school and choose a more respectable career than that of press agent.

We pretty much lose track of this career in the 1930s except for learning that Lou made his mark in the field of radio, as an inventor of quiz shows, including the popular show *Quiz Kids*. On the basis of this radio work, Lou was tapped to become the director of the Office of War Information in 1942. The new job required his moving to New York, and it made possible a new, grander phase for the Cowan family. When I read Paul's book, with its weakness for 1940s-ish populist affirmations about a mystical and mythical America, a fuzzy place without ethnic or class conflicts, I think of his father, who used his media experience in trying to enlist support at home for the Allied war effort. The same middlebrow style of Lou Cowan's wartime propaganda informed the new quiz shows that he produced after the war, when he was back in radio and then later in television.

Paul Cowan includes some fascinating pages on his father's career in the 1950s, when Paul was studying at Choate and at Harvard and Lou was in his heyday at CBS TV. We learn from the son about family discussions related to Lou's taking the job as president of CBS, and how he saw himself in those years. The reader might get the idea from Paul's exposition that Lou Cowan was a frustrated intellectual who would have used the media to educate the public but for the demands of CBS's top executives. But we get a different view in Joan Shelley Rubin's *The Making of Middlebrow Culture* (1992), in which Lou Cowan is seen as one of those who allowed the better impulses of the old genteel culture to be co-opted by the booming new postwar consumer culture.

Paul Cowan maintains that shows like *The Quiz Kids* helped to make American children eager to learn and that other programs like it served as an antidote in the fifties to the anti-intellectualism engendered by the McCarthyite red scare. Even the big-money quiz show *The $64,000 Question* is made to seem as if it were the university of the air. That program led to Lou Cowan's downfall when the pervasive rigging of TV quiz shows was revealed. Lou Cowan may well have been innocent of the rigging, as Paul insists, but it can hardly be said that he resisted the trend to splashiness that was so different from the relative innocence of radio talk shows in the forties.

Lou Cowan was forced to resign as president of CBS TV in 1959. This scandal seems, in retrospect, to have been inevitable as the exposure that Louis Cowan's entire life up to that point had been devoted to fending off. It is surely possible that Louis Cowan was not involved in the rigging, but his conduct in the case remains mysterious. Asked to resign by CBS's top brass, he simply withdrew from the field, never writing a book or launching a legal case to vindicate his name. And he never subsequently attempted a comeback. His curious behavior confirms his son's sense of the man as oddly vulnerable despite his worldly success. For the seventeen years that remained of Lou Cowan's life, he mainly involved himself in teaching, at Brandeis and the journalism school of Columbia University, and in volunteer assignments with the organized Jewish community. It was as if Lou Cowan was free, finally, to give expression to his Jewish idealism.

The devastating scandal marked a milestone in Paul Cowan's project of disassimilation. The quiz show scandal and CBS's sacking of his father was an illustration of the establishment culture from which Paul had always been in flight. As if to express his difference, he increasingly separated himself from everything that he had come to regard as cold or slick or superficial. In this book, which devotes six pages to Paul's stint in the Peace Corps and about that much space to his six months in Israel, there is hardly any mention of his four years at Harvard or his postgraduate year at the University of Chicago. The reason is that, if the corporate world was unfeeling, the professors, as he saw it, were excessively abstract and theoretical in their approach to life.

Paul Cowan also firmly distanced himself from "the movement" of the 1960s, in which he had his start. He seems to have felt that the good days of the New Left had ended fairly early, perhaps by 1966 or 1967. His book includes example after example of gods that failed, American icons from which the author needed to disassimilate. But he remained ever loyal to his father during the latter's lifetime, and after his death in 1976 he tried even harder to bind his father to him, as if discontinuity were the worst possible fate. But what has Lou Cowan's very American rise and fall to do with Paul's retrieval of Judaism and the Jewish past?

On the one hand, we have the son, devoted to authenticity and so bent on not repeating his parents' lives that he chooses the way of downward social mobility—although no one should confuse the comfortable upper-middle-class world of New York's Upper West Side with being down and out in the manner, say, of the younger George Orwell.

Still, the difference between Paul Cowan and his parents remains significant. As a journalist he worked for the raffish *Village Voice,* not the *New York Times;* and as a reporter he invariably sought authenticity among the poor and marginalized, who seemed to the boy from Park Avenue to have a more fierce engagement with "reality" than the wealthy people among whom he grew up.

On the other hand, there is the father, devoted as a PR man and then as a producer of entertainment for television to a sanitized version of things. How did this remarkable son protect in his own consciousness the image of this equally remarkable father, even while choosing his very different path? It seems that the holes in the father's life story bred in the son a will, as he says, to "heal the rift," so that there would be no break in the relations between them such as occurred in the relation between Lou Cowan and his father. Paul Cowan was very attached to his father, perhaps more than if the father had been more candid about himself.

The main consequence for Paul Cowan of his father's editing of the past was a restless search, ending usually with disillusionment, for something to believe in. Dad, the smoothie, buttered up the show biz crowd at Sardi's in the days of his glory, but his son needed to find a reality more substantial. The 1960s were Paul's years of idealistic striving but also of repeated disappointment. After the civil rights movement let him down, so did the New Left and then the Peace Corps. After he left the last of these, he wrote a book entitled *The Making of an Un-American* (1970). It was a record of disenchantment. The title itself suggests a commitment to disassimilation, a reversal of his father's journey.

In *An Orphan in History* Cowan frequently invokes the novelist John Dos Passos. Perhaps he was responding to the sardonic portrayal of the PR man and World War I propagandist J. Ward Moorehouse in Dos Passos's trilogy *U.S.A.* Certainly Louis Cowan was a far more decent, honorable man than Moorehouse, but both made their way in the world by sweet-talking. A repeatedly baffled, disenchanted Paul might have become a latter-day version of another Dos Passos character, Vag, with whom the *U.S.A.* trilogy ends. If the disillusioning pattern of the 1960s had repeated itself in the two subsequent decades of his life, Cowan might have become a spiritual drifter, an emotional vagabond, a man without a home or a people.

An Orphan in History is about how the author averted that fate. After the death of his parents in a fire in 1976, Cowan's preoccupation with his father's past intensified. He took on reporting assignments that led to his meeting with a Hasidic rabbi on the Lower East Side of New York who functioned for him as a substitute father and as the master in a rite of initiation into Judaism. In Paul's own language, his rabbi was a genuine mitzvah man, a bestower of goodness out of the wealth of his unshakable faith. Paul Cowan does not himself claim any such faith in this book—he specifically remarks that it was his wife, not he, who fell in love with Judaism as a religion. For Cowan, Judaism meant continuity and community more than it meant a supernatural faith. The important thing is that his Hasidic rabbi-mentor gave him an alternative to the feckless Jake Cohen who was his grandfather and to the smooth-talking Lou Cowan who was his father. And at the same time he could continue to love these imperfect but well-meaning forebears.

Paul Cowan was able now to throw in his lot with something that stood on an ancient foundation. His lifelong mourning—first for his own lost self, later for his parents—could come to an end. His need was too great for him to entertain postmodernist doubts like Eva Hoffman's about whether any foundation could be real or could guarantee the stability and continuity of his own self. He had finally found something that would not let him down, as had the left-wing politics of the 1960s.

It is a moving story, this narrative of the son committed to protecting his father's image within himself while at the same time rescuing himself from spiritual drift. The charm of the story, as Paul Cowan tells it, is that his new commitment allows the coexistence of his Jewish and American selves: "Now I am an American and a Jew. I live at once in the years 1982 and 5743, the Jewish year in which I am publishing this book. I am Paul Cowan, the New York–bred son of Louis Cowan and Pauline Spiegel Cowan, Chicago-born, very American, very successful parents; and I am Saul Cohen, the descendant of rabbis in Germany and Lithuania."

The rhythm and diction of this passage derive from the opening paragraph of Saul Bellow's *The Adventures of Augie March,* rather than from, say, Genesis. And we recall the frequent objection to Bellow's novel, that its optimism is too theoretical, wished for rather than justified in the texture of the novel.

Certainly it seems a romantic ideal, this notion of having it both ways, Jewish and American, of having it all. But I think Paul Cowan was right in seeing his Americanness as at least as important as his newly embraced Jewishness. I wonder what might have been the next stops in his spiritual pilgrimage if Cowan had lived to a healthy old age. Dos Passos, whom he admired and whom he resembled in many ways, moved from left-wing radicalism in the early 1930s to celebration of American libertarian values in his later writing. It's not likely that Cowan would have become a right-winger like Dos Passos had he lived. But he might have continued to feel himself less and less an outsider. His personal trajectory, toward ethnic self-affirmation, has become our contemporary paradigm. His way of being Jewish now looks to be a characteristic way of being American for nearly all the ethnic groups in our emerging multicultural society. Particularism has become our way of being like everybody else. Nowadays nothing could be more un-American than trying to assimilate to an ideal American type, when the supposed exemplars of that type themselves feel like members of a marginalized group. John Updike's characters feel quite as out of the mainstream as Philip Roth's.

There was a deep sentimentality about the image of America in the propaganda disseminated by Louis Cowan during World War II, and there is a parallel sentimentality in Paul Cowan's way of inserting himself into the Walt Whitman–Carl Sandburg populist tradition. In the foreword to *An Orphan in History,* Cowan merges himself not only with Frankie Ruggio the Italian but also with the progeny of a Scandinavian fisherman, Per Hansa, and a Cuban cigar maker, Jose Martinez, all immigrants to America, all constituents of the great American rainbow. Paul Cowan inaugurated his career as a writer with *The Making of an Un-American,* an autobiographical account of the loss of illusions. It may be that anyone who writes a book with such a title in his late twenties is likely to have earlier taken for granted that his identity was totally interwoven with the fabric of his homeland. As a civil rights activist and New Left radical, Cowan was able to take a great deal for granted about his privileged place in the social order he opposed. The greatest privilege conferred by his upbringing may not have been money or status but a certainty about belonging that itself enabled the stance of opposition. True, that certainty expressed itself in a kind of populist national mysticism rather than a cult of "we happy few." But the main thing is that a prodigal of this kind is likely to come home.

Thus *An Orphan in History* is not about being an orphan but about getting your family back, reclaiming your legacy. That family consists not only of the Cohens from whom Lou Cowan had fled, and not only the other born-again Jews who shared the synagogue and school and day-care center Paul and Rachel Cowan established in their West Side neighborhood. The family is also all the other children and grandchildren of immigrants, hyphenated Americans who have successfully made the case in recent years that coming from somewhere else is what America has always been about.

Many Jewish American writers are writing about themselves these days, and their theme is often the retrieval of their Jewish religious and cultural legacy. The whole burgeoning field of Jewish studies is one major expression of this turn. The question remains whether the current retrieval will prove any more lasting than previous Jewish religious and cultural reawakenings. It is inevitable that in America the recovery of Jewish roots will take an American form. But one hopes that this return and the writing it engenders will seem in retrospect more than a fashion, that it will not appear as a type of middlebrow conformity, like the greater part of the "radical" literature of the 1930s or the recovery of Americanness during the war years. The lightness of being is lighter in America than anywhere else, and nothing is easier at present than ethnic correctness.

Revisiting Morrie
Were His Last Words Too Good to Be True?

No doubt it is imprudent to write critically of Morris "Morrie" Schwartz, who became a national icon as a victim of amyotrophic lateral sclerosis—the fatal neurodegenerative disease (better known as Lou Gehrig's disease or ALS) that leads, usually in two to four years, to the atrophy of all the body's voluntary muscles, including those that make it possible to breathe. Providing an example of how to live in the shadow of death, Morrie was interviewed by Ted Koppel on three separate *Nightline* TV shows in his final year, 1996, and his reflections on love and death were tape-recorded by former students of his (Morrie had been a popular professor of sociology at Brandeis for more than three decades). The tapes became the basis for two books—*Morrie: In His Own Words* (1999) and Mitch Albom's *Tuesdays with Morrie: An Old Man, a Young Man, and Life's Greatest Lesson* (1997)—the latter of which

Though this essay appears toward the end of the book, where Mark wanted it, it was among those closest to Mark's heart. Mark was put off by both the sentimentality of Mitch Albom's *Tuesdays with Morrie* and the adoration that book received from readers and critics, and he felt strongly that another view of ALS and its horrors was in order. Even after this article was published in the *Forward* in January 2002, the public adulation of *Morrie* remained a preoccupation of his, and he continued to rework the essay. As late as March 22, 2003, just a week before his death, Mark asked that extended thoughts about Morrie be appended. Some of his last-hour writing was fragmentary and first draft, but some of it was as pungent and provocative as the original, and we've incorporated some if its paragraphs into this essay. Eds.

was made into a movie that won an Emmy Award and, the last time I checked, had nearly five million copies in print. In the process, Morrie became a much-revered figure.

Obviously, Morrie is a hard guy to criticize. And when I say Morrie, of course, I mean Morrie as presented to us by Mitch Albom. Morrie was a well-meaning and loving person whose message has brought inspiration and consolation to many people. But I think I have a right to express myself. I, too, have ALS. My version of ALS, progressive bulbar palsy, which first attacks the mouth and throat, is considered more devastating than Morrie's, since most people would rather be confined to a wheelchair than not be able to speak. Morrie was still talking it up nearly to the end. (My own legs and arms will eventually go the way of my speech and swallowing.) Most important, bulbar patients usually die sooner than patients who are first afflicted in their limbs because their respiratory muscles usually atrophy faster.

But even if our diseases were identical, I would still find Morrie's "wisdom" not all that wise. His message seems to me mainly a blend of middlebrow platitudes with New Age spirituality, and his huge sales prove less that Morrie was a sage than that in his final months he was saying things that people wanted to hear.

I am not being hard on Morrie simply because I want to contest his primacy as an ALS sufferer. The world has seen enough rivalry among victims. It is more to the point that professionally I am a literary critic, and criticism (as well as analysis, appreciation, interpretation) is what critics do. That Morrie is himself uncritical is, in fact, part of my objection to him. Morrie urges his own nonjudgmental stance on everybody else—especially urging dying patients to think affirmatively—but there is a limit to the usefulness of such an upbeat message. I think that people suffering from fatal diseases such as ALS are better served by straight talk than by Morrie's homilies. Personally, I can deal better with extreme experience—what is already here and what is to come—when it is described as objectively as possible than when it is rendered with a moralistic glow. The actual experience of ALS is at odds with Morrie's message of sweetness and light. Your mind is not affected, but over time your body ceases to do what you wish it to. My own suffering from ALS has been mostly emotional, stemming from the frustration of becoming increasingly unable to transform my thoughts into speech that can be understood. Demoralization and a sense of helplessness follow from the progressive irrelevance of one's will. Cognitive functioning remains unimpaired, so you can be aware of all the things you can no longer do.

At this point, my breathing is so diminished that I am in home hospice care. I no longer go to the hospital for checkups; recently, when my feeding tube broke, paramedics came to my apartment, wrapped me up, and delivered me by ambulance to the emergency room, where the tube was surgically reimplanted in my stomach. The single most frightening event since losing my capacity for speech has been radical weakening of the fingers I use for "talking" using E-triloquist, my artificial speech software. I now have splints to keep my hands from further clawing and have a "scanner" that will make my speech machine still usable after I can no longer type. The scanner involves a switcher and will slow me down considerably, but it is assuring that I will still be able to communicate. Notwithstanding my various mechanical aids, I find it hard to keep panic at bay as helplessness descends.

That is me. What about Morrie? He is skimpy in his direct account of living with ALS. For him ALS is mostly an occasion to discourse on the larger issue of how to cope with the prospect of death. Insofar as Morrie's message derives from traditional religious and philosophical sources, much of it is predicated on familiar Western affirmations and ethical imperatives. Thus he urges persons with fatal diseases to take moral stock and become loving, forgiving, compassionate, and gentle to persons to whom they previously were ambivalent.

Where Morrie is somewhat more original is in playing moral therapist. He takes advantage of the authority with which ALS endows him to teach other sufferers how to comfort themselves. Morrie says, "It's very important to be kind and loving to yourself. You're the only self you've got, so to speak." Persons living with the prospect of early death, who may be inclined to blame themselves for their condition, may find some comfort in being given permission to be kind to themselves. But it is hard to imagine truly traumatized persons being touched at a deep level by such counseling. My hospice care has included a chaplain. That person has enabled me, in just two visits so far, to penetrate to deep places heretofore inaccessible to me. I cannot imagine that reading and rereading Morrie would accomplish remotely as much.

Morrie's argument, to the extent that it has a logic, is about the relationship between part and whole. He emphasizes individual self-consciousness as the key to his psycho-moral code, but then he says that each of us ought also to feel that we are part of humanity as a whole, part of nature, and fated to live on after death in a condition of spiritual oneness. It is here, in passing from psychological self-awareness to spiritual connectedness, that he rides off the rails into light-minded New Age spirituality.

For instance, one of the few anecdotes he has to tell is a story told by his meditation teacher to illustrate the idea of spiritual connectedness. "There is a little wave . . . bobbing up and down in the ocean off the shore. All of a sudden, he realizes he's going to crash into the shore . . . he's now moving toward the shore, and he'll be annihilated." At this point another wave tells him not to despair because "you're not a wave; you're part of the ocean." The point is that we do not suffer individual deaths; rather, we are part of something larger than ourselves and immortal.

Walt Whitman wrote poems affirming our being part of the ocean and eternity and so forth. But Whitman also wrote great poems of doubt, such as "As I Ebb'd with the Ocean of Life." Whitman's poetry is immortal and Morrie's "wisdom" ephemeral because the poet acknowledges the fact of death whereas the would-be guru writes it off with reassuring allegories and banal aphorisms. In a saturnalia of self-help syncretism, he invokes Jesus, meditation practices, Martin Buber's "I and Thou," Buddhism, the Indian philosopher Krishnamurti, Jewish mysticism, W. H. Auden, and the Beatles, all on behalf of his self-described mantra: "Love each other or die."

Love may be said to be Morrie's great subject, but his version of love is strictly chicken soup. One of his weakest chapters, the chapter on marriage, is symptomatic of his universalizing impulse. For all his invocations of love he has so little to say about his wife and sons. He attends much more closely to his relationship to himself. He has nothing to say, for instance, on how his relationship to his wife may have differed from his friendship with the Brandeis colleagues who seem always to be visiting him. Perhaps his wife's sense of privacy militated against personal revelations, but it is more likely, I think, that Morrie's middlebrow guruism is incompatible with a life in which an intense relationship with one person is at the center.

At the close of his last interview on *Nightline,* Morrie rolled his eyes heavenward and said to Ted Koppel: "I'm bargaining with Him up there now. I'm asking Him, 'Do I get to be one of the angels?'" If he so managed, it is as a Hallmark greeting card angel, his message adorned with bows and ribbons. In dilating endlessly on goodness, Morrie doesn't say enough about suffering and evil. Unfortunately, opposites such as goodness and evil remain abstract unless we can consider them in relationship to each other. That is why Morrie is unable to illuminate the question of love. In what has been reported, he does not ever face up to the rage and hatred that are inevitably evoked by a degenerative disease as debilitating as ALS.

Morrie's major work in sociology had been carried out several decades before he came down with ALS. It concerned the social relations between mental patients and their professional caretakers. In the final phase of his life, he acted out the role of caretaker, more to the well than to the sick. He explained how to live in the face of death. But he did not offer his counsel as a scientific advisor, as Dr. Sherwin Nuland has so brilliantly done; or as a religious philosopher, as Boethius did; or as a writer of fiction, like Tolstoy in "The Death of Ivan Ilych." In his late seventies, when he developed ALS, Morrie came forth as a one-man adjunct of Hallmark's greeting card department.

In the old days, New York's public intellectuals would have quickly stepped in to expose Morrie's trivial pursuits. The art critic Clement Greenberg was one of the most brilliant of the first generation of New York intellectuals. In 1939 he published in *Partisan Review* a seminal essay, "Avant Garde and Kitsch." *Tuesdays with Morrie* is pure kitsch, sentimental and sometimes pretentious slush that Vladimir Nabokov referred to by a Russian word, *poshlust,* five years later in his book on Gogol. But now that we dwell in a sea of kitsch and so many literature professors rely on it for their subject matter—their specialty is called cultural studies—we are not likely to see such foolishness called by its right name.

No doubt I reacted as negatively to *Tuesdays with Morrie* as I did because it did so little justice to the debilitating experience I was suffering. But I have a lot invested, also, in a certain human development that Morrie implicitly repudiated with his sickly transcendentalism. That development involved growing out of narrow, parochial beginnings and finding a new home in the world of ideas and a realistic, critical attitude toward life and one's own and other persons' integration of their ideas, moral attitudes, and implicit choices about an ideal self and society. Who could be sentimental about such a project, living a life through one's reading and creating a self through writing in which one dealt with one's traumas and at the same time tried to do justice to the texts under review and the ideas and theories that enabled one's critique. Such a kind of writing could never sell enough books to achieve bestseller status, much less hang up there on the charts year after year. This was how-to writing after a manner of speaking, but the "how to" it argued for did not call for dissolving all the difficulties and complexities in a strawberry-smelling bubble bath.

I find myself depressed a good part of the time. At other times I'm furious—at receptionists, health insurance people, airline reservationists, and "friends" who have mysteriously vanished since I became sick. I think about the friends in a poem by George MacBeth (who himself died of ALS at age sixty) titled "Laughter in Hell":

> One f**ker was even crying. I'll do the crying,
> Sonny boy, you stand and listen. Give
> Me a break. Friends!
> I'd rather have enemies.

Like MacBeth, I understand that I am displacing my rage to hapless people who have difficulty dealing with emotions. But I find it hard taking seriously anyone who has had ALS and does not acknowledge the negative feelings that are an inevitable part of the experience unless one is committed, heart and mind, to repressing them. Morrie's love contains too much schmaltz to provide nourishment to a person near the end of the line. A better book would probe the varieties of love: gratitude, tenderness, loyalty, the fierceness and intensity that do not suddenly disappear with one's capacity for speech, the joy in the presence and happiness of one's loved ones, the affection and concern for one's offspring. There is so much to say that Morrie does not begin to say. But to do justice to the variety and complexity of love in extreme circumstances would require a different kind of book.

The Art of the Obituary

Some newspaper readers start their days with the sports section or the crossword puzzle. I start with the death notices. My favorite American paper is the *New York Times,* partly because it's the best at obituaries. I doubt I am alone in my fascination with obits, but people don't talk about the recently deceased as they do about the Yankees or the Lakers. Cultural studies professors write articles about comic strips and hip-hop, but nobody writes about the obituary as either a literary form or an expression of social mores.

My own interest in obituaries is easy enough to understand. I have a terminal illness, amyotrophic lateral sclerosis. ALS, more familiarly known as Lou Gehrig's disease, is a neurodegenerative muscular disease that usually claims its victims' lives within two to four years of diagnosis. My own illness was discovered about a year and a half ago, so you might be reading my own obit before too long.

Being terminally ill, however, hasn't made me obsess about my own obituary; it has merely intensified my longstanding interest in other people's obits. As a scholar specializing in literary history, I have always read obituaries as minibiographies—stories of lives, not of deaths. At their best, obituaries strip away the nonessentials in order to disclose the inner form of their subjects' personal dramas. Few things fascinate me more than the trajectories of human lives.

I was therefore as pleased as can be when, several years ago, I was introduced to the obit editors at the London *Guardian* by an American friend who wrote occasional obits for them, and was asked to try my

This essay appeared in *American Scholar* 71.4 (Autumn 2002): 91–96.

hand. Before I became sick with ALS, I wrote about a dozen obits of American writers for the *Guardian*. Most of these have not yet been published, because their subjects are still alive. They were written, in newspaper lingo, as "advance obits." I was paid, as it were, for inventory that went into storage, from which it would be extracted when one of my notables died.

Several of my subjects are in their eighties and nineties, whereas I just turned sixty-three. I get up every morning to see if one of them has died in the hope, frustrated each time, that I will finally see my name in print and receive acknowledgment for my work. When I see that they have all survived another day, I think to myself, Dammit! Every day my muscles weaken further; I have to take food through a tube inserted in my stomach; I can no longer speak; diminishing strength in my hands is beginning to threaten my ability to dress myself. Meanwhile, the subjects of my as-yet-unpublished obits are still touting their books and accepting prizes and receiving honorary degrees. Who would have thought, when I wrote about these buggers, that they would outlive me? Am I angry about my fate? Dear reader, would you be? But maybe I'll get lucky and one or two will die before me.

My obits for the *Guardian,* like most British newspaper obits, are not straight, chronological accounts. In order to provide some sense of the subject's personality, they include a good deal of interpretation and evaluation. Though in writing them I never violated the taboo against speaking ill of the dead, neither did I pretend to the perfect objectivity of the *New York Times*. But I didn't go nearly as far as some of my British colleagues at the *Guardian* and the *Independent* who have led the shift from the formal standard once set by the stiffly solemn obits in the *Times* of London. My obits, and those of my American friend, place us, as authors, firmly in the background, whereas many Brit-on-Brit obits are now "appreciations" informed by the writer's friendship with the deceased. They often refer to the dead person by his or her first name. The impression they create is that of an intimate society in which everyone who matters knows everyone else. You get a feeling for what Gertrude Stein once called England's "daily island life," with its predictable rituals and secure social hierarchy.

In his excellent "Essay upon Epitaphs," William Wordsworth argued that the epitaph form reflected a desire to render eternal the memory of the deceased. The original impulse for inscriptions upon tombs, he said, arose from a belief in immortality. It might seem that the modern obituary had its origins in such sentiments, which were formalized in the poetic epitaph, a literary genre that had its heyday in the seventeenth and eighteenth centuries. In fact, obituaries as a form did not begin until later and were a far more modest way of acknowledging the dead. At the start, in the late eighteenth century, a periodical's obituary column was a mere list of recently deceased worthies. With the expansion of the popular press and the reading public, these notices gradually expanded to the length of our modern newspaper obits.

Even now, a substantial part of each day's obit section is devoted to brief death notices of the old-fashioned sort. My local paper distinguishes between the "paid death notice" and the "unpaid news obituary." In the former case, family or friends of the deceased compose the notice, which usually runs only a few lines. It may suggest something about our modern secular culture that you place this notice through the paper's classified advertising department, as if the deceased were a used car you were trying to sell. When it comes to the unpaid news obit, the relatives of the deceased are also often involved in "selling," persuading the news staff that their dead son or mother deserves to be written up because of his or her contribution to the community. Of course, there are figures for whom no such pleading is necessary. If your father was Joe Bonanno or John Gotti, he will end up in the paper when he's dead because he was in the paper when he was alive.

American obituaries reflect a very different sense of time from the eye-on-eternity perspective of the traditional poetic epitaph. Like the modern newspaper itself, the obit section strives to be timely and topical. The obits in the *New York Times* are written as news stories. The understanding is that the recently dead are part of a passing show and that, like the front page headlines themselves, they will be replaced tomorrow by new objects of interest.

At the other end of the spectrum is London's *Daily Telegraph*, which, by encouraging us to remember its obituary subjects as comic figures, may come closer to conferring Wordsworthian immortality than any other paper in the world.

But Wordsworth could never have anticipated the emergence of the humorous obituary. That innovation in the tradition of death writing can be credited to Hugh Massingberd, who became the *Telegraph*'s obituary editor in the mid-1980s. Massingberd had previously been the editor of Burke's peerage publications, a background that equipped him well for the right-leaning *Telegraph,* with its sympathetic attitudes toward England's hereditary aristocracy. As it turned out, Massingberd's obits page devoted a great deal of attention to recently deceased lords and baronets, but showed little of the piety toward them that one might have anticipated.

The Very Best of the Daily Telegraph Books of Obituaries, published in London last year, is Massingberd's sixth compilation of the paper's obits, all so well written that they are likely to make a small place for themselves in English literary history. A best-seller in the United Kingdom, *The Very Best* is remarkable for the same charm, wit, and explosive irreverence that distinguished earlier *Telegraph* compilations, whose subtitles, including *Heroes and Adventurers, Entertainers,* and *Rogues,* suggest a readership interested more in eccentric characters than in Nobel Prize winners. Thus, we find the Third Lord Moynihan, whose "chief occupations were bongo-drummer, confidence trickster, brothel keeper, drug-smuggler and police informer" and who "provided, through his character and career, ample ammunition for critics of the hereditary principle."

Not all the *Telegraph*'s obits are of peers; plenty of scoundrels and oddballs can be found in the lower regions of show business and journalism. The former newspaperman Graham Mason, for example, found his true calling as "the drunkest man in the Coach and Horses, the pub in Soho where, in the half century after the Second World War, a tragicomedy was played out nightly by its regulars." The *Telegraph* doesn't cast Mason's life in tragic terms; on the contrary, his mishaps are presented as farce.

The *Telegraph*'s most recent anthology also includes an obit of the memoirist Barbara Skelton, who caught the editor's eye less because of her writing than because of the "petulant promiscuity" it revealed. Skelton was sexually involved with several renowned figures in mid-twentieth-century literary London, including the book critic Cyril Connolly and the publisher George Weidenfeld, both of whom she married, as well as the drama critic Kenneth Tynan. Skelton's "peculiarly incisive malignity," in the words of the novelist Anthony Powell, seems not to have discouraged King Farouk of Egypt, with whom she also had an affair, as she did later in life with a French journalist, Bernard Frank, whose favors she shared with the novelist Françoise Sagan.

The *Telegraph*'s obituary of Skelton amuses and entertains; it makes no attempt to garner our sympathy. To appreciate the difference between British and American obituaries, one need only look at the headline from the recent *New York Times* obituary of another troubled woman writer notable for her well-written memoirs: "Caroline Knapp, Writer, 42; Chronicled Struggles and Joys," and then, in smaller type, "A columnist whose memoirs portrayed alcoholism and sweet lessons from her dog." After a dip into the *Telegraph* compilations, one might suspect the *Times* editors of irony at Ms. Knapp's expense. In fact, they were playing it perfectly straight in linking her drinking problem and her canine solution. The obit quotes from a book of hers: "I'm thirty-eight and I'm single, and I'm having my most intense and gratifying relationship with a dog. But we all learn about love in different ways, and this happens to be mine." Maybe if I get a dog and write about it, I will feel better about my illness. I will definitely be in a better position to make a claim on the interest of the editor of the *Times* obit section.

A week before the *Times* honored Caroline Knapp, it featured an obit of Lois Gould, at the center of whose writing life was the sudden death of her husband, a *Times* reporter. The dead man had left among his effects a diary written in code. Gould unlocked the code and thereby discovered that her late husband had been a serial adulterer who had chosen many of his lovers from among Gould's own friends. According to the *Times*, Gould's first novel, which was based on this painful experience, "offered a raw, darkly comic portrait of [the main character's] emotional life, her grief, rage, amphetamine popping and suicidal depression, along with frank depictions of her sexual life, which ran the gamut from quiet marital frustration to ardent masturbation." Gould built her subsequent reputation on telling all, chiefly in novels but also in a memoir of her difficult relationship with her mother.

Ever since Sylvia Plath, the royal road to fame for American women writers has been the confessional mode. Not all have taken that path, but writers of only moderate talent have received more recognition and enjoyed greater sales than their contemporaries when they told stories of emotional suffering and attempts at suicide. That leads me to think about how a truly loving husband married to a novelist memoirist might best plan to insure his wife's financial well-being after his death. A career of infidelities, documented in a diary, might be just the thing, although few financial consultants are likely to recommend it. In today's market, louche conduct and emotional anguish (transmuted into your widow's best-selling prose) may be worth a lot more than a portfolio of stocks.

I find the *Telegraph* obits of Barbara Skelton and her ilk altogether more appealing than those of the *Times*'s women, partly because the *Telegraph*'s ladies caused quite as much pain to their men as they got from them. Take, for example, Laura Riding, a minor poet who was Robert Graves's lover. The *Telegraph* cheerfully calls her "man-eating" and notes that she led a life "of cleverness unsanctified by humility, of power unredeemed by benevolence, and above all of human presumption swallowed up in the vast indifference of eternity." I know how our sympathies are supposed to run, but are dragons like Skelton and Riding so much less common than victims like Knapp and Gould?

The *Telegraph* obits may turn off American readers because of their cool indifference to the emotional distress of the families of their subjects. I have no doubt that Skelton, Riding, and whole battalions of men in these anthologies did suffer greatly, but their obits don't portray them with the aim of awakening the reader's compassion. Rather, the short lives in the *Telegraph* take as their models the characters in the British comic tradition from Shakespeare to Henry Fielding to Charles Dickens to Oscar Wilde to P. G. Wodehouse. In such comedy, externality is the great thing. You wouldn't be disposed to laugh while reading the obits of Barbara Skelton and Graham Mason if the emphasis were on their subjective pain.

I have enough pain of my own to make me grateful for the British revolution in obituary rhetoric, which has succeeded in making the *Telegraph* compilations such entertaining bedtime reading. I would be unlikely to keep the *Times* obit page by my bedside; its abundance of respect and paucity of anecdotes would weigh me down. But it isn't solely a literary issue, this contrast between the American fascination with psychological interiority and the British tendency to conceive of identity from the outside. Clearly it has a cultural-historical dimension as well.

The present period of British comic irreverence began shortly after the end of the Second World War, when the nation's great empire collapsed, and with it the class structure that had supported it. England's jokers have been flourishing ever since. To be sure, there were postwar writers (including John Osborne and the other Angry Young Men of the fifties) who were irritable rather than funny. But by the sixties, the antiestablishment stage review *Beyond the Fringe* and the magazine *Private Eye* had set the new tone in satire.

The politics of postimperial humor are surprising. The serious-minded obits in the left-leaning *Guardian* are well done, but not nearly as enjoyable as those in the *Telegraph*. How is it that the latter paper, traditionally associated with the values of the old class order, has chosen to make a home for such impudent obituaries?

Many Englishmen feel nostalgic for the old ways, but they also feel free to make fun of figures who call to mind that past and to laugh about their nation's diminished role. Indeed, part of the appeal of British obits to American readers is their near-total irrelevance to our more pressurized world. With so many enemies wanting to bring us down, we are far too anxious about our role as global leader to be ironic.

America presents itself officially as a deeply pious nation, and that image is reflected in our newspapers' dull obituaries. But the underlying mood of the nation is probably more accurately expressed in the nihilistic anarchical style of American satiric novels, typically a mix of grief, rage, and madness. The English—think of *Monty Python*—prefer goofiness. The *Telegraph* obits don't go in for denunciation; they merely poke fun at traditional British types—clergymen, peers, army officers, who, even in their roguishness and eccentricity, call to mind a lost world. That they don't measure up to the standard of British rectitude in the great age of empire doesn't keep us from feeling fond of them.

American satirists display greater acerbity, in some cases, even fury and hatred. And our cultural commentary is far more extreme than the Brits'. No wonder, given the nearly daily exposure of outrageous misbehavior at the top of our major institutions. Still, it might induce more useful national self-reflection if we had a few more laughs.

What we need is something other than the solemnity with which our newspapers speak of the dead and the hysteria-infused vindictiveness with which our novelists target the living. We could do worse than to learn a spirit of forgiveness and fun from the Brits. The period near the end of life is a good time to divert ourselves. And the end itself is the

best time for others to write about our lives with humor. I would welcome any American writer's attempt to apply the arts of amusement in
an obit about me.

V

LAST WORDS

Why Are English Departments Still Fighting the Culture Wars?

Everyone has heard about the culture wars that have torn apart university departments of English. But it was still shocking to read a *New York Times* article a few months ago about how animosity between traditional and theory-oriented professors at Columbia University has decimated its once-great department.

Similar antagonisms have created bedlam in a surprisingly large number of American departments of English. My own feelings about English-department life may be surmised from the fact that, in 1990, I jumped ship to take a full-time position in religion and literature in the Divinity School at the University of Chicago.

I was at ease teaching literature in a religious-studies setting because there was no pressure to reduce literature to the circumstances of material culture, or to race, class, and gender. The same could hardly be said about many cutting-edge English departments. During my years at Chicago, I was also an associate (nonvoting) member of the English department, but my real commitment was always to the Divinity School.

This essay appeared originally in the *Chronicle of Higher Education*, September 20, 2002. Mark never mentioned this for possible inclusion in the book, but we've decided to include it because, as a kind of capsule *apologia pro vita sua*, it helps explain why he was happy to leave "English" in 1990 and join the University of Chicago Divinity School, which he found more intellectually congenial and more collegial. Eds.

The usual explanation for the divisiveness in English is twofold. First, starting with the invasion of French poststructuralism in the 1960s, advanced literary interpretation changed from being formalist in method and traditionalist in ideology to a brand of French theory whose major distinguishing characteristic seemed to be that it required you to spend more time reading the theorists than reading the canonical texts of Western literature. The second major explanation for the culture wars is that they basically have been about politics, set off when '60s radicals took their battles from the streets into university departments.

But the culture wars have petered out in many departments. Why so much less so in English? I suggest that the bitterness of the canon wars, and so much else in academic literary studies, has had a great deal to do with the kind of people who become English professors. Here I need to appeal to my own experience.

My introduction to life in an English department was at Boston University, in the late '60s and early '70s. Those were some of the most intense years of the anti–Vietnam War movement and the youth counterculture, and the department was divided. The rather modest radicalism of the assistant professors antagonized many of the elders. Several tenured professors sympathized with our cause, but the dominant wing preferred to get on with business as usual, without the rumpus of sit-ins and all the rest. Their idea was that we young ones had veered from the proper—that is, aesthetic—focus of literary education.

My purpose is not to rehash that intradepartmental clash. In any case, it more often took the form of personal conflicts than of reasoned debate. For example, when I offered my congratulations to one of the most aggressive of the antiradicals, who had just received an invitation to join a highly prestigious English department, that professor spit out: "I'm not going anywhere. I'm going to stay here long enough to see you all buried."

"Professor X's" virulent hatred might be understood in terms of a unique personal psychopathology. But it's more illuminating to see Professor X's attitude in terms of a shared disposition among literary academics, who tend to stake their professional and personal identities on their readings—their evaluations and interpretations—of texts.

But do English professors identify themselves with their theories and methods more than do their colleagues in, say, history or economics? I think so. Professor X detested the department's "radicals" because Professor X regarded literature and a proper approach to it as the key to truth and reality.

Of course, there are as many permutations of an English professor's personal identification with texts as there are English professors. The point is that the archetypal English-department academic, in contrast to academics in other fields, is involved in a quest to know himself or herself and arrive at a more intimate relationship with the good, the true, and the real. So English professors tend to experience alternative approaches to the truth as they see it as a personal affront, and cause for counterattack. The personal truly is political.

After leaving Boston University, I had a chance to observe another aspect of the culture of personality that is endemic to English-department life. The University of Wisconsin at Milwaukee, where I taught from 1974 to 1987, had set up the Center for Twentieth Century Studies. It wasn't a department—it didn't grant degrees or offer courses—but was more like a European intellectual salon, providing an enviable social milieu as well as cultural enrichment. For the most part, the center's director managed to keep the tension between the theorists and the traditionalists in check. But what always struck me most about the center was the snobbishness it encouraged and satisfied.

The hunger for social status has always seemed to me more pronounced in English professors than in other academics. In the first few decades of the twentieth century, for example, one way that American English professors sought to distinguish themselves from their commonplace countrymen was through a genteel Anglophilia, which paralyzed academic literary study. Jews could rarely be found in prestigious English departments until the 1950s, because it was thought that they lacked the cultural background to properly understand John Milton or Henry David Thoreau. No such questions arose in physics departments or in the social sciences, where a more tolerant culture prevailed.

Nowadays, that urge for cultural distinction has been displaced by zeal to demonstrate radical political piety. Yet, the two forms of status seeking aren't so different. Whether literature professors have sought acknowledgment for their cultural superiority or for their political correctness, they seem to have always insisted on their spiritual distinction.

That is because the role of moral tutor in the United States has fallen to professors of English nearly as much as to the clergy. For the first sixty years or so of the last century, college English teachers were in a better position than pastors and priests—in our mass democracy of recent immigrants—to refine the manners and morals of the immigrants' progeny. Far from reinforcing old values, professors helped their students to separate from their parents and transcend the past. Professors of English began to derive a sense of their specialness by enabling students to rise above the materialistic values of their uneducated parents, who were striving to establish themselves in the New World. The objects of their attention have changed, but English professors continue to seem to feel as if they are uniquely responsible for the spiritual condition of the nation.

I spent a few years, 1987–90, at the University of Illinois at Chicago. The wannabes at UIC hadn't been as fortunate as my former colleagues in Milwaukee. Those who had been at UIC a long time suffered from a sense that the brave new world of literary theory had been rendered inaccessible to them by an indifferent university administration. They weren't wrong about the administration. Still, it was uncomfortable working among persons whose sense of self-esteem was so damaged and who, as a consequence, directed toward the world, including newcomers like me, a free-floating resentment.

It is necessary to keep in mind the social as well as the personal side of such wounded narcissism. Western intellectuals like Diderot and Voltaire once were literary generalists who, nevertheless, were also trenchant social and political critics. Contemporary critics, some of whom aspire to be "public intellectuals" like Sartre and Camus, have been compelled by economic changes to seek refuge in the universities. As their critical idiom has become more and more technical and specialized, they have exercised less and less influence on the general culture. But they still want to be noticed. It is almost as if they live in the shadow of the great literary-political intellectuals of the past, and are constantly trying to measure up. Their solution has been to achieve celebrity in the self-enclosed world of academic literary studies.

The baby boomers have prevailed. Now there are fewer clashes within cutting-edge English departments, because nearly everyone is a theorist or cultural-studies specialist. The victors don't always present a pretty picture. Baby-boom and younger academics in English often project a sanctimony about their secular political-cultural convictions that I never see when my Divinity School colleagues touch on their religious beliefs. Their moralism strikes me as being at odds with their obsession with intradepartmental power plays and their rapt attention to new fashions in criticism and whatever will advance their careers.

Upon Retirement

I thank my friends and colleagues—and I include my former students among my present friends. I also thank Sandra Peppers, who has been a supportive and loyal friend from the time I came to the Divinity School. I am writing these words before the retirement ceremony, but I think it's probably safe to thank all of you for saying nice things about me. I shall probably wish, after the ceremony is over, that I had a CD of what you all have said to and about me. On the other hand, let's face it, this event inevitably has about it a certain sadness insofar as it is a farewell ceremony. Given my fatal illness, which I will say more about as I go on, this event could be thought of as a "living funeral." It differs from a conventional funeral in that I get to hear the wonderful things most people miss. So before I do anything else, I want to say that I am glad I am alive to hear what has been said about me this afternoon; I am grateful to the dean and you in this room for acknowledging me in this way; and I thank the staff for once again laying a table with such fine fare. I have no doubt about it: a living funeral is always going to be better than the other kind.

Mark formally retired from teaching at the conclusion of the winter quarter, 2002. A reception was held in his honor on February 7 in Swift Common Room at which colleagues, students, and friends gathered to offer their reflections on his tenure at the Divinity School and on his seminal contributions to scholarship on modern American literature, Jewish American writing, and twentieth-century literary theory and criticism. Due to his compromised ability to speak, Mark's words were delivered by Jean. The separate section on Lou Gehrig was written three months later, in May. This talk was first published in the *Criterion*, the publication of the University of Chicago Divinity School, Spring 2002.

I am very glad to be alive to hear what my friends have said, but I feel some dismay about being the object of a farewell ceremony. This event has quite properly been billed a "retirement" party. I am indeed retiring from classroom teaching because my illness has destroyed my capacity to speak intelligibly.

Still, bidding farewell to teaching is not the same thing as bidding farewell to the Divinity School community, which has meant so much to me, or ceasing to be a member of the University of Chicago faculty. Formally, a professor on total disability, like me, remains on this university's faculty but as an "inactive employee." I think of my redefined role as one of "inactive service."

But how can a person who is not active serve? And "inactive service" may come to seem even more of an oxymoron as this disease advances, possibly leaving me paralyzed in a wheelchair or confined to bed. My disease, amyotrophic lateral sclerosis, or ALS, stripped the baseball hero Lou Gehrig of his strength as the New York Yankees' "Iron Horse," and ultimately it deprived New York Senator Jacob Javits and the British movie star David Niven of their impressive bearing. But a scholar who is also a writer does not depend upon physical stamina or an impressive personal appearance. Even if paralyzed, he can continue writing with the aid of extraordinary recent technology.

I can still do what I love most to do: I can still hug my wife and meet downtown with my son and cherish my friends. I can still get around and occasionally make it to lectures in Swift Hall and see some of you for lunch or a slurpee or smoothie. (ALS-caused difficulty in swallowing has led me to these latter creamy treats, which I had never heard of before my illness.)

Above all, I can still write. One of my projects involves finishing up a collection of my own essays of twenty-five years about Jewish writing in America. And when I am not writing about Jews, I am writing about my experience of ALS. My two projects are not totally separate. In the case of the Jewish intellectuals and novelists, I am writing about what they have had to say about love and death; and in trying to write candidly about my experience of ALS, I am also writing about love and death.

The love I write about is for persons like yourselves who have been supportive in a variety of ways. But above all, it will be about my relationship with Jean Kathryn Carney, my wife, who is now reading my words to you. I apologize to Jean for perversely assigning her the awkward role of telling you what I plan to write about her. And it will be about my relationship with my son, Joe, which has become more open and strong than I ever imagined this relationship could be. Like Lou Gehrig, my people have been stepping up to the plate. This brings me back to the idea of "inactive service." If I can in my writing be as simple, direct, and honest as possible about my experience as an ALS sufferer, perhaps that writing may make a difference in some people's lives and thereby make those people grateful, not to me alone, but to the Divinity School, where I learned to be a better person. That seems to me the best chance I have of serving though I am "inactive." And, as I have said, I continue strongly to wish to be of service.

Now that I have said something about my present projects, please bear with me as I say a word about my teaching aims as they evolved in Religion and Literature. When I came to the Divinity School in 1990, it marked a great change for me. During my preceding twenty-five years of full-time university teaching, I had always been a professor of English. During that time, I had no doubts about the central role of religion in literature, but I had not felt a need to theorize their relations or to devise a method appropriate to the study of Religion and Literature as an academic discipline. But coming to Swift Hall to teach in RL, I did feel the need to conceptualize "religion" and "literature," not as separate terms, but as a single area of study.

What, then, could I bring to the subject? After some years of trying to find my way, and sometimes stumbling badly, I decided that the most valuable thing I could do for our students was to adapt the method I had learned and used in my pre-Divinity years as a professor of English. Rhetorical reading is my name for this method. Sometimes I call it "close reading." Broadly conceived, the rhetorical analysis of literary texts embraces both formalist approaches, like that of one famous Yale literary critic, Cleanth Brooks, and the antiformalism of another famous Yale teacher, Paul de Man. The main thing is very close attention to the text, like the very close attention to the Bible enjoined by those Protestants who originated the idea of *sola scriptura*. I think that, whether you are a Protestant or not, for a student of Religion and Literature there is no possibility of anything like grace unless you begin with a close reading of texts.

The association of reading and transcendence may seem far-fetched. Please consider, then, another way of making the point. For some of us, reading texts may be more than a cognitive activity. It is nothing less than a way of being in the world. Now, there is rhetorical reading broadly conceived, as I have been describing it. But there is also a specific kind of rhetorical reading that requires knowledge of a distinct method of inquiry, with its own technical terms and tradition. I am thinking in particular of the rhetorical reading of medieval and early modern literature that is informed by the interpretative tradition that runs from Aristotle to Cicero to St. Augustine, and from Quintilian up to Dante. The rhetorical scholars who work on Dante and early modern texts are often persons lucky to have been educated in Catholic institutions in which the study of theology, philosophy, and rhetoric has been central. The church fathers they have studied in their theology classes are often, like Augustine, the most original and imaginative rhetoricians. People like me, who have not received such training, have had to educate ourselves and improvise as we go along. Sometimes, instead of drawing from a solid foundation of tradition, we fly on a wing and a prayer. But, although it may sound like it, such literary interpretation is not necessarily anarchical or irresponsible. The fact is, some of the most illuminating of modern rhetoricians make it up as they go along, though they do it so much more brilliantly than those of us who have been inspired by them. Their flexibility is necessary especially in dealing with modernist texts from Baudelaire and Mallarmé to the present because that literature, even when informed by religious sensibility, rarely manifests religion in an orthodox, easily recognizable form. The most famous school of literary interpretation developed at the University of Chicago took its lead from the poetics and rhetoric of Aristotle. I wasn't myself trained in that school, and have learned more from modern-day American rhetoricians like Kenneth Burke and Harold Bloom. These are highly eccentric interpreters, but as long as you resist buying into their Rube Goldberg–like systems, you can learn a lot from them about how to read literary texts. And both of them, in very different ways, have written illuminatingly about the relations between religion and literature. I have hardly been super-trendy, and I have not been an unambivalent convert to the ultra-new, mainly French-inspired styles of reading. But I have always believed that their close attention to metaphor and language generally makes the new rhetoricians very suggestive. And you can use their disparate methods to read theological texts as well as secular literary texts.

My topic here is rhetorical critics and criticism that I have taught and applied in my Divinity School teaching, and not Lionel Trilling or other New York intellectuals who were oriented to the interrelationships of politics and culture and who have been the focus of my research and writing. Partly, it is the case that I am a divided man, but mainly I have thought my students might learn more from the rhetoricians. Indeed, I think a student can be forever changed as a reader just by studying the modern rhetoricians whose last names start with the letter *B*. I am not an authority on all the figures I will name, but here is my list of killer *B*s, most of whom I have taught: first the Americans, a long list including Burke, Bloom, R. P. Blackmur, and the U of C's own Wayne Booth; and then a few French masters: Roland Barthes, Gaston Bachelard, and Maurice Blanchot; and still other European *B*s, notably Walter Benjamin and Mikhail Bakhtin. For my queen *B*, let me introduce you to an independent scholar whose work is less known than that of the men I have cited. Marjorie O'Rourke Boyle has from the start of her career made religious issues and theological texts her central concern. Whereas the men have offered us methods that we can apply to religious studies, Boyle, who has written extensively on language in Erasmus and Luther, has from the start worked in the field of religion and rhetoric. A typically learned new essay of hers appears in a pathbreaking anthology, *Rhetorical Invention and Religious Inquiry* (2000). That book, which has been edited by two scholars with University of Chicago credentials, makes clear to what an extent this university has been at the vanguard of rhetoric and religion studies. I myself am honored to be one of the seventeen contributors, half of whom—including David Tracy, Wayne Booth, and Paul Ricoeur—are U of C people. I have conceived my task, then, as that of helping my students become better readers. It may seem a modest goal, but, properly executed, a course in rhetorical reading might well be part of a core program in religious studies. In such a course, students would study not only religion and literature but also the languages of theology and ethics. And, as Bruce Lincoln's recent, prize-winning book, *Theorizing Myth,* helps us to see, self-consciousness about language also has the power of illuminating the history of religions as a discipline. If the previous part of this occasion has been a living funeral, the part to come may be regarded as a kind of wake—but unlike at Finnegan's wake, I am vertical not horizontal.

So how do you talk to a guy who has ALS? First of all, my hearing is unimpaired. Ditto for my cognitive functioning, such as it is. And I can still make hoarse, guttural noises, though I am better at vowels than consonants, and I am absolutely incapable of pronouncing *C* words like "caretaker." But if I can't make a particular word clear, I can write it on a notebook and show it to you. I possess but resist using a laptop speech synthesizer, partly because the artificial sound of my synthesized speech creates the effect of a foreigner who didn't pay enough attention in his courses on English as a Second Language.

I want to say a few more words about ALS, or Lou Gehrig's disease, because if you know where I am, you are likely to feel you can approach me with less anxiety. ALS is a neurodegenerative disease in which one muscle after another atrophies. Most victims avoid quadriplegia only because their respiratory muscles give out first. It is a disease quite unlike cancer in that nobody ever gets better. That has a positive side. Technology-obsessed doctors can't put you through the rigors of chemotherapy or radiation or other treatments that may or may not help a cancer patient but may, due to their side effects, make that patient's life a living hell. My version of ALS is called progressive bulbar palsy, which means that its effects are first seen in the lower facial muscles and the throat. And that is why it is hard for me to speak. It also affects my swallowing, though (as you can see) it has not caused me to lose weight. What I would emphasize is that although ALS is ultimately a devastating disease, at this stage, apart from its effect on my speaking, swallowing, and breathing, I don't feel myself to be in terrible physical shape. As you can see, I can get around, and I am in less pain than some of you here today who suffer from sciatica or gout. ALS is a neuromuscular disease, not a neurosensory disease, so it doesn't come with painful sensations.

I won't talk anymore about the emotional effects of ALS except to say that I feel as if I have become more open in regard to myself and to others than earlier in my life. And that trust has enabled some of you to be more direct and forthcoming with me. People have expressed themselves to me in different ways, and I have been grateful for your support and affection, however communicated.

With ALS inevitably consuming a greater part of my time, I am glad to have people thinking of me and praying for me. If you want to give your thoughts and prayers a focus, please pray for Krupnick to continue to be able to keep in touch with his feelings and to keep working on his writing assignments. An extension of the due date would be nice, but I can't count on being allowed extra time. There is something some of you can do for me. Hear me when I say that I wish as long as I can to be part of the general life of the Divinity School and the university. Encourage me to get my thoughts on paper or, more precisely, the computer monitor. And if I seem to be falling silent or getting out of touch, I hope you will e-mail me and draw me out of my self-bemusement or gloom.

May 5, 2002

It is three months since the farewell reception. In the past week, I have been reading and thinking about Lou Gehrig, whose name has been associated with ALS for over six decades. I want here, by way of a coda, to add a few thoughts about Gehrig and myself.

Gehrig had come to be known as the Yankees' Iron Horse because he had set a record by playing in 2,130 consecutive games over the course of his fifteen-year career in baseball. By June 1939, however, he was flagging badly and went with his wife to the Mayo Clinic for a checkup. There he received the bad news. He was suffering from ALS, an obscure motor neuron disease that inevitably led to paralysis. His career as a baseball player was over.

Gehrig's wife always insisted she and the doctors shield him from the prognosis which accompanies that disease: ALS is incurable and fatal and the average time to live after diagnosis is two to four years. In fact, Gehrig died two years after the trip to the Mayo Clinic. His death occurred seventeen days before what would have been his thirty-eighth birthday. I have thought that Gehrig's condition of not knowing might lie behind his famous words on July 4, 1939. Those words were part of his short speech to the sixty thousand fans who crowded into Yankee Stadium on Lou Gehrig Appreciation Day.

After first appearing too emotionally overcome to speak, Gehrig began: "Fans, for the past two weeks you have been reading about a bad break I got. Yet today I consider myself the luckiest man on the face of the earth." These words have become an indelible part of baseball history. I would myself like to feel a sense of identification with Lou's courage and evident nobility of character. But I'm afraid that, apart from ALS, all I have in common with him is that as a boy I was a lefty first-baseman. Deeply happy as I was to be acknowledged at the farewell reception, I also know too much about the likely future to have repeated Lou's statement that he considered himself the luckiest man on the face of the earth. I can imagine being a lot luckier, and I haven't wanted to kid myself or you.

But it strikes me now, maybe Lou did know what was happening to him and where it was leading, and that he spoke as he did despite that knowledge. Also, it may be that I share his sentiments more than I have acknowledged to myself. Lou said he had been lucky because of the people he had been able to associate with as a Yankee: the management, the coaches, his teammates, rival team players, the ball boys, the groundskeepers, and above all the fans.

Lou had started out poor, as the child of German immigrants living in the Yorkville section of Manhattan. He had obviously come a very long way. Unlike Babe Ruth, his roguish teammate, Lou was always a straight arrow, grateful for the rewards that came to him. His humility informs the peroration of his speech: "So I close in saying that I might have had a bad break, but I have an awful lot to live for. Thank you."

Lou's short speech has often been called the Gettysburg Address of baseball. I am incapable of his wonderful rhetoric. Still, I find myself feeling now rather as Lou said he felt at his farewell event. I feel lucky when I think about my students, colleagues, the staff at the Divinity School, and other friends at this university and outside it; and I feel lucky when I think about my wife and son, who were there, as always, since my illness began, to provide emotional support on the Appreciation Day held for me by the Divinity School.

Afterword
Biographical Summary
Publications
Index

Afterword

MARK SHECHNER

It is a hard paradox that we develop by moving toward death.
Lionel Trilling

My work in criticism is mainly disguised and not-so-disguised spiritual autobiography.
Mark Krupnick

Starting Out in Irvington

As usual it was Mark who broke the ice with a letter in October 2002. Not that there was much ice to break so much as the lassitude that could afflict the both of us, me more than Mark. Mark's basic instincts were gregarious, and it was he who always took up the conversation after a silence, by a timely letter or e-mail or offprint. It was always a treat to hear from Mark. Not only did he check in with customary ebullience, but also his very presence reassured me that there remained room in the profession that we had both chosen, or fallen into, for creativity, imagination, and humor. As a bonus for me, he invariably delivered the news from the world of ideas.

This letter wasn't the usual sunny hello, accompanied by an offprint or request for help with a draft, but an announcement that he was dying of ALS, amyotrophic lateral sclerosis, popularly known as Lou Gehrig's disease, a neurodegenerative illness that attacks the voluntary muscles and is always fatal. Mark had known of his illness for eighteen months, and I had only just found out. "According to the clinic where I go I have to reckon on only months not years to live. I'd give you my phone number, but an early muscle loss was my ability to speak." As I was to learn, his physical condition was horrible beyond this laconic announcement. Mark had lost not only the power of speech but also the swallowing

287

reflex, and he spent much of his time on a noninvasive ventilator, a machine that forced air into his lungs. He had only limited use of his hands, which allowed him to type away, sometimes with a single finger, at his correspondence, and to continue to work on the book he was close to finishing: *Jewish Writing and the Deep Places of the Imagination.* The keyboard had become virtually his last mode of communication, as it was attached to a speech synthesizer, and e-mail was his lifeline to the world.

I have little up-close experience of death and dying and tend to grow uneasy in the presence of sick people. I'd make a lousy doctor. Mark was way ahead of me in this matter, having had time to get his priorities in order and to figure out what he needed from his friends, of which he had so many. He wanted friendship, of course, and beyond that practical help. From himself he wanted only to remain as he had been: a scholar, a critic, and a writer, working as though there was no good reason to stop. There needed to be ever so much stoicism and Spartan renunciation about all of this, though Mark never spoke of his book and his determination to finish it in clichéd terms: of fortitude or guts or any of that. Nor, after the initial letter, was there much about himself, unless in response to a direct question. He kept his personal tribulations out of the e-mails, but then, I would ask and he would tell me, in bruising detail, about everything from his hands to his breathing to the rage he felt at it all. But there was no self-dramatizing. No doubt he had in mind the example of Morris "Morrie" Schwartz, the Brandeis University sociology professor whose death of ALS in 1995 was the occasion of a best-selling book by sportswriter Mitch Albom, *Tuesdays with Morrie,* which Mark felt had sentimentalized what he knew to be a hideous way to die. Mark simply elected to remain what he already was: a working critic and intellectual, and to press on with his work because it was there to be done. He wanted one more book to represent his thinking in its maturity, and he was bent on finishing.

I began to receive essays and to piece them together. It was quickly apparent that there had come into Mark's writing an equanimity and focus that was taking him to another level of clarity. From the time we had first met some three decades ago I had admired Mark as a thinker as much as I had enjoyed him as a friend, though the two can't be separated. In his last years, however, Mark had shifted into a higher gear; the essays I was reading were startlingly original and exploratory, freer in expression and more probing, as Mark knew they were. He was urgent about getting them into print before his death, and I found it only natural to volunteer to help him out and, if need be, see the book through publication. Mark died on March 29, 2003, just seven days after his last e-mail to me. And though there were loose ends to be tied up, the book was finished and I had it all on disk. I raced to print up a rough copy for him to see, and it arrived at his home on March 29, but he knew that the book was done, that it was under contract, and that it had editors who would do the rest: his wife, Jean, and me.

Mark and I were contemporaries; he was only a year older and, as I was to discover only in working on this book, we had spent our early childhoods within walking distance of each other. Mark grew up on Webster Street in Irvington, New Jersey, I on Hawthorne Avenue in Newark, and if you call up either of them on Mapquest, you can get both streets in the same frame. Could we have encountered each other in some playground, on some ball field, in some candy store or library or museum as children? I don't rule it out, though this short trip across postal zones was virtually a border crossing. My neighborhood of Newark was overwhelmingly Jewish and upwardly mobile. That my family remained in Newark in the late 1940s meant that we had a way to go before moving to higher ground: to Maplewood, the Oranges, and to those places that Philip Roth in *American Pastoral* calls collectively Old Rimrock. The store names around me—Galoff, Chaplowitz, Tabatchnik— gave my street the appearance of a transplanted Eastern European shtetl, and in some ways it was: tightly knit, suspicious of outsiders, gossipy, and shot through with jealousies and more than just a little community hush-hush. There were rumored to be mobsters. My mother knew all the other mothers in my grammar school class, and indeed she had gone to high school with some of them at South Side (now Malcolm X Shabazz High School). I was obliged to sing Yiddish songs for the barber before I could have my hair cut, and he always hummed a Yiddish niggun while cutting my hair, stopping only to take a puff of his cigarette or take a bet over the phone. The landlord was the grocer downstairs, Galoff, and when our mousetrap clamped shut over a mouse, it was my job to take it downstairs and plant myself before Galoff as he weighed Mrs. Resnick's stewing hen, with the pencil casually tucked behind his ear. "My mom says please do something about this."

But Irvington was truly foreign soil and a little scary to us. Strongly German American in population, it was a place from which marauders would barge in periodically looking for Jewish kids to kick around. Everyone is familiar with the fight song of the local high school, Weequahic, since it appeared in Philip Roth's *Portnoy's Complaint:* "Ikey, Mikey, Jake, and Sam, / We're the boys who eat no ham. / We play football, we play soccer—/And we keep matzohs in our locker! / Aye Aye, Aye, Weequahic High!" Irvington's was different, at least as I was taught it: "We never stagger, we never fall, / We live on wood alcohol. / When we yell we yell like hell, / 'Cause we come from Irvington." Well, that is where Mark grew up, a boy who ate no ham (figuratively) among the drinkers of wood alcohol who yelled like hell (again, figuratively). You can bet he didn't sing Yiddish songs for his barber, unless his mother drove him over to Hawthorne Avenue for his haircuts. No doubt it was on Webster Street that he developed that self-ironic humor that reminded me of a dozen kids I played stickball with. If I could hear his voice now I'd listen hard for the posts and beams of the Essex County accent—that strange jointure of aggression and complaint—beneath the intricate overlays of Harvard, Brandeis, Milwaukee, and Chicago.

I do not recall the details of getting to know Mark, though in his files there is a letter from my colleague Leslie Fiedler in 1976 offering to introduce us after Mark's essay on Philip Rahv had appeared in the *New Review.* I'm sure that Mark wrote first, and I'd guess that there are dozens of others around the country—around the world—who can claim much the same thing, that Mark initiated their contact, even their friendship. Ideas for Mark were powerful adhesives; they bound people together. And we had plenty to talk about. We had both written about *Partisan Review* and the New York intellectuals. We were both looking for ways to fashion careers in the academy without becoming entirely captive to it. There may have been some illusions in that self-image on both accounts; we normally traded these avowals of disaffection in the bustling hallways of the Modern Language Association convention between sessions, not at, say, the Cedar Tavern between punch-outs.

But we were earnest for all that. The search for models of intelligence beyond the academy had led us to our secular rabbis and informal apprenticeships. For Mark, that rabbi would be the critic he had once dealt with harshly, Lionel Trilling, while for me it would be one of those splendid minor writers who appear in New York intellectual history, Isaac Rosenfeld. Those labors, and the conversations that formed around them, made for a bond, such that when Mark published his book on Trilling in 1986, *Lionel Trilling and the Fate of Cultural Criticism*, I volunteered to review it for the *Nation*.

Over several decades we'd meet at conferences. Sometimes this was planned but mainly it was happenstance. I last saw Mark in 1996, at a conference on Bernard Malamud at Oregon State University in Corvallis. Nothing particular about the conference itself stands out in my memory half so much as the conviviality that seemed to follow Mark around. Mark was an inspired conversationalist, by which I don't mean talker. He was not a raconteur; he did not hold forth. He didn't corner you with his exploits. He had mastered conversation, that rare skill that involves listening as much as it does speaking. Over the course of an evening, a group's conversation would gravitate toward him, in part because he seemed so alert, so up-to-date, and so effortlessly available. At play too were some indefinable erotics of sociability, so that by an evening's conclusion you were convinced that you had gotten beneath the surface and made a friend. Often enough that was exactly what happened.

Six years is a long time to be out of touch with a friend, a loss that can't be made up now. During those years Mark was settling into a happy collegial environment in the Divinity School of the University of Chicago, where he had moved in 1990 from the English Department at the University of Illinois at Chicago. By all accounts, he flourished there and began preparing the ground for a book that would lead him, as he put it in a phrase taken from Lionel Trilling, into "the deep places of the imagination." But the book did not come entirely into focus until after he had been diagnosed with ALS in March 2001. From that point on, the writing had to compete with many things, including drastically reduced physical powers and a move from the house in Flossmoor in Chicago's far south suburbs to an apartment in the Hancock Building on Chicago's near North Side, in order to be near Jean's office.

Though many of these essays predate Mark's illness, the longest and most impressive of them were written under its shadow, Mark's hands slowed and weakened, his breath slowed and weakened, his body beset by God-knows-what torments. Some of the chapter drafts I have are dated February and March 2003. It sounds melodramatic but surely it is accurate to regard the completion of this book as a fierce act of will on Mark's part. However, I much prefer to think of this writing as a marshaling of intelligence and insight, a breakthrough into regions of perception that do not reflect so much his consciousness of impending death as his consciousness of his strength. A phrase from Mark's essay on Philip Roth's novel *Sabbath's Theater* describes well my own sense of Mark in this book. "[The book] is a triumph of fantasy, emotion, and instinct. Roth was able to reach down far into the deep places of imagination. In this unique novel, Roth reached down within himself to the deepest springs of his being, which freed his imagination as never before or since." Mark could have been talking about himself here, and maybe he was. There is much covert self-assessment going on in these essays about others, and certainly what Mark says about *Sabbath's Theater* applies equally to *Jewish Writing and the Deep Places of the Imagination*. It is a triumph of emotion and instinct. For "fantasy," substitute "disciplined intelligence."

Modern Occasions

Mark was all of thirty-one and an assistant professor at Boston University when he leaped feet first from the cruise ship Academia into the flaming sea of cultural polemics. It was 1970, and, together with young novelist Alan Lelchuk, he had been recruited by Philip Rahv to be an associate editor on Rahv's new venture, the journal *Modern Occasions*. Mark's essay on Rahv in this volume, "He Never Learned to Swim," is a vivid account of the *Modern Occasions* moment in his life, complete with dinners with Rahv and Philip Roth: "It was like Lenny Bruce meeting Doctor Johnson." Rahv, who had been Mark's PhD advisor at Brandeis University two years earlier, had broken with *Partisan Review* and drummed up backing for a new journal that would be committed to both revolutionary political ideas and literary modernism. More than thirty years earlier, Rahv had played a pivotal role in the history of the New York intellectuals, and had been, indeed, a paterfamilias to a crowd that now and then thought of itself as a family, dysfunctional though it might have been. Together with William Phillips he founded *Partisan Review* in 1934 under the sponsorship of the New York John Reed Club, a cultural arm of the Communist Party in the United States, and three years later stole the magazine away from the party to reestablish it as a voice of an independent, literary left, which was nominally Trotskyist but given mainly to the broadening of radical social views by importing avant-garde art into the arena of Marxist polemics. *Partisan Review* quickly became a rallying point for anti-Stalinist radicals and a clearinghouse for new directions in a time of political and intellectual confusion. Its rise to prominence in the 1940s, when it was instrumental in loosening the grip of Proletarian and Popular Front thinking on "the liberal imagination," was due largely to Rahv and Phillips. With considerable deftness they presided over a restless coalition of radical and avant-garde elements and tried to make art's contribution to consciousness seem more valuable than its incitement to action. "Like other Marxist critics of his time," Mark would later write about him, "[Rahv] was concerned above all with reconciling his revolutionary politics with an admiration for decidedly illiberal modernist writers. The solution was to minimize the professed beliefs of the reactionary writers he liked and to adapt them for his own cause."

After a long editorial marriage of more than thirty years, however, Rahv and Phillips had finally fallen out in the 1960s over the issue of the counterculture and the "new sensibility," which Phillips had embraced out of a desire to keep the graying *Partisan Review* in the thick of the action. Rahv's mood, insurrectionary on the one hand and deeply antagonistic toward the New Left and the counterculture on the other, demanded its own forum, and Mark would note of Rahv that his mood "was very close to that of Saul Bellow's *Mr. Sammler's Planet,* which came out at this time. His revulsion against the pornographers, the 'swingers,' the black militants, the patrons of pop, the publicists of apocalypse—was total." But then of course the conundrum: "How could you be against all the characteristic features of the emergent culture and continue to call yourself a radical?"

The inaugural issue of *Modern Occasions* in fall 1970, which headlined the "Salad Days" section of Philip Roth's novel *My Life as a Man,* along with essays by or interviews with Mary McCarthy, Noam Chomsky, Robert Lowell, and Hilton Kramer, found Mark in the review pages taking aim at two of literary postmodernism's favorite sons, John Barth and Donald Barthelme. The books under review were *City Life,* one of Barthelme's jaunty miscellanies, and Barth's *Lost in the Funhouse,* subtitled *Fiction for Print, Tape, Live Voice.* Though both books had garnered a modicum of critical acclaim and academic buzz, they were light entertainments at best, fashionable symptoms of a period that had an affection for the aleatory and the capricious and was against interpretation. Formally inventive and textually playful, they were typical products of postmodernism's R&D workshop for tailoring a radical consciousness for short attention spans. Postmodernism announced a literary renaissance of fabulation, of metafiction, of "art and joy," as one acolyte called it, though Mark saw in Barth and Barthelme a surrender to fashion, labyrinths for labyrinths' sake, "as empty as they are complicated." What the contemporary avant-garde appeared to offer as fresh and disturbing visions were only gestures of surrender, "ostrich-like denials of reality, holidays in the funhouse." Mark wrote, "The typical new experimental story or novel is turning out to be a labyrinth of mirrors where the artist's imagination confronts nothing but endless reflections of itself—squirming and preening and trying on faces—and where no one searches for Ariadne's thread and the way out, because entrapment, indeed despair, have turned out to be so much fun. The jokes and poses of imagination at the end of its tether have become both means and end in the new fiction, but the comedy has already begun to wear thin."

As I write this, thirty-four years later, Mark's brisk dismissal holds up remarkably well as a prescient, if somewhat cantankerous and hortatory, criticism. (It should be noted that though Mark was a great fan of the master Vladimir Nabokov, his enchantment did not carry over to any of Nabokov's homegrown imitators.) Certainly John Barth's star fell quickly, and Barthelme, the more elegant stylist of the two, never made the leap from playfulness to engagement with his time that his admirers hoped would be forthcoming. He remained, in Mark's words, "a parodist and a pastiche artist." Mark's review was auspicious: it had phrasing and bite, and one could imagine Mark, out on a different limb in life's garden of forking paths, becoming an acerbic critic of contemporary fiction, scattering anathemas while rendering sharp judgments: a younger John Aldridge or Yvor Winters, calling literature to account and refusing to be taken in by shoddy goods or facile pyrotechnics.

That didn't happen. The very next review Mark wrote, in the second issue of *Modern Occasions,* became a cause célèbre that altered the direction of his professional life. It was a review of Lionel Trilling's anthology

Literary Criticism: An Introductory Reader. Trilling (1905–75) in his later years had been turning his energies in an increasingly professional and institutional direction. The probing and influential essays of the 1940s and after, published in *The Liberal Imagination* (1950), *The Opposing Self* (1955), *A Gathering of Fugitives* (1956), and *Beyond Culture* (1965), had given way to textbook publication. In 1967, he came out with the three-volume anthology of world literature for college freshmen, *The Experience of Literature,* whose prefaces alone, republished in 1979, came to 302 pages, making it one of his longer books. It was an attempt to outline a great tradition, in drama (Sophocles to Brecht), poetry (Wyatt to Lowell), and fiction, largely modern, from Hawthorne to Malamud. It was a labor of summing up, a tour de force of erudition that established Trilling as one of the most wide-ranging, not to say tireless, literary minds of his era.

Literary Criticism: An Introductory Reader was a less arduous affair. An introduction to criticism for undergraduates featuring forty-five essays in criticism, from Plato to Susan Sontag, it was a guided tour to Western thought, to Western *mind,* that, coming at the end of the 1960s, loomed above the landscape like one of those brooding Tolkien-esque towers that the sixties themselves were all about bringing down. The book has nothing in it of the intellectual journalism that Trilling himself so successfully practiced, and only Susan Sontag was summoned to speak for the New York intellectuals, on being "against interpretation." In confronting this particular version of Trilling and finding it wanting, Mark was nothing if not a man of his generation.

Mark's review was a smash and grab attack on the master. At a time when a certain decorum still shaped polemics on culture, it was an act of lèse-majesté. Mark dealt harshly with Trilling's "reverence for the customary and the established" and his "increasingly priggish distaste for less elevated conditions of being." Trilling, Mark wrote, had come on the scene in *The Liberal Imagination* as a figure of agonistic thought, a dialectician of the spirit, whose favorite image of the critic confronting the great books of modern literature was Jacob wrestling with the angel. "But increasingly the critic as spiritual wrestler seemed eager to come to terms, to renounce the trials of the will and bathe in 'the sentiment of being'—a condition of spirit exemplified, in Trilling's view, by writers as oddly different as Wordsworth and William Dean Howells. *Increasingly there was evident in Trilling's criticism the desire for rest, the will to discontinue willing, the impulse to disengagement"* (italics mine).

Mark's indictment singled out in particular Trilling's aloofness, his mandarinism, his detached passivity, and his tragic sense of life: "A case can be made that a certain amount of distortion of the text enters into all the literary criticism that lasts, but what remains disturbing about Trilling's essays is his incapacity to respond fully to any subject but that of loss and defeat, which he proceeds to dignify in the rhetoric of tragic grandeur." And as for that, "Tragedy . . . becomes a rationalization for giving in too easily." Turning the screw yet another notch, "An enervating overrefinement and preciosity are not lacking in his long introduction to the present anthology, in which literary criticism is conceived as a kind of connoisseurship, involving acts of assessment no different fundamentally than in the case of Japanese swords or Greek and Chinese urns."

Such criticisms had been leveled before. Trilling's fussy choreographies of equivocation had become notorious. The meticulous balancing of literary issues on the scale of his own sensibility could be infuriating. Trilling's disengagement while at the epicenter of upheaval at Columbia University in the 1960s was often ruefully noted, though given his exquisite sense of irony, one finds it hard to distinguish the appearance of fastidiousness from a calculated decision to resist being "impaled upon the present" (Philip Roth's phrase), because a tragic stance and aesthetic distance were just what the present called for. Rather than a posture of retreat, the tragic sense of life was the tonic, the antidote to the sound and the fury surrounding Columbia University. That would have been Trilling at his most dialectical, but also at his most Jewish: the Moishe Kapoyr—Moishe "backwards"—who says "yin" just because all others are chanting "yang."

And yet, rereading Trilling's introduction to *Literary Criticism* decades later, I too am struck by the donnish remoteness and wooden phrasing: a writing in which all the fire of the personal has been doused. Here is how one section begins: "The intention of judgment is a salient motive of all critical theories. They undertake to say what literary excellence consists in and how discriminations between various degrees of excellence are to be made." One senses that this is only a voice speaking through Trilling, a collective Ivy League Olympianism pouring out through his typewriter. And did the undergraduate reader for whom Trilling was writing such things even exist anymore? This was a far cry from the Trilling of the great essays, on Babel, Keats, "Freud and Literature," "Art and Neurosis," and "Joyce in His Letters." This was a more fatigued and institutionally embalmed voice. Mark was impatient, the streets were still smoldering, and he wasn't going to sit still for this.

The timing could not have been worse, and the association with the truculent and self-destructive Rahv did not help. In 1970, Trilling was, if not the most celebrated literary critic living in America — that honor belonged to Edmund Wilson — surely the most influential by virtue of his professorship at Columbia, coupled with his eminence in New York intellectual life. He had credit both uptown and downtown. The review drew a crushing response. Hilton Kramer, who until then had been an ally of Rahv's in his battle against William Phillips, withdrew his support from *Modern Occasions.* "Rahv," Mark wrote about it later, "probably could have sacrificed me and attempted to mollify Kramer, but he let him go with a delighted snort and some choice remarks about petty-bourgeois fetishists of culture." Diana Trilling, ferocious in her defense of her husband's reputation, would later write in her memoir of him, *The Beginning of the Journey,* "Featured in [*Modern Occasions*] first issue was an extended attack upon Lionel by a then-unknown teacher of English, Mark Krupnick. Like 'The Duchess' Red Shoes,' Delmore Schwartz's attack on Lionel in *Partisan Review,* Krupnick's piece was of course solicited and predesigned." How, she surely reasoned, could a rookie like Mark, so inexperienced in the decorum of intellectual warfare, have the acumen, the background, the discipline, and the chutzpah to take on someone like Lionel Trilling, unless Coach Rahv were calling signals from the sideline? Was Mark put up to it? She certainly thought so.

This drama didn't play out in a vacuum. Though Mark and *Modern Occasions* were located in Boston, there was a sense in which it was taking place at Columbia. On the one side was Trilling himself, whose major essay collections were more than just extended meditations on books: they were a climate of thought, an ethos, a serious reconsideration of what we meant (whoever "we" were) by such key terms as *modernism, liberalism, reality, culture, imagination, sincerity, authenticity, self, will, spirit,* and *mind.* When Trilling died in 1975 it was generally conceded that a literary office had fallen vacant. Trilling had long since become something more than just a critic; he was an icon, even that rarest of creatures, an academic celebrity. He even looked the part. Ambiguously Jewish and Waspy looking all at once and in his later years maned in white locks, looking mournful and intelligent, he was photogenic as hell. Even when he spoke for no one but himself he was taken for a spokesman, even a standard reference, a coiner of commonplaces that stuck to literature: "variousness and possibility," "the divided self," "the liberal imagination," "the tragic sense of life." He was the gold standard. His first collection of essays, *The Liberal Imagination,* had set the tone for the retreat from Popular Front liberalism that had dominated the 1930s and, under the broad umbrella of "progressivism," had maintained even after the war a stranglehold on what the word "liberal" was taken to mean. The book redefined "liberalism" in so sweeping and irrefutable a way that Popular Frontism had nowhere to go but into the dustbin of failed sentimentalities, where it ceased ever afterward to stir any heart that did not stubbornly beat to the rhythm of "The Internationale."

Like most New York intellectuals, Trilling styled himself a modernist, even though he distrusted modernism and was more at home with the nineteenth century, whose complex ideas and thick textures, its concerns with decency, order, respectability, were more congenial to his temperament. He shared with the others the view of literature as the expression of history, politics, class, and the Zeitgeist and kept steady watch over the fever chart of what his circle called "the culture," which consisted largely of the opinions and social habits of the eastern, liberal intelligentsia. But he was also a scholar and a teacher, a historian of modern social thought whose early books on Matthew Arnold (1939) and E. M. Forster (1943) and later studies of Freud gave him credentials in the Modern Language Association and International Psychoanalytic Association. As if that were not enough, as an editor of the Readers' Subscription—a Book-of-the-Month Club for highbrows—Trilling enjoyed a successful venture into the commercial end of letters. Was there anything about him that could not be unequivocally honored?

Or had the parade just moved on? The 1960s had just come to a close, leaving cities, institutions, citadels, icons, and happy intellectual families shattered, and *Modern Occasions* itself was a symptom of the shattering and finally a victim of it as well. In the spring of 1968 Columbia University had undergone one of the bitterest upheavals of any university in

America. The prevailing antiwar anxiety and tension over the murder of Martin Luther King on April 4 of that year had been raised to a fever pitch by local issues, most particularly the university's plans to buy up surrounding property in a predominantly black neighborhood in order to build a gym. While in less mutinous times this might not have exercised a white and privileged student population, in the context of the sixties, with its ruling perception that Mississippi was a metaphor for all America, sometimes spelled *Amerika* or even *Amerikkka,* it had an incendiary effect and student radicals seized on it as evidence that Columbia University was also the enemy, a voracious slumlord that bore significant responsibility for the problems of Harlem.

As I write this I have in front of me two contemporary accounts of the 1968 Columbia uprising: Mark Rudd's "Columbia: Notes on the Spring Rebellion" and Diana Trilling's "On the Steps of Low Library," which appears in her collection of essays, *We Must March My Darlings.* Neither of these testifies directly about either Mark Krupnick or Lionel Trilling, but they set the mood for the moment three years later when Mark would read Trilling and erupt. Rudd's essay, with its epigraph by Che Guevara, "Revolution is the best education for honorable men," is very much a screed on the failures of a liberalism that had gotten everyone to this pass. Mrs. Trilling's is a fearful reflection from within the liberal temple of reason on what it felt like to have one's values trashed and one's certainties outflanked by more aggressive, primordial tones and sensibilities. Perhaps nothing better characterizes that face-off than Mrs. Trilling's account of Rudd's leaving his headquarters in Ferris Booth Hall to hear the latest meliorative proposal of the faculty and greeting it "with a stunning economy: 'Bullshit.'"

Strip away Mark's erudition, his keen sensitivity to Lionel Trilling's place in intellectual history, and his understanding of the ethos in which Trilling worked, his review of *Literary Criticism: An Introduction* surely sounded as summary and accusing as Mark Rudd's "bullshit," some three years before. That is one side of seeing Mark's review and its aftermath through the filter of the Columbia experience. Another—and this can only be speculation—is that *Literary Criticism* was the book that came out of Trilling's experience of the Columbia uprising. This was surely the project that he was at work on in 1968 between disruptions and emergency faculty meetings. Something in its chilled phrasing, its eye on posterity, its posture of being a monument to Western Civilization, might well have been inspired by the attack on that very civilization that Trilling had worked so tirelessly to become a part of. Having taken a long route from the outside, as a Freudian and a Jew with a history of youthful leftism, to join the intellectual establishment, to be the first Jew to be tenured in English at Columbia, Trilling was hardly prepared to be anything but a pillar of that establishment from then on. Books that in the reading may seem to lack all personal dramatics may be no less dramatic in their impassivity than books that wear their hearts on their dust jackets. From the viewpoint of an aspiring Jewish intellectual of the 1960s, *Literary Criticism: An Introduction* must have looked like an act of refusal, even counterrevolution, and so Mark took it to be.

Mark would remain with *Modern Occasions* until the end, the sixth issue of the magazine in spring 1972, making two more contributions. One was in the spring 1971 issue, an editorial screed against *Commentary* magazine and its sharp right turn under the editorship of Norman Podhoretz. Titled "The Fifties Revisited" it noted with alarm *Commentary*'s increasing conservatism and its stand against, among other things, the New Left intellectuals. Mark hardly needed prodding from Rahv to complain bitterly of the intellectual class's "increasingly sterile and curmudgeonly conservatism characterized by a spirit of lamentation, rancorousness, meanness of spirit, and mourning for a lost world." I can't say that I would ever characterize Mark as a man of the Left; he was never a party man of any sort, and nobody's action faction would ever claim him. But that he was and remained throughout his career a man of the anti-Right is certain, and what he had to say about Norman Podhoretz and *Commentary* in 1971 he might have said at any time from then up until his death in 2003. In that he remained steadfast.

In the Spring 1972 issue, which would turn out to be the last gasp of *Modern Occasions*, Mark turned his attention to Henry James in an essay that is so unlike his polemical pieces that one might wonder if they were written by the same person. Titled "Henry James' Curiosity," it is a rather patient, Trillingesque look at James's obscurity, which raises the question of whether James "leaves his meanings blank because he is in the dark." It was an early study for a book on James that Mark would write over the next several years and never publish. The subject of Mark and Henry James demands a section of its own, and I'll reserve any comment on this essay for later.

The high point of Mark's career as a firebrand did not appear, however, in *Modern Occasions* at all but in the *New York Review of Books,* where Mark was given an opportunity to review Quentin Anderson's book *The Imperial Self* in 1971. So heated was Mark's assault on Anderson, a colleague of Trilling's at Columbia, that by comparison, the reviews of Trilling and Podhoretz seem like bedtime stories. *Modern Occasions* had a limited readership and, for all that Philip Roth and Saul Bellow made contributions, it was something of a curiosity. The *New York Review,* by contrast, was smack dead center in the intellectual life and sported left and anti-Vietnam War credentials. If Mark was going to earn his stripes as an enfant terrible of his generation, here was the chance, and he came flying out of his corner.

The Imperial Self was going to take the heat for everything that ailed American society; it was guilty above all of what the academy these days calls "patriarchy," and though that epithet had not yet been coined for literary study, Mark was prepared for its advent, calling the book "a book for embattled fathers." What was wrong with it? What wasn't? Basic conception? "*The Imperial Self* is an imperial mingling of literary criticism, cultural history, spiritual autobiography, ideological polemic, and sermon." Style? "The result is a book as personal, obsessed, tendentious, repetitive, and tediously apocalyptic as [D. H.] Lawrence at his worst—without being nearly so original." Scholarship? "Anderson's readings of Emerson, Whitman, and James are often incomprehensible when they are not simply distorted, because he sees these nineteenth-century figures as versions of [Norman O.] Brown." Attitude? "*The Imperial Self* bangs the drum for normalcy as if it were a new discovery or about to go out of style." That was no country for old men! Up against the wall! The assignment was a tryout, and after such a disemboweling the *New York Review* never assigned Mark another book. A provocative footnote to this dustup was Mark's organizing a panel on "The Achievement of Lionel Trilling" for the Modern Language Association in 1976, to which he invited Anderson, Robert Boyers (editor of *Salmagundi*), and Denis Donoghue, one of his mentors at Darwin College, Cambridge. What did they say to each other?

The collapse of *Modern Occasions* coincided with Mark's failure to gain tenure at Boston University. Mark would later write bitterly of Philip Rahv's refusal to speak up on his behalf in his tenure battle. Indeed, the entire episode would send him packing, and he spent the academic years 1972–74 in England, lecturing in the American Studies Program at the University of Keele and studying psychoanalysis at the Hampstead Institute with Anna Freud. The *Modern Occasions* moment took up something more than two years in Mark's life, and yet it was a defining experience, out front in public where all could see. It took a while for him to revisit Trilling's work, and when he did so he weighed in with *Lionel Trilling and the Fate of Cultural Criticism* (1986). By that time he'd had his edges rubbed smooth by academic life and had even cycled through the world of high theory along the way.

Art as Restitution: Henry James

> [Lambert Strether] wakes up to [his loss] in conditions that press the spring of a terrible question. Would there yet perhaps be time for reparation?
>
> Henry James, Preface to *The Ambassadors.*

When Mark was not broadcasting polemics, he had his sights set on being a Henry James scholar, and much of his research after receiving his PhD was devoted to James. After two sojourns to England, as a student at Darwin College in 1965–66 and as a teacher at the University of Keele in 1972–74, Mark had come to admire the Jamesean persona, socially and intellectually at ease in both England and America. Among his first publications was a review in the *Nation* in 1969 of volume 4 of Leon Edel's biography of James, and we may recall that "Henry James' Curiosity" was his final contribution to *Modern Occasions* in 1972. By 1976, Mark had completed a book-length manuscript: "Henry James: Art as Restitution." The book was given a contract by Seabury Press and then rejected, after a negative reading by Frederick Crews made its publication untenable, at least as submitted. Though snippets from the book did find publication as stand-alone articles (see Publications), the manuscript disappeared into Mark's files and never came out.

"Henry James: Art as Restitution" was for the most part a close reading of James's stories and novels. Selected passages are patiently anatomized and meaning is teased out of minor details of image and phrasing. But this explication is conducted with Freudian suspicion, after the manner of a case history, like Freud's Rat Man or Dora. James's novels are read as symptoms and keys to their author's ruling passions, recurring obsessions, and vulnerabilities. Given characters who prefer dreaming their lives to living them, some who display, as Mark put it, "an immense appetite for emptiness," and given an imagination obsessed by failure, silence, and absence, James fairly begged for psychological profiling. As Mark would see it, James's vapors would lift once unmasked as sublimations — as civilized embodiments of conflicts taking place somewhere deep in the author's psyche.

Appropriately, Mark began with James's dreaming. "The beginning and ending of Henry James's creative career are linked by two dreams, one a nightmare associated with James's thirteenth year, the other a death-bed hallucination when the writer was seventy-three. Together these dreams reveal the central fantasy of James's life and illuminate the major preoccupations of his fiction. The continuity of James's career is the continuity of the wishes revealed in these dreams. A man's 'past, present and future are strung together, as it were, on the thread of the wish that runs through them,' as Freud writes in his essay on 'The Creative Writer and Day-Dreaming.'"

The first is a childhood dream of being awakened by something awful outside his bedroom door and springing out of bed to confront the attacker, who flees. In pursuing the intruder, the young dreamer finds himself in the Galerie d'Apollon of the Louvre, "a room named for the painting by Delacroix of 'Apollo's Victory over the Python.'" The dream has its own portentous sound track, thunder and lightning, that reveals the setting, the "triumphant turning of the tables," but "it is also a spotlight illuminating the dream itself and . . . the immortality of the child's mind which had vibrated many years before in the Galerie d'Apollon to the grandeur of style."

Mark glosses the dream as follows. "The dream of Galerie d'Apollon is a dream of triumphant aggression worthy of the triumphal glory of the First Empire. It expresses a wish for conquest over passivity and dread, a wish to be heroic in the grand style." There is nothing of ambivalence here; the dreamer is only thirteen. Thus, "The power and the glory are Napoleonic, but James's method is Wordsworthian: he is celebrating neither his own aggression nor the museum world of Paris but his own unconquerable mind."

The second dream is actually a hallucination experienced by James in 1916, as he lay on his deathbed after suffering two strokes. In that hallucination, the identification with Napoleon is complete and "the Napoleonic campaigns had become identified in James's mind with his art." The dreams of triumph are resonant from the alpha of James's life to the omega, only late in life they have become megalomaniacal, fantasies of total identification with Napoleon himself. Is there a primal dimension to this dreaming, an Oedipal plot? Yes, in the Apollo dream the dreamer "revenges himself on his gentle, ineffectual father and on a once-formidable American intellectual tradition." There is anxiety and the wish for restitution here as well. Oedipal desires have this inevitable downside.

It is pointless to belabor Mark's method here or follow his reading through some 158 densely packed pages of analysis, with texts—*The Ambassadors,* "The Aspern Papers," "The Beast in the Jungle," *The American*—standing in for dreams. One can see the method here plainly enough: the bold analytic slashes, the presumption of knowing James's mind through a survey of fantasies, the authority of Freud himself brought to bear on questions of interpretation, and all texts sooner or later connected at the heart to James's personal myths.

Frederick Crews, an erstwhile Freudian critic and author of a psychoanalytic reading of Nathaniel Hawthorne, *The Sins of the Fathers,* had recently turned against psychoanalytic theory and may not have been the most sympathetic referee available, but he was a judicious reader whose report could not be dismissed. He praised Mark's manuscript as "a provocative study that probably deserves publication—though not, I think, in its present form. . . . Krupnick is a skillful critic who writes effectively, and his thesis about restitution in James is cogent and significant. His insight into the destructive, negative force of 'love' and transcendence in James's fiction is acute, and it constitutes a welcome antidote to the usual worshipful style of criticism. . . . And there are many eloquent passages. . . . Krupnick can make a point with tactful decisiveness."

But then fell the other shoe. Crews sliced away at the book's originality, its execution, its significance, its research—Mark seemed to be unfamiliar with the extant James scholarship—and its psychoanalytic apparatus, which he found "jarringly dogmatic" and "arbitrary, tacked-on exercises in Freudian 'real meaning.'" "Despite this," he concluded, "I repeat my profession of faith in the thesis of this book; I hope it *will* become a book. At present, however, it is too desultory and too arbitrary to be judged successful." The door was left open for revision, though it would have required Mark to scrap the single most critical feature of his method, the quest for Freudian "real meaning," and Mark, in electing to neither rewrite the book nor seek another publisher, seems to have assented to Crews's critique.

What had gone wrong? Possibly Mark was barking up the wrong literary tree. James was other, inexorably. There was a poor fit between James's patrician sensibilities and Mark's own as a son of the textile business, and no amount of close textual analysis or psychoanalytic guesswork was going to bridge that gap. Indeed, Mark was to write to Denis Donoghue in November 1976, speaking of R. P. Blackmur, "I'm down on Blackmur right now as part of my swing away from Henry James and pure sensibility."

Moreover, Mark was working in handcuffs. He was an assistant professor at the University of Wisconsin–Milwaukee and still uncertain about how much liberty was really his. He might be free to hazard a diagnosis of James, using Freud's authority to home in on James's recurring personal mythos or his dreams of conquest and restitution, but not yet free enough to make a fuss over James's discouraging habit of casting Jews like himself as hook-nosed and rapacious. Whatever else James might have meant, he was an icon of modernity to the postwar generation of critics, and a young Jewish critic out to earn his spurs by coming to grips with the master might feel a bit circumspect about a novelist who would say in *The American Scene* of the downtown Jews who made him nervous:

> What struck me in the flaring streets (over and beyond the everywhere insistent, defiant, unhumorous, exotic face) was the blaze of the shops addressed to the New Jerusalem wants and the splendour with which these were taken for granted; the only thing indeed a little ambiguous was just this look of the trap too brilliantly, too candidly baited for the wary side of Israel itself. It is not *for* Israel, in general, that Israel so artfully shines—yet its being moved to do so, at last, in that luxurious

style, might be precisely the grand side of the city of redemption. Who can tell . . . what the genius of Israel may, or may not, really be up to?

In this instance, the genius of Israel was trying to decode the neurotic preoccupations of Boston and finding in the process that other things were more interesting to him, mainly a chance to take up once again the Lionel Trilling enigma, which he had already begun doing, even as he was preparing the James book for publication. Indeed, Mark had committed himself to organizing and chairing the MLA special session on Trilling that December, and all his energies were now channeled in that direction. Among the consequences of this venture was that Mark would not deal again in depth with fiction until the writing of "'A Shit-Filled Life': Philip Roth's *Sabbath's Theater*" for this volume. As for psychoanalysis, it would go into hibernation for a spell, though Mark would be in need of what he had learned in editing the book on Jacques Derrida in 1983, *Displacement: Derrida and After.* Freud and psychoanalysis, never abandoned, needed a longer period of gestation, and they would emerge many years later, in the essays in this book, as fully integrated into Mark's own sensibility, his habits of reading, and a far cry from "tacked-on exercises in Freudian 'real meaning.'"

The project, however, was anything but a total loss. In the James manuscript, Mark tried out a method of writing that is not well suited to periodical publication: the long fetch of thought, with ideas unwinding gradually over the course of a chapter rather than in quick, temperamental bursts, as in the broadside or the review. It is the style of the Trilling book and of the longer essays in this book. As for cautionary lessons, I'd venture to say that Mark learned something about projects in which he had a low personal investment as well as the drawbacks of totalizing intellectual systems. The book on Lionel Trilling marked as much a turn away from system as it did from polemics. Mark had given himself up in the James book to something that was too narrow a channel for his own expansive and ironic cast of mind, and he was not going to do it again. Decorum? Renunciation? With Saul Bellow out there impaled on eros in *Herzog* and Philip Roth blazing a trail of hand jobs in *Portnoy's Complaint?* In the long run, Bellow and Roth would prove to be so much more invigorating to Mark, and even the modulations of Lionel Trilling would prove to be more enlivening than James. In his essay on Cynthia Ozick in this volume, Mark speaks of her taking her veneration of Henry James too far, "losing herself in the process." Is he not speaking of his own younger self?

Derrida and Displacement: The Ordeal of Clarity

Mark entered public life as a feuilletonist, a writer of slashing broadsides, and had *Modern Occasions* become a going concern he might have remained one. He was a quick study and had a quick temper and a style to match and could say "bullshit" in fifteen hundred words with the best of them. That impulse and the ability to crank out a riposte never left him, and when anything struck him as false, he could rev up the old son-of-Rahv jets and return to form in a flash. Toward the end of his life, when suffering horribly with ALS, he was so appalled by the adulation that had greeted Mitch Albom's book about the last days of fellow ALS sufferer Morrie Schwartz, *Tuesdays with Morrie,* that he whipped off a "bullshit" as impassioned as the review of Quentin Anderson thirty years earlier.

Indeed, during his two years in England in 1972–74, Mark was furiously busy as a book reviewer, mainly for the *Times Higher Education Supplement,* for which he reviewed books on psychology (C. G. Jung, Erik Erikson) and literary criticism. The prose tended to be slashing and aggressive; he was still very much the enragé. Writing about a Festschrift for critic William K. Wimsatt, he informed his British readers that in the American academy "the professors huddle inside their departments and the students mass at the barricades. . . . With their [the professors'] retreat literature ceases to be a part of general culture and becomes the private possession of the conserving class, which displays all the unattractive characteristics of a beleaguered elite: rigidity, exclusiveness, a concern for its privileges. It loses contact with history and warns against the death of reason." Much of Mark's writing during this exile was like that; how was he ever going to come home and assume his place among the beleaguered elite?

Returning from England in 1974 and taking a position at the University of Wisconsin at Milwaukee, Mark returned to the academy, and though he had mixed feelings about it, he allowed his writing to flow largely in professional channels. He abandoned the feuilleton and began to cultivate the reflective essay that puzzled through a chain of interlocked ideas over many pages. In the late 1970s and early 1980s he published critical essays on Trilling, Podhoretz, Alfred Kazin, the *Menorah Journal* (where Lionel Trilling had his start as a writer), Edmund Wilson, Daniel Bell, Clement Greenberg, cultural criticism, criticism as an institution, and President Reagan's visit to Bitburg, and he edited *Displacement: Derrida and After.* Mark had taken the bit between his teeth and become a productive critic, his attention moving easily from reflections on the New York intellectuals to concerns more central to the professional conduct of literary studies. In those years it meant "theory."

A search for Mark Krupnick on Amazon.com's new citation database turns up unexpected results. Of some ninety references to Mark, nine are to the Trilling book, a handful to specific individual essays, and seventy-two to *Displacement.* Precious few of those references are to Mark himself, while the greater bulk are to one or more of the seven contributors, Gayatri Chakravorty Spivak in particular. No doubt that explains how Mark's name finds its way into the bibliographies of books with titles like *Leaky Bodies and Boundaries: Feminism, Postmodernism and (Bio)Ethics* and *Transvestism, Masculinity, and Latin-American Literature: Genders Share Flesh.* That is surely not where Mark anticipated finding himself when he started out. How far from *Modern Occasions* had he traveled?

Anyone who was in the literary academy in the early 1980s knows exactly how Mark got there. All he had to do was go with the flow, and if that metaphor suggests a certain insensate drifting along with the currents of fashion, let's bear in mind what that current was. It was a riptide of influence flowing from east to west, from Europe to America, in currents so powerful that they rearranged the topography of whole disciplines, as though they were the sandy shorelines of coastal islands. Though Deconstruction had been flowing through much of the 1970s (Jacques Derrida's *Of Grammatology* was published in French in 1967, in English in 1976), it was the monumental *Deconstruction and Criticism* in 1979, with contributions by Derrida, Paul de Man, J. Hillis Miller, Harold Bloom, and Geoffrey Hartman, that threw a challenge to the literary community. Paris had established a beachhead in New Haven. Deal with it.

The pressures on the literary academy then were enormous, and they emanated not from the top down—by ukase from a ministry of thought—but from all around: from colleagues who appeared to have outflanked one theoretically and by graduate students who saw a revolution taking place in their time and feared that if they didn't latch onto its coattails they might find themselves exiled from the academy. Such fears were justified. The French invasion carried enormous institutional weight, and the threat it implied, "Adapt or be written off," was real enough.

Mark felt the pressure. He was in midcareer, but the main line of his work had begun to feel passé. Even as he labored over his book on Lionel Trilling, he calculated that he couldn't continue to puzzle through the Trilling mystique or fret over Rahv or Clement Greenberg or Norman Podhoretz to the end of the millennium. That way lay a one-way ticket to the undergraduate classroom. According to Jean, recalling those days, "He loved his way of working but began to feel that he was becoming a 'fuddy-duddy,' and that perhaps he was missing out on the excitement of the new." It happened that Mark found himself in one of the flagship institutions of the 1960s, the Center for Twentieth Century Studies at the University of Wisconsin at Milwaukee. Styling itself a workshop of cutting-edge ideas, it brought Mark into contact with the major conversations in criticism and theory. During those years he immersed himself in the new voices that were working a change in the literary academy: Edward Said, Ihab Hassan, Theodor Adorno, Paul de Man, Harold Bloom, Jürgen Habermas, Michel Foucault, Susan Sontag, Roland Barthes, and Geoffrey Hartman, as well as Jacques Derrida, and with the support of colleagues and the pressure from students, Mark hitched a ride on the Deconstruction express. *Displacement: Derrida and After* is a collection of seven essays, by Greg Ulmer, Herman Rapaport, Tom Conley, Susan Handelman, Paul de Man, Michael Ryan, and Gayatri Chakravorty Spivak, a mix of seasoned veterans and emerging scholars. Mark did most of the work on it in 1980–82, when he was a fellow of the Institute for the Advanced Study of Religion at the Divinity School at the University of Chicago. It was as up-to-date as one could get, and, as the Amazon.com list indicates, the book has had a lingering shelf life.

I find it disconcerting to encounter Mark, who was addicted to lucidity, joining forces with the great Gallic fog machine, and while his publication vita indicates that Deconstruction left no paper trail after 1983, I have to wonder what he was telling himself as he worked on this book. He doesn't betray much here; his two introductory essays, one to the book itself and one to a section of three essays, are among the least polemical or self-disclosing writing he ever did. Mark took up the clarity issue in "Introduction: Sensible Language," a preface to three of the essays, in which he freely admits that in Derridean discourse sensible language is "a joke really, for the criticism of Derrida and his American exponents is by no means 'sensible' as that word would have been understood by earlier English-language critics like Edmund Wilson and Lionel Trilling or T. S. Eliot and F. R. Leavis. There are few echoes in Derridean writing of their older humanist positives, such as sincerity, tradition, clarity." However, he adds, "A too accommodating idea of reason and sense have been precisely the enemies Derridean criticism has been seeking to undermine. But what a crisis of critical language the revolt against *clarté* has brought about. Is there no way back to 'sensible' language as Jane Austen, say, would have understood the word?" "Not soon," is his answer.

Mark seems to have been of two minds about this project. On the one hand he was responding to the real danger of superannuation by radically updating his skills with a new and revolutionary instrument. It is difficult in any case to remain cutting edge in a profession in which world views and the favored tools of analysis are in such rapid flux and fashion is capricious and fleeting. Deconstruction may not have been the only game in town, but it was the big one. To be in literary studies just then and profess ignorance of Deconstruction was tantamount to being a physicist today and claiming never to have heard of String Theory.

One problem, however, was the language in which Derrida and his followers wrote. It often appears to have been cobbled whimsically together, a language that no one ever spoke except in formal academic costume, and had neither the rude familiarity of the English vernacular nor the formal propriety of the well-prepared second language. So much of it seems to be a made-up language that fleshes out the bones of English syntax with the tissues of a French-Latin vocabulary. It is virtually a new professional Lingua Franca—an Esperanto for lit critters—and Mark had to teach himself how to speak it. Which he did. Mark's sentences became permeated with the jargon du jour. Certain attitudes are "privileged"; theory is "problematized"; the role of the "marginal" reader is "to contest and demoralize authority"; older language is "placed under erasure." Mark knew full well the hazards of that language, and, after *Displacement,* he never again had recourse to it. However, I don't get the impression that Mark was up to nothing more than angling for relevance. He was endlessly curious, always eager to find out what was new and what it had in store for him. There was never a time when Mark was not serious about educating himself, and even as he lay dying and was writing this book, his reading included the latest Derrida: *The Gift of Death* and *The Work of Mourning.* In addition, there was another, more enduring, purpose for which the project served him well: reengagement with Freud.

Mark came to the Derrida project well schooled in Freud, and was familiar, for example, with early psychoanalytic formulations of the nervous system as a flow of psychic energy or "cathexes" from one idea to another. The "signifying chains" of Derrida had their precursors in the "associative pathways" of Freud's 1895 "Project for a Scientific Psychology." After *The Interpretation of Dreams* (1900), however, these bound and unbound energies became verbal processes and the transfer of charges became their mobility. It was Freud who first "decentered" thinking itself, observing, "The dream is, as it were, differently centered from the dream-thoughts—its content has different elements as its central point." Whether the fundamental assumptions of Deconstruction truly are rooted in Freud I can't say, but it appears that for Mark, Deconstruction's analytical authority lay in its Freudian credentials.

Mark, in all, cut an odd figure as a pitchman for Deconstruction, rather like a bartender who knows what is in every drink but won't touch the stuff himself. Neither before nor after this book did he read a text deconstructively or practice anything that remotely resembled a "dissemination" of phrases—the linking of words together on the basis of sound or "clang" associations. In his role as an intellectual cartographer and historian, he quickly and quietly distanced himself from the book and the knowledge he had taken such pains to acquire and articulate. His friend and contributor to the volume, Herman Rapaport, recalls that while Mark was "an unlikely candidate as editor of such a volume . . . he was dogged and patient with those materials and really tried hard to get a firm grasp of what terms and ideas meant." Apparently he did that well enough to have earned a letter of heartfelt praise from Derrida himself, who wrote to Mark, "I am struck by the extraordinary quality of the work it contains, by the uncompromising rigor, the quality, and, let me insist on this, by the generosity with which I am discussed or presented—particularly by yourself in the very remarkable and rich introduction I have just read."

Nor was that the complete story. Mark continued to read Derrida and to teach him at the Divinity School. "I think," observes Jean, "he read Derrida not as a system or even as coherent theory but as a source of evocative phrases that opened a door for him to think in ways he wouldn't have on his own," and as noted above, he continued to read Derrida's later writing. And there was a side to Derrida apart from the system that he found appealing. As Jean recalls, there was Mark's feeling for "the Jewishness of Derrida and ultimately a love for the complexity of thought." Mark was learning to become what his friend Gerald Graff has described as an "insider-outsider," learning what he needed to know about many things but never joining up.

The work on *Displacement* was a furlough from the longer, abiding labor on the Trilling book, in which Freud looms large. When Mark returned to reflect broadly on the state of institutionalized criticism, in 1985 and 1986, Derrida, displacement, and Deconstruction were barely on his radar at all. In an essay published in 1986 titled "Criticism as an Institution," he spoke mainly about two intellectual "schools" of the postwar years, the New York intellectuals and the Institute for Social Research or Frankfurt School, whose coexistence in New York in the 1940s could have led to a joining of forces but did not, a loss to both.

The details of the argument are less important than Mark's familiarity with the major features in the intellectual landscape and his singling out as the heirs to the New York intellectual legacy two contemporary figures: Susan Sontag, who began her career by declaring herself to be "against interpretation," and Edward Said, a Palestinian and an opponent of Israel, who is nevertheless "in the structure" of the Jewish New York intellectual, in being radical, homeless, different, and alienated. That both made Mark uneasy was held in their favor. Their effect was to rattle the received culture of interpretation, to challenge tradition, to promote heterodoxy, and to arouse discomfort. Sontag and Said were arguably carrying on the legacy of worldly criticism that had passed through Trilling from Arnold and the Victorians. Both were writers of the immediate, responding to pressing political situations in the real world—Vietnam, the Middle East—writing often as engaged journalists. The world's hardness was always with them.

Mark would observe in an essay published in 1985, just two years after *Displacement:* "After twenty years of floating about the skies of philosophical abstraction, criticism would do well to touch down and recover contact with the concrete, ground level virtues of the older literary journalism. Criticism has forgotten recently that, like literature itself, it must ultimately derive its strength from contact with the earth." And he would declare, "Theory in America has temporarily lost its momentum." He adds, "American critics in the next decade will be less disposed than in recent years to sound like philosophers."

In Susan Sontag and Edward Said, Mark found what he most needed in the wake of the Derrida book: reassurance that his own tradition, one of native radical thought formulated as reasoned discourse, was alive and well in America, and that his commitment to the New York intellectual tradition was not musty and antiquarian. It was a way of being in and of the moment and standing for a tradition of critical thinking that had the weight and tenacity to hold its own against the French invasion and to restore criticism, as he would say in one of these essays, "to a larger, more confident role in the general life of the culture."

Lionel Trilling and the Fate of Cultural Criticism

> "The self for Trilling is always a conscious, personal achievement, an expression of free will. We may inherit our genes, but we make our selves."
>
> Mark Krupnick

The durable work that Mark was doing, even as he edited the volume on displacement, was *Lionel Trilling and the Fate of Cultural Criticism,* which was published in 1986. I think that in the Trilling book Mark was after something larger than just setting the record straight or making amends. Rather, using Trilling as a measuring stick, Mark engaged himself in an elaborate course of self-education in relation to a literary "father," a "strong critic" who might serve as an analogue to those "strong poets" described in Harold Bloom's *The Anxiety of Influence,* who shaped the history of poetry through the powerful counter-reactions they provoked in the souls of younger poets. Mark would respond to these strong critics—Trilling was but one of several—all his life, from the first reviews to the essays in this book, since what needed to be born out of the encounter with them was nothing less than Mark himself.

Trilling looked decidedly more attractive from the perspective of the Balkanized academy, with its baffling proliferation of -isms, its weakness for Paris fashions, and, as Mark would observe, the "preening triviality" that accompanied the theory invasion. "Instead of striving for a totalizing view, what Matthew Arnold called an 'intellectual deliverance,' advanced academic theory has disintegrated—without much sign of regret—into myriad 'fields' and sects." Seen from the viewpoint of such an academy, "This polarization [between literary journalism and academic prose] has had the effect of canceling the middle ground where literature and social thought might meet." Mark also needed a model for a complex vision and a modest voice, and Henry James— whose mind was so fine, as T. S. Eliot had quipped, that no idea could violate it—would not do.

"I missed Trilling's leadership at the time," Mark wrote in *Lionel Trilling and the Fate of Cultural Criticism,* "and wrote about him with some bitterness in 1971. I am not disposed to judge him as harshly now as I did fifteen years ago. Given the uncertainties Trilling had about nearly everything, it was right for him to turn to history for understanding rather than to trumpet opinions about which he was unsure simply because, in his intellectual milieu, everyone was supposed to have a ready opinion about everything." As we will see, Mark turned decisively away from polemics as a calling, from the whole notion that thinking creatively about history, culture, and identity required one to have a ready and combative point of view. But then, jettisoning ready opinion, what else was there?

That question is the key to Mark's mature writing. What was there beyond opinion itself, beyond posture, stance, engagement, and how did Trilling point toward an answer? *Lionel Trilling and the Fate of Cultural Criticism* is the opening of that question, which Mark undertook in the spirit of cautious, probing inquiry. The Trilling whom Mark

encountered was one who devoted his life to discovering an adequate relation to ideas, and, even more critically, an adequate relation to himself.

Mark wrote of Trilling: "He conceives of his personal identity as
being intimately involved with his relation to advanced ideas. He wants
to be able to 'give the credence of my senses' to these ideas or better ones
so that society will seem real to him. But the ultimate goal of his quest
for an adequate theory remains personal. If society can be made to seem
more intelligible and manageable, he will then feel more anchored and
real in relation to that society." It is not at all surprising that the book on
Trilling should also be, in part, a book about Mark and that the Trilling
he discovered was one whose particular steps toward becoming himself
were of the greatest personal interest to Mark. Lionel Trilling comes
into view as a man who had been self-created through his relation to
books. "The self for Trilling," he observed, "is always a conscious, personal achievement, an expression of free will. We may inherit our genes,
but we make our selves."

Lionel Trilling and the Fate of Cultural Criticism was far from being a
one-dimensional study of a literary critic in search of himself by a literary critic in search of himself. It was a full-featured study of Trilling's
mind, a mind in evolution, restless and ill at ease with itself. It disclosed,
to use a jargon prevalent in the 1980s, a "decentered" Trilling who could
say with Kafka, "What have I in common with the Jews? I scarcely have
anything in common with myself." But then there was nothing quite so
au courant about Mark's book; nothing in its jargon suggested that Mark
was out to postmodernize Lionel Trilling, to bring his self-confessed
ambivalences up to date and repackage him for a new generation of
scholars who had cut their teeth on *Tel Quel*. Mark's purposes were sim-
pler and more direct: to model Trilling from the inside, to get behind the
masks, the sententiae, the buzzwords, and see plainly the core of ambivalence that had brought such a tension into Trilling's essays.

But Trilling proved to be an elusive guide to Trilling. Though "the
self" and its formation was the central preoccupation of his career, it
was always abstracted, "*the* self," never *my*self. The first person singular
pronoun remained foreign to him, a ball that was always out of play, visible to the eye but bouncing around in foul territory. As Mark was quick
to point out, Trilling presented himself as self-fashioned and yet always
at the ready to alter the pattern. (Was he a tailor's son for nothing?)

Long before deconstruction became a fashion in the academy, Trilling was practicing it on himself, defending positions from one essay to the next that seemed to stand in opposition to each other, suggesting a turn of mind that Mark characterized as exhibiting an "allergy to closure." There was Trilling the Dionysus wannabe and Trilling the archaic torso of Apollo; Trilling who celebrated freedom from the conditioned life and Trilling who bemoaned the lightness of culture; there was Trilling who extolled the historical imagination and Trilling who invoked time-less mythic themes; there was Trilling who celebrated "the opposing self" and Trilling who exalted the middle class and defended William Dean Howells and Howells's American belief in the "more smiling as-pects of life," Trilling who led the charge against the Popular Front in the 1940s and Trilling who confessed two decades later to fatigue before the vulgarities of "the movement." "Not having a fixed, easily summar-ized position is for Trilling itself a kind of position." And again, "We need to speak not of fixed ideological positions but of alternations and fluctuations of mood. Trilling refines and corrects the culture by per-forming these operations first on himself."

What kind of a father was that? Was this not maddening? Was this the house in which Mark, having left his father's home on Webster Street, was going to live? Whatever it was that Mark finally responded to in this long immersion in Trilling and which surfaces boldly in *Deep Places* was not the fussiness, the conspicuous ambivalence, the meander-ing positions and fluctuating moods, the dissolving ego. It was the stur-diness of the work itself, the lessons in applied psychoanalysis, the depths Trilling could reach in his portraits of artists, in "The Poet as Hero: Keats in His Letters," "Freud: Within and Beyond Culture," "Emma and the Legend of Jane Austen," "Isaac Babel," and "Joyce in His Letters." These were durable goods indeed, as the recent publica-tion of Trilling's major essays under the title of *The Moral Obligation to Be Intelligent* amply testifies. Mark wrote about the polemical Trilling, the Trilling of opinions and their discontents, but what he absorbed through his very skin was another Trilling, the portraitist, the character analyst, the writer of indelible cameos, the Trilling who without fanfare plumbed the deep places of the imagination by immersing himself in the lives of others. Here Mark found the occluded Trilling, the novelist manqué but also the novelist redux, who was far more adept at creating characters in his critical essays than ever he had been in his stories and his novel. This was also Trilling the psychoanalyst, applying what he had gathered from Freud and from his own years on the couch. And it was also Trilling the rabbi of character, as understood by the nineteenth century, a composite of reason, durability, rectitude, and judgment. In absorbing these lessons, Mark was his talmid.

The Deep Places of the Imagination

The question of how a book is conceived out of the tangle of thoughts that precede it may be unanswerable. This book, *Jewish Writing and the Deep Places of the Imagination,* existed in Mark's mind in some form as early as the 1980s, after he published the Trilling book and realized that much of what he had to say was out of place there. The years after 1986 were hectic with activity, and there can be little doubt that Mark wrote some of his essays with an eye toward their eventual collection. Why he hesitated is also not difficult to imagine.

Essay collections from all but superstars in literary studies are a tough sell to publishers because they are a tough sell to readers. The library purchases that could once be counted on to underwrite academic publications are in steep decline, and with general interest in literary scholarship at an all-time low, writers are hard-pressed to find a publisher willing to take a loss, even in exchange for the abstract benefits of prestige. Mark entertained his own doubts. Just who was the audience for essays titled "Criticism as an Institution," "Middlebrowism in the Academy," "Edward Said: Discourse and Palestinian Rage," or "Cynthia Ozick as the Jewish T. S. Eliot"? As original as some of these essays were, Mark must surely have wondered who would take an avid interest in them. And what about the book's identity, its handle? There was an abundance of essays but what unified them? What was their unique signature, their collective name?

A terminal illness dissolves such scruples. "Death," Thomas More wrote from his cell in the Tower of London, "wonderfully focuses the mind," and it certainly did that for Mark. Though some essays in this book predate Mark's illness and other late essays revise and update earlier ones, the core of this book is recent. Mark died on March 29, 2003, and portions of this book were dated as late as March 23. To cite some specifics and to give a sense of Mark's focus and determination in the last months of his life, despite obstacles that stun the imagination, the dates I have for the completion of some of the essays in this book are as follows: "A Shit-Filled Life," January 6; both Cynthia Ozick and Geoffrey Hartman, March 14; Roth and "We Are Here to Be Humiliated," March 18; a revision of his essay on *Tuesdays with Morrie,* March 22; revisions of his essay on Diana Trilling, March 23. In his last months, Mark wrestled with his introduction through many drafts; he struggled with hands that were failing him; he was on oxygen and fought to catch his breath.

Mark spent the better part of the 1980s and 1990s writing essays of two very different sorts: landscapes and portraits. In the aftermath of the Derrida book, whether on assignment or out of a personal need for clarity, Mark wrote several essays on the state of critical thought, both in the academy and in the realm of journalism. With titles like "The Two Worlds of Cultural Criticism," "Criticism as an Institution," and "Middlebrowism in the Academy," they were summary reports, virtually satellite photos of the critical terrain. They were also fingers on the pulse of New York intellectual life itself. Did the intellectual radicalism that had evolved in *Partisan Review,* turned stridently to the right in *Commentary,* and flamed out in *Modern Occasions* have anything left to say for itself? Mark's discovery of Susan Sontag and Edward Said as innovators in the free-style New York fashion was the meager solace he needed to soldier on. Subsequently he would add Cynthia Ozick and Philip Roth.

Right along, however, Mark had been composing portraits. His elegiac and disillusioned memoir of Philip Rahv, "He Never Learned to Swim," was the first of them. Written in white heat and remembered injury, it was a cross between a god-that-failed testimony and a case history. (If this portrait of the editor as a "manic-impressive"—Delmore Schwartz's stinging phrase—owed anything to Freud, however, it was more to Lucien than to Sigmund.) It was the first of Mark's ruminations on a literary father figure in relation to himself, and in its combination of nostalgia and resentment it displayed an intimacy and animus that his landscape writing could never match. Efforts they may have been to write his own *Liberal Imagination,* the landscapes lacked the one ingredient that Mark always needed for his best writing: room for himself. Starting out in the 1980s, Mark would move portraiture to the forefront of his writing: how alien it was to continental postmodernism, in which the artist had been eclipsed by *le texte*. Even before starting to work on this book, Mark composed portraits of Alfred Kazin, Edmund Wilson (twice), Daniel Bell, Irving Howe for *The Dictionary of Literary Biography*, Cynthia Ozick, Hannah Arendt for *The Cambridge Guide to Women's Writing in English*, and shorter review-essays on Edward Said, Diana Trilling, and Michael Walzer. *Lionel Trilling and the Fate of Cultural Criticism* was the centerpiece of his gallery. So congenial had the personal element in criticism become that by the late 1990s Mark had latched on with the London *Guardian* as a writer of obituaries. "Few things fascinate me more," he confessed in his essay on obituary writing, "than the trajectories of human lives." No one less than Derrida, we might note, has become an exemplary writer of obituaries and eulogies in his later years.

This was stubbornly unfashionable work. Since this biographical writing picked up speed in the late 1980s (the *DLB* essay on Irving Howe appeared in 1988) and was in full stride in the 1990s, we might notice that in 1990 Mark left the English Department at the University of Illinois' Chicago campus for the Divinity School at the University of Chicago, where he would be relieved of the pressure to be theoretically *au courant* and hermeneutically correct. Could this turn to portraiture be deemed conservatism on Mark's part? Maybe so, though I think in such a context terms like liberal and conservative, radical and reactionary, left, right, and center simply fail us. What do they describe? Are conservative and right (i.e., the opposite of left) always musty, always defensive, always rear guard? Always *ancien régime?* It is best to simply say that Mark was standing firm by his own sensibility and style and was determined to work things through on his terms.

One was to find his way beyond the topical. There are many directions to go with that, including into Olympian historiography, but Mark's compass was already set. He was going to line the gallery with character studies of Jewish writers who had plumbed their own depths, braved the hazards of self-knowledge, and heroically laid themselves open to their readers. Possibly Mark was generalizing from the example of Freud, who had declared in *The Interpretation of Dreams* that the basic insights of psychoanalysis had emerged from the analysis of himself that he had embarked on after the death of his father. But he turned first to Trilling, who had used the phrase in a 1946 essay, "The Function of the Little Magazine," in which he contrasted "the great literature of European modernism—Proust, Joyce, Mann, etc.—with what he regarded as the drearily unimaginative American writing of the forepart of the twentieth century."

Trilling had an easy enough time singling out literature that did not touch down in those deep places. "It is clear," Mark noted, "that he had in mind older figures like Theodore Dreiser and Sherwood Anderson, especially their writing in the 1930s, and younger socially oriented novelists like John Steinbeck, especially the latter's Pulitzer prize-winning bestseller *The Grapes of Wrath* (1939). He was especially interested in the appeal of these writers to a group he referred to as the 'liberal educated class.'" Identifying a literature that does draw inspiration from the depths is another matter, and neither Trilling nor Mark had a ready formula for that. Much of Mark's essay looks at Trilling's essay on Isaac Babel, published in 1955 as the introduction to *The Collected Stories of Isaac Babel* and reprinted in *Beyond Culture* (1965).

Only in that essay, Mark pointed out, did Trilling deal with a Jew. Wide-ranging though Trilling's attentions were, his canon revolved around English and American authors: Hemingway, Dreiser, Kipling, James, Austen, Keats, Dos Passos, Orwell. Babel was anomalous among these, a Jewish Russian story writer, son of an Odessa businessman, who, in his youth, embraced the Russian Revolution, joined the Red Army as a journalist, and wrote reports for a divisional newspaper, *The Red Cavalryman*. As a journalist and a Jew, "with spectacles on his nose and autumn in his heart," riding with General Budyonny's Cossack Cavalry, he learned to admire his opposite type, the Cossacks, even as they pillaged the bedraggled and vulnerable Jewish villages along the Russian-Polish border. Out of that experience came the stories collected under the title of *Red Cavalry*. Those stories, in their understated passion, their tension and economy, have become monuments of European modernism, not to say world literature.

> Babel was a Jew and thus, as Trilling understood him, one who "conceived his ideal character to consist in his being intellectual, pacific, humane." On the other hand, he was powerfully drawn to the Cossacks even though to the Jews "the Cossack was physical, violent, without

mind or manners." In the Jewish imagination, the Cossack stood for "animal violence" and "aimless destructiveness." There was a potential political dimension to the detestation of the Cossack. If the Jew "thought beyond his own ethnic and religious group, he knew that the Cossack was the enemy not only of the Jew—although him especially— but of all men who thought of freedom; he was the natural and appropriate instrument of ruthless oppression."

Trilling, as Mark saw it, was speaking not simply of Babel but of some fascination with untamed elements within himself. As the Cossacks were releasing agents for Babel, giving him a purchase on a way of life alien to his own, Babel in turn served as one for Trilling, though only in imagination. "That is, he admired Babel's original imagination and genius as Babel admired the uninhibited instinct-life and pre-modern authenticity of the Cossacks. The suffocatingly respectable middle-class society in which Trilling was raised was as far as can be from what Babel remembered as the 'gay, rowdy, noisy and multilingual' world of his Odessa." Writing a decade later in *The Experience of Literature* about Babel's story "Di Grasso," in which a crime of passion occurs in the theater when an actor leaps across the stage to sink his teeth into the throat of a rival in love, Trilling ruminated on Babel's "lyric joy in the midst of violence." Babel himself glossed the passage: "There is more justice in outbursts of noble passion that in all the joyless rules that run the world."

For Trilling, however, the act's violence struck him less than its grace: "By way of analogy to Di Grasso's great leap, Trilling adduces the great leaps of the dancer Nijinsky, whose seeming ability to fly across the stage gave his audience a precious 'intimation of freedom from the bondage of our human condition.'" (I have not read anywhere that Trilling was a baseball fan, but what might he have thought of the great center fielders of his lifetime: DiMaggio, Mantle, Mays, Snider, for their great leaps, their flying protests against the bondage of gravity and the human condition, in the process of which they sometimes crashed against the outfield fences of reality?) Did this admiration of grace, spontaneity, and energy disclose something reckless and antinomian in Trilling, a repressed desire welling up into consciousness in the guise of aesthetic appreciation? "When he referred to imagination's deep places, he had in mind what Arnold called the 'buried life' and Freud the unconscious.

But tapping into the depths, where lie the springs of our being, precisely enables the elevation, the sublimity, of Di Grasso's leap. Elevation is the effect, the creative act, enabled by the imagination's plumbing of its own depths."

If Trilling had given Mark his career at the beginning, a transfigured Trilling helped to revitalize it at the end. If the Trilling of stasis, disengagement, and tragic grandeur, who could not respond fully "to any subject but that of loss and defeat," first roused Mark to protest, the Trilling of instinct and grace buoyed him up later on. "Lionel Trilling and the Deep Places of the Imagination" is not only in my view the best writing Mark ever did about Trilling, it also gave him this book. For one thing, it gave him a subject, subjectivity itself. It gave him license, in effect, to go soul hunting, and the essays that accompany it, on Geoffrey Hartman, Cynthia Ozick, and Philip Roth, take their freedom to probe and speculate from what he found he could do with Trilling. It also gave him a method. It is not exactly an applied psychoanalysis that he performs here or anywhere else, and it is most obligingly unsystematic. Mark gives all his authors credit for self-awareness; they dream being awake. He performs a sinuous rumination, a meandering descent into some fissure in a writer's work that allows him a richer, and darker, apprehension of it, but never with assurances of homing in on "Freudian real meaning." He reads with the empathy of the secret sharer, who has been there himself and knows the experience.

"'A Shit-Filled Life': Philip Roth's *Sabbath's Theater*," "Geoffrey Hartman, Wordsworth, and Holocaust Testimonies," and "Cynthia Ozick: Embarrassments" were written with a common purpose—to pay homage to the masters from whom he had learned—and a common method: the patient, unstructured penetration of an oeuvre in search of some region of tenderness and urgency, some hidden part that illuminates the whole. He wanted to understand the writer's power by looking at how it draws upon the writer's vulnerability.

On the face of it, that sounds like the application of Edmund Wilson's wound and bow thesis, that the artist's power and insight develop as compensatory gifts for psychic wounds that had left the artist feeling damaged. Trilling himself had rejected that idea in his essay, "Art and Neurosis," in which he argued that the artist was healthy, at least in his or her art, and that to explain art as symptom or compensation was to explain it away. In these essays Mark didn't directly take up the issue either way, and in any case he was losing his taste for abstractions that were not grounded in flesh and blood and the sensible world. His time was short and he wanted to have his say about four writers who had come to matter to him and to sound their depths using the tools he had at hand. Living in Chicago, he had adopted the knockabout Chicago manner and might have said with Bellow's Augie March. "[I] go at things as I have taught myself, free-style, and will make the record in my own way."

To write about Cynthia Ozick and engage her from a different angle, Mark revisited an essay he had published in 1991, on Ozick as "the Jewish T. S. Eliot" (see Publications). "Writing about Cynthia Ozick twelve years ago, I thought of her as she had presented herself in the late 1960s and through the '70s, as a Jewish writer with a self-consciously Jewish agenda." Without denying any of this, Mark was no longer willing to see Ozick entirely through the lens of her opinions, which no longer felt adequate to the job of understanding her. "My present conception of Ozick is quite different from the one she proposed of herself and that I uncritically took over from her. Rather than seeing Ozick as a public and polemical writer chiefly concerned with Jewishness and Judaism, I now think of her as much more personal in her emphases."

Though Mark had taken his title, "Embarrassments," from Henry James's story collection of 1896, a year after he had been jeered by playgoers on the opening night of *Guy Domville,* he applied it to the prevailing emotional temper of Ozick's own more self-revealing stories and essays. The principal story is "Puttermesser Paired" from *The Puttermesser Papers,* and essays are from her alliteratively titled miscellanies: *Art and Ardor* (1983), *Metaphor and Memory* (1991), *Fame and Folly* (1996), and *Quarrel and Quandary* (2000). They are in particular "Justice (Again) to Edith Wharton," "Mrs. Virginia Woolf: A Madwoman of the Master," and the autobiographical "A Drugstore in Winter" (*Art and Ardor*), "Alfred Chester's Wig: Images Standing Fast" *(Fame and Folly),* "Lovesickness," "A Drugstore Eden," and "A Portrait of the Artist as a Warm Body" *(Quarrel and Quandary).* Mark hopscotches through Ozick's career, as a psychoanalyst might, picking out a story here and essays there to catch the subterranean life wherever it breaks the surface. In doing that, Mark follows Ozick's own lead: "The best of her essays are remarkable in displaying a fiction writer's gift for summing up her biographical subject in a certain image or ruling passion."

The ruling passion is humiliation, which Mark finds in the essay on Virginia Woolf, who is said to have been humiliated by her husband, Leonard, whose sexual indifference to her drove her into the arms of her aggressively lesbian friend, Vita Sackville-West. Edith Wharton, on the other hand, was the one who dealt out the humiliating blows to her husband, Teddy, who eventually went mad and was not spared the humiliation of his madness by Edith. When he got out of line he found himself, in Ozick's words, "replaced in bed by a writing board." The smoking gun, however, is Ozick's essay on her former school friend Alfred Chester, a promising young writer whose lack of body hair as a result of a childhood disease was a narcissistic wound that obliged him to wear a yellow wig to conceal his baldness. Here we have humiliation writ large: Chester's humiliation and his lifetime of rejection by women, and Ozick's double humiliation as the woman who was attracted to him and rejected and whose career was so much more plodding than his at the outset.

In 1946, Ozick and Chester were students together at NYU and rivals as well. "I wanted more than anything else to beat him," she wrote. She was also infatuated with him and was hurt when he did not take her attentions seriously. After graduation, she was awed by his successes, as he went off to join the *Paris Review* crowd and be fiction editor of the influential journal *Botteghe Oscure*. Mark notes, "The pain of unrequited affection is intensified for Ozick by their continuing literary competitiveness, in which she is unambiguously the loser." He finds there and elsewhere this experience of defeat and humiliation and quest for vindication.

Was Mark here attempting to take Ozick down a notch, after having earlier lionized her as the Jewish American T. S. Eliot and her writing as a contemporary embodiment of "Jewish moral seriousness and the Jewish commitment to history"? Wasn't it prudent to leave things that way? In an e-mail message to me during our midwinter correspondence Mark had spoken of Ozick as a friend and had given no hints of any shadows on that friendship. Was he taking it back? Is this exposure of Ozick's embarrassments an act of friendship? Homage by unfamiliar means?

I think the last. For reasons that are built into Jewish American literary culture and its nervous propensity to circle the wagons around its icons, Ozick over the years has been both beneficiary and victim of obscene amounts of hagiography. Her ethical pronouncements on art and politics, including her fierce defense of Israel, have created around her an aura, that of the indignant prophet bearing torahs of righteousness and high culture that has made it hard for readers to see her plain, though she had taken pains to make herself visible in all due plainness. Mark's own earlier essay, for all its exposure of the contradictions in her attitude toward art, indulged in the hagiographic impulse, and as this later essay shows, he was impatient with it.

Here Mark takes Ozick's own invitation to see her through some lens other than her Judaism or her aesthetic militancy and to observe her instead through her womanhood, which she describes in essays and fiction as aggrieved. In electing to portray Ozick as wounded in her self-esteem, Mark is hardly dredging for unconscious material: for Freud's repressed infantile wishes. He just chooses to read what Ozick herself has put before us and to place a higher value on the confessional side of her writing than on the critical. In this he pays respect to a writer who is not after all the Jewish Henry James or T. S. Eliot (though maybe more the Jewish J. Alfred Prufrock), for she will have nothing of their neurasthenia, their mandarin fastidiousness, or their repulsion toward the Jew who, in Eliot's poem, squats on the windowsill. Despite her absorption in literature, she has elected to be a Puttermesser (Yiddish for butterknife), a druggist's daughter, and a despondent rival and to speak of being at times heartsick, haunted by memories, and embarrassed. "Ozick, so often described as if she were an ideological dogmatist, turns out to be emotionally quite complex." Rather than undercutting her art, this is just a way to see it in a human context, calling to mind Isaac Rosenfeld's aphorism: "I hold the conviction—it amounts to something of a theory—that embarrassment represents the true state of affairs, & the sooner we strike shame, the sooner we draw blood." Ozick's striking shame in order to draw blood is the spirit that Mark finally wished to stress, and he came to value her efforts at self-detranscendance, at slipping out from behind her high-culture armor to play at being a dreamy, bookish, harried heroine named Puttermesser, a woman with periodontal disease who reads thick nineteenth-century novels and carries an umbrella.

That Mark's Jewish identity was secular did not mean that it was tepid. Mark responded most profoundly to Jewish writers with whom he felt a spiritual affinity, whose Jewishness was more cultural than observant and consisted of bookish secular pursuits. His sole extended excursion away from Jewish intellectual life was the Derrida book, and one wonders whether Mark's interest there did not lie partly in Derrida's own occluded Jewishness. It is clear, though, from everything Mark wrote that he held most dear a brand of Jewish intelligence that might be described as post-Enlightenment. It was open and fractious, curious and worldly, tempered by age-old habits of panic and responsibility, and it answered to the requirements of "variousness and possibility." And it led him to an engagement with Jewish thinkers across the centuries, both those within the tradition—Rashi, Martin Buber, Gershom Sholem, Moshe Idel, Cynthia Ozick—and those whom Isaac Deutscher had famously called the "non-Jewish" Jews—Walter Benjamin, Derrida, Hartman, and of course Rahv, Trilling, Howe, and the New York intellectuals. An alternative title for this book could be *Varieties of Jewish Experience*.

But if normative Judaism held little appeal for Mark, Jewish consciousness was everything. From the summers Mark devoted to teaching Jewish American literature at seminars sponsored by the NEH to his immersion in Jewish intellectual life, his sense of self was saturated with his Jewishness and with the legacies of history and thought that it brought with it. In the writers he adopted as his mentors—call them fathers, rabbis—it was invariably the clarification of Jewishness and the expansion of its boundaries that he sought. (Cynthia Ozick is not exempted by gender from being a rabbi in this instance. That is how she existed "structurally" for Mark.) Edmund Wilson was as close as he ever came to taking on a non-Jewish rabbi, and significantly Mark's essay on Wilson was about the latter's philo-Semitism. Mark's adoption of Geoffrey Hartman and Hartman's Holocaust studies was yet another phase of expanding Jewish awareness.

Hartman's visit to the Divinity School at the University of Chicago in 2000 and Mark's growing friendship with him led to "Geoffrey Hartman, Wordsworth, and Holocaust Testimonies" in this book. I find it the most intimate essay in the book but also the most difficult. The intimacy may have something to do with Mark's drawing closer to Hartman than he ever had or could to Roth, Ozick, or Trilling. The difficulty reflects the range of Hartman's scholarship, the subtlety and complexity of his mind, the dense layering of his interests, and his sometimes elliptical prose. "Logic," Mark wrote, "has never been his strong suit." Hartman is not as intellectually accessible as Ozick or Roth—though far more accessible personally—and we need to bear in mind that later that year, 2000, Mark first took ill and his immersion in Hartman's writing was not pursued casually.

Geoffrey Hartman is one of those members of the literary academy who came to Jewish studies only after starting as something else. Mark must be accounted another, having been trained as an Americanist, with a PhD dissertation on Stephen Crane and Edith Wharton. Whatever this may mean as a commentary on the literary academy, in which Jewish literary studies is normally peripheral to the curriculum, it is a trademark of post-Enlightenment Jewishness itself, the freedom of Jews to take part openly in the life of Western civilization and their eager reaction to the opportunity. Hartman entered academic life as a Wordsworth scholar, his earliest books included *The Unmediated Vision: An Interpretation of Wordsworth, Hopkins, Rilke, and Valery* (1954) and *Wordsworth's Poetry 1787–1814* (1964). His early years too were devoted to critical theory, and he would eventually come to be known, along with his colleagues J. Hillis Miller, Paul de Man, and Harold Bloom, as one of the "Yale Critics," as though that signaled a uniform approach and intention, which it did not.

It was neither Wordsworth studies nor essays on critical method, however, that deeply drew Mark into Hartman's writing, but Hartman's work with the Fortunoff Video Archive for Holocaust Testimonies at Yale, of which he was a founder and continues to be a project director, and his writing about the ethics and phenomenology of witnessing. From that involvement have come *Holocaust Remembrance: The Shapes of Memory* (edited, 1994) and *The Longest Shadow: In the Aftermath of the Holocaust* (1996), a universe undreamt of by Wordsworth. The question immediately arises: Has Hartman's career been of a piece, its apparent eclecticism knitted together by subterranean threads, or is this another case of a Jewish intellectual turning attention in midcareer to Jewishness?

What Mark uncovered is an intellectual life rooted in trauma and loss and integrated by poetry and scholarship. Hartman suffered a series of devastating shocks as a child in Germany. His parents divorced when he was just a year old, and later, in 1939, his mother, who had placed him in an orphanage from which he was to go to England on a Kindertransport, left for the United States when she was able to get a visa for herself but not for him. The nine-year-old Hartman—his name then was Gert Heumann—was rescued by a Children's Transport financed by British Jews that took him to a group home in the English countryside, where he spent the war years. "Brought up without father and mother," Hartman wrote, "I would let no one else fill the vacuum."

Poetry and scholarship, however, would serve as anodynes, in particular the involvement with Wordsworth's poetry, which evoked the Buckinghamshire countryside where Hartman felt at home, "my life somehow part of its life." English Romantic literature, Wordsworth in particular, restored that childhood bond to the nurturing English countryside: "Hartman's tie to Wordsworth is remarkable for its intimacy. The poet of the Lake District propped him up when he was a child and his supports were few, and it is as if he has continued to be part of Hartman's being."

Despite the legendary obliquity of Hartman's prose—his rejection of the "hegemonic" conversational style—and his lifetime of engagement with continental theory, the Wordsworth and Holocaust phases of his writing have been intensely personal, and the project of reparation and restoration in the study of Holocaust testimonies is continuous with the nurturing poetry of Wordsworth. "Hartman is not interested in the Holocaust testimonies as straightforward historical narratives. Rather, he watches for the surfacing of a long-forgotten trauma, and the subject's self-reflective imaginative response in the present. Here, too, Wordsworth's poems provide some clues and constitute the link between the earlier and the later Hartman."

Mark was less receptive, however, to those portions of Hartman's career, in books like *Beyond Formalism: Literary Essays 1958–1970* (1973) and *Criticism in the Wilderness: The Study of Literature Today* (1980), devoted to critical thought and the chastisement of the Anglo-American tradition for its resistance to theory. Remarking on Hartman's idea of the Holocaust archive as constituting an "affective community," Mark observed, "It is just theory, after all, and we have been drowning in theory for some time now." The Hartman who drew his strength from contact with the earth was the Hartman who appealed to him most.

Trauma and repair, then, were the keys to Hartman's career, and Mark was willing to extend them globally to his entire intellectual life, including his investments in philosophy. "If we consider the spirit of attentiveness in the light of Hartman's own biography, it would seem a response to the long trauma of separation from his mother that I would guess to be the founding experience of his personality."

For all that, Hartman is not driven by unconscious pressures but rather is aware of his complexities and of having made of memory, witness, and interpretation duties and burdens. The larger design of which it all partakes is an overarching "consciousness of consciousness" that Hartman identifies as the project of Wordsworth himself. "If we ask, then, what might induce a literary scholar who has been a great interpreter of Wordsworth to expand his study to embrace the video testimonies of Holocaust survivors, our answer might be that his fascination with the poet's 'consciousness of consciousness' might well find a worthy complement in his new interest in the process by which survivor-interviewees awaken and respond to their suppressed memories as they tell their stories. It may be that both objects of study speak to 'the wish' Hartman describes as latent in most of us 'for strong, identity-shaping memories.'"

In effect, Freud's return of the repressed, the great law of dreams, jokes, and neurotic symptoms, has been transferred from psychodynamics to public life as a duty and an ethical imperative. The project of recovery (as both restoration and convalescence) is now the goal of research and organized memory. Hartman spoke of "the burden of how to be a witness to the witness—how to attend, value, and interpret the testimonies—clearly falls on all for whom Nazism's 'culture of death' is a frightening riddle. There is a duty of reception."

For Mark, Hartman represented a port of entry into an area of Jewish identity, the Holocaust, and it was the kind of entry that best suited him: through ideas and not visceral response. True, Cynthia Ozick deals also with the Holocaust, most notably in her novels *The Shawl* and *The Messiah of Stockholm*, and Mark did use those books in his teaching. But as a writer, Mark couldn't use Ozick as a guide to thinking about the Holocaust, and wound up using Ozick as guide to Ozick herself. In Hartman's case, the personal was the historical, and the scholarship was grounded in loss and grief, his own as well as the catastrophe that befell Europe's Jews. Mark in time came to see Hartman as one of his ego-ideals, an embodiment of what he hoped he might be, and he wrote in one of his many notes on Hartman, "I would say that Hartman's criticism conforms to Oscar Wilde's description of the highest criticism: 'the record of one's own soul.'" From one perspective, that criticism extends Wordsworth's "consciousness of consciousness," the development of a sensibility that is adequate to the world that it perceives. From another it is obedience to the Jewish injunction to repair the world, "tikkun olam," which the kabbalists understood as both a social and a spiritual practice, doing service to society while also liberating the divine spark within oneself. This doesn't make of Geoffrey Hartman either a Zaddik or a missionary, but it does lend the weight of Jewish tradition to his scholarship and allow us to see, as Mark did, the scholarship as fully integrated with the life.

What then do we make of Mark's interest in Philip Roth and of his taking *Sabbath's Theater* for his model book, its being by all accounts the most abrasive of Roth's fictions since *Portnoy's Complaint?* Maybe the question is self-answering. If the deep places of the imagination are what we seek, then Roth, who of all modern writers has most consistently turned himself inside out in the service of his art, is our man and *Sabbbath's Theater* his signature book.

Sabbath's Theater features Morris "Mickey" Sabbath, a broken-down street performer who does puppet routines with his hands alone in his Indecent Theater routine. He has been known to unbutton the blouses of young women on the street; engage in phone sex with an undergraduate at a women's college; celebrate the disappearance of his first wife by bedding a friend in just hours; steal underclothes from a host's teenage daughter and money from the hostess; urinate on the grave of his deceased lover, the Croatian earth-mother Drenka Balich. Something elemental is going on, which I have come to think of as Roth's war with the normal in an era of rehabilitation. *Sabbath's Theater* would appear to be the latest word—maybe even the last word—on Roth's romance with the incurable self, his shot across the bow of an age that is all gung ho for "healing" and "wellness." Mark too saw the book as something exceptional: a psychic disburdening, a bottoming out, and found it emblematic of Roth's career from the late 1990s to the present. "In his writing during the past fifteen years or so, Philip Roth has continued to be a writer with little interest in dreams or traditional ideas of beauty, except if represented in the shape of the female breast. He has increasingly found loss, humiliation, and death at the heart of things. And increasingly reductive in his sense of reality, he has found the most basic, most elemental principle of things in excrement. The protagonists of his most recent books have been in the end overcome by storms of shit. It might seem excessive to say that Roth was invoking shit more than as a metaphor, but it is an important literal fact in the doomed careers in some of his main characters."

Though Mark's is a focused study of a single book, his broader meaning is plain: something—many things—happened to Roth from the late '8os and after, and his books throughout the '90s record, with seismographic precision, a collapse of morale. We need only reflect on what we do know—the death of his father, the dissolution of his marriage to Claire Bloom and his brief institutionalization afterward, his harrowing episode with the pain killer Halcion, his cardiac surgery—and wonder how he survived with his creative faculties intact. *Sabbath's Theater* in 1995 gives us the deepest penetration into that collapse by expanding on a single metaphor for how it felt to Roth.

Mark's admiration of *Sabbath's* is twofold. For one thing, the book is more internally consistent than the "American problem" novels that followed it: *American Pastoral, I Married a Communist,* and *The Human Stain.* It is not so vitiated by sidetracks, subplots, evasions, clunky narrative strategies, pasteboard characterizations (Merry Levov, Les Farley, Delphine Roux), and in particular by the "irrepressible zest for sermonizing" by which Roth has been increasingly overcome. Moreover, it is more personal than the others; it appears to be hot-wired directly into Roth's own troubled core, in which Mark finds humiliation and defeat. He finds in *Sabbath* a novel built on "increments of excrement" and therefore a sequel to Roth's memoir of his father's last year in *Patrimony.* He cites the scene in which Roth's father, visiting his rural Connecticut home, at one point slips away from the company and goes upstairs. "When he does not reappear, Philip mounts the stairs himself and discovers his father in a state of shock. Repeatedly moaning 'I beshat myself,' the old man stands in his son's bathroom surrounded by the effects of the volcanic eruption of his bowels: 'The shit was everywhere.' Philip ends his inventory of stain with striking detail: 'It was even on the tips of the bristles of my toothbrush hanging in the holder over the sink.'"

The father is ashamed. "Don't tell the children. . . . Don't tell Claire." Mark writes: "To honor his father's wish, the son seeks no help in cleaning up the mess. He even gets down on his hands and knees, and with a bucket of hot water and Spic and Span goes to work with that toothbrush trying to clean flecks of shit from where they have lodged in the crevices between the planks of the floor." Roth goes to work meticulously cleaning up after his father and reflects, "So that was the patrimony. And not because cleaning it up was symbolic of something else but because it wasn't, because it was nothing less or more than the lived reality that it was. There was my patrimony: not the money, not the tefillin, not the shaving mug, but the shit."

The publication of *Patrimony* in 1991 ushered in a decade of robust publishing for Roth, being followed in assembly-line succession by *Operation Shylock* (1993), *Sabbath's Theater* (1995), *American Pastoral* (1997), *I Married a Communist* (1998), and *The Human Stain* (2000). From Mark's angle of vision, this outburst of creativity reveals a personal crisis that unleashed in Roth "an extremism of subject-matter and style that goes far beyond the artistic self-liberation he achieved in *Portnoy's Complaint.*" Part of that extremism is an openness, as never before, to the "shit-filled life," which pervades the novels of the '90s, and even lends a title to *The Human Stain.* In the words of that novel's Faunia Farley, who is so terribly familiar with defeat, "We leave a stain, we leave a trail, we leave our imprint. Impurity, cruelty, abuse, error, excrement, semen—there's no other way to be here."

Mark concludes: "*Sabbath's Theater* will someday receive the honor it deserves. It is not didactic fiction propelled by argument like [Saul Bellow's] *Herzog* and is free of Roth's own tendency in recent novels to preach cultural jeremiads. Also, its nihilism is not doctrinal. Rather, it is a triumph of fantasy, emotion, instinct. Roth was able to reach down far into the deep places of imagination. In this unique novel, Roth reached down within himself to the deepest springs of his being, which freed his imagination as never before or since. The result, as with Mickey Sabbath himself, was a giant surge of energy, but, unlike in the case of Sabbath, energy not so anarchical that it ran away with itself and turned the book into a mess."

As someone who has himself written extensively about Roth, I find Mark's reading of him persuasive and revealing, not to say reflective of

Mark's own creative surge after the onset of his illness. It is curious that over the course of Mark's long and productive career he seldom lingered over individual works of literature; neither his landscapes nor his portraits gave much play to the individual novel. This essay on Roth is a notable exception and is remarkable for its pungency and its insight and for its unflinching determination to zero in on Roth's shit.

The essays on Trilling, Ozick, Hartman, and Roth were the major productions of Mark's illness and were written expressly with this book in mind. Some others were written before and some reviews and shorter essays also during this period, though not necessarily for this book. I'll have a word about just three and let the rest speak for themselves. Mark was at work on three essays in the weeks before his death, once he had finished with Hartman and Ozick in mid–March. In addition to his introduction, Mark was updating two earlier essays that he felt were incomplete. One was the essay on Mitch Albom's *Tuesdays with Morrie* that he had initially published in the *Forward* in January 2002. It was a scathing editorial on a book about another ALS sufferer, Brandeis sociology professor Morrie Schwartz, whose dying was chronicled by sportswriter Mitch Albom and was turned, as Mark saw it, into pure schmaltz. "After his last interview on *Nightline*," Mark wrote, "Morris rolled his eyes heavenward and said to Mr. Koppel, 'I'm bargaining with Him up there now. I'm asking Him, "Do I get to be one of the angels?"' If he so managed, it is as a Hallmark greeting card angel, his message adorned with bows and ribbons." Months later, Mark continued to fume at all the denial that went into the secular canonization of *Tuesdays with Morrie,* whose cover hailed it as "the runaway best seller that changed millions of lives," and which opened as a play Off Broadway in November 2002. Mark was more in tune with the words of poet George Mac-Beth, who also had died of ALS, from a poem titled "Laughter in Hell."

> One f**ker was even crying. I'll do the crying,
> Sonny boy, you stand and listen. Give
> Me a break. Friends!
> I'd rather have enemies.

That was the spirit that Mark preferred, a refusal to go gently, and the resemblance to Roth's Mickey Sabbath can't be mistaken. The text of Mark's late addition to the Morrie essay was a bit ragged, but some of it has been appended to that essay as it appears in this book.

Mark was also dissatisfied with the essay on Diana Trilling, which appeared in *Salmagundi* in 1994 as his review of her memoir of her marriage to Lionel Trilling: *The Beginning of the Journey*. He was revising it right up until he lost the power to type entirely, and the version of that essay that appears in this book was found by Jean on Mark's computer, dated March 23, 2003, just six days before he died. The 1994 version of this review was irritable enough, but given Mark's let-'er-rip temper at the end, however, his anger is a good deal fiercer and his remarks more personal in his final version of the review. And even then it doesn't approach the agitation of private notes he kept on his relationship with Mrs. Trilling over many years. Without delving too extensively into those notes, it does seem appropriate to say that after Mark's review of Lionel Trilling's *Literary Criticism: An Introductory Reader*, Mrs. Trilling regarded Mark as an adversary and treated him accordingly. He complained in private: "My file is full of letters from her, letters that were wholly gratuitous in that they were not prompted by letters of my own, that can only be regarded as attempts to stifle my research and intimidate me." She had warned him against citing letters of her husband's that he had seen in the Low Library archive, and threatened legal action. Mark took those threats seriously enough to retain a lawyer and to get counsel on the legality of using the materials he had seen. Beyond that, friends of Lionel Trilling's informed Mark that they preferred not to speak with him for fear of offending Mrs. Trilling. Mark was uncertain of whether they were being deferential before the fact or had been asked not to cooperate. Mark kept pages of furious, steaming notes about Diana Trilling that never had an outlet in print, nor could they. However you may choose to read his last-minute revision of his essay "The Trillings: A Marriage of True Minds?" be assured that Mark was, even at the last hour, observing restraint. So far as I know, that essay contains the last words he wrote for this book, and even as he may have desired to let fly, finally, he declared the book finished and let the matter rest.

Morrie Schwartz might have spent his last hours bargaining with God, but Mark spent his bargaining for time. He devoted what he had to bestowing blessings on the fathers who had taught him how to employ his talents and to settling scores with others, leaving this book of celebrations and anathemas as his legacy. There is ever so much solid intellectual nourishment to be encountered here, but I'll refrain from commenting on it all.

August 27, 2004

Biographical Summary

MARK SHECHNER

It has been said of intellectuals that they conduct their educations in public, and that was true of Mark. His writing was not the expression of a mind that had barricaded itself in and was forever issuing bulletins from behind its fortifications, but the probing of someone who was ever alert to variousness and possibility and was charting his course on the fly. This book, with its spectrum of heroes from Philip Roth to Geoffrey Hartman, is evidence enough of that. In a sense, Mark lived that way, ever the student. Not that he lacked a significant private life—of course he had one, and a full and eventful one it was—but in a way that is unique to those who live by words, his life took on significance and direction from his reading, his writing, his teaching, and the dialogues that formed around them.

Mark lived for ideas, and the dramas that unfold in this book are dramas of thought. That his ideas had tendrils buried deep in his life is a bromide that describes nearly all of us—I am, therefore I think—but just as certainly in Mark's case ideas furnished him with purpose and justification, not to say tension and pleasure. Indeed, Mark's own self-presentation at the beginning of this book is an intellectual's introduction, listing the journals he read in the Lamont Library Reading Room at Harvard before saying a word about his childhood. Jean remembers dinnertime at their house as a time for catching up with ideas as the stuff of regular conversation. Even in the months before his death, Mark was reading Derrida on death, in *The Gift of Death* and *The Work of Mourning*. I regarded Mark when I knew him as a model of how an intellectual life might be conducted: curious, challenging, heedless of disciplinary constraints, and always in gear, qualities that are abundantly displayed in these essays. He lived, it seems, more in the interrogative mood than in the declarative.

For Jewish children of Mark's generation, families were launching pads to worlds that were as strange to the parents as the moons of Saturn, strange even to themselves. Mark's father Jack (anglicized from Jacob), who had emigrated from Ukraine at the age of eighteen—where he had witnessed, among other horrors, his sister being raped by Cossacks—was in the furniture fabric goods business in Newark and president of his own firm, National Textiles, which provided textiles to the White House of John F. Kennedy. Mark's sister Elyse remembers: "He was a middleman between the mills and the decorators. I think he was very proud that he had a successful business. Once in a while my father would take us to the store on a Saturday and Sunday to pack up the books of fabrics that he bought from the mills." To Mark he seemed remote, and Mark would recall being driven to school by his father without a word being exchanged. Of Alfred Kazin's spiritual longing he later wrote that it "plainly had its source in his traumatic experience of silence as a very young boy: 'Speak, Father, speak!'" Though Jack Krupnick was a loyal reader of the Yiddish press, the *Forward* in particular, there were few books in the house (Mark would remember some *Reader's Digest* volumes), something Mark would lament in later years. His mother, Betty (anglicized from Bertha), after marriage took care of the home and the children. Mark may have lamented these beginnings as a vacuum, yet, such an upbringing and its outcome was an almost paradigmatic Jewish-academic childhood. During the first three decades after World War II, the shmata business supplied the academy with a virtual army of its children. Without dry goods, where would scholarship in America have been?

Mark went off first to private school and then to Harvard and Brandeis before taking his first academic position at Boston University in 1968. Elyse, the older of his two sisters, five and a half years Mark's junior, became an artist and Janice (Krupnick Suzman), eleven years younger, a psychologist. It may even be that growing up in Irvington where his parents, disdainful of the local high school, sent him to the private, elite Newark Academy, made the critical difference in Mark's life. Newark Academy, founded in 1774, but with roots going back to the 1730s and the Reverend Aaron Burr, was the stepping-stone to Harvard and Harvard the intro to graduate study at Brandeis and Brandeis the intro to Philip Rahv and *Modern Occasions*. And from there to a life. How contingent everything was!

What looks on a vita to be a straight path, however, was in reality jagged and improvisational. As Mark's friend Eric Homberger would write of him in an obituary in the *Guardian,* "He went on to Harvard University to read English, and, taking a break from its oppressive earnestness, lived for two years in Greenwich Village, handicapping horses on the sports desk of the *New York Post,* and hanging out at the Cedar Street Tavern, the favorite bar of the younger abstract expressionists." In 1958, moreover, when he was nineteen, Mark drove across country, as he recalled in his essay on Alfred Kazin and Irving Howe, "starting in San Francisco, picking up odd jobs down the California coast. I identified with Kazin's Whitmanesque effort to absorb American culture into himself and assume an American voice." It was the late fifties, after all; Kerouac, Ginsberg, Kesey, and the beats were reinventing consciousness for young Americans, and to be out there on the highway looking for adventure was the literary thing to do, even if you weren't born to be wild. Books supplied all the authority you needed to take to the open road.

For a while, anyway. Mark returned to Harvard in 1960 and graduated Phi Beta Kappa in American history and literature two years later. After taking his MA and PhD in English at Brandeis University—writing a PhD dissertation on Stephen Crane and Edith Wharton under the direction of Philip Rahv—he won a Fulbright scholarship and spent 1965–66 studying at Darwin College, a new graduate college that was part of the University of Cambridge. There, as Patrick Parrinder recalls, Graham Hough, then dean of the college, was one of his mentors, as was Denis Donoghue, with whom he studied modern poetry. He must have cut quite a figure, this American with the "spanking new Volvo car in Cambridge" that he drove to London on the weekends. This son of the rag business felt at home in England, and as Parrinder recalls, "One of his great loves was Henry James and the Jamesian persona, socially and intellectually at ease on both sides of the Atlantic." He returned to the States for his first full-time job at Smith College, one of the Seven Sisters schools that, before coeducation, were counterparts to the all-male colleges of the Ivy League.

Typically, wherever he went Mark made lasting friends. From his Harvard days he maintained ties with Charles Maier, now a history professor at Harvard, and writer Paul Cowan, for whom he wrote a tender obituary that is included here in his essay "Assimilation in Recent Jewish American Autobiographies." His tutor, Joel Porte, now a professor of English at Cornell University, has remained a lifelong friend as well, as did his professor, Daniel Aaron. From the Darwin College days he made lasting friendships with Patrick Parrinder, now a professor at Reading University, and Eric Homberger, now a professor at the University of Keele. From the Brandeis years, poet Allen Grossman, now teaching at Johns Hopkins University, became a close and lasting confidant.

In 1968, Mark was hired as an assistant professor of English at Boston University, where he taught until 1972, the last two years of which he was also engaged with *Modern Occasions*. During his five years at BU he was witness to the student upheaval caused by the emergence of the counterculture (Trilling's "modernism in the streets") and the rebellion against the war in Vietnam, and inevitably some of it spilled over into the department itself as it did throughout the American academy. He also took courses at the Boston Psychoanalytic Institute with the first-year class. The decision of an ailing and defeated Philip Rahv to shut down *Modern Occasions* coincided with Mark's department at BU voting down his application for promotion to tenure. The failure to gain tenure may have owed something to departmental politics and the generational fissures that virtually defined the era. Citing an instance, Mark recalled years later, "when I offered my congratulations to one of the most aggressive of the antiradicals, who had just received an invitation to join a highly prestigious English department, that professor spit out: 'I'm not going anywhere. I'm going to stay here long enough to see you all buried.'" Mark felt at the time that his senior colleague Helen Vendler had led the resistance to his promotion, but a purely professional explanation doesn't demand personalities. While Mark's antiwar views and reputation as a literary sansculotte could not have made his senior colleagues comfortable with him, his publication record, public and spectacular though it may have been (essays and reviews in the *Nation, TLS, Modern Occasions,* the *New York Review of Books*), was entirely in literary journalism, in a profession that, then more than now, demanded refereed articles and a published book as evidence of one's scholarly bona fides. Joel Porte, Mark's tutor at Harvard's Leverett House, remembers, "Of course Mark was not conventionally productive during those years. In any case, the atmosphere at John Silber's BU was not a happy one and I knew Mark would move on to better things." Suddenly cut loose from his Boston moorings, Mark was off again to England with an NEH grant, to study psychoanalytic theory and study with Anna Freud and her staff at her child therapy clinic in Hampstead, North London.

During his London sojourn, while formally attached to the Hampstead clinic, Mark gravitated to the nearby Tavistock Center for friends, where the clinicians and students were mainly up-to-date English, not World War II–era Viennese in their culture as at the Hampstead. Feeling at home in England and momentarily on furlough from the crisis in America, he decided to remain a second year and took a position as visiting lecturer in the Department of American Studies at the University of Keele, a "redbrick" university in industrial Staffordshire. The time abroad was a healing respite from the turbulence at home, personal as well as national, though it also meant missing out on some major political dramas, including the Watergate scandal and the impeachment of a president.

On his return to America in fall 1974, Mark took an assistant professorship in English at the University of Wisconsin–Milwaukee, which housed the Center for Twentieth Century Studies, an avant-garde institution devoted to cross-disciplinary research in the humanities. It was an ideal place for Mark to reboot his career. If he bridled at the conservatism at Boston University, where ideological lines would be hardened after John Silber became president in 1971, the shoe would be on the other foot at UW–M, where the center prided itself on being cutting edge and devoted to emerging perspectives and discourses, especially those of European design. "It wasn't a department—it didn't grant degrees or offer courses," Mark later wrote about it, "but was more like a European intellectual salon, providing an enviable social milieu as well as cultural enrichment." He added, "But what always struck me most about the center was the snobbishness it encouraged and satisfied." (See the chapter "Why Are English Departments Still Fighting the Culture Wars?")

It is beyond imagining that BU as it was in the 1970s could have provided incentive or breathing space for *Displacement: Derrida and After,* a book so obviously authorized by the progressive ardor and exploratory freedom at UW–M in those days. No doubt the ecumenism of the center allowed Mark to test the waters of theory without feeling obliged to take the full plunge.

I have little information about Mark as a teacher and colleague during the University of Wisconsin–Milwaukee years, though professionally he was productive, as evidenced by the two books that established his reputation, the Derrida and the Trilling, and a bumper crop of essays on critics and the critical environment of American life that were spun off of the Trilling research. There too he gained promotions to tenure in 1977 and to full professor in 1985. For one year also, 1978–79, he served as acting director of the center. And personally he was solidifying the persona that he would maintain ever after, which Gerald Graff characterizes as the "insider-outsider."

But Mark also didn't live in Milwaukee for long, and it may be that his productivity was enabled by his frequent absences. After just a year there, Mark met Jean Carney, who was then a reporter for the *Milwaukee Journal,* and as Jean remembers, "We immediately started plotting our exit." Jean was at a party for a friend who was getting married and Mark crashed the party with a date. The date must have called a taxi, as Mark and his new friend wound up sitting in a car all night talking. Mark and Jean married in 1977 and moved to Chicago the year after the birth of their son, Joseph, in 1978, so that Jean could attend graduate school in human development at the University of Chicago.

In 1987 Mark was bailed out of his bus ride by an appointment in the English Department at the University of Illinois at Chicago, where he remained for three years and even served for a year, 1989–90, as acting head. Coming from the open intellectual community of UW–M to a department that was in a state of flux and uncertainty, Mark experienced a profound sense of shock. As for Mark's year as acting head, his colleague at UIC Michael Lieb reports, "Mark hated every minute of it." A decade after that experience, Mark would write about how uncomfortable he was "working among persons whose sense of self-esteem was so damaged and who, as a consequence, directed toward the world, including newcomers like me, a free-floating resentment." By then, plotting an exit had become Mark's academic modus operandi.

This exit would be made possible by an offer to join the Divinity School at the University of Chicago in fall 1990, where Mark would teach until his retirement in 2002. Mark had had a prior relationship with the Divinity School a decade earlier when, on leave from UW–M in 1980–82, he had an office there where he did the bulk of the research that led to the Derrida collection. There, by Mark's own account, he experienced a revival of intellectual vitality, in an environment that was at once fertile with ideas and free from parochialism. Though the emphases differed, the Divinity School shared with the center in Milwaukee a bracing eclecticism and cosmopolitan ethos. Mark found it to be virtually a humanities institute unto itself, in which even his contribution as a secular scholar was welcome. "I was at ease teaching literature in a religious-studies setting," Mark wrote in the "Culture Wars" essay, "because there was no pressure to reduce literature to the circumstances of material culture, or to race, class, and gender."

At the time, I had assumed that this move signaled Mark's deepening commitment to Jewish studies and maybe even a turn toward tradition, if not religion itself. Was he going to show up at the MLA wearing tefillin? I recall one of our conversations in the nineties being about kaballah and Jewish mysticism, after my own belated discovery of Gershom Scholem, and he had replied with something like, "Scholem is old news. Have you read Moshe Idel?" That clearly was the influence of the Divinity School working on him, but how? When I asked him in January 2003, he responded by e-mail, "It would be nice to say that my move to the Divinity School had to do with desire to deepen and enrich my life; actually, it had more to do with my loathing of UIC and having pleasant memories of my two years (1980–82) when I had an office at the Divinity School; they had just opened the Institute for the Advanced Study of Religion with Martin Marty running it and were sympathetic to my Trilling project. I did like the people there but had no intention of widening my scope so as to take in Bible or theology or Jewish history or anything else. In fact, I haven't learned Yiddish or Hebrew since I've been there, and I don't think I've become less secular-minded."

And yet widen his scope he did. He absorbed the Divinity School and the University of Chicago in copious draughts. Among his papers Mark kept a list of courses taught during his years at the Divinity School, and besides the courses we might expect, on Modern Jewish American Writing, American Autobiography, and two on Henry James, we find Judaic Civilization III (which included, at the urging of his TA, texts by Martin Buber, Franz Rosenzweig, and Gershom Scholem),

Recent Theory and Hermeneutics (with Anthony Yu), Poetic Theory of Harold Bloom (with whom Mark also maintained a correspondence), and Literary Theory since Kant (a course that included some of his "killer *B*s": R. P. Blackmur, Kenneth Burke, Harold Bloom, Wayne Booth, Roland Barthes, Gaston Bachelard, Maurice Blanchot, Walter Benjamin, and Mikhail Bakhtin). And publications began to appear in places like *Journal of Religion* and *Christian Century* and *Shofar.* At the time he retired, Mark was scheduled to coteach courses with Bruce Lincoln and visiting novelist (and since Nobel Laureate) J. M. Coetzee. He also expanded his critical horizons to include the kinds of rhetorical criticism for which the University of Chicago was famed. Add to this his regular NEH seminar on Jewish American writers.

Certainly there was a great strain in this need to change the upholstery of his mind every several years, and as Michael Lieb would report, there were times, certainly at the beginning, when Mark felt that he was in over his head. Working up Buber, Rashi, Benjamin, and Blanchot, not to say Hartman, while also teaching James and Bellow, is not a stroll in Hyde Park. And there was an inevitable sense of vertigo, for as Bruce Lincoln noted to me in a correspondence, "He never quite knew what to make of it, nor how and why he was supposed to fit in. He was alienated in ways, but not ways that were particularly painful, at least not most of the time. Rather, his stance was mildly ironic." But then, Mark being Mark, to be mildly ironic was only to be himself, and in the e-mail cited previously Mark declared simply, "No question, these have been the best years of my life, especially the last five; even with death looming."

The preceding is at best a reference book citation of certain raw information about Mark, but as I have been writing this there have been many voices in my head, and this is the moment to let them speak. So much of what registered with people about Mark were the tone and texture of his presence: the grace, the poise, the humor, the generosity, the warmth, and always the gentle irony. Joel Porte, who knew Mark longer than almost anyone not family, recalls that "when I knew him at Leverett House, Harvard, he was, of course, a little older than the other students; but even taking that into account, he seemed wise beyond his years. And yet his humor and wry way of looking at things saved him from ever being ponderous. He always had a twinkle in his eye—a very piercing eye." In a letter to me, Richard Rosengarten, Mark's colleague at the Divinity School, had this to say about Mark's presence: "He had a kind of shambling debonair disposition that was quite elegant but sufficiently understated to avoid ostentation. Wryness and wit were his constant companions." Martin Marty, with whom Mark had cotaught a seminar on literature and religion in America in the 1950s, noted in his contribution to the retirement ceremony Mark's insistence on "irresolution," which "inspires him to be cautious in the judgments he makes, open to the many voices in conversation at this school and beyond, careful not to sound too sure of himself in a world where the Big Answers are and will remain elusive." Wendy Doniger welcomed his thoughtfulness in reading her own writing about Indian mythology: "His extraordinary literary taste, his true eye for narrative in all forms, his interest in writing as much as in scholarship, all of this made him a sharp and appreciative reader; with a kind of boyish enthusiasm." A characterization that I find particularly telling about what a long strange trip it had been is this by his colleague Bruce Lincoln, who at the ceremony offered this rendition of Mark's vision of Mark. "If anything, I suspect he saw himself as an urbane and witty occasional critic, a clever and intriguing character in a comedy of manners, short story, or soap opera, perhaps, or conceivably in a narrative of paratactic structure (a term he taught me in the class we offered together, and defined as a story of episodic nature, in which 'it's just one goddam thing after another')." To return to Richard Rosengarten's letter on Mark's cast of mind: "When I think about Mark's contributions to our intellectual life, I think first and most important that he continually brought to our attention both the challenges and the real virtues of close reading. Mark had big ideas, but he was, in a profound way, an intellectual miniaturist: he called everyone's attention back to the local, the particular, and insisted that there were riches to be discovered there by the patient and the persistent." Norman Finkelstein, poet and professor of English at Xavier University, who was Mark's student in an NEH seminar in 1990, remembers "how [Mark's students] were touched by him." Mark "had the enviable ability to tease out the most salient issues regarding each text, author, and cultural milieu that we studied. His choice of readings was pitch perfect. And despite his obvious intelligence and low-key confidence, he never presumed, like some ideological critics suffering from the 'will to knowledge' syndrome, to know more than the work and its author. Yet he did not enshrine the writing either. Each session was an exploration, an unfolding, and possessed a virtually aggadic charm."

Not to be neglected is the other Mark, the private Mark, and colleague Paul Mendes-Flohr noted, as many did, Mark's devotion to his family, describing how on their perambulations around campus Mark "would pause to tell me about the joy he takes in his son's and wife's achievements: his eyes—very expressive eyes, indeed—would twinkle with an infectious delight as he spoke of them, his wife and son, who are understandably his most precious companions."

To Joseph, the connections between the work and the life are abundantly plain. He writes in a letter to me, "For my father the 'deep places' came to represent a primal will to stay alive—whatever humiliation he endured, however much he needed to escape through humor, and to whatever extent he needed to rely on his loved ones—to finish this book and share his love with the world and my mother and me." Jean, recalling Mark's packing books at the house in Flossmoor in preparation for the move to an apartment in the Hancock Building: "There was a sensuous elegance to his system, characteristic but for its astonishing slowness. He put aside the cane and took each book in his hands, feeling his way into its upholstery by pressing his fingertips into the cover, the binding, the paper. I have seen him make those moves thousands of times. It's the way that his father taught him to feel his way into fabric when he took him to New York's 'rag district' on buying trips for the family textile business. Mark always said that he 'felt his way into a text,' and the process with every new book began with gently creasing the front and back covers, going through the book page by page, folding pages back and forth, getting the book ready to rest in his hands."

I acknowledge help in writing this capsule biography first of all to Mark himself who, in addition to an exchange of e-mails during the last half year of his life, also wrote, in January 2003, a self-obit, portions of which Jean gave to the press after his death. A good deal of what appeared in obits in the *Guardian* in England, the *Chicago Tribune*, the *Chicago Sun-Times*, and the University of Chicago's press release owe details to Mark's press release about himself. Eric Homberger's obituary in the *Guardian* draws both on Mark's writing and on his own long friendship with Mark, and I've cribbed freely from it as well. On the occasion of Mark's retirement, the Divinity School's publication, the *Criterion*, dedicated the better part of its Spring 2002 issue to Mark, and after his death published memorial essays in the Spring 2003 issue, and I have drawn freely from several of them.

For material about Mark's days in Irvington, at Harvard, Darwin College, University of Keele, UW–M, UIC, and finally at the University of Chicago, I've leaned heavily on conversations and personal correspondences with Mark's colleagues and friends, including Eric Homberger, Norman Finkelstein, Allen Grossman, Gerald Graff, Michael Lieb, Richard Stern, Richard Rosengarten, Bruce Lincoln, Joel Porte, and Patrick Parrinder as well as the tributes that appeared in two issues of the *Criterion*, which are available on-line at http://divinity.uchicago.edu/research/criterion/. I wish I could reprint all of these letters and tributes in their entirety. Suzanne Geissler Bowles, historian of early New Jersey, has helped me with information about Newark Academy. For so much else I have relied on the hours of discussion and e-mail with Mark's widow and my co-editor, Jean K. Carney, son, Joe Krupnick, and sister, Elyse Krupnick. My thanks to them all for their patience and good-natured support.

Among Mark's own essays, I have drawn freely from his introduction to this book, his essay on Alfred Kazin and Irving Howe, his essay on Philip Rahv, his farewell talk at the Divinity School retirement party for him in 2002, and his *apologia pro vita sua*, "Why Are English Departments Still Fighting the Culture Wars?"

•

Publications

This publication list for Mark is based on a vita that Mark kept, which was neither inclusive nor always entirely accurate. We've made efforts to fill in a few blanks and to correct some mistakes, but because some citations are impossible to check and some of Mark's publications are either unknown or minor or can't be retrieved, we estimate that well over a hundred publications are not on this list. In some cases also we've kept inaccurate but identifying versions of titles that Mark added for clarification, such as "Fathers, Sons, and New York Intellectuals (Daniel Bell)."

It probably is of no long-term scholarly interest to know that Mark wrote about egg donors for the *Chicago Sun-Times,* travel to the Marquesas for the *Wall Street Journal,* obituaries for literary scholar Walter Jackson Bate and hotel proprietress (of the Algonquin) Mary Bodne for the *Guardian* in London, or was a steady book reviewer for the *Chicago Tribune.* We've admitted a handful of these reviews: Mark's review of the correspondence of Mary McCarthy and Hannah Arendt and his obituary for poet Joseph Brodsky were essays in miniature. But to admit more than a handful is to open a floodgate, and we've decided to keep this list compact rather than dilute major items with those of transient interest.

Books

Editor, *Displacement: Derrida and After.* Bloomington: Indiana University Press, 1983. Paperback reprint, 1987.

Lionel Trilling and the Fate of Cultural Criticism. Evanston, IL: Northwestern University Press, 1986.

Special Issues

Editor and Introduction, special section on "Religion and Literature." *Journal of Religion* 74 (July 1994).

Selected Essays and Reviews

"The Sanctuary of the Imagination." Review of *Henry James: The Treacherous Years, 1895–1901,* by Leon Edel. *Nation,* July 14, 1969.

"Notes from the Funhouse: Recent American Fiction." *Modern Occasions* 1.1 (Fall 1970): 108–12.

"Lionel Trilling: Criticism and Illusion." *Modern Occasions* 1.2 (Winter 1971): 282–87.

"The Fifties Revisited." *Modern Occasions* 1.3 (Spring 1971): 313–16.

"It's Your Fault, Henry James." Review of *The Imperial Self: An Essay in American Literary and Cultural History,* by Quentin Anderson. *New York Review of Books,* September 23, 1971.

"Henry James's Curiosity." *Modern Occasions* 2.2 (Spring 1972): 168–80.

"The Artist as Anti-Neurotic." Review of *The Dynamics of Creation,* by Anthony Storr. *Times Higher Education Supplement* (London), December 15, 1972.

"Scaling Down and Demystifying the Master." Review of *The Air of Reality: New Essays on Henry James,* ed. John Goode. *Times Literary Supplement,* January 1, 1973.

"Jung's Parson's Letters." Review of *Letters: 1906–1950,* by C. G. Jung. *Times Higher Education Supplement* (London), March 16, 1973.

"Well Wrought Urns and the English Department." Review of *Literary Theory and Structure: Essays in Honor of William K. Wimsatt,* ed. Frank Brady, John Palmer, and Martin Price. *Times Higher Education Supplement* (London), April 13, 1973.

"Erik Erikson and the Diversity of Father Images." Review of *Erik Erikson: The Growth of His Work,* by Robert Coles. *Times Higher Education Supplement* (London), May 1973.

"He Never Learned to Swim: A Memoir of Philip Rahv." *New Review* (London) 2 (January 1976): 33–39.

"'The Beast in the Jungle' and the Dilemma of Narcissus." *Southern Review* 9 (July 1976): 113–20.

"Playing with the Silence: Henry James's Poetics of Loss." *Forum* 13 (Winter 1976): 37–42.

"*The Golden Bowl:* Henry James's Novel about Nothing." *English Studies* 57 (December 1976): 533–40.

"Alfred Kazin: An American Life." *Salmagundi* 44–45 (Spring–Summer 1979): 197–204.

"The *Menorah Journal* Group and the Origins of Modern Jewish-American Radicalism." *Modern Jewish Studies Annual* 3 (Winter 1979): 56–67. Reprinted in *A Quest for Social Justice,* ed. Ralph Aderman. Madison: University of Wisconsin Press, 1983.

"Lionel Trilling, Freud, and the Fifties." *Humanities in Society* 3 (Summer 1980): 265–81.

"The Neoconservative Imagination (Norman Podhoretz)." *Salmagundi* 47–48 (Winter–Spring 1980): 202–8.

"Edmund Wilson." *Salmagundi* 50–51 (Fall 1980–Winter 1981): 315–21.

"The New York Intellectuals: Losing Touch with Tradition." *Christian Century,* June 1981.

"Fathers, Sons, and New York Intellectuals (Daniel Bell)." *Salmagundi* 54 (Fall 1981): 106–20.

"Art and Politics Once More (Clement Greenberg)." *Bennington Review* 12 (Winter 1981–82): 23–26.

"Lionel Trilling, 'Culture,' and Jewishness." *Denver Quarterly* 18 (Autumn 1983): 106–22.

"The Two Worlds of Cultural Criticism." In *Criticism in the University,* ed. Gerald Graff and Reginald Gibbons, 159–69. Evanston, IL: Northwestern University Press, 1985.

"Walking in Our Sleep: Bitburg and the Post-1939 Generation." *Christian Century,* June 1985. Reprinted in *Bitburg in Moral and Political Perspective,* ed. Geoffrey Hartman. Bloomington: Indiana University Press, 1986.

"Criticism as an Institution." In *Crisis of Modernity: Recent Critical Theories of Culture and Society in the United States and West Germany,* ed. Gunter H. Lenz and Kurt L. Shell, 156–76. Frankfurt am Main: Campus Verlag; Boulder, CO: Westview Press, 1986.

"Irving Howe." In *Dictionary of Literary Biography: Modern American Critics,* ed. Gregory Jay, 167–75. Detroit: Gale Research, 1988.

"Middlebrowism in the Academy." *American Quarterly* 40 (June 1988): 229–39.

"Lionel Trilling and the Politics of Style." In *American Literary Landscapes: The Fiction and the Fact,* ed. Ian F. A. Bell and D. K. Adams, 152–70. London: Vision Press; New York: St. Martin's Press, 1988.

"The Critic and His Connections: The Case of Michael Walzer." *American Literary History* 1 (Fall 1989): 689–98.

"Edward Said: Discourse and Palestinian Rage." *Tikkun* 4 (November–December 1989): 21–24.

"Cynthia Ozick as the Jewish T. S. Eliot." *Soundings* 74 (Fall–Winter 1991): 351–68.

"Assimilation in Recent American Jewish Autobiographies." *Contemporary Literature* 34 (Fall 1993): 451–74.

"Jewish Jacobites: Henry James's Presence in the Fiction of Philip Roth and Cynthia Ozick." In *Traditions, Voices, and Dreams: The American Novel since the 1960s,* ed. Melvin J. Friedman and Ben Siegel, 89–107. Newark: University of Delaware Press, 1994.

"Steiner's Literary Journalism: The Heart of the Maze." *New England Review* 15 (Spring 1993). Reprinted in *Reading George Steiner,* ed. Nathan A. Scott Jr. and Ronald Sharp, 43–57. Baltimore, MD: Johns Hopkins University Press, 1994.

"A Marriage of True Minds." Review of Diana Trilling's *The Beginning of the Journey. Salmagundi* 103 (Summer 1994): 213–24.

"How Shaw, Kipling, Joyce and Company Looked at Jews: Reading Jewish Literature after Shylock." Review of *Constructions of "the Jew" in English Literature and Society: Racial Representations, 1875–1945,* by Bryan Cheyette. *Forward,* July 15, 1994.

"Saul Bellow in *Humboldt's Gift.*" *Salmagundi* 106–7 (Spring–Summer 1995): 85–88.

"Corresponding Virtues: The Letters of Hannah Arendt and Mary McCarthy." *Chicago Tribune,* March 26, 1995.

"Irving Howe," "Philip Rahv," and "Lionel Trilling." In *A Companion to American Thought,* ed. Richard Wightman Fox and James Kloppenberg. Oxford, England, and Cambridge, MA: Blackwell, 1995.

"Jewish-American Literature." In *New Immigrant Literatures in the United States,* ed. Alpana Sharma Knippling, 295–308. Westport, CT: Greenwood Press: 1996.

"An Exile's 'Soul Quest': Remembering Joseph Brodsky." *Chicago Tribune,* February 11, 1996.

"The Troubles of Henry James: How a Master of the Short Story Responded to an 'Age of Trash Triumphant.'" *Chicago Tribune,* March 3, 1996.

"Edmund Wilson and Gentile Philo-Semitism." In *Edmund Wilson: Centennial Reflections,* ed. Lewis M. Dabney, 70–88. Princeton, NJ: Princeton University Press, 1997.

"Marshall McLuhan Revisited: Media Guru as Catholic Modernist." *Modernism/Modernity* 5 (September 1998): 107–28.

"Jewish Autobiographies and the Counter-Example of Philip Roth." In *American Literary Dimensions: Essays in Honor of Melvin J. Friedman,* ed. Ben Siegel and Jay L. Halio, 155–67. Newark: University of Delaware Press, 1999.

"Hannah Arendt." In *The Cambridge Guide to Women's Writing in English,* ed. Lorna Sage. Cambridge: Cambridge Univ. Press, 1999.

"Diagnosing Trilling: Why the Critics Are Wrong." *Chronicle of Higher Education,* June 4, 1999.

"Philo-Semitism in the American Grain." In *Rhetorical Invention and Religious Inquiry: New Perspectives,* ed. Walter Jost and Wendy Olmsted, 356–80. New Haven, CT: Yale University Press, 2000.

"Religion and the Modern Novel: What My Japanese Students Helped Me to See." *Commonweal,* May 5, 2000.

"Stain of Sanctimony." Reviews of *The Human Stain,* by Philip Roth, and *The Day After: A Retrospective on Religious Dissent in the Presidential Crisis,* by Gabriel J. Fackre. *Christian Century,* September 13–20, 2000.

"A Chicagoan, Born and Bred." Review of *Bellow: A Biography,* by James Atlas. *Commonweal,* February 23, 2001.

"Saul Bellow and Modern American Fiction." *Comparative Literature: East and West* (Sichuan University, China) 3 (Summer 2001): 1–17.

"Death and Men of Letters: Measuring Roth and Bellow by the Way They Handle the Final Question." *Forward,* July 6, 2001.

"Revisiting Morrie: Were His Last Words Too Good to Be True?" *Forward,* January 25, 2002.

"Listmania in *Humboldt's Gift.*" *Literary Imagination* 4.1 (Winter 2002): 60–67.

"Upon Retirement." *Criterion: A Publication of the University of Chicago Divinity School* 41, no. 2 (Spring 2002).

"Why Are English Departments Still Fighting the Culture Wars?" *Chronicle of Higher Education,* September 20, 2002.

"The Art of the Obituary." *American Scholar* 71.4 (Autumn 2002): 91–96.

"Jewish Intellectuals and 'The Deep Places of the Imagination.'" *Shofar,*
   March 23, 2003.

Other

Review-essays, shorter reviews, op-ed pieces, obituaries, and short arti-
   cles in the *Times* (London), the *Nation, New York Review of Books,
   Christian Century, American Literature, New York Times Book Re-
   view, Commonweal, Salmagundi,* the *Forward, Journal of Religion,
   Chicago Tribune, Chronicle of Higher Education, Chicago Sun-Times,
   Wall Street Journal,* and the *Guardian* (London).

Index